# Applied Macroeconometrics

CARLO A. FAVERO



OXFORD
UNIVERSITY PRESS

*This book has been printed digitally and produced in a standard specification in order to ensure its continuing availability*

**OXFORD**
UNIVERSITY PRESS

Great Clarendon Street, Oxford OX2 6DP

Oxford University Press is a department of the University of Oxford.
It furthers the University's objective of excellence in research, scholarship,
and education by publishing worldwide in

Oxford New York

Auckland Cape Town Dar es Salaam Hong Kong Karachi
Kuala Lumpur Madrid Melbourne Mexico City Nairobi
New Delhi Shanghai Taipei Toronto

With offices in

Argentina Austria Brazil Chile Czech Republic France Greece
Guatemala Hungary Italy Japan South Korea Poland Portugal
Singapore Switzerland Thailand Turkey Ukraine Vietnam



Published in the United States
by Oxford University Press Inc., New York



Reprinted 2008



ISBN 978-0-19-829685-0

# PREFACE

The objective of this book is the discussion and the practical illustration of techniques used in applied macroeconometrics. The plural here is as appropriate as ever in that the profession does not currently share a common view on the methodology of applied macroeconometrics. The different approaches are regarded as alternative, in fact it is very rare to see a combination of them applied by the same authors, it is also very difficult to see a combination of them published in the same journal, with the notable exception of the *Journal of Applied Econometrics*. Interestingly, up to the 1970s there was consensus, regarding both the theoretical foundation and the empirical specification of macroeconometric modelling. The consensus was represented by the Cowles Commission approach which broke down in the 1970s when, as Pesaran and Smith(1995) put it, it was discovered that this type of models

> ... did not represent the data...did not represent the theory... were ineffective for practical purposes of forecasting and policy...

The Cowles Commission approach was then substituted by a number of prominent methods of empirical research: the LSE (London School of Economics) approach, the VAR(vector autoregressive model) approach, and the intertemporal optimization/calibration approach. We shall discuss and illustrate the empirical research strategy of these three alternative approaches by interpreting them as different proposals to solve problems observed in the Cowles Commission approach. The presentation of each methodological approach is paired with extensive discussions and replications of the relevant empirical work. The bulk of empirical illustrations is related to the monetary transmission mechanism by considering benchmark dataset for the US and European economies. This choice allows us to have a common benchmark to address explicitly the differences in questions and answers provided by the different schools of thought.

## Plan of the book

Our presentation is based on the conviction that one of the oldest concepts in econometrics, namely identification, provides a natural unified framework to discuss the collapse of Cowles Commission models and the alternative strategies currently adopted in applied research. Therefore, in the first part of the book we introduce time-series models and discuss extensively the importance of identification for time-series models. In the second part of the book we illustrate the Cowles Commission approach and the LSE, VAR, and intertemporal optimization/calibration approaches providing applications.

Chapter 1 serves the purposes of giving a quick revision of basic econometrics and of introducing macroeconometrics. This is done by analysing the economic problem of convergence and growth by using the dataset and replicating the results reported in Mankiw, Romer and Weil (1992). Traditional issues in econometrics, with particular emphasis on the mis-specification problem, are revised using the cross-section dataset of the cited article. The importance of time-series in econometrics is then stressed by illustrating the potential of the application of time-series methodology to the Mankiw, Romer and Weil dataset.

Chapters 2 and 3 form the econometric basis for the illustration of all the different approaches to time-series. The discussion starts with the problems of temporal dependence of time-series and its impact on the properties of the estimator, the solution provided by asymptotic theory for stationary time-series is then discussed. Non-stationarity is introduced as the reason for the impossibility of using asymptotic theory to fix dependence. Cointegration is then considered as the solution in that it allows to specify a cointegrated VAR as the baseline stationary statistical model for non-stationary time-series. On such a statistical model the fundamental problem of identification is discussed, with a separate treatment of identification of long-run equilibrium relationships and short-run simultaneous feedback. Within this common statistical framework, we introduce the criticisms to Cowles Commission econometrics and our analysis of the alternative econometric methodologies currently used by the profession. Chapter 4 illustrates the Cowles Commission approach by considering specification, estimation and simulation of a simple IS-LM-AS-AD model fitted to US data. Chapter 5 illustrates the LSE methodology by introducing the diagnosis of the Cowles Commission problems provided within this approach as well as the proposed solution. Chapters 6, 7, and 8 apply the same strategy to VAR, intertemporal optimization GMM approach and calibration. The chapter on calibration would not exist in this actual format without the contribution of Marco Maffezzoli, who is jointly responsible for this section. Marco and I have jointly taught the advanced econometrics option in Bocconi's Master of Economics course, the book has greatly benefited from this experience.

### Data, programmes and exercises

Data, programmes and exercises are available from the section of my homepage devoted to the book at the following address:

**http://www.igier.uni-bocconi.it/personal/favero/homepage.htm**

Applications presented in the book are performed by using different packages, such as E-views, Pc-Give, Pc-Fiml, RATS and Matlab. The data are provided in the appropriate format for the package used in the application and also in Excel format, to leave the reader free to experiment with the preferred software.

Exercises are not yet available at the date of publication of the book, but I plan to include them in the site as part of a project of continuous updating of the book. I really hope that the website will grow over time, also with contributions by the readers.

**Acknowledgements**

This book reflects my research and draws heavily from joint work with many co-authors. My grateful thanks go to Fabio-Cesare Bagliano, Vladimiro Ceci, Rudi Dornbusch, Francesco Franco, Francesco Giavazzi, David Hendry, Fabrizio Iacone, Jack Lucchetti, Marco Maffezzoli, Alessandro Missale, Anton Muscatelli, Luca Papi, Hashem Pesaran, Marco Pifferi, Riccardo Rovelli, Giorgio Primiceri, Sunil Sharma, Luigi Spaventa, Franco Spinelli, Guido Tabellini.

Over the years many colleagues have influenced and shaped my perception of how applied macroeconomics is and should be done. I am especially indebted to Larry Christiano, James Davidson, Roger Farmer, Carlo Giannini, Clive Granger, Luigi Guiso, James Hamilton, David Hendry, Soren Johansen, Katarina Juselius, Rocco Mosconi, John Muellbauer, Paolo Paruolo, Bahram Pesaran, Hashem Pesaran, Lucrezia Reichlin, Alan Timmermann, Mike Wickens and Harald Uhlig for having commented constructively on my work and having helped my understanding of different methodologies.

My work has benefited from comments by many students, especially those attending the Master of Economics course (MEc) at Bocconi University, some of them have also been involved in writing, documenting, and indexing the book. Special thanks to Gani Aldashev, Marco Aiolfi, and Giorgio Primiceri for their help. Marco Aiolfi has also made available some interesting exercises on optimal monetary policy along with the Matlab codes for their solution.

I firmly believe that the main motivation for my book is the promotion of cross-fertilization among different methodologies in applied macroeconometrics. A number of institutions have offered me the possibility of meeting and exchanging ideas with researchers from very different backgrounds. I am glad to acknowledge my debt to the Center For Economic Policy Research, to the Innocenzo Gasparini Institute for Economic Research. Acknowledging a debt to IGIER usually means also acknowledging a debt to Ornella Bissoli, and I make no exception. Centro Interuniversitario di Econometria has played an important role in facilitating circulation of ideas among Italian econometricians, within this group Roberto Golinelli and Jack Lucchetti have provided extensive and extremely useful comments on draft chapters. I am also very grateful to Christian Zimmermann for his effort in constructing and developing the Quantitative Macroeconomics and Real Business Cycle home page, a great website for getting in touch with research on applied macroeconometrics:

**http://ideas.uqam.ca/QMRBC/index.html**

Colleagues at Queen Mary Westfield College, University of Ancona and Bocconi University have granted me over the years the possibility of working in friendly and open-minded environments. Special thanks to Chris Gilbert, Jonathan Haskel, Chris Martin, Steve Pollock, Jack Lucchetti, Matteo Manera, Massimiliano Marcellino and Bruno Sitzia.

I also owe much to the modelling team of the Italian Treasury, with which I worked on the construction of ITEM (the Italian Treasury Econometric Model), for giving me the opportunity of learning a lot on the application of macroeconometrics to policy analysis. Many thanks to Riccardo Fiorito, Francesco Nucci, Ottavio Ricchi and Flavio Padrini.

*Applied Macroeconometrics* reflects the path of my research until 1999, and develops considerably ( I believe) on views and ideas expressed in a previous book in Italian entitled *Econometria*, edited by Nuova Italia Scientifica (now Carocci editore) in 1996. I am grateful to Gianluca Mori of Carocci for his support for the old project, and for allowing me to develop freely the new one.

There is a group of people who are the constant reference point of my work. This group includes Francesca, Vittoria and Angelo Raimondo Favero, Caterina, Alessandro and Simone Mancuso, Lorenzo Fornasetti, Emma and Riccardo Missale, Arianna Pucci, Kiki Signorini, Sophie and Sacha Martin, Ino and Ivan Badanjak, Alessandro and Edoardo Zorzoli, Benjamin and Leo Vlassenroot. My deep thanks to all of them.

I also owe much to Massimo Fuggetta, my personal guru, for his spiritual guidance.

Financial support from MURST (Italian Ministry for University and Scientific Research) is gratefully acknowledged.

CONTENTS


**1 Applied Macroeconometrics: an introduction** 1

1.1 Introduction 1

1.2 From theory to data: the neo-classical growth model 1

1.3 Estimation problem: ordinary least squares 3

1.4 OLS estimation of the Solow growth model 9

1.5 Residual analysis 10

1.6 Elements of distribution theory 12

1.7 Inference in the linear regression model 14

1.8 Estimation under linear constraints 19

1.9 The effects of mis-specification 22

1.10 Human capital in Solow's growth model 24

1.11 Importance of time-series in macroeconomics 26

1.12 Alternative research strategies in macroeconometrics 28

1.13 References 30

**2 Probabilistic structure of time-series data** 31

2.1 Introduction: what is a time-series? 31

2.2 Analysing time-series: fundamentals 34

2.3 Persistence: Monte-Carlo experiment 40

2.4 Traditional solution: asymptotic theory 42

2.5 Stochastic trends and spurious regressions 44

2.6 Univariate decompositions of time-series 50

2.7 Multivariate decompositions and dynamic models 56

2.8 Multivariate cointegration: an application to US data 71

2.9 Multivariate decompositions: some considerations 79

2.10 References 81

**3 Identification problem in macroeconometrics** 85

3.1 Introduction 85

3.2 Identification in the Cowles Commission approach 88

3.3 Great critiques 91

3.4 Identification in LSE methodology 94

3.5 Identification in VAR methodology 96

3.6 Identification in intertemporally optimized models 99

3.7 References 101

**4 Cowles Commission approach** 103

4.1 Introduction 103

4.2 Estimation in the Cowles Commission approach 103

4.3 Simulation 117
4.4 Policy evaluation 118
4.5 A model of the monetary transmisssion mechanism 120
4.6 Assessing econometric evaluation of monetary policy 126
4.7 What is wrong with econometric policy evaluation? 128
4.8 References 130

**5 LSE approach** 132
5.1 Introduction 132
5.2 The LSE diagnosis 133
5.3 Reduction process 134
5.4 Test, test and test 137
5.5 Testing a Cowles Commission model 140
5.6 Searching for a congruent specification 142
5.7 Cointegration analysis 144
5.8 Specifying a structural model 144
5.9 A model of the monetary transmission mechanism 153
5.10 Simulating monetary policy 154
5.11 What have we learned? 158
5.12 References 160

**6 VAR approach** 162
6.1 Introduction: why VAR models? 162
6.2 Identification and estimation 164
6.3 Why shocks? 172
6.4 Description of VAR models 174
6.5 Monetary policy in closed economies 176
6.6 Monetary policy in open economies 180
6.7 VAR and non-VAR measures of monetary policy 191
6.8 Empirical results 201
6.9 Conclusions 207
6.10 References 210

**7 Intertemporal Optimization and GMM method** 214
7.1 Introduction 214
7.2 Euler equations and closed form solutions 215
7.3 Estimating Euler equations: the GMM method 219
7.4 The limits to Euler equation–GMM approach 225
7.5 Application to the consumer's problem 228
7.6 GMM and monetary policy rules 229
7.7 Interest rate rules and central banks' preferences 235
7.8 References 238

**8 Calibration (with M. Maffezzoli)** 241
8.1 Introduction 241
8.2 Model design 242

8.3 Dynamic equilibrium 245
8.4 An IS–LM interpretation 247
8.5 Choice of parameters 248
8.6 Calibration 253
8.7 Model solution 255
8.8 Implementation 262
8.9 Model evaluation 266
8.10 Policy analysis 274
8.11 References 275

**Index** 278

# 1

# APPLIED MACROECONOMETRICS: AN INTRODUCTION

## 1.1 Introduction

Once upon a time there was consensus on both the theoretical foundations of macroeconomics and the correct approach to macroeconometric modelling. Such a consensus, built around the Cowles Commission approach to model building, broke down dramatically at the beginning of the 1970s when it became clear that '...the models did not represent the data...did not represent the theory... were ineffective for practical purposes of forecasting and policy...', Pesaran and Smith(1995) . The breakdown of consensus has been rather spectacular, but, as Faust and Whiteman(1997) put it

> ...even more impressive are the deep rifts that have emerged over the proper way to tease empirical facts from macroeconomic data....

This book has the ambitious aim of discussing and illustrating the different approaches currently taken by the profession in applied macroeconometrics. We concentrate on the (large) subset of macroeconometrics dealing with time-series data. It is fair to say that the emergence of those deep rifts has been paired with a clear awareness of the specificity of time-series data. We shall discuss the emergence of a plurality of approaches in macroeconomic modelling within a framework provided by the statistical analysis of time-series data. We start with an introduction, which reviews the basics in econometrics, describes the interaction between theory and data in applied work, and illustrates the importance of using time-series instead of cross-section data in macroeconometrics.

## 1.2 From theory to data: the neo-classical growth model

Consider the Solow model of growth.[1] This model takes as given the saving rate, $s$, the rate of growth of population, $n$, while technology, $A$, grows at a constant rate $g$. There are two inputs: capital, $K$, and labour, $L$, paid their respective marginal productivities. Output, $Y$, is determined by a Cobb–Douglas function with constant returns to scale

$$Y_t = K_t^{\alpha} \left(A_t L_t\right)^{1-\alpha}, \qquad 0 < \alpha < 1,$$

$$L_t = L_{t-1} \left(1 + n\right), \qquad (1.1)$$

$$A_t = A_{t-1} \left(1 + g\right). \qquad (1.2)$$

[1]The original reference is Solow (1956). The data and the empirical analysis of this chapter replicate the results reported in Mankiw, Romer and Weil (1992). For an excellent introduction to macroeconomic models of growth, see Barro and Sala-i-Martin (1995) and Farmer (1998).

Note that the number of effective unit of labour grows (approximately) at the rate $(n+g)$. The model is built by considering the production function together with two accounting identities and an *ad hoc* relation between savings and output. The two accounting identities are

$$S_t \equiv I_t, \tag{1.3}$$

$$K_t \equiv K_{t-1}(1-\delta) + I_t, \tag{1.4}$$

where $I$ denotes investment, $S$ denotes savings, and $\delta$ represents the rate of depreciation of the capital stock $K$. Equation (1.3) immediately clarifies that we are considering a closed economy with no government sector.

The relationship between output and saving is determined by assuming a constant marginal propensity to save $s$

$$\frac{S}{Y} = s. \tag{1.5}$$

We define as $k$ and $y$, respectively, the stock of capital per effective unit of labour $(K/AL)$ and the level of output per effective unit of labour $(Y/AL)$. By using all the equations in the model we have

$$k_t(1+n)(1+g) = k_{t-1}(1-\delta) + sk_t^{\alpha}. \tag{1.6}$$

Equation (1.6) determines the pattern over time of the stock of capital per effective unit of labour. From this relation we can pin down the steady-state value of $k$, by setting $k^* = k_{t+i}$ for each $i$

$$k^* = \left(\frac{s}{n+g+\delta}\right)^{\frac{1}{1-\alpha}}. \tag{1.7}$$

Equation (1.7) shows that the steady-state $k$ is positively related to the saving rate and negatively related to the rate of growth of population, the rate of technological progress, and the rate of depreciation of capital.

By substituting (1.7) in the production function and taking logarithms, we derive the per capita steady-state output growth as:

$$\ln\left(\frac{Y_t^*}{L_t}\right) = \ln A_0 + gt + \frac{\alpha}{1-\alpha}\ln(s) - \frac{\alpha}{1-\alpha}\ln(n+g+\delta). \tag{1.8}$$

Equation (1.7) makes specific predictions on the impact on output of the saving rate and the rate of population growth, the rate of technological progress, and the rate of depreciation of capital.

It is natural at this stage to raise a question on the empirical support to such well-specified predictions. Mankiw, Romer, and Weil (1992) chose to test the model on data from a cross-section of countries. Such data are available from a database constructed by Summers and Heston (1988), which contains series on real output, private and government consumption, investment, and population for virtually all countries in the world, excluding planned economies. The data are available at annual frequencies. Mankiw, Romer and Weil concentrate on the variables of interest between 1960 and 1985. The rate of growth of population, $n$, is measured by the average rate of growth of population in working age (15-64 years old). The rate of savings, $s$, is measured by the ratio of investment to GDP. $n$ and $s$ are averages for the period 1960-85. $y$ is measured by the log of GDP per working age person in 1985. $(g + \delta)$ is not directly observable and is assumed constant at a value of 0.05. We concentrate on a sample of 75 countries labelled 'Intermediate' by the authors and obtained by considering non-oil producing countries with populations above one million in 1960 and reliable data, thus excluding from the sample oil producers (as the bulk of their GDP is not value added but extraction of existing resources), small countries, and countries with low-quality data (receiving a grade of 'D' from Summers and Heston). The data are contained, in Excel format, in the file mrw.xls.

Now we have data and equation $\ln y_i$, which makes specific, theory-based predictions on the relations between variables in our dataset. How can we empirically test the Solow model?

The first point to note is that (1.8) has no stochastic structure. Mankiw, Romer, and Weil add such structure to the data by concentrating on the term $A$ and on the difference between $Y$ and $Y^*$. $A$ reflects not only the state of technology but also other factors, such as natural resources, climate, and institutions; therefore the following specification is adopted:

$$\ln A_0 = a + v_i, \tag{1.9}$$

where $a$ is a constant and $\varepsilon_i$ represents a country-specific shock. Moreover, if deviation of observed output from equilibrium output can be modelled as an i.i.d. disturbance, we have

$$\ln y_i = \ln y_i^* + u_i \tag{1.10}$$

By substituting from (1.9) and 1.10 into (1.8) we have:

$$\begin{aligned} \ln y_i &= a + gt + \frac{\alpha}{1-\alpha} \ln (s_i) - \frac{\alpha}{1-\alpha} \ln (n_i + g + \delta) + \varepsilon_i, \\ \varepsilon_i &= u_i + v_i \end{aligned} \tag{1.11}$$

which forms the basis for the empirical investigation.

## 1.3 Estimation problem: ordinary least squares

The basis for an empirical test of the predictions of Solow's model is the estimation of (1.11). Consider the following model on our sample of 75 countries:

$$\ln y_i = \beta_0 + \beta_1 \ln (s_i) + \beta_2 \ln (n_i + g + \delta) + \varepsilon_i. \tag{1.12}$$

If Solow's model describes the data correctly, then the parameter $\beta_0$ should capture the term $a + gt$, which is a constant on the cross-section of data, while

$\beta_1$ should be equal to $\frac{\alpha}{1-\alpha}$ and $\beta_2$ should instead take the value of $-\frac{\alpha}{1-\alpha}$. Independent information on factor shares can be used to assess the magnitude of the estimated coefficient. Mankiw, Romer, and Weil claim that the data on factor shares suggest $\frac{1}{3}$ as a plausible value for $\alpha$ and, therefore, the elasticities of $y_i$ with respect to $s_i$ and $(n_i + g + \delta)$ should be, respectively, 0.5 and -0.5. Moreover, under the null of the validity of Solow's model, we have a testable restriction on the parameters, namely, $\beta_1 = -\beta_2$.

To illustrate how estimation can be performed, consider the following general representation of our model:

$$\mathbf{y} = \mathbf{X}\boldsymbol{\beta} + \boldsymbol{\epsilon},$$

$$\mathbf{y} = \begin{pmatrix} y_1 \\ \cdot \\ \cdot \\ \cdot \\ y_N \end{pmatrix}, \quad \mathbf{X} = \begin{pmatrix} x_{11} & x_{12} & \cdot\cdot & x_{1k} \\ \cdot & \cdot & \cdot\cdot & \cdot \\ \cdot & \cdot & \cdot\cdot & \cdot \\ \cdot & \cdot & \cdot\cdot & \cdot \\ x_{N1} & x_{N2} & \cdot\cdot & x_{Nk} \end{pmatrix},$$

$$\boldsymbol{\beta} = \begin{pmatrix} \beta_1 \\ \cdot \\ \cdot \\ \cdot \\ \beta_k \end{pmatrix}, \quad \boldsymbol{\epsilon} = \begin{pmatrix} \varepsilon_1 \\ \cdot \\ \cdot \\ \cdot \\ \varepsilon_N \end{pmatrix}.$$

In our case $N = 75$, $k = 3$, the vector $\mathbf{y}$ contains 75 observations on per capita GDP while matrix $\mathbf{X}$ is $(75 \times 3)$. Note that the first column of $\mathbf{X}$ consists entirely of ones, the second contains observations on $\ln(s_i)$, while the third contains observations on $\ln(n_i + g + \delta)$. The vector $\boldsymbol{\beta}$ contains three parameters: a constant and the two elasticities of interest in our economic problem.

The simplest way to derive estimates of the parameters of interest is the ordinary least squares (OLS) method. Such a method chooses values for the unknown parameter to minimize the magnitude of the non-observable components. Define the following quantity:

$$\mathbf{e}(\boldsymbol{\beta}) = \mathbf{y} - \mathbf{X}\boldsymbol{\beta},$$

where $\mathbf{e}(\boldsymbol{\beta})$ is a $(n \times 1)$ vector. If we treat $\mathbf{X}\boldsymbol{\beta}$, as a (conditional) prediction for $\mathbf{y}$, then we can consider $\mathbf{e}(\boldsymbol{\beta})$ as a forecasting error. The sum of the squared errors is then

$$\mathbf{S}(\boldsymbol{\beta}) = \mathbf{e}(\boldsymbol{\beta})' \mathbf{e}(\boldsymbol{\beta}).$$

The OLS method produces an estimator of $\boldsymbol{\beta}$, $\widehat{\boldsymbol{\beta}}$, defined as follows:

$$\mathbf{S}\left(\widehat{\boldsymbol{\beta}}\right) = \min_{\boldsymbol{\beta}} \mathbf{e}(\boldsymbol{\beta})' \mathbf{e}(\boldsymbol{\beta}).$$

Given $\widehat{\boldsymbol{\beta}}$, we can define an associated vector of residual $\widehat{\epsilon}$ as $\widehat{\epsilon} = \mathbf{y} - \mathbf{X}\widehat{\boldsymbol{\beta}}$. The OLS estimator is derived by considering the necessary and sufficient conditions for $\widehat{\boldsymbol{\beta}}$ to be a unique minimum for $\mathbf{S}$:

1. $\mathbf{X}'\widehat{\epsilon} = 0$;
2. $\text{rank}(\mathbf{X}) = k$.

Condition 1 imposes orthogonality between the right-hand side variables on the OLS residuals, and ensures that residuals have an average of zero when a constant is included among the regressors. Condition 2 requires that the columns of the $\mathbf{X}$ matrix are linearly independent: no variable in $\mathbf{X}$ can be expressed as a linear combination of the other variables in $\mathbf{X}$.

From 1 we derive an expression for the OLS estimates:

$$\mathbf{X}'\widehat{\epsilon} = \mathbf{X}'\left(\mathbf{y} - \mathbf{X}\widehat{\boldsymbol{\beta}}\right) = \mathbf{X}'\mathbf{y} - \mathbf{X}'\mathbf{X}\widehat{\boldsymbol{\beta}} = 0,$$
$$\widehat{\boldsymbol{\beta}} = \left(\mathbf{X}'\mathbf{X}\right)^{-1}\mathbf{X}'\mathbf{y}.$$

### 1.3.1 *Properties of the OLS estimates*

We have derived the OLS estimator without any assumption on the statistical structure of the data. However, the statistical structure of the data is needed not to derive the estimator but to define its properties. To illustrate them, we refer to the basic concepts of mean and variance of vector variables.

Given a generic vector of variables, $\mathbf{x}$,

$$\mathbf{x} = \begin{pmatrix} x_1 \\ . \\ . \\ . \\ x_n \end{pmatrix},$$

we define the mean vector $E(\mathbf{x})$ and the mean matrix of outer products $E(\mathbf{x}\mathbf{x}')$ as:

$$E(\mathbf{x}) = \begin{pmatrix} E(x_1) \\ . \\ . \\ . \\ E(x_n) \end{pmatrix},$$

$$E(\mathbf{x}\mathbf{x}') = E\begin{pmatrix} x_1^2 & x_1x_2 & .. & x_1x_n \\ . & x_2^2 & .. & x_2x_n \\ . & . & .. & . \\ . & . & .. & . \\ x_nx_1 & x_nx_2 & .. & x_n^2 \end{pmatrix}$$

$$= \begin{pmatrix} E(x_1^2) & E(x_1x_2) & .. & E(x_1x_n) \\ . & E(x_2^2) & .. & E(x_2x_n) \\ . & . & .. & . \\ . & . & .. & . \\ E(x_nx_1) & E(x_nx_2) & .. & E(x_n^2) \end{pmatrix}.$$

The variance-covariance matrix of $\mathbf{x}$ is the defined as:

$$\begin{aligned} var(\mathbf{x}) &= E(\mathbf{x}-E(\mathbf{x}))\,E(\mathbf{x}-E(\mathbf{x}))' \\ &= E(\mathbf{x}\mathbf{x}') - E(\mathbf{x})\,E(\mathbf{x})'. \end{aligned}$$

Note that the variance-covariance matrix is symmetric and positive definite, by construction. Given an arbitrary $\mathbf{A}$ vector of dimension $n$, we have:

$$var(\mathbf{A}'\mathbf{x}) = \mathbf{A}'var(\mathbf{x})\,\mathbf{A}.$$

The first relevant hypothesis for the derivation of the statistical properties of OLS regards the relationship between disturbances and regressors in the estimated equation. This hypothesis is constructed in two parts: first we assume that $E(\mathbf{y}_i \mid \mathbf{x}_i) = \mathbf{x}_i'\boldsymbol{\beta}$, ruling out the contemporaneous correlation between residuals and regressors (which is therefore valid if there are no omitted variables correlated with the regressors), second we assume that the components of the available sample are independently drawn. The second assumption guarantees the equivalence between $E(\mathbf{y}_i \mid \mathbf{x}_i) = \mathbf{x}_i'\boldsymbol{\beta}$ and $E(\mathbf{y}_i \mid \mathbf{x}_1, ..., \mathbf{x}_i, ..., \mathbf{x}_n) = \mathbf{x}_i'\boldsymbol{\beta}$. Using vector notation, we have:

$$E(\mathbf{y} \mid \mathbf{X}) = \mathbf{X}\boldsymbol{\beta},$$

which is equivalent to

$$E(\boldsymbol{\epsilon} \mid \mathbf{X}) = \mathbf{0}. \tag{1.13}$$

Note that hypothesis (1.13) is very demanding. It implies that

$$E(\epsilon_i \mid \mathbf{x}_1, ...\mathbf{x}_i, ...\mathbf{x}_n) = 0 \quad (i = 1, ...n).$$

The conditional mean is, in general, a non-linear function of $(\mathbf{x}_1, ..., \mathbf{x}_i, ..., \mathbf{x}_n)$ and (1.13) requires that such a function is a constant of zero. Note that (1.13) requires that each regressor is orthogonal not only to the error term associated with the same observation ($E(x_{ik}\varepsilon_i) = 0$ for all $k$), but also to the error tem associated with each other observation ($E(x_{jk}\varepsilon_i) = 0$ for all $j \neq k$). This statement is proved by using the properties of conditional expectations.

Since $E(\epsilon \mid \mathbf{X}) = \mathbf{0}$ implies, from the law of iterated expectations, that $E(\epsilon) = \mathbf{0}$, we have

$$E(\varepsilon_i \mid x_{jk}) = E[E(\varepsilon_i \mid \mathbf{x}) \mid x_{jk}] = 0. \tag{1.14}$$

Then

$$\begin{aligned} E(\varepsilon_i x_{jk}) &= E[E(\varepsilon_i x_{jk} \mid x_{jk})] && (1.15)\\ &= E[x_{jk}E(\varepsilon_i \mid x_{jk})] && (1.16)\\ &= 0. && (1.17)\end{aligned}$$

In the context of the Solow model, (1.13) requires that $s$ and $n$ are independent from $\epsilon$. Such a hypothesis is clearly false in any time-series model when the time-series shows some degree of persistence (which is always true in practice). Think of a simplest time-series model for a generic variable $y$:

$$y_t = a_0 + a_1 y_{t-1} + u_t.$$

Clearly, if $a_1 \neq 0$, then, $E(u_{t-1} \mid y_{t-1}) \neq 0$ although it is still true that $E(u_t \mid y_{t-1}) = 0$, and (1.13) breaks down, without any omitted variable problem.

This is why we use a cross-section example in our introductory chapter. We shall then complicate the framework to deal properly with time-series observations.

The second hypothesis defines the constancy of the conditional variance of shocks:

$$E(\epsilon'\epsilon \mid \mathbf{X}) = \sigma^2 I, \tag{1.18}$$

where $\sigma^2$ is a constant independent from $\mathbf{X}$.

The third hypothesis is the one already introduced, which guarantees that the OLS estimator can be derived:

$$rank(\mathbf{X}) = k. \tag{1.19}$$

Under hypotheses (1.13) – (1.19) we can derive the properties of the OLS estimator.

**Property 1: unbiasedness**
The conditional expectation (with respect to $\mathbf{X}$) of the OLS estimates is the vector of unknown parameters $\boldsymbol{\beta}$:

$$\begin{aligned}\widehat{\boldsymbol{\beta}} &= (\mathbf{X}'\mathbf{X})^{-1}\mathbf{X}'(\mathbf{X}\boldsymbol{\beta}+\epsilon)\\ &= \boldsymbol{\beta}+(\mathbf{X}'\mathbf{X})^{-1}\mathbf{X}'\epsilon\\ E\left(\widehat{\boldsymbol{\beta}}\mid\mathbf{X}\right) &= \boldsymbol{\beta}+(\mathbf{X}'\mathbf{X})^{-1}\mathbf{X}'E(\epsilon\mid\mathbf{X})\\ &= \boldsymbol{\beta},\end{aligned}$$

by hypothesis (1.13).

**Property 2: variance of OLS**
The conditional variance of the OLS estimator is $\sigma^2(\mathbf{X}'\mathbf{X})^{-1}$:

$$\begin{aligned}var\left(\widehat{\boldsymbol{\beta}}\mid\mathbf{X}\right) &= E\left(\left(\widehat{\boldsymbol{\beta}}-\boldsymbol{\beta}\right)\left(\widehat{\boldsymbol{\beta}}-\boldsymbol{\beta}\right)'\mid\mathbf{X}\right)\\ &= E\left((\mathbf{X}'\mathbf{X})^{-1}\mathbf{X}'\epsilon\epsilon'\mathbf{X}(\mathbf{X}'\mathbf{X})^{-1}\mid\mathbf{X}\right)\\ &= (\mathbf{X}'\mathbf{X})^{-1}\mathbf{X}'E(\epsilon\epsilon'\mid\mathbf{X})\mathbf{X}(\mathbf{X}'\mathbf{X})^{-1}\\ &= (\mathbf{X}'\mathbf{X})^{-1}\mathbf{X}'\sigma^2 I\mathbf{X}(\mathbf{X}'\mathbf{X})^{-1}\\ &= \sigma^2(\mathbf{X}'\mathbf{X})^{-1}.\end{aligned}$$

**Property 3: Gauss-Markov theorem**
The OLS estimator is the most efficient in the class of linear unbiased estimators.

Consider the class of linear estimators:

$$\boldsymbol{\beta}_L = \mathbf{L}\mathbf{y}.$$

This class is defined by the set of matrices $(k\times n)$ $\mathbf{L}$, which are fixed when conditioning upon $\mathbf{X}$. $\mathbf{L}$ does not depend on $\mathbf{y}$. Therefore we have:

$$\begin{aligned}E(\boldsymbol{\beta}_L\mid\mathbf{X}) &= E(\mathbf{L}\mathbf{X}\boldsymbol{\beta}+\mathbf{L}\varepsilon\mid\mathbf{X})\\ &= \mathbf{L}\mathbf{X}\boldsymbol{\beta},\end{aligned}$$

and $\mathbf{L}\mathbf{X}\boldsymbol{\beta}=\boldsymbol{\beta}$ only if $\mathbf{L}\mathbf{X}=\mathbf{I}_k$. Such a condition is obviously satisfied by the OLS estimator, which is obtained by setting $\mathbf{L}=(\mathbf{X}'\mathbf{X})^{-1}\mathbf{X}'$. The variance of the general estimator in the class of linear unbiased estimators is readily obtained as:

$$\begin{aligned}var(\boldsymbol{\beta}_L\mid\mathbf{X}) &= E\left(\mathbf{L}\varepsilon\varepsilon'\mathbf{L}'\mid\mathbf{X}\right)\\ &= \sigma^2\mathbf{L}\mathbf{L}'.\end{aligned}$$

To show that the OLS estimator is the most efficient within this class we have to show that the variance of the OLS estimator differs from the variance of the generic estimator in the class by a positive semidefinite matrix.

To this aim define $\mathbf{D} = \mathbf{L} - (\mathbf{X}'\mathbf{X})^{-1}\mathbf{X}'$; $\mathbf{LX} = \mathbf{I}$ requires $\mathbf{DX} = \mathbf{0}$.

$$\begin{aligned}\mathbf{LL}' &= \left((\mathbf{X}'\mathbf{X})^{-1}\mathbf{X}' + \mathbf{D}\right)\left(\mathbf{X}(\mathbf{X}'\mathbf{X})^{-1} + \mathbf{D}'\right) \\ &= (\mathbf{X}'\mathbf{X})^{-1}\mathbf{X}'\mathbf{X}(\mathbf{X}'\mathbf{X})^{-1} + (\mathbf{X}'\mathbf{X})^{-1}\mathbf{X}'\mathbf{D}' + \\ &\quad + \mathbf{DX}(\mathbf{X}'\mathbf{X})^{-1} + \mathbf{DD}' \\ &= (\mathbf{X}'\mathbf{X})^{-1} + \mathbf{DD}',\end{aligned}$$

from which we have that

$$var(\boldsymbol{\beta}_L \mid \mathbf{X}) = var\left(\widehat{\boldsymbol{\beta}} \mid \mathbf{X}\right) + \sigma^2\mathbf{DD}',$$

which proves the point. For any given matrix $\mathbf{D}$, (not necessarily square), the symmetric matrix $\mathbf{DD}'$ is positive semidefinite.

## 1.4 OLS estimation of the Solow growth model

Table 1.1 reports the results of the application of the OLS to the Solow growth model. We report point estimates along with standard errors (square roots of the elements in the principal diagonal of the variance-covariance matrix of the OLS estimates). The table is based on a regression run by using E-Views and exactly replicates the results in Table 1 of Mankiw, Romer, and Weil (1992: 414).

TABLE 1.1: The estimation of the Solow model

| Variable | Coefficient | Std. Error | t-ratio | Prob. |
|---|---|---|---|---|
| C | 5.367698 | 1.540082 | 3.485333 | 0.0008 |
| $\ln(s)$ | 1.325353 | 0.170611 | 7.768281 | 0.0000 |
| $\ln(n+g+\delta)$ | -2.013390 | 0.532830 | -3.778672 | 0.0003 |

$R^2$ 0.601703 S.E. of regression 0.609456

$\ln(s)$: log of savings rate (defined as LNS in mrw.xls)

$\ln(n+g+\delta)$ : log of 0.05 + rate of growth of population (defined as LNNGD in mrw.xls)

Let's consider the results. First, we have specified a model by deriving it directly from the theory and we have estimated it to derive empirical evidence on the validity of the model's prediction. Adoption of this strategy for research makes the residuals of the estimated model informative in that they reflect the impact of all variables omitted from the chosen specification. The analysis of residuals can be revealing on the mis-specification of the estimated model.

Second, the coefficients have the expected sign but do not exactly satisfy the restrictions implied by the theory. The absolute values of the point estimates of the two elasticities are different, and their magnitude does not match available information on the capital-output ratio. The authors observe that the empirical observation of a capital-output ratio of about one third is consistent with an elasticity of the pro-capita output with respect to the saving rate of about 0.5 and elasticity of the per capita output with respect to $(n+g+\delta)$ of about $-0.5$. The natural question at this point relates to the nature of estimated parameters. Given that they are random variables, one can try and derive their distribution in order to test statistically the hypotheses of economic interest. An interesting general hypothesis regards the significance of the estimated coefficients, while more specific hypotheses are of interest in testing the prediction of the theory (in our case, $\beta_1 = -\beta_2$, $\beta_1 = 0.5$, $\beta_2 = -0.5$).

## 1.5 Residual analysis

Consider the following representation:

$$\begin{aligned} \widehat{\boldsymbol{\epsilon}} &= \mathbf{y} - \mathbf{X}\widehat{\boldsymbol{\beta}} \\ &= \mathbf{y} - \mathbf{X}\left(\mathbf{X}'\mathbf{X}\right)^{-1}\mathbf{X}'\mathbf{y} = \mathbf{M}\mathbf{y}, \end{aligned}$$

where $\mathbf{M} = \mathbf{I}_n - \mathbf{Q}$, and $\mathbf{Q} = \mathbf{X}\left(\mathbf{X}'\mathbf{X}\right)^{-1}\mathbf{X}'$. The $(n \times n)$ matrices $\mathbf{M}$ and $\mathbf{Q}$, have the following properties:

1. they are symmetric: $\mathbf{M}' = \mathbf{M}, \mathbf{Q}' = \mathbf{Q}$;
2. they are idempotent: $\mathbf{QQ} = \mathbf{Q}, \mathbf{MM} = \mathbf{M}$;
3. $\mathbf{MX} = \mathbf{0}, \mathbf{MQ} = \mathbf{0}, \mathbf{QX} = \mathbf{X}$.

Note that the OLS projection for $\mathbf{y}$ can be written as $\widehat{\mathbf{y}} = \mathbf{X}\widehat{\boldsymbol{\beta}} = \mathbf{Q}\mathbf{y}$, and that $\widehat{\boldsymbol{\epsilon}} = \mathbf{M}\mathbf{y}$, from which we have the known result of orthogonality between the OLS residuals and regressors. We also have $\mathbf{My} = \mathbf{MX}\boldsymbol{\beta} + \mathbf{M}\boldsymbol{\epsilon} = \mathbf{M}\boldsymbol{\epsilon}$, given that $\mathbf{MX} = \mathbf{0}$. Therefore we have a very well-specified relation between the OLS residuals and the errors in the model $\widehat{\boldsymbol{\epsilon}} = \mathbf{M}\boldsymbol{\epsilon}$, which cannot be used to derive the errors given the residuals, since the $\mathbf{M}$ matrix is not invertible.

We can re-write the sum of squared residuals as:

$$S\left(\widehat{\boldsymbol{\beta}}\right) = \widehat{\boldsymbol{\epsilon}}'\widehat{\boldsymbol{\epsilon}} = \boldsymbol{\epsilon}'\mathbf{M}'\mathbf{M}\boldsymbol{\epsilon} = \boldsymbol{\epsilon}'\mathbf{M}\boldsymbol{\epsilon}.$$

$S\left(\widehat{\boldsymbol{\beta}}\right)$ is an obvious candidate for the construction of an estimate for $\sigma^2$. To derive an estimate of $\sigma^2$ from $S\left(\widehat{\boldsymbol{\beta}}\right)$, we introduce the concept of trace. The trace of a square matrix is the sum of all elements on its principal diagonal. The following properties are relevant:

1. given any two square matrices $\mathbf{A}$ and $\mathbf{B}$, $tr\left(\mathbf{A} + \mathbf{B}\right) = tr\mathbf{A} + tr\mathbf{B}$;
2. given any two matrices $\mathbf{A}$ and $\mathbf{B}$, $tr\left(\mathbf{AB}\right) = tr\left(\mathbf{BA}\right)$;
3. the rank of an idempotent matrix is equal to its trace.

Using property 2 together with the fact that a scalar coincides with its trace, we have:

$$\boldsymbol{\epsilon}'\mathbf{M}\boldsymbol{\epsilon} = tr\left(\boldsymbol{\epsilon}'\mathbf{M}\boldsymbol{\epsilon}\right) = tr\left(\mathbf{M}\boldsymbol{\epsilon}\boldsymbol{\epsilon}'\right).$$

Now we analyse the expected value of $S\left(\widehat{\boldsymbol{\beta}}\right)$, conditional upon $\mathbf{X}$:

$$\begin{aligned} E\left(S\left(\widehat{\boldsymbol{\beta}}\right) \mid \mathbf{X}\right) &= E\left(tr\mathbf{M}\boldsymbol{\epsilon}\boldsymbol{\epsilon}' \mid \mathbf{X}\right) \\ &= tr E\left(\mathbf{M}\boldsymbol{\epsilon}\boldsymbol{\epsilon}' \mid \mathbf{X}\right) \\ &= tr\mathbf{M}\left(E\boldsymbol{\epsilon}\boldsymbol{\epsilon}' \mid \mathbf{X}\right) \\ &= \sigma^2 tr\mathbf{M}. \end{aligned}$$

From properties 1 and 2 we have:

$$\begin{aligned} tr\mathbf{M} &= tr\mathbf{I}_n - tr\left(\mathbf{X}\left(\mathbf{X}'\mathbf{X}\right)^{-1}\mathbf{X}'\right) \\ &= n - tr\left(\mathbf{X}'\mathbf{X}\left(\mathbf{X}'\mathbf{X}\right)^{-1}\right) \\ &= n - k. \end{aligned}$$

Therefore, an unbiased estimate of $\sigma^2$ is given by $s^2 = S\left(\widehat{\boldsymbol{\beta}}\right)/(n-k)$.

These results allow us to construct the standard errors for the estimated OLS parameters reported in the second column of Table 1.1.

Using the result of orthogonality between the OLS projections and residuals, we can write:

$$var\left(\mathbf{y}\right) = var\left(\widehat{\mathbf{y}}\right) + var\left(\widehat{\boldsymbol{\epsilon}}\right),$$

from which we can derive the following residual-based indicator of the goodness of fit:

$$R^2 = \frac{var\left(\widehat{\mathbf{y}}\right)}{var\left(\mathbf{y}\right)} = 1 - \frac{var\left(\widehat{\boldsymbol{\epsilon}}\right)}{var\left(\mathbf{y}\right)}.$$

The information contained in $R^2$ is associated with the information contained in the standard error of the regression, which is the square root of the estimated variance of OLS residuals.

Note that, when a model is estimated in logarithms, residuals and, consequently, the standard error of the regression do not depend on the unit of measure in which the variables are expressed. In fact, we have:

$$\begin{aligned} \widehat{\boldsymbol{\epsilon}} &= \log\left(\mathbf{y}\right) - \log\left(\widehat{\mathbf{y}}\right) \\ &= \log\left(\frac{\mathbf{y}}{\widehat{\mathbf{y}}}\right) = \log\left(1 + \frac{\mathbf{y} - \widehat{\mathbf{y}}}{\widehat{\mathbf{y}}}\right) \simeq \frac{\mathbf{y} - \widehat{\mathbf{y}}}{\widehat{\mathbf{y}}}. \end{aligned}$$

When the model is not specified in logarithms, standard errors are usually intepreted by dividing them by the mean of the dependent variable.

## 1.6 Elements of distribution theory

We consider the distribution of a generic $n$-dimensional vector $\mathbf{z}$, together with the derived distribution of the vector $\mathbf{x} = g(\mathbf{z})$ which admits the inverse $\mathbf{z} = h(\mathbf{x})$, with $h = g^{-1}$. If $prob(z_1 < z < z_2) = \int_{z_1}^{z_2} f(z)\,dz$, and $prob(x_1 < x < x_2) = \int_{x_1}^{x_2} f^*(x)\,dx$, then:

$$f^*(x) = f(h(x))\,J,$$

where $J = \begin{vmatrix} \frac{\partial h_1}{\partial x_1} & \cdots & \frac{\partial h_n}{\partial x_1} \\ \cdots & \cdots & \cdots \\ \frac{\partial h_1}{\partial x_n} & \cdots & \frac{\partial h_n}{\partial x_n} \end{vmatrix} = \left|\frac{\partial \mathbf{h}}{\partial \mathbf{x}'}\right|.$

### 1.6.1 *The normal distribution*

The standardized normal univariate has the following distribution:

$$f(z) = \frac{1}{\sqrt{2\pi}} \exp\left(-\frac{1}{2}z^2\right),$$
$$E(z) = 0, \qquad var(z) = 1.$$

By considering the transformation $x = \sigma z + \mu$, we derive the distribution of the univariate normal as:

$$f(x) = \frac{1}{\sigma\sqrt{2\pi}} \exp\left(-\frac{(x-\mu)^2}{2\sigma^2}\right),$$
$$E(x) = \mu, \qquad var(x) = \sigma^2.$$

Consider now the vector $\mathbf{z} = (z_1, z_2, ..., z_n)$, such that

$$f(\mathbf{z}) = \prod_{i=1}^{n} f(z_i) = (2\pi)^{-\frac{n}{2}} \exp\left(-\frac{1}{2}\mathbf{z}'\mathbf{z}\right).$$

$\mathbf{z}$ is, by construction, a vector of normal independent variables with zero mean and identity variance covariance matrix. The conventional notation is $\mathbf{z} \sim \mathbf{N}(0, I_n)$.

Consider now the linear transformation,

$$\mathbf{x} = \mathbf{A}\mathbf{z} + \boldsymbol{\mu},$$

where $\mathbf{A}$ is an $(n \times n)$ invertible matrix. We consider the following transformation $\mathbf{z} = \mathbf{A}^{-1}(\mathbf{x} - \boldsymbol{\mu})$ with Jacobian $J = \left|\mathbf{A}^{-1}\right| = \frac{1}{|\mathbf{A}|}$. By applying the formula for the transformation of variables, we have:

$$f(\mathbf{x}) = (2\pi)^{-\frac{n}{2}} \left|\mathbf{A}^{-1}\right| \exp\left(-\frac{1}{2}(\mathbf{x} - \boldsymbol{\mu})' \mathbf{A}^{-1\prime}\mathbf{A}^{-1}(\mathbf{x} - \boldsymbol{\mu})\right),$$

which, by defining the positive definite matrix $\Sigma = \mathbf{AA}'$, equals

$$f(\mathbf{x}) = (2\pi)^{-\frac{n}{2}} \left|\Sigma^{-\frac{1}{2}}\right| \exp\left(-\frac{1}{2}(\mathbf{x}-\boldsymbol{\mu})'\Sigma^{-1}(\mathbf{x}-\boldsymbol{\mu})\right). \tag{1.20}$$

The conventional notation for the multivariate normal is $\mathbf{x} \sim \mathrm{N}(\boldsymbol{\mu}, \Sigma)$. A useful theorem relates to the multivariate normal:

**Theorem 1.1** *For any* $\mathbf{x} \sim \mathrm{N}(\boldsymbol{\mu}, \Sigma)$, *given any* $(m \times n)$ $\mathbf{B}$ *matrix and any* $(m \times 1)$ *vector,* $\mathbf{d}$, *if* $\mathbf{y} = \mathbf{Bx} + \mathbf{d}$, *this implies* $\mathbf{y} \sim \mathrm{N}(\mathbf{B}\boldsymbol{\mu} + \mathbf{d}, \mathbf{B}\Sigma\mathbf{B}')$.

Consider a partitioning of an $n$-variate normal vector in two sub-vectors of dimensions $n_1$ and $n - n_1$:

$$\begin{pmatrix} \mathbf{x}_1 \\ \mathbf{x}_2 \end{pmatrix} \sim \mathrm{N}\left(\begin{pmatrix} \boldsymbol{\mu}_1 \\ \boldsymbol{\mu}_2 \end{pmatrix}, \begin{pmatrix} \Sigma_{11} & \Sigma_{12} \\ \Sigma_{21} & \Sigma_{22} \end{pmatrix}\right).$$

By applying the theorem, we obtain two results:

1. $\mathbf{x}_1 \sim \mathrm{N}(\boldsymbol{\mu}_1, \Sigma_{11})$, which follows from applying the theorem in the case $\mathbf{d} = \mathbf{0}$, $\mathbf{B} = (I_{n_1} \ \ \mathbf{0})$;
2. $(\mathbf{x}_1 \mid \mathbf{x}_2) \sim \mathrm{N}\left(\boldsymbol{\mu}_1 + \Sigma_{12}\Sigma_{22}^{-1}(\mathbf{x}_2 - \boldsymbol{\mu}_2), \Sigma_{11} - \Sigma_{12}\Sigma_{22}^{-1}\Sigma_{21}\right)$, which is obtained by applying the theorem to the case $\mathbf{d} = \Sigma_{12}\Sigma_{22}^{-1}\mathbf{x}_2$, $\mathbf{B} = \left(I_{n_1} \ \ -\Sigma_{12}\Sigma_{22}^{-1}\right)$.

Result 2 shows clearly that the absence of correlation is equivalent to independence within the framework of a multivariate normal. This result is justified by the fact that the normal distribution is entirely described by its first two moments.

### 1.6.2 *Distributions derived from the normal*

Consider $\mathbf{z} \sim \mathrm{N}(0, I_n)$, an $n$-variate standard normal. The distribution of $\omega = \mathbf{z}'\mathbf{z}$ is defined as a $\chi^2(n)$ distribution with $n$ degrees of freedom. Consider two vectors $\mathbf{z}_1$ and $\mathbf{z}_2$ of dimensions $n_1$ and $n_2$ respectively, with the following distribution:

$$\begin{pmatrix} \mathbf{z}_1 \\ \mathbf{z}_2 \end{pmatrix} \sim \mathrm{N}\left(\begin{pmatrix} 0 \\ 0 \end{pmatrix}, \begin{pmatrix} I_{n_1} & 0 \\ 0 & I_{n_2} \end{pmatrix}\right).$$

We have $\omega_1 = \mathbf{z}_1'\mathbf{z}_1 \sim \chi^2(n_1)$, $\omega_2 = \mathbf{z}_2'\mathbf{z}_2 \sim \chi^2(n_2)$, and $\omega_1 + \omega_2 = \mathbf{z}_1'\mathbf{z}_1 + \mathbf{z}_2'\mathbf{z}_2 \sim \chi^2(n_1 + n_2)$. In general, the sum of two independent $\chi^2(n)$ distributions is in itself distributed as $\chi^2$ with a number of degrees of freedom equal to the sum of the degrees of freedom of the two $\chi^2$.

Our discussion of the multivariate normal concludes that if $\mathbf{x} \sim \mathrm{N}(\boldsymbol{\mu}, \Sigma)$, then $(\mathbf{x} - \boldsymbol{\mu})'\Sigma^{-1}(\mathbf{x} - \boldsymbol{\mu}) \sim \chi^2(n)$.

A related result establishes that if $\mathbf{z} \sim \mathrm{N}(0, I_n)$ and $\mathbf{M}$ is a symmetric idempotent $(n \times n)$ matrix of rank $r$, then $\mathbf{z}'\mathbf{Mz} \sim \chi^2(r)$.

Another distribution related to the normal is the $F$-distribution. The $F$-distribution is obtained as the ratio of two independent $\chi^2$ divided by the respective degrees of freedom. Given $\omega_1 \sim \chi^2(n_1)$, and $\omega_2 \sim \chi^2(n_2)$, we have:

$$\frac{\omega_1/n_1}{\omega_2/n_2} \sim F(n_1, n_2).$$

The Student's $t-$distribution is then defined as:

$$t_n = \sqrt{F(1,n)}.$$

Another useful result establishes that two quadratic forms in the standard multivariate normal, $\mathbf{z}'\mathbf{M}\mathbf{z}$ and $\mathbf{z}'\mathbf{Q}\mathbf{z}$, are independent if $\mathbf{MQ} = \mathbf{0}$. We can finally state the following theorem, which is fundamental to the statistical inference in the linear model:

**Theorem 1.2** *If* $\mathbf{z} \sim \mathbf{N}(0, I_n)$, $\mathbf{M}$ *and* $\mathbf{Q}$ *are symmetric and idempotent matrices of ranks* $r$ *and* $s$ *respectively and* $\mathbf{MQ} = \mathbf{0}$, *then* $\frac{\mathbf{z}'\mathbf{Q}\mathbf{z}}{\mathbf{z}'\mathbf{M}\mathbf{z}}\frac{r}{s} \sim \mathbf{F}(s,r)$.

## 1.7 Inference in the linear regression model

To perform inference in the linear regression model, we need a further hypothesis to specify the distribution of $\mathbf{y}$ conditional upon $\mathbf{X}$:

$$y \mid \mathbf{X} \sim \mathbf{N}\left(\mathbf{X}\boldsymbol{\beta}, \sigma^2 I\right), \tag{1.21}$$

or, equivalently

$$\epsilon \mid \mathbf{X} \sim \mathbf{N}\left(\mathbf{0}, \sigma^2 I\right). \tag{1.22}$$

Given (1.21) we can immediately derive the distribution of $\left(\widehat{\boldsymbol{\beta}} \mid \mathbf{X}\right)$ which, being a linear combination of a normal distribution, is also normal:

$$\left(\widehat{\boldsymbol{\beta}} \mid \mathbf{X}\right) \sim \mathbf{N}\left(\boldsymbol{\beta}, \sigma^2 \left(\mathbf{X}'\mathbf{X}\right)^{-1}\right). \tag{1.23}$$

Equation (1.23) constitutes the basis to construct confidence intervals and to perform hypothesis testing in the linear regression model. Consider the following expression:

$$\begin{aligned}\frac{\left(\widehat{\boldsymbol{\beta}} - \boldsymbol{\beta}\right)' \mathbf{X}'\mathbf{X} \left(\widehat{\boldsymbol{\beta}} - \boldsymbol{\beta}\right)}{\sigma^2} &= \frac{\epsilon'\mathbf{X}\left(\mathbf{X}'\mathbf{X}\right)^{-1}\mathbf{X}'\mathbf{X}\left(\mathbf{X}'\mathbf{X}\right)^{-1}\mathbf{X}'\epsilon}{\sigma^2} \\ &= \frac{\epsilon'\mathbf{Q}\epsilon}{\sigma^2},\end{aligned}$$

and, applying the results derived in the previous section, we know that

$$\frac{\epsilon'\mathbf{Q}\epsilon}{\sigma^2} \mid \mathbf{X} \sim \chi^2(k). \tag{1.24}$$

Equation (1.24) is not useful in practice, as we do not know $\sigma^2$. However, we know that

$$\frac{S\left(\widehat{\boldsymbol{\beta}}\right) \mid \mathbf{X}}{\sigma^2} = \frac{\boldsymbol{\epsilon}'\mathbf{M}\boldsymbol{\epsilon}}{\sigma^2} \mid \mathbf{X} \sim \chi^2 (T-k). \tag{1.25}$$

Since $\mathbf{MQ} = \mathbf{0}$, we know the distribution of the ratio of (1.24) and (1.25); moreover, taking the ratio, we get rid of the unknown term $\sigma^2$:

$$\frac{\left(\widehat{\boldsymbol{\beta}} - \boldsymbol{\beta}\right)' \mathbf{X}'\mathbf{X} \left(\widehat{\boldsymbol{\beta}} - \boldsymbol{\beta}\right) / \sigma^2}{s^2/\sigma^2} = \frac{\boldsymbol{\epsilon}'\mathbf{Q}\boldsymbol{\epsilon}}{\boldsymbol{\epsilon}'\mathbf{M}\boldsymbol{\epsilon}} (T-k) \sim kF(k, T-k). \tag{1.26}$$

We use result (1.26) to obtain from the tables of the $F$-distribution the critical value $F_\alpha^* (k, T-k)$ such that

$$prob\left[F(k, T-k) > F_\alpha^* (k, T-k)\right] = \alpha, \qquad 0 < \alpha < 1,$$

for different values of $\alpha$ we are in the position of evaluating exactly an inequality of the following form:

$$prob\left\{\left(\widehat{\boldsymbol{\beta}} - \boldsymbol{\beta}\right)' \mathbf{X}'\mathbf{X} \left(\widehat{\boldsymbol{\beta}} - \boldsymbol{\beta}\right) \leq ks^2 F_\alpha^* (k, T-k)\right\} = 1 - \alpha,$$

which defines confidence intervals for $\boldsymbol{\beta}$ centred upon $\widehat{\boldsymbol{\beta}}$. Hypothesis testing is strictly linked to the derivation of confidence intervals. When testing the hypothesis, we aim at rejecting the validity of restrictions imposed on the model on the basis of the sample evidence. Within this framework, (1.13) – (1.23) are the maintained hypothesis and the restricted version of the model is identified with the null hypothesis $H_0$. Following the Neyman–Pearson approach to hypothesis testing, one derives a statistic with known distribution under the null. Then the probability of the first-type error (rejecting $H_0$ when it is true) is fixed at $\alpha$. For example, we use a test at the level $\alpha$ of the null hypothesis $\boldsymbol{\beta} = \boldsymbol{\beta}_0$, based on the $F$-statistic, when we do not reject the null $H_0$ if $\boldsymbol{\beta}_0$ lies within the confidence interval associated with the probability $1 - \alpha$. However, in practice, this is not a useful way of proceeding, as the economic hypotheses of interest rarely involve a number of restrictions equal to the number of estimated parameters. Reconsider Solow's growth model: we have three estimated parameters and only one restriction.

The general case of interest to the economist is the one when we have $r$ restrictions on the vector of parameters with $r < k$. If we limit our interest to the class of linear restrictions, we can express them as

$$H_0 = \mathbf{R}\boldsymbol{\beta} = \mathbf{r},$$

where $\mathbf{R}$ is an $(r \times k)$ matrix of parameters with rank $k$ and $\mathbf{r}$ is an $(r \times 1)$ vector of parameters. To illustrate how $\mathbf{R}$ and $\mathbf{r}$ are constructed, we consider the baseline case of the Solow model; we want to impose the restriction $\beta_1 = -\beta_2$ on the following specification:

$$\ln y_i = \beta_0 + \beta_1 \ln(s_i) + \beta_2 \ln(n_i + g + \delta) + \varepsilon_i, \qquad (1.27)$$

$$\mathbf{R}\boldsymbol{\beta} = \mathbf{r},$$

$$(0\ 1\ 1)\begin{pmatrix}\beta_0\\ \beta_1\\ \beta_2\end{pmatrix} = (0).$$

The distribution of a known statistic under the null is derived by applying known results.

If $\left(\widehat{\boldsymbol{\beta}} \mid \mathbf{X}\right) \sim \mathbf{N}\left(\boldsymbol{\beta}, \sigma^2 (\mathbf{X}'\mathbf{X})^{-1}\right)$, then:

$$\left(\mathbf{R}\widehat{\boldsymbol{\beta}} - \mathbf{r} \mid \mathbf{X}\right) \sim \mathbf{N}\left(\mathbf{R}\boldsymbol{\beta} - \mathbf{r}, \sigma^2 \mathbf{R}(\mathbf{X}'\mathbf{X})^{-1}\mathbf{R}'\right). \qquad (1.28)$$

The test is constructed by deriving the distribution of (1.28) under the null $\mathbf{R}\boldsymbol{\beta} - \mathbf{r} = \mathbf{0}$.

Given that

$$\left(\mathbf{R}\widehat{\boldsymbol{\beta}} - \mathbf{r} \mid \mathbf{X}\right) = \mathbf{R}\boldsymbol{\beta} - \mathbf{r} + \mathbf{R}(\mathbf{X}'\mathbf{X})^{-1}\mathbf{X}'\mathbf{u},$$

under $H_0$, we have:

$$\begin{aligned}&\left(\mathbf{R}\widehat{\boldsymbol{\beta}} - \mathbf{r}\right)'\left(\mathbf{R}(\mathbf{X}'\mathbf{X})^{-1}\mathbf{R}'\right)^{-1}\left(\mathbf{R}\widehat{\boldsymbol{\beta}} - \mathbf{r}\right)\\ &= \boldsymbol{\epsilon}'\mathbf{X}(\mathbf{X}'\mathbf{X})^{-1}\mathbf{R}'\left(\mathbf{R}(\mathbf{X}'\mathbf{X})^{-1}\mathbf{R}'\right)^{-1}\mathbf{R}(\mathbf{X}'\mathbf{X})^{-1}\mathbf{X}'\boldsymbol{\epsilon}\\ &= \boldsymbol{\epsilon}'\mathbf{P}\boldsymbol{\epsilon}.\end{aligned}$$

where $\mathbf{P}$ is a symmetric idempotent matrix of rank $r$, orthogonal to $\mathbf{M}$.

Then

$$\frac{\left(\mathbf{R}\widehat{\boldsymbol{\beta}} - \mathbf{r}\right)'\left(\mathbf{R}(\mathbf{X}'\mathbf{X})^{-1}\mathbf{R}'\right)^{-1}\left(\mathbf{R}\widehat{\boldsymbol{\beta}} - \mathbf{r}\right)}{s^2} \sim r\mathbf{F}(r, T-k), \qquad \text{under } H_0,$$

which can be used to test the relevant hypothesis. We report the application of this methodology to our economic case of interest in Table 1.2.

TABLE 1.2. Testing linear restrictions on equation (1.12)

| | $F(n_1, n_2)$ | Probability |
|---|---|---|
| $\beta_1 = -\beta_2$ : | $F(1, 72) = 1.255627$ | 0.26 |
| $\beta_1 = 0.5$, $\beta_2 = -0.5$ : | $F(2, 72) = 23.48172$ | 0.00 |

The null hypothesis $\beta_1 = -\beta_2$ cannot be rejected for values of $\alpha$ smaller than 0.2662; therefore such a hypothesis cannot be rejected at the conventional 5%. While the null hypothesis $\beta_1 = 0.5$, $\beta_2 = -0.5$ is rejected at the conventional 5%, and also at the 1%. Note that in Table 1.1 we have already reported the $t$-values on estimated coefficients, which did reject the null hypothesis of the coefficient being equal to zero at conventional critical levels. An interesting specific case of the test of the validity of restrictions on estimated coefficients is testing for the significance of the subset of coefficients, which we discuss in the next section.

### 1.7.1 *Testing the significance of the subset of coefficients*

In the general framework to test linear restrictions we set $\mathbf{r} = \mathbf{0}$, $\mathbf{R} = \left[ I_r \; 0 \right]$, and partition $\boldsymbol{\beta}$ in a corresponding way into $\left[ \boldsymbol{\beta}_1 \; \boldsymbol{\beta}_2 \right]$. In this case the restriction $\mathbf{R}\boldsymbol{\beta} - \mathbf{r} = \mathbf{0}$ is equivalent to $\boldsymbol{\beta}_1 = 0$ in the partitioned regression model

$$\mathbf{y} = \mathbf{X}_1\boldsymbol{\beta}_1 + \mathbf{X}_2\boldsymbol{\beta}_2 + \boldsymbol{\epsilon},$$

in which partitioning creates two blocks of dimension $r$ and $k - r$.

Before proceeding to the discussion of hypothesis testing, it is useful to derive the formula for the OLS estimator in the partitioned regression model. To obtain such results we partition the 'normal equations' $\mathbf{X}'\mathbf{X}\widehat{\boldsymbol{\beta}} = \mathbf{X}'\mathbf{y}$ as:

$$\begin{pmatrix} \mathbf{X}_1' \\ \mathbf{X}_2' \end{pmatrix} \begin{pmatrix} \mathbf{X}_1 & \mathbf{X}_2 \end{pmatrix} \begin{pmatrix} \widehat{\boldsymbol{\beta}}_1 \\ \widehat{\boldsymbol{\beta}}_2 \end{pmatrix} = \begin{pmatrix} \mathbf{X}_1' \\ \mathbf{X}_2' \end{pmatrix} \mathbf{y},$$

or, equivalently,

$$\begin{pmatrix} \mathbf{X}_1'\mathbf{X}_1 & \mathbf{X}_1'\mathbf{X}_2 \\ \mathbf{X}_2'\mathbf{X}_1 & \mathbf{X}_2'\mathbf{X}_2 \end{pmatrix} \begin{pmatrix} \widehat{\boldsymbol{\beta}}_1 \\ \widehat{\boldsymbol{\beta}}_2 \end{pmatrix} = \begin{pmatrix} \mathbf{X}_1'\mathbf{y} \\ \mathbf{X}_2'\mathbf{y} \end{pmatrix}. \tag{1.29}$$

System (1.29) can be resolved in two stages by first deriving an expression $\widehat{\boldsymbol{\beta}}_2$ as:

$$\widehat{\boldsymbol{\beta}}_2 = (\mathbf{X}_2'\mathbf{X}_2)^{-1} \left( \mathbf{X}_2'\mathbf{y} - \mathbf{X}_2'\mathbf{X}_1\widehat{\boldsymbol{\beta}}_1 \right),$$

and then by substituting it in the first equation of (1.29) to obtain

$$\mathbf{X}_1'\mathbf{X}_1\widehat{\boldsymbol{\beta}}_1 + \mathbf{X}_1'\mathbf{X}_2 (\mathbf{X}_2'\mathbf{X}_2)^{-1} \left( \mathbf{X}_2'\mathbf{y} - \mathbf{X}_2'\mathbf{X}_1\widehat{\boldsymbol{\beta}}_1 \right) = \mathbf{X}_1'\mathbf{y},$$

from which:[2]

[2] Note that the expression for the estimator can be obtained by applying the formula of the partitioned inverse directly on the normal equations:
$$\begin{pmatrix} A & B \\ C & D \end{pmatrix}^{-1} = \begin{pmatrix} E & -EBD^{-1} \\ -D^{-1}CE & D^{-1} + D^{-1}CEBD^{-1} \end{pmatrix}, \; E = \left(A - BD^{-1}C\right)^{-1}.$$

$$\widehat{\beta}_1 = (\mathbf{X}_1'\mathbf{M}_2\mathbf{X}_1)^{-1}\mathbf{X}_1'\mathbf{M}_2\mathbf{y}$$
$$\mathbf{M}_2 = \left(\mathbf{I} - \mathbf{X}_2(\mathbf{X}_2'\mathbf{X}_2)^{-1}\mathbf{X}_2'\right).$$

Note that, as $\mathbf{M}_2$ is idempotent, we can also write:

$$\widehat{\beta}_1 = (\mathbf{X}_1'\mathbf{M}_2'\mathbf{M}_2\mathbf{X}_1)^{-1}\mathbf{X}_1'\mathbf{M}_2'\mathbf{M}_2\mathbf{y},$$

and $\widehat{\beta}_1$can be interpreted as the vector of OLS coefficients of the regression of $\mathbf{y}$ on the matrix of residuals of the regression of $\mathbf{X}_1$ on $\mathbf{X}_2$. Thus, an OLS regression on two regressors is equivalent to two OLS regressions on a single regressor (Frisch-Waugh theorem).

Finally, consider the residuals of the partitioned model:

$$\widehat{\epsilon} = \mathbf{y} - \mathbf{X}_1\widehat{\beta}_1 - \mathbf{X}_2\widehat{\beta}_2,$$
$$\widehat{\epsilon} = \mathbf{y} - \mathbf{X}_1\widehat{\beta} - \mathbf{X}_2(\mathbf{X}_2'\mathbf{X}_2)^{-1}\left(\mathbf{X}_2'\mathbf{y} - \mathbf{X}_2'\mathbf{X}_1\widehat{\beta}_1\right),$$
$$\begin{aligned}\widehat{\epsilon} &= \mathbf{M}_2\mathbf{y} - \mathbf{M}_2\mathbf{X}_1\widehat{\beta}_1 \\ &= \mathbf{M}_2\mathbf{y} - \mathbf{M}_2\mathbf{X}_1(\mathbf{X}_1'\mathbf{M}_2\mathbf{X}_1)^{-1}\mathbf{X}_1'\mathbf{M}_2\mathbf{y} \\ &= \left(\mathbf{M}_2 - \mathbf{M}_2\mathbf{X}_1(\mathbf{X}_1'\mathbf{M}_2\mathbf{X}_1)^{-1}\mathbf{X}_1'\mathbf{M}_2\right)\mathbf{y},\end{aligned}$$

however, we already know that $\widehat{\epsilon} = \mathbf{M}\mathbf{y}$, therefore,

$$\mathbf{M} = \left(\mathbf{M}_2 - \mathbf{M}_2\mathbf{X}_1(\mathbf{X}_1'\mathbf{M}_2\mathbf{X}_1)^{-1}\mathbf{X}_1'\mathbf{M}_2\right). \tag{1.30}$$

Now reconsider testing for our null of interest. Under $H_0$, $\mathbf{X}_1$ has no additional explicatory power for $\mathbf{y}$ with respect to $\mathbf{X}_2$, therefore:

$$H_0\text{: } \mathbf{y} = \mathbf{X}_2\beta_2 + \epsilon, \qquad (\epsilon \mid \mathbf{X}_1, \mathbf{X}_2) \sim N\left(0, \sigma^2 I\right).$$

Note that the statement

$$\mathbf{y} = \mathbf{X}_2\gamma_2 + \epsilon, \qquad (\epsilon \mid \mathbf{X}_2) \sim N\left(0, \sigma^2 I\right),$$

is always true under our maintained hypotheses. However, in general $\gamma_2 \neq \beta_2$.To derive a statistic to test $H_0$ remember that the general matrix $\mathbf{R}(\mathbf{X}'\mathbf{X})^{-1}\mathbf{R}'$ is the upper left block of $(\mathbf{X}'\mathbf{X})^{-1}$, which we can now write as $(\mathbf{X}_1'\mathbf{M}_2\mathbf{X}_1)^{-1}$. The statistic then takes the form

$$\frac{\widehat{\beta}_1'(\mathbf{X}_1'\mathbf{M}_2\mathbf{X}_1)\widehat{\beta}_1}{rs^2} = \frac{\mathbf{y}'\mathbf{M}_2\mathbf{X}_1(\mathbf{X}_1'\mathbf{M}_2\mathbf{X}_1)^{-1}\mathbf{X}_1'\mathbf{M}_2\mathbf{y}}{\mathbf{y}'\mathbf{M}\mathbf{y}}\frac{T-k}{r} \sim F(T-k, r).$$

Given (1.30), (1.29) can be re-written as:

$$\frac{\mathbf{y}'\mathbf{M}_2\mathbf{y} - \mathbf{y}'\mathbf{M}\mathbf{y}}{\mathbf{y}'\mathbf{M}\mathbf{y}}\frac{T-k}{r} \sim F(T-k, r), \tag{1.31}$$

where the denominator is the sum of the squared residuals in the unconstrained model, while the numerator is the difference between the sum of residuals in the constrained model and the sum of residuals in the unconstrained model.

Consider the limit case $r = 1$ and $\beta_1$ is a scalar. The $F$-statistic takes the form

$$\frac{\widehat{\beta}_1^2}{s^2\left(\mathbf{X}_1'\mathbf{M}_2\mathbf{X}_1\right)} \sim F\left(T-k, r\right), \text{ under } H_0,$$

where $\left(\mathbf{X}_1'\mathbf{M}_2\mathbf{X}_1\right)^{-1}$ is element $(1,1)$ of the matrix $\left(\mathbf{X}'\mathbf{X}\right)^{-1}$.

Using the result on the relation between the $F$ and the Student's $t$-distribution:

$$\frac{\widehat{\beta}_1}{s\left(\mathbf{X}_1'\mathbf{M}_2\mathbf{X}_1\right)^{1/2}} \sim t\left(T-k\right) \text{ under } H_0.$$

Therefore, an immediate test of significance of the coefficient can be performed, as it is in Table 1.1, by taking the ratio of each estimated coefficient and the associated standard error.

Let us reconsider our results on the Solow growth model. We cannot reject the null of the validity of the model, but the point estimates are far from the predicted coefficient on the basis of theory.

Two questions naturally rise at this stage. First, what is the impact on our coefficient of having estimated the model without imposing the theoretical restrictions? Second, is it possible to explain the discrepancies between the estimated elasticities and the ones predicted by the theory on the basis of the mis-specification of the model, i.e. of the omission from the estimated model of some variables relevant to explain $\mathbf{y}$?

In the following two sections we discuss these two questions in turn.

## 1.8 Estimation under linear constraints

In this section we analyse the impact on the OLS estimator of a mis-specification deriving from ignoring the existence of constraints on an estimated parameter. To analyse the mis-specification, we introduce the difference between the estimated model and the data generating process (DGP).

The estimated model is the linear model analysed up to now:

$$\mathbf{y} = \mathbf{X}\boldsymbol{\beta} + \boldsymbol{\epsilon},$$

while the DGP is instead:

$$\mathbf{y} = \mathbf{X}\boldsymbol{\beta} + \boldsymbol{\epsilon}, \quad \textit{subject to } \mathbf{R}\boldsymbol{\beta} - \mathbf{r} = \mathbf{0},$$

where the constraints are expressed using the so called implicit form. A useful alternative way of expressing constraints, known as the 'explicit form' has been expressed by Sargan (1988):

$$\boldsymbol{\beta} = \mathbf{S}\boldsymbol{\theta} + \mathbf{s},$$

where $\mathbf{S}$ is a $(k \times (k-r))$ matrix of rank $k-r$ and $\mathbf{s}$ is a $k \times 1$ vector.

To show how constraints are specified in the two alternatives let us reconsider the restrictions of the Solow growth model, $\beta_1 = -\beta_2$ on the following specification:

$$\ln y_i = \beta_0 + \beta_1 \ln(s_i) + \beta_2 \ln(n_i + g + \delta) + \varepsilon_i. \tag{1.32}$$

Using $\mathbf{R}\boldsymbol{\beta} - \mathbf{r} = \mathbf{0}$:

$$\begin{pmatrix} 0 & 1 & 1 \end{pmatrix} \begin{pmatrix} \beta_0 \\ \beta_1 \\ \beta_2 \end{pmatrix} = (0),$$

while using $\boldsymbol{\beta} = \mathbf{S}\boldsymbol{\theta} + \mathbf{s}$:

$$\begin{pmatrix} \beta_0 \\ \beta_1 \\ \beta_2 \end{pmatrix} = \begin{pmatrix} 1 & 0 \\ 0 & 1 \\ 0 & -1 \end{pmatrix} \begin{pmatrix} \beta_0 \\ \beta_1 \end{pmatrix} + \begin{pmatrix} 0 \\ 0 \\ 0 \end{pmatrix}.$$

In practice the constraints in the explicit form are written by considering $\boldsymbol{\theta}$ as the vector of free parameters. Note that there is no unique way of expressing constraints in the explicit form, in our case the same constraint can be imposed as:

$$\begin{pmatrix} \beta_0 \\ \beta_1 \\ \beta_2 \end{pmatrix} = \begin{pmatrix} 1 & 0 \\ 0 & -1 \\ 0 & 1 \end{pmatrix} \begin{pmatrix} \beta_0 \\ \beta_2 \end{pmatrix} + \begin{pmatrix} 0 \\ 0 \\ 0 \end{pmatrix}.$$

As the two alternatives are indifferent, $\mathbf{R}\boldsymbol{\beta} - \mathbf{r} = \mathbf{0}$ and $\mathbf{RS}\boldsymbol{\theta} + \mathbf{Rs} - \mathbf{r} = \mathbf{0}$ are equivalent, which implies:

1. $\mathbf{RS} = \mathbf{0}$;
2. $\mathbf{Rs} - \mathbf{r} = \mathbf{0}$.

We use the explicit form of imposing constraints to derive the restricted least squares (RLS) estimators, and to evaluate the consistency and relative efficiency of OLS and RLS.

### 1.8.1 *The restricted least squares (RLS) estimator*

To construct RLS, substitute the constraint in the original model to obtain:

$$\mathbf{y} - \mathbf{Xs} = \mathbf{XS}\boldsymbol{\theta} + \boldsymbol{\epsilon}. \tag{1.33}$$

Equation (1.33) is equivalent to:

$$\mathbf{y}^* = \mathbf{X}^*\boldsymbol{\theta} + \boldsymbol{\epsilon}, \tag{1.34}$$

where $\mathbf{y}^* = \mathbf{y} - \mathbf{Xs}$, $\mathbf{X}^* = \mathbf{XS}$.

Note that the transformed model features the same residuals with the original model; therefore, if hypotheses (1.13) – (1.21) hold for the original model, they also hold for the transformed. We apply OLS to the transformed model to obtain:

$$\begin{aligned}\widehat{\boldsymbol{\theta}} &= \left(\mathbf{X}^{*\prime}\mathbf{X}^{*}\right)^{-1}\mathbf{X}^{*\prime}\mathbf{y}^{*} \\ &= \left(\mathbf{S}'\mathbf{X}'\mathbf{X}\mathbf{S}\right)^{-1}\mathbf{S}'\mathbf{X}'\left(\mathbf{y}-\mathbf{X}\mathbf{s}\right).\end{aligned} \tag{1.35}$$

From (1.35) the RLS estimation is easily obtained by applying the transformation $\widehat{\boldsymbol{\beta}}^{rls} = \mathbf{S}\widehat{\boldsymbol{\theta}} + \mathbf{s}$. Similarly, the variance of the RLS estimator is easily obtained as:

$$\begin{aligned}var\left(\widehat{\boldsymbol{\theta}} \mid \mathbf{X}\right) &= \sigma^2\left(\mathbf{X}^{*\prime}\mathbf{X}^{*}\right)^{-1} = \sigma^2\left(\mathbf{S}'\mathbf{X}'\mathbf{X}\mathbf{S}\right)^{-1}, \\ var\left(\widehat{\boldsymbol{\beta}}^{rls} \mid \mathbf{X}\right) &= var\left(\mathbf{S}\widehat{\boldsymbol{\theta}} + \mathbf{s} \mid \mathbf{X}\right) \\ &= \mathbf{S}\, var\left(\widehat{\boldsymbol{\theta}} \mid \mathbf{X}\right)\mathbf{S}' \\ &= \sigma^2\mathbf{S}\left(\mathbf{S}'\mathbf{X}'\mathbf{X}\mathbf{S}\right)^{-1}\mathbf{S}'.\end{aligned}$$

We report in Table 1.3 the RLS estimator of the Solow growth model. By comparing tables, we note that the estimated coefficients are very close but the estimates in Table 1.3 are more precise. We also note that the hypothesis $\beta_1 = 0.5, \beta_2 = -0.5$ is still rejected, despite our imposition of the theory-based constraint on our estimated coefficients.

TABLE 1.3. The estimation of the constrained Solow model

| Variable | Coefficient | Std. Error | t-ratio | Prob. |
|---|---|---|---|---|
| C | 7.0857 | 0.1453 | 48.65 | 0.0000 |
| lns-lnngd | 1.43687 | 0.13882 | 10.35 | 0.0000 |
| $R^2$ 0.594 | S.E. of regression 0.61 | | | |

This observation leads to the discussion of the properties of OLS and RLS in the case of a DGP with constraints.

**Unbiasedness**

Under the assumed DGP, both estimators are unbiased, since such properties depend on the validity of hypotheses (1.13) – (1.21), which is not affected by the imposition of constraints on parameters.

**Efficiency**

Obviously, if we interpret RLS as the OLS estimator on the transformed model (1.35) we immediately derive the results that the RLS is the most efficient estimator, as the hypotheses for the validity of the Gauss Markov theorem are satisfied when OLS is applied to (1.35). Note that by posing $\mathbf{L} = (\mathbf{X}'\mathbf{X})^{-1}\mathbf{X}'$ in the context of the transformed model, we do not generally obtain OLS but an estimator whose conditional variance with respect to $\mathbf{X}$, coincides with the conditional variance of the OLS estimator.

We support this intuition with a formal argument by showing that the difference between the variance of the OLS estimator and the variance of the RLS estimator is a positive semidefinite matrix.

$$var\left(\widehat{\beta} \mid \mathbf{X}\right) - var\left(\widehat{\beta}^{rls} \mid \mathbf{X}\right) = \sigma^2 (\mathbf{X}'\mathbf{X})^{-1} - \sigma^2 \mathbf{S} (\mathbf{S}'\mathbf{X}'\mathbf{X}\mathbf{S})^{-1} \mathbf{S}'.$$

Define $\mathbf{A}$ as:

$$\mathbf{A} = (\mathbf{X}'\mathbf{X})^{-1} - \mathbf{S} (\mathbf{S}'\mathbf{X}'\mathbf{X}\mathbf{S})^{-1} \mathbf{S}'.$$

Given that

$$\begin{aligned}
\mathbf{A}\mathbf{X}'\mathbf{X}\mathbf{A} &= \left((\mathbf{X}'\mathbf{X})^{-1} - \mathbf{S} (\mathbf{S}'\mathbf{X}'\mathbf{X}\mathbf{S})^{-1} \mathbf{S}'\right) \mathbf{X}'\mathbf{X} \left((\mathbf{X}'\mathbf{X})^{-1} - \mathbf{S} (\mathbf{S}'\mathbf{X}'\mathbf{X}\mathbf{S})^{-1} \mathbf{S}'\right) \\
&= (\mathbf{X}'\mathbf{X})^{-1} - 2\mathbf{S} (\mathbf{S}'\mathbf{X}'\mathbf{X}\mathbf{S})^{-1} \mathbf{S}' + \mathbf{S} (\mathbf{S}'\mathbf{X}'\mathbf{X}\mathbf{S})^{-1} \mathbf{S}'\mathbf{S} (\mathbf{S}'\mathbf{X}'\mathbf{X}\mathbf{S})^{-1} \mathbf{S}' \\
&= (\mathbf{X}'\mathbf{X})^{-1} - \mathbf{S} (\mathbf{S}'\mathbf{X}'\mathbf{X}\mathbf{S})^{-1} \mathbf{S}' \\
&= \mathbf{A},
\end{aligned}$$

$\mathbf{A}$ is positive semidefinite, being the product of a matrix and its transpose.

The OLS estimator ignores available information and therefore is less efficient than the RLS estimator. However, there is no difference between the two estimators in terms of unbiasedness.

So far we have evaluated the gains of imposing true restrictions. A related interesting exercise is the evaluation of the loss from imposing false restrictions.

## 1.9 The effects of mis-specification

We consider two general cases of mis-specification to evaluate empirically their relevance in the case of the Solow model. We take first the case of under-parameterization (the estimated model omits variables included in the DGP) to move on to over-parameterization (the estimated model includes more variables than the DGP). We evaluate the effects of mis-specification on the OLS estimators by using results from the partitioned regression model.

### 1.9.1 *Under-parameterization*

Given the DGP:

$$\mathbf{y} = \mathbf{X}_1\boldsymbol{\beta}_1 + \mathbf{X}_2\boldsymbol{\beta}_2 + \boldsymbol{\epsilon}, \tag{1.36}$$

for which hypotheses (1.13) – (1.21) hold, the following model is estimated:

$$\mathbf{y} = \mathbf{X}_1\boldsymbol{\beta}_1 + \boldsymbol{\nu}. \tag{1.37}$$

The OLS estimates are given by the following expression:

$$\widehat{\boldsymbol{\beta}}_1^{up} = (\mathbf{X}_1'\mathbf{X}_1)^{-1}\mathbf{X}_1'\mathbf{y}, \tag{1.38}$$

while the OLS estimates which are obtained by estimation of the DGP, are:

$$\widehat{\boldsymbol{\beta}}_1 = (\mathbf{X}_1'\mathbf{M}_2\mathbf{X}_1)^{-1}\mathbf{X}_1'\mathbf{M}_2\mathbf{y}. \tag{1.39}$$

The estimates in (1.39) are best linear unbiased estimators (BLUE) by construction, while the estimates in (1.38) are biased unless $\mathbf{X}_1$and $\mathbf{X}_2$ are uncorrelated. To show this, consider:

$$\widehat{\boldsymbol{\beta}}_1 = (\mathbf{X}_1'\mathbf{X}_1)^{-1}\left(\mathbf{X}_1'\mathbf{y} - \mathbf{X}_1'\mathbf{X}_2\widehat{\boldsymbol{\beta}}_2\right) \tag{1.40}$$

$$= \widehat{\boldsymbol{\beta}}_1^{up} + \widehat{\mathbf{D}}\widehat{\boldsymbol{\beta}}_2, \tag{1.41}$$

where $\widehat{\mathbf{D}}$ is the vector of coefficients in the regression of $\mathbf{X}_2$ on $\mathbf{X}_1$ and $\widehat{\boldsymbol{\beta}}_2$ is the OLS estimator obtained by fitting the DGP.

To provide further interpretation of these results, note that if

$$E(\mathbf{y} \mid \mathbf{X}_1, \mathbf{X}_2) = \mathbf{X}_1\boldsymbol{\beta}_1 + \mathbf{X}_2\boldsymbol{\beta}_2,$$
$$E(\mathbf{X}_1 \mid \mathbf{X}_2) = \mathbf{X}_1\mathbf{D},$$

then,

$$E(\mathbf{y} \mid \mathbf{X}_1) = \mathbf{X}_1\boldsymbol{\beta}_1 + \mathbf{X}_1\mathbf{D}\boldsymbol{\beta}_2 = \mathbf{X}_1\boldsymbol{\alpha}.$$

Therefore the OLS estimator in the under-parameterized model is a biased estimator of $\boldsymbol{\beta}_1$, but an unbiased estimator of $\boldsymbol{\alpha}$. Then, if the objective of the model is forecasting and $\mathbf{X}_1$ is more easily observed than $\mathbf{X}_2$, the under-parameterized model can be safely used. On the other hand, if the objective of the model is to test specific predictions on parameters (as in case of Solow's model), the use of the under-parameterized model delivers biased results. When we are interested in the effect of $\mathbf{X}_1$ on $\mathbf{y}$, independently from other factors, it is crucial to control the effects of omitted variables.

### 1.9.2 *Over-parameterization*

Given the DGP,

$$\mathbf{y} = \mathbf{X}_1\boldsymbol{\beta}_1 + \boldsymbol{\epsilon}, \tag{1.42}$$

for which hypotheses (1.13) – (1.21) hold, the following model is estimated:

$$\mathbf{y} = \mathbf{X}_1\boldsymbol{\beta}_1 + \mathbf{X}_2\boldsymbol{\beta}_2 + \mathbf{v}. \tag{1.43}$$

The OLS estimator of the over-parameterized model is

$$\widehat{\beta}_1^{op} = \left(\mathbf{X}_1'\mathbf{M}_2\mathbf{X}_1\right)^{-1}\mathbf{X}_1'\mathbf{M}_2\mathbf{y}, \tag{1.44}$$

while, by estimating the DGP, we obtain:

$$\widehat{\beta}_1 = \left(\mathbf{X}_1'\mathbf{X}_1\right)^{-1}\mathbf{X}_1'\mathbf{y}. \tag{1.45}$$

By substituting $\mathbf{y}$ from the DGP, one finds that both estimators are unbiased and the difference is now made by the variance. In fact we have:

$$var\left(\widehat{\beta}_1^{op} \mid \mathbf{X}_1, \mathbf{X}_2\right) = \sigma^2\left(\mathbf{X}_1'\mathbf{M}_2\mathbf{X}_1\right)^{-1}, \tag{1.46}$$

$$var\left(\widehat{\beta}_1 \mid \mathbf{X}_1, \mathbf{X}_2\right) = \sigma^2\left(\mathbf{X}_1'\mathbf{X}_1\right)^{-1}. \tag{1.47}$$

One can show that the estimator derived from the correct model is more efficient. The difference between the two variance-covariance matrices is a positive semidefinite matrix. To show this, remember that if two matrices $\mathbf{A}$ and $\mathbf{B}$ are positive definite and $\mathbf{A}-\mathbf{B}$ is positive semidefinite, then also the matrix $\mathbf{B}^{-1}-\mathbf{A}^{-1}$ is positive semidefinite. We have to show that $\mathbf{X}_1'\mathbf{X}_1-\mathbf{X}_1'\mathbf{M}_2\mathbf{X}_1$ is a positive semidefinite matrix. Such a result is almost immediate:

$$\begin{aligned}\mathbf{X}_1'\mathbf{X}_1-\mathbf{X}_1'\mathbf{M}_2\mathbf{X}_1 &= \mathbf{X}_1'\left(\mathbf{I}-\mathbf{M}_2\right)\mathbf{X}_1\\ &= \mathbf{X}_1'\mathbf{Q}_2\mathbf{X}_1 = \mathbf{X}_1'\mathbf{Q}_2\mathbf{Q}_2\mathbf{X}_1.\end{aligned}$$

We conclude that over-parameterization impacts on the efficiency of estimators and the power of the tests of hypotheses.

## 1.10 Human capital in Solow's growth model

Let us reconsider the estimated elasticities in Solow's model. We have seen that the theory-implied restriction on the equality of elasticities cannot be rejected, but imposing such a constraint does not solve the problem of the implausibly high values for the point estimates of elasticities. Our discussion of the effect of omitted variables on the OLS estimation illustrates a potential solution to the problem. Mankiw, Romer, and Weil follow this lead and point out that human capital could be the relevant omitted variable. To illustrate the impact of human capital on Solow's model, let us augment our simple specification to consider three inputs: physical capital, $K$, human capital, $H$, and labour, $L$. By keeping a constant returns-to-scale Cobb-Douglas production function, we have:

$$Y_t = K_t^{\alpha}H_t^{\beta}\left(A_tL_t\right)^{1-\alpha-\beta}. \tag{1.48}$$

Define as $s_k$ and $s_h$ the fractions of output invested in physical and human capital, respectively. We maintain all the other original assumptions in Solow's model and assume that physical and human capital depreciate at the same speed.

The evolution of the economy over time is now governed by two dynamic equations:

$$k_t(1+n)(1+g) = k_{t-1}(1-\delta) + s_k y_t, \tag{1.49}$$
$$h_t(1+n)(1+g) = h_{t-1}(1-\delta) + s_h y_t. \tag{1.50}$$

By assuming $\alpha + \beta < 1$, we can derive the steady state of the economy represented by the two following relationships:

$$k^* = \left(\frac{s_k^{1-\beta} s_h^{\beta}}{n+g+\delta}\right)^{\frac{1}{1-\alpha-\beta}}, \tag{1.51}$$

$$h^* = \left(\frac{s_k^{1-\alpha} s_h^{\alpha}}{n+g+\delta}\right)^{\frac{1}{1-\alpha-\beta}}. \tag{1.52}$$

By substituting these two relationships in the production function and taking logarithms, we find an expression for the per capita level of output in the steady state:

$$\ln\left(\frac{Y_t}{L_t}\right)^* = \ln A_0 + gt + \frac{\alpha}{1-\alpha-\beta}\ln(s_k) + \tag{1.53}$$
$$+\frac{\beta}{1-\alpha-\beta}\ln(s_h) - \frac{\alpha+\beta}{1-\alpha-\beta}\ln(n+g+\delta).$$

Equation (1.53) shows how per capita output depends on the rate of growth of population, the rate of accumulation of human capital, and the rate of accumulation of physical capital. Equation (1.53) nests (1.7), and illustrates how the direct estimation of (1.7) might deliver biased estimates of the parameters of interest as a consequence of under-parameterization. Mankiw, Romer, and Weil construct a proxy for the rate of accumulation of human capital by merging two datasets to obtain a measure of the percentage of working-age population that is in secondary school. They call such variable SCHOOL and include its logarithm in the regression. In this case, even if SCHOOL is only proportional to $s_h$, it can be safely used in the estimation of the equation of interest as only the constant is affected. On the other hand, if SCHOOL is measured with error, the measurement error will deliver bias in the estimates only if it is correlated with the other regressors.

The results of the estimation of the augmented Solow model are reported in Table 1.4.

TABLE 1.4. The estimation of the augmented Solow model

| Variable | Coefficient | Std. Error | t-ratio | Prob. |
|---|---|---|---|---|
| C | 4.451 | 1.153 | 3.859 | 0.0002 |
| lns | 0.709 | 0.15 | 4.725 | 0.0000 |
| lnngd | -1.497 | 0.402 | -3.719 | 0.0004 |
| lsch | 0.728 | 0.095 | 7.666 | 0.0000 |
| $R^2$ 0.782 | S.E. of regression 0.45 | | | |

Note that all the model-based restrictions on coefficients cannot be rejected and that estimated parameters are compatible with values of about $\frac{1}{3}$ for $\alpha$ and $\beta$. Such values are deemed to be reasonable by Mankiw, Romer, and Weil who conclude that the estimation of Solow's model without human capital can be considered as a benchmark case to illustrate the effect of under-parameterization.

## 1.11 Importance of time-series in macroeconomics

Results obtained so far are based on a cross-sectional analysis of different countries, without using information on the time-series behaviour of relevant variables. However, most of the interesting questions in macroeconomics are answered by analysing the time-series. The Solow model predicts that each economy converges to its own steady state. The obvious implication is that, over time, differences in per capita output of countries featuring the same rates of capital accumulation and growth of population should disappear. The empirical validity of such a prediction has been heavily questioned. Recently an alternative theory of growth has developed: the endogenous growth theory, see Lucas (1988) and Barro and Sala-i-Martin (1995). Such a theory basically modifies the neoclassical growth model by introducing constant returns to scale in the production function for output in effective units of labour ($\alpha+\beta=1$, instead of $\alpha+\beta<1$). In such types of models the steady-state level of output is undefined.[3] Therefore, differences between countries can persist indefinitely even if they share the same rates of accumulation of capital and population growth.

If one considers time-series data, one easily discriminates between the two models on the basis of their different predictions. Consider the $i$-th country in our sample. If we have $t=1,...,T$ time-series observations on the relevant variables, we can estimate the $\lambda_i$ parameter in the following model:

$$\Delta \ln y_{i,t} = \lambda_i \left(\ln y_{i,t-1} - \ln y^*_{i,t-1}\right) + \varepsilon_{it} \tag{1.54}$$
$$\Delta \ln y_{i,t} = \left(\ln y_{i,t} - \ln y_{i,t-1}\right).$$

[3] The non-existence of equilibrium generates some problems for the construction of a theory of distribution. These problems are solved by introducing the idea of an aggregate production function different from the one faced by the specific firm. Productivity gains at the firm level are not exogenous, as they depend on the general level of industrialization of the society (theory of the 'learning by doing'). For a lucid discussion of this point see Farmer (1998).

The neo-classical growth model predicts $\lambda_i < 0$, while the endogenous growth model predicts $\lambda_i > 0$.

$\lambda_i < 0$ warrants convergence of $y$ to its steady state (which is time variant in that the rates of accumulation of capital and population growth might vary over time). While in the case $\lambda_i > 0$, we do not have convergence of $y$ to its steady state. The main complication in estimating and testing the model of interest within a time-series context is that the hypothesis $E(\epsilon \mid \mathbf{X}) = 0$ does not hold and the derivation of properties of estimators and statistical distribution for hypotheses testing requires a new appropriate framework, which we discuss in the following chapter.

To reinforce our point on the importance of time-series in evaluating macroeconomic theories, we evaluate the loss of information when $\lambda_i$ is estimated by using the 75 cross-sectional observations used so far.

We can re-write (1.54) as

$$\ln y_{i,t} = (1 + \lambda_i) \ln y_{i,t-1} + \lambda_i \ln y^*_{i,t-1} + \varepsilon_{it}. \tag{1.55}$$

By recursively substituting in (1.55), we have,

$$\ln y_{i,t} - \ln y_{i,0} = -\left(1 - (1 + \lambda_i)^t\right) \ln y_{i,0} - \lambda_i \ln y_i^* \sum_{j=0}^{t-1} (1 + \lambda_i)^j + \tag{1.56}$$
$$+ \sum_{j=0}^{t} (1 + \lambda_i)^j \varepsilon_{i,t-1},$$

which is equivalent to,

$$\ln y_{i,t} - \ln y_{i,0} = -\left(1 - (1 + \lambda_i)^t\right) \ln y_{i,0} + \left(1 - (1 + \lambda_i)^t\right) \ln y_i^* + v_t \tag{1.57}$$
$$v_t = \sum_{j=0}^{t} (1 + \lambda_i)^j \varepsilon_{i,t-1}.$$

So far we have taken the steady state to be constant. By adding to this assumption $\lambda_i = \lambda$, we impose its constancy across countries. It is possible to estimate (1.57) on our cross-section of 75 countries by taking as a dependent variable the difference between initial and final output. Mankiw, Romer, and Weil do so by taking the difference between output in 1985 and output in 1960. Note that the error term in the cross-sectional model is much larger than the error term in the time-series model, being the cumulation of 25 time-series residuals. We report Mankiw, Romer, and Weil in Table 1.5. Note that we compare three models: the unconditional convergence model, and two conditional convergence models (Solow and augmented Solow). As expected, the results on the estimation of $\lambda$ change as the specification is changed. The richer model gives a point estimate for $\lambda$ of $-0.02$, giving some support to the neo-classical model (what is the standard error associated to this point estimate?).

TABLE 1.5. Testing convergence (dep.var. lyl85-ly60)

| Variable | Unconditional | Solow | Augmented Solow |
|---|---|---|---|
| Constant | 0.568 (0.432) | 2.26 (0.847) | 2.48 (0.795) |
| lyl60 | -0.002 (0.054) | -0.23 (0.056) | -0.36 (0.066) |
| lns | - | 0.65 (0.103) | 0.55 (0.101) |
| lnngd | - | -0.45 (0.304) | -0.54 (0.286) |
| lnsch | - | - | 0.27 (0.079) |
| $R^2$ | 0.00002 | 0.38 | 0.47 |
| $\sigma$ | 0.41 | 0.32 | 0.30 |
| $\lambda$ | -0.0078 | -0.01 | -0.018 |

## 1.12 Alternative research strategies in macroeconometrics

Some final remarks on the research strategy behind the empirical work considered so far are useful to set out the general framework for the organization of the material in this book. The starting point of the research strategy of Mankiw, Romer, and Weil is a theoretical model. The estimated empirical relation is derived from the solution of the model. As the estimation of the relation explicitly derived from Solow's growth model delivers disappointing results, the authors consider a modification of the model by introducing human capital in the original framework. Such a modification generates satisfactory empirical results and is capable of explaining the empirical failure of the original specification. At this point the authors have their message and are able to convey it to the profession.

Any empirical research strategy is based on the combination of theoretical analysis and work on the data to produce models of economies. We have shown that time-series are the most natural empirical counterpart of variables in macroeconomic models. In the next chapter we discuss the statistical framework necessary to analyse time-series.

We shall then introduce identification; the crucial stage of research in applied macroeconometrics where theory and statistical analysis of the data meet. In fact, one can understand the different approaches currently adopted in applied empirical work in macroeconomics as different solutions to the identification problem. On the basis of the working knowledge of fundamentals built in these two introductory chapters, we shall consider the different approaches to applied macroeconometrics. We start with the Cowles Commission approach, by discussing a model of the monetary transmission mechanism built on the most famous *ad hoc* framework (the IS-LM model augmented by some supply function) imposed on the data to ask the time-honoured question 'what does monetary policy do?'. Such a model is designed to identify the impact of monetary policy variables on macroeconomic quantities. The exercise aims to determine the value to assign to the monetary instruments to achieve a given target for the macroeconomic variables. Exogeneity of the policy variables is assumed on the ground that these are the instruments controlled by the policymaker. We illustrate how the model is used by estimating a small model of the US economy and replicating the empirical failure of the generation of macroeconometric models in achieving the objective of their simulation. Such a failure has been rationalized in different ways, leading to different approaches to replace the Cowles Commission research program.

The LSE approach (see Hendry 1996) explains the failure of the Cowles Commission methodology by the lack of attention to the statistical model underlying the particular econometric structure adopted to analyse the effect of alternative monetary policies. The LSE methodology considers econometric policy evaluation an interesting and feasible exercise. However, the way in which the Cowles Commission approach deals with a legitimate question is seen as incorrect. The lack of sufficient interest for the statistical model is interpreted as the root of the failure of the Cowles Commission approach to provide an acceptable answer to an interesting question. The diagnosis is a careful diagnostic checking on the specification adopted. By applying the LSE approach to the same problem faced by the Cowles Commission model, we shall show its merits and limits.

Differently from the LSE explanation of traditional structural modelling, the two most famous and demolishing critiques, due to Lucas (1976) and Sims (1980), concentrate on the weak theoretical basis for the Cowles Commission models. The Lucas critique explains the failure of structural models when the coefficient describing the impact of monetary policy on the macroeconomic variables of interest depends on the monetary policy regimes. In this case, no model estimated under a specific regime can be used to simulate the effects of a different monetary policy regime. Such a situation is naturally generated when intertemporal optimization determines agents' behaviour. The Sims critique attacks identification from a different perspective, pointing out that the restrictions needed to support exogeneity in structural models of the Cowles Commission type are 'incredible' in an environment where agents optimize intertemporally.

The natural conclusion of these two critiques is that one should undertake policy simulation not on the basis of structural econometric models but rather of simulation of model economies based on microeconomic foundations. However, econometrics still play an important role for the selection of the appropriate model economy and the estimation of the deep parameters describing taste and technology, that are independent from expectations.

The research program initiated by Sims led to the estimation of VAR models in empirical macroeconomics. VAR models of the transmission mechanism are not estimated to yield advice on the best monetary policy; instead, they are estimated to provide empirical evidence on the response of macroeconomic variables to monetary policy impulses to discriminate between alternative theoretical models of the economy. One should identify monetary policy actions using theory-free restrictions and taking into account the potential endogeneity of policy instruments.

The generalized method of moments (GMM) is the econometric methodology naturally applied to the first-order conditions for the solution of intertemporal optimization problems to derive estimates of the deep parameters in the economy.

Once deep parameters of interest are estimated, the micro-founded model can be calibrated and the effect of relevant economic policies can then be assessed.

We devote three final chapters to VAR models, GMM estimation and calibration to illustrate the strategy of empirical research in macroeconomics consistent with the view that policy advice should be based on the simulation of theoretical models considering explicitly the intertemporal optimization problem of agents.

## 1.13 References

Barro, R. J., and Sala-i-Martin, X. (1995). *Economic Growth.* The MIT Press.

Farmer, R. (1998). *Macroeconomics.* South-Western Publishing.

Faust, J. and Whiteman, C. H. (1996). 'General-to-specific procedures for fitting a data-admissible, theory-inspired, congruent, parsimonious, encompassing, weakly-exogenous, identified, structural model to the DGP: a translation and a critique'. Board of Governors of the Federal Reserve System, International Finance Discussion Papers, 576.

Hendry, D. H. F. (1996). *Dynamic Econometrics.* Oxford University Press, Oxford.

Lucas, R. E. Jr. (1976). 'Econometric Policy Evaluation: A Critique'. In K. Brunner and A. Meltzer (eds.) *The Phillips curve and labor markets,* Amsterdam: North-Holland.

Lucas, R. E. (1988). 'On the Mechanics of Economic Development'. *Journal of Monetary Economics*, 22: 3-42.

Mankiw, G., Romer, D., and Weil, D. (1992). 'A Contribution to the Empirics of Economic Growth'. *Quarterly Journal of Economics*, 408-438.

Pesaran, M. H., and Smith, R. (1995). 'The role of theory in econometrics'. *Journal of Econometrics*, 67: 61-79.

Sims, C. A. (1980). 'Macroeconomics and Reality'. *Econometrica*, 48: 1-48.

Solow, R. (1956). 'A Contribution to the Theory of Economic Growth'. *Quarterly Journal of Economics*, 70: 65-94.

# 2

# PROBABILISTIC STRUCTURE OF TIME-SERIES DATA

## 2.1 Introduction: what is a time-series?

In the previous chapter we introduced time-series to show that time-series violates one of the fundamental properties necessary to perform valid estimation and inference in the linear model. In this chapter we shall discuss this issue at greater depth and length by precisely defining time-series and the fundamental concepts used to analyse them, illustrating how the problem introduced can be resolved in the context of stationary time-series, and, finally, extend our discussion to non-stationarity and cointegration.

Time-series is a sequence

$$\{x_1, x_2, ..., x_T\} \text{ or } \{x_t\}, \ t = 1, ..., T,$$

where $t$ is an index denoting the period in time in which $x$ occurs. We shall treat $x_t$ as a random variable; hence, a time-series is a sequence of random variables ordered in time. Such a sequence is known as a stochastic process. The probability structure of a sequence of random variables is determined by the joint distribution of a stochastic process. A possible probability model for such a joint distribution is:

$$x_t = \epsilon_t, \ \epsilon_t \sim n.i.d. \left(0, \sigma_\epsilon^2\right),$$

i.e., $x_t$ is normally independently distributed over time with constant variance and zero mean. In other words, $x_t$ is a *white-noise* process. A white-noise process is not a proper model for macroeconomic time-series because it does not feature their most common characteristic, namely persistence. Consider the dataset usuk.xls which contains, in Excel format, retrieved from Datastream, quarterly time-series data for nominal and real personal disposable income and consumption in the UK and the US over the sample period 1959:1–1998:1:

ukpdispid: personal disposable income in the UK at constant 1992 prices;
uspdispid: personal disposable income in the US at constant 1992 prices;
uscndurb: consumption of durable goods in the US at current prices;
uscndurb: consumption of durable goods in the US at constant 1992 prices;
uscnnondb: consumption of non-durable goods in the US at current prices;
uscnnondd: consumption of non-durable goods in the US at constant 1992 prices;
uscnservb: consumption of services in the US at current prices;
uscnservd: consumption of services in the US at constant 1992 prices.

All series are adjusted for seasonality. To assess the behaviour of a typical economic time-series against the benchmark of the white-noise process, we import all series in an E-Views workfile and run the following routine:

```
smpl 1959:1 1998:1
genr lyus=log(uspdispid)
genr WN=8.03+0.36*nrnd
plot WN lyus
```

The routine generates the logarithm of the US real disposable income and an artificial series defined as a constant (8.03) plus a normal random variable with zero mean and standard deviation of 0.36, where 8.03 and 0.36 are respectively the sample mean and the sample standard deviation of `lyus`. Having generated the series the program plots them.

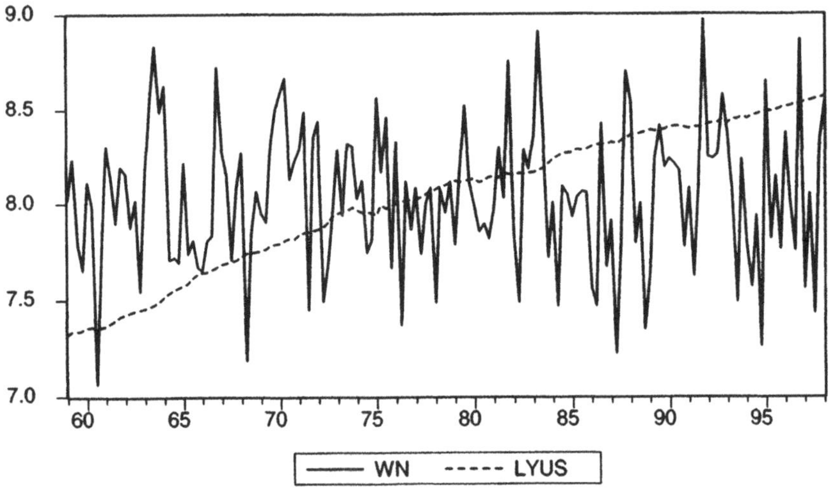


FIG. 2.1. A white-noise process and the logarithm of US real disposable income

Figure 2.1 clearly shows that the white noise model does not capture the property of persistence that motivates the study of time-series. To construct more realistic models one should use combinations of $\epsilon_t$. We concentrate on a class of models created by taking linear combinations of the white noise, the autoregressive moving average (ARMA) models:

$$
\begin{aligned}
AR(1): &\quad x_t = \rho x_{t-1} + \epsilon_t, \\
MA(1): &\quad x_t = \epsilon_t + \theta \epsilon_{t-1}, \\
AR(p): &\quad x_t = \rho_1 x_{t-1} + \rho_2 x_{t-2} + \ldots + \rho_p x_{t-p} + \epsilon_t, \\
MA(q): &\quad x_t = \epsilon_t + \theta_1 \epsilon_{t-1} + \ldots + \theta_q \epsilon_{t-q}, \\
ARMA(p,q): &\quad x_t = \rho_1 x_{t-1} + \ldots + \rho_p x_{t-p} + \theta_1 \epsilon_{t-1} + \ldots + \theta_q \epsilon_{t-q}.
\end{aligned}
$$

Unless it is already clear, we show why ARMA models are obtained by taking linear combinations of the white noise in the next section, where we discuss the necessary fundamentals to analyse time-series.

Note that each of these models can be easily put to action to generate the equivalent time-series by modifying appropriately and running the following program in E-Views, which generates an AR(1) series:

```
smpl 1 1
genr X=0
smpl 2 200
series x=0.5*x(-1)+NRND
```

The program generates a sample of 200 observations from an AR(1) model with $\rho = 0.5$. The series is first initialized for the first observations, the command `series` then generates the series for the specified process, each observation being 0.5 times the previous observation plus a random disturbance drawn from a serially independent standard normal distribution.

The time-series behaviour of the generated series X is plotted in Figure 2.2.

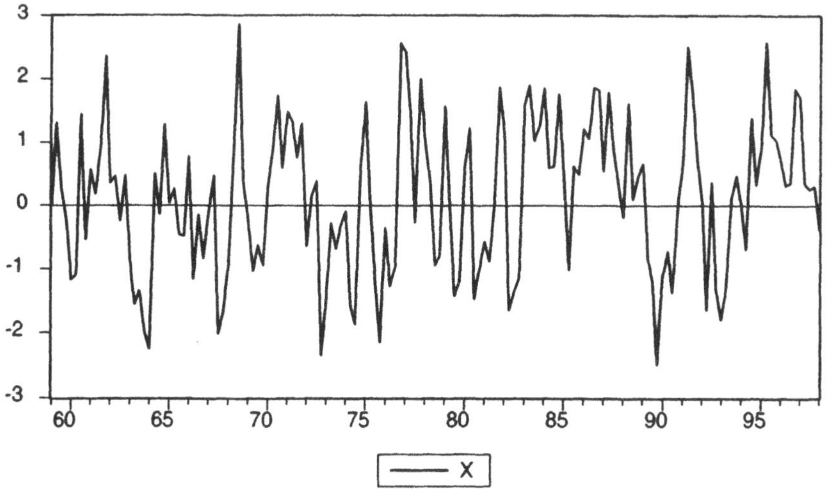


FIG. 2.2. A stationary AR(1) process

The following modified version of the program will generate an ARMA(1,1) series:

```
smpl 1 1
genr X=0
smpl 1 200
genr u=NRND
smpl 2 200
series x=0.5*x(-1) +u +0.4*u(-1)
```

## 2.2 Analysing time-series: fundamentals

To illustrate empirically all the fundamentals we consider a specific member of the ARMA family, the AR model with drift,

$$\begin{aligned} x_t &= \rho_0 + \rho_1 x_{t-1} + \epsilon_t, \\ \epsilon_t &\sim n.i.d.\left(0, \sigma_\epsilon^2\right). \end{aligned} \tag{2.1}$$

Given that each realization of our stochastic process is a random variable, the first relevant fundamental is the density of each observation. In particular, we distinguish between conditional and unconditional densities. Having introduced these two concepts, we define and discuss stationarity, generalize the form of our specific member to the whole family of ARMA models, and conclude this section with a discussion of deterministic and stochastic trends and de-trending methods. Note that at this introductory stage we concentrate almost exclusively on univariate models, for the sake of exposition. After the completion of our introductory tour, we shall concentrate on multivariate models, which are the focus of this book.

### 2.2.1 *Conditional and unconditional densities*

We distinguish between conditional and unconditional densities of a time-series. The unconditional density is obtained under the hypothesis that no observation on the time-series is available, while conditional densities are based on the observation of some realization of random variables. In the case of time-series, we derive unconditional density by putting ourselves at the moment preceding the observation of any realization of the time-series. At that moment the information set contains only the knowledge of the process generating the observations. As observations become available, we can compute conditional densities. As distributions are summarized by their moments, let us illustrate the difference between conditional and unconditional densities by looking at our AR(1) model.

The moments of the density of $x_t$ conditional upon $x_{t-1}$ are immediately obtained from (2.1):

$$\begin{aligned} E\left(x_t \mid x_{t-1}\right) &= \rho_0 + \rho_1 x_{t-1}, \\ Var\left(x_t \mid x_{t-1}\right) &= \sigma_\epsilon^2, \\ Cov\left[\left(x_t \mid x_{t-1}\right), \left(x_{t-j} \mid x_{t-j-1}\right)\right] &= 0 \ \text{ for each } j. \end{aligned}$$

To derive the moments of the density of $x_t$ conditional upon $x_{t-2}$, we need to substitute $x_{t-2}$ from (2.1) for $x_{t-1}$:

$$\begin{aligned}
E(x_t \mid x_{t-2}) &= \rho_0 + \rho_0\rho_1 + \rho_1^2 x_{t-2}, \\
Var(x_t \mid x_{t-2}) &= \sigma_\epsilon^2 \left(1 + \rho_1^2\right), \\
Cov\left[(x_t \mid x_{t-2}), (x_{t-j} \mid x_{t-j-2})\right] &= \rho_1 \sigma_\epsilon^2, \quad \text{for } j = 1, \\
Cov\left[(x_t \mid x_{t-2}), (x_{t-j} \mid x_{t-j-2})\right] &= 0, \quad \text{for } j > 1.
\end{aligned}$$

Finally, unconditional moments are derived by substituting recursively from (2.1) to express $x_t$ as a function of information available at time $t_0$, the moment before we start observing realizations of our process.

$$\begin{aligned}
E(x_t) &= \rho_0 \left(1 + \rho_1 + \rho_1^2 + \ldots + \rho_1^{t-1}\right) + \rho_1^t x_0, \\
Var(x_t) &= \sigma_\epsilon^2 \left(1 + \rho_1^2 + \rho_1^4 + \ldots + \rho_1^{2t-2}\right), \\
\gamma(j) &= Cov(x_t, x_{t-j}) = \rho_1^j Var(x_t), \\
\rho(j) &= \frac{Cov(x_t, x_{t-j})}{\sqrt{Var(x_t)\, Var(x_{t-1})}} = \frac{\rho_1^j Var(x_t)}{\sqrt{Var(x_t)\, Var(x_{t-1})}}.
\end{aligned}$$

Note that $\gamma(j)$ and $\rho(j)$ are functions of $j$, known respectively as the autocovariance function and the autocorrelation function.

### 2.2.2 *Stationarity*

A stochastic process is strictly stationary if its joint density function does not depend on time. More formally, a stochastic process is stationary if, for each $j_1, j_2, \ldots, j_n$, the joint distribution,

$$f\left(x_t, x_{t+j_1}, x_{t+j_2}, x_{t+j_n}\right),$$

does not depend on $t$.

A stochastic process is covariance stationary if its two first unconditional moments do not depend on time, i.e. if the following relations are satisfied for each $h, i, j$:

$$\begin{aligned}
E(x_t) &= E(x_{t+h}) = \mu, \\
E\left(x_t^2\right) &= E\left(x_{t+h}^2\right) = \mu_2, \\
E\left(x_{t+i}x_{t+j}\right) &= \mu_{ij}.
\end{aligned}$$

In the case of our AR(1) process, the condition for stationarity is $|\rho_1| < 1$. When such a condition is satisfied, we have:

$$\begin{aligned}
E(x_t) &= E(x_{t+h}) = \frac{\rho_0}{1 - \rho_1}, \\
Var(x_t) &= Var(x_{t+h}) = \frac{\sigma_\epsilon^2}{1 - \rho_1^2}, \\
Cov(x_t, x_{t-j}) &= \rho_1^j Var(x_t).
\end{aligned}$$

On the other hand, when $|\rho_1| = 1$, the process is obviously non-stationary:

$$E(x_t) = \rho_0 t + x_0,$$
$$Var(x_t) = \sigma_\epsilon^2 t,$$
$$Cov(x_t, x_{t-j}) = \sigma_\epsilon^2 (t - j).$$

To illustrate graphically the properties of different AR processes we generate, using the above program in E-Views, we generate three AR process with $\rho_1$ set to 0.6 (series X1), 0.8 (series X2), and 1 (series X3) respectively. To allow direct comparison, we exclude a drift in all processes, so for all of them we have $\rho_0 = 0$. The time-series behaviour of the three processes is reported in Figure 2.3.

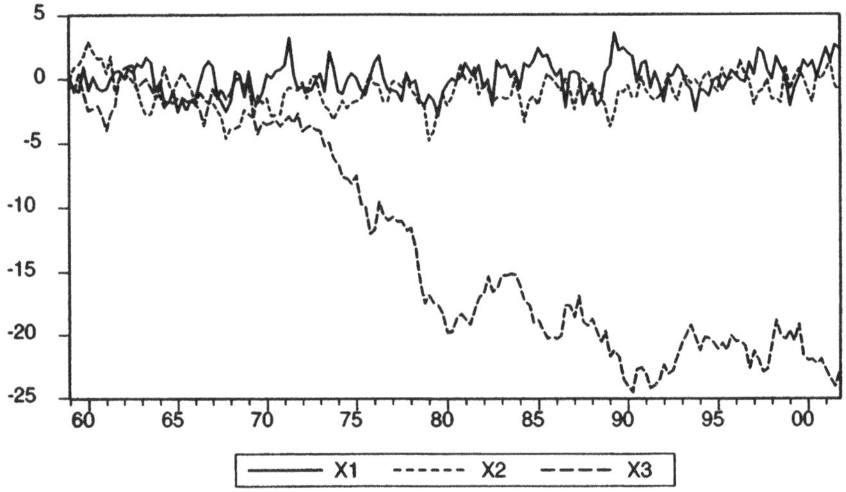


FIG. 2.3. First order autoregressive processes with $\rho_1 = 0.6$ (X1), $\rho_1 = 0.8$ (X2), $\rho_1 = 1$ (X3)

Note that X1 and X2 tend to revert quickly towards their unconditional means. The unconditional mean of X3 is also zero but X3 does not show any tendency for reverting towards its mean; on the contrary, as the sample size grows, the variance of X3 increases without any bound.

### 2.2.3 *ARMA processes*

Before introducing the fundamentals of time-series, we have asserted that white-noise processes are too simplistic to describe economic time-series and one can obtain a closer fit by considering combinations of white noises. We have then introduced ARMA models and discussed the fundamentals to understand their properties, but we have not yet shown that ARMA models represent combinations of white-noise processes. We show this by considering a time-series as a polynomial distributed lag of a white-noise process:

$$\begin{aligned} x_t &= \epsilon_t + b_1\epsilon_{t-1} + b_2\epsilon_{t-2} + \ldots + b_n\epsilon_{t-n} \\ &= \left(1 + b_1 L + b_2 L^2 + \ldots + b_n L^n\right)\epsilon_t \\ &= b(L)\epsilon_t, \end{aligned}$$

where $L$ is the lag operator. The Wold decomposition theorem, which states that any stationary stochastic process can be expressed as the sum of a deterministic and a stochastic moving-average component, warrants generality of our representation. However, in order to describe successfully a time-series, a very high order in the polynomial $b(L)$ is required. This feature can be problematic for estimation, given the usual limitations for sample sizes. This potential problem is resolved, if the polynomial $b(L)$ can be represented as the ratio of two polynomials of lower order:

$$\begin{aligned} x_t = b(L)\,\epsilon_t &= \frac{a(L)}{c(L)}\epsilon_t, \\ c(L)\,x_t &= a(L)\,\epsilon_t. \end{aligned} \tag{2.2}$$

Equation (2.2) is an ARMA process. The process is stationary when the roots of $c(L)$ lie outside the unit circle. The MA component is invertible when the roots of $a(L)$ lie outside the unit circle. Invertibility of the MA component allows it to be represented as an autoregressive process.

To illustrate how the autocovariance and the autocorrelation functions of an ARMA model are derived, we consider the simplest case, the ARMA(1,1) process:

$$\begin{aligned} x_t &= c_1 x_{t-1} + \epsilon_t + a_1\epsilon_{t-1}, \qquad (2.3) \\ (1 - c_1 L)\,x_t &= (1 + a_1 L)\,\epsilon_t. \end{aligned}$$

Equation (2.3) is equivalent to:

$$\begin{aligned} x_t &= \frac{1 + a_1 L}{1 - c_1 L}\epsilon_t \\ &= (1 + a_1 L)\left(1 + c_1 L + (c_1 L)^2 + \ldots\right)\epsilon_t \\ &= \left[1 + (a_1 + c_1)\,L + c_1\,(a_1 + c_1)\,L^2 + c_1^2\,(a_1 + c_1)\,L^3 + \ldots\right]\epsilon_t. \end{aligned}$$

Then,

$$Var(x_t) = \left[1 + (a_1 + c_1)^2 + c_1^2 (a_1 + c_1)^2 + ...\right] \sigma_\epsilon^2$$
$$= \left[1 + \frac{(a_1 + c_1)^2}{1 - c_1^2}\right] \sigma_\epsilon^2,$$
$$Cov(x_t, x_{t-1}) = \left[(a_1 + c_1) + c_1 (a_1 + c_1) + c_1^2 (a_1 + c_1) + ...\right] \sigma_\epsilon^2$$
$$= \left[(a_1 + c_1) + \frac{c_1 (a_1 + c_1)^2}{1 - c_1^2}\right] \sigma_\epsilon^2.$$

Hence,

$$\rho(1) = \frac{Cov(x_t, x_{t-1})}{Var(x_t)}$$
$$= \frac{(1 + a_1 c_1)(a_1 + c_1)}{1 + c_1^2 + 2a_1 c_1}.$$

Successive values for $\rho(j)$ are obtained from the recurrent relation $\rho(j) = c_1 \rho(j-1)$ for $j \geq 2$.

To illustrate the difference between an AR and an ARMA process, we generate an AR(0.7) process and an ARMA(0.7, 0.4) process in E-Views. The two autocorrelation functions (for lags up to 10) are reported in Table 2.1.

TABLE 2.1. Autocorrelation functions

| AR(0.7) | ARMA(0.7,0.4) |
|---|---|
| 0.712 | 0.836 |
| 0.561 | 0.639 |
| 0.437 | 0.491 |
| 0.304 | 0.364 |
| 0.254 | 0.305 |
| 0.270 | 0.305 |
| 0.270 | 0.313 |
| 0.298 | 0.326 |
| 0.279 | 0.323 |
| 0.296 | 0.316 |

Note that the autocorrelation of the ARMA(1,1) process is higher than the autocorrelation of the AR(1) process, because $a_1 > 0$.

### 2.2.4 *Deterministic and stochastic trends*

Figure 2.1 at the beginning of this chapter shows that macroeconomic time-series, besides being persistent, often feature upward trends. Non-stationarity of time-series is a possible manifestation of a trend. Consider, for example, the random walk process with a drift:

$$x_t = a_0 + x_{t-1} + \epsilon_t,$$
$$\epsilon_t \sim n.i.d. \left(0, \sigma_\epsilon^2\right).$$

Recursive substitution yields

$$x_t = x_0 + a_0 t + \sum_{i=0}^{t-1} \epsilon_{t-i}, \tag{2.4}$$

which shows that the non-stationary series contains both a deterministic $(a_0 t)$ and a stochastic $\left(\sum_{i=0}^{t-1} \epsilon_{t-i}\right)$ trend.

An easy way to make a non-stationary series stationary is differencing:

$$\Delta x_t = x_t - x_{t-1} = (1 - L)\, x_t = a_0 + \epsilon_t.$$

In general, if a time-series needs to be differenced $d$ times to become stationary, then it is integrated of order $d$ or I($d$). Our random walk is I(1). When the $d$-th difference of a time-series $x$, $\Delta^d x_t$, can be represented by an ARMA$(p, q)$ model, we say that $x_t$ is an integrated moving-average process of order $p, d, q$ and denote it as ARIMA$(p, d, q)$.

Compare the behaviour of an integrated process with that of a trend stationary process. Trend stationary processes feature only a deterministic trend:

$$z_t = \alpha + \beta t + \epsilon_t. \tag{2.5}$$

The $z_t$ process is non-stationary, but the non-stationarity is removed simply by regressing $z_t$ on the deterministic trend. Unlike this, for integrated processes like (2.4) the removal of the deterministic trend does not deliver a stationary time-series. Deterministic trends have no memory while integrated variables have an infinite one. Both integrated variable and deterministic trend exhibit systematic variations, but in the latter case the variation is predictable, whereas in the other one it is not. This point is easily seen in Figure 2.4, where we report three series for a sample of 200 observations. The series are generated in E-Views by running the following program:

```
smpl 1 1
genr ST1=0
genr ST2=0
smpl 2 200
series ST1=0.1+ST1(-1)+nrnd
series ST2=0.1+ST2(-1)+nrnd
series DT=0.1*@trend+nrnd
```

We have a deterministic trend (DT) generated by simulating equation (2.5) with $\alpha = 0, \beta = 0.1$, and a white noise independently distributed as a standard normal (**nrnd**), and two integrated series (ST1 and ST2), which are random walks with a drift of 0.1. The only difference between ST1 and ST2 is in the realizations from the error terms, which are different drawings from the same serially independent standard normal distribution.

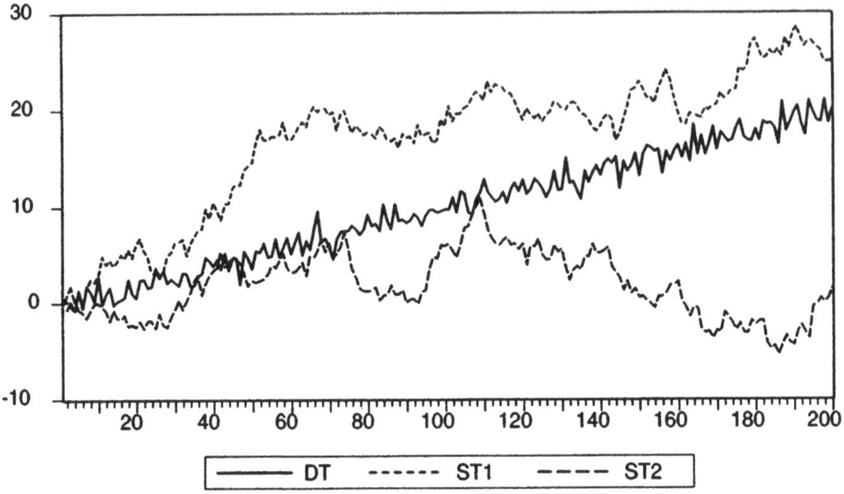


FIG. 2.4. Deterministic (DT) and stochastic (ST1 and ST2) trends

## 2.3 Persistence: Monte-Carlo experiment

Persistence of time-series destroys one of the crucial properties for implementing valid estimation and inference in the linear model. We have already seen that in the context of the linear model

$$\mathbf{y} = \mathbf{X}\boldsymbol{\beta} + \boldsymbol{\epsilon}.$$

The following property is required to implement valid estimation and inference

$$E(\boldsymbol{\epsilon} \mid \mathbf{X}) = \mathbf{0}. \tag{2.6}$$

Hypothesis (2.6) implies that

$$E(\epsilon_i \mid \mathbf{x}_1, \ldots \mathbf{x}_i, \ldots, \mathbf{x}_n) = 0, \quad (i = 1, \ldots, n).$$

Think of the simplest time-series model for a generic variable $y$:

$$y_t = a_0 + a_1 y_{t-1} + \epsilon_t.$$

Clearly, if $a_1 \neq 0$, then, although it is still true that $E(\epsilon_t \mid y_{t-1}) = 0$, $E(\epsilon_{t-1} \mid y_{t-1}) \neq 0$ and (2.6) breaks down.

How serious is the problem? To assess intuitively the consequences of persistence, we construct a small Monte-Carlo simulation on the short sample properties of the OLS estimator of the parameters in an AR(1) process.

A Monte-Carlo simulation is based on the generation of a sample from a known data generating process (DGP). First we generate a set of random numbers from a given distribution (here a normally independent white-noise disturbance) for a sample size of interest (200 observations) and then construct the process of interest (in our case, an AR(1) process). When a sample of observations on the process of interest is available, then we can estimate the relevant parameters and compare their fitted values with the known true value. For this reason the Monte-Carlo simulation is a sort of controlled experiment. The only potential problem with this procedure is that the set of random numbers drawn is just one possible outcome and the estimates are dependent on the sequence of simulated white-noise residuals. To overcome this problem in a Monte-Carlo study, the DGP is replicated many times. For each replication we obtain a set of estimates, and compute averages across replications of the estimated parameters, to assess these averages against the known true values.

Our Monte-Carlo simulation is performed by running the following program in E-Views:

```
genr a1sum=0
for !i=1 to 500
smpl 1 1
genr y{!i}=10
smpl 2 200
series y{!i}=1+0.9*y{!i}(-1)+nrnd
equation eq.ls y{!i}=c(1)+c(2)*y{!i}(-1)
eq.rls(c,s)
genr a1sum=a1sum+R_c2
next
genr a1mean=a1sum/500
```

The first line of the program generates a series to store the values of the estimated $a_1$ in each replication. In the next step we set a counter to keep track of the replications (in this specific case we have 500 of them). The loop for the five hundred replications is then set. In each replication we generate a sample of two hundred observations from an AR(1) and then estimate the autoregressive parameters. Note that such estimation is performed recursively starting with a sample of five observations and then by adding one observation at a time until the last one. The series of these estimates is stored at each replication with the command `eq.rls(c,s)`. At the end we have 500 hundred series each containing a series of 195 estimated parameters (the first being the parameter estimated on the sample 1-5, the second the parameter estimated on the sample 1-6, the last one the parameter estimated on the full sample). We report the averages across replications in Figure 2.5.

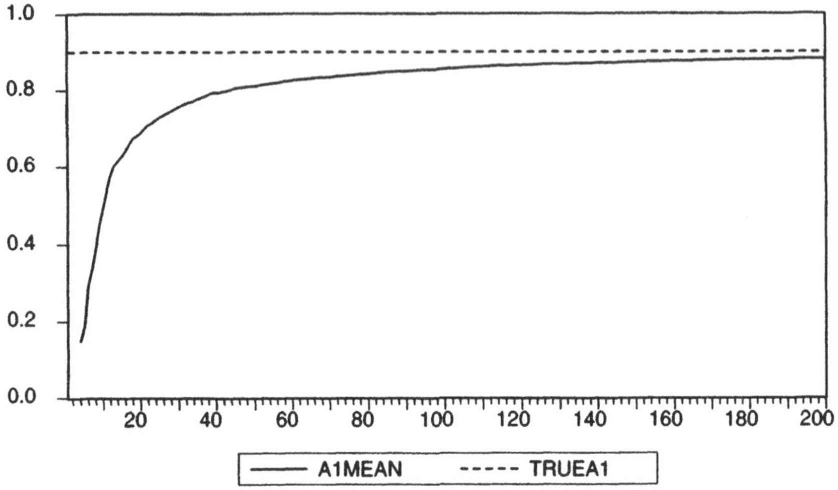


FIG. 2.5. Small sample bias

From the figure we note that the estimate of $a_1$ is heavily biased in small samples, but the bias decreases as the sample gets larger, and disappears eventually. One can show analytically that the average of the OLS estimate of $a_1$ is $a_1 \left(1 - \frac{2}{T}\right)$. This is an interesting result, which can be generalized. For stationary time-series, the correlation, which destroys the orthogonality between residuals and regressors in the linear regression model, tends to disappear as the distance between observations increases. Therefore, as we shall show in the next section, the finite sample results can be extended to time-series by considering large samples. Such an aim is obtained by introducing asymptotic theory.

## 2.4 Traditional solution: asymptotic theory

Stationary time-series feature time-independent distributions, as a consequence, the effect of any specific innovation disappears as time elapses. We show in this section that the intuition of the simple Monte-Carlo simulation can be extended and asymptotic theory can be used to perform valid estimation and inference when modelling *stationary* time-series.

### 2.4.1 *Basic elements of asymptotic theory*

In this section we introduce the elements of asymptotic theory necessary to illustrate how the results in estimation and inference for the linear model applied to cross-sectional data in Chapter 1 can be extended to time-series models.[1]

Consider a sequence $\{X_T\}$ of random variables with the associated sequence of distribution functions $\{F_T\} = F_1, ..., F_T$, we give the following definitions of convergence for $X_T$.

2.4.1.1 *Convergence in distribution.* Given a random variable $X$ with distribution function $F$, $X_T$ converges in distribution to $X$ if the following equality is satisfied:

$$\lim_{T\to\infty} P\{X_T < x_0\} = P\{X < x_0\},$$

for all $x_0$, where the function $F(x)$ is continuous.

2.4.1.2 *Convergence in probability.* Given a random variable $X$ with distribution function $F$, $X_T$ converges in probability to $X$ if, for each $\epsilon > 0$, the following relation holds:

$$\lim_{T\to\infty} P\{|X_T - X| < \epsilon\} = 1.$$

Note that convergence in probability implies convergence in distribution.

2.4.1.3 *Central limit theorem (formulation of Lindeberg–Levy).* Given a sequence $\{X_T\}$ of identically and independently distributed random variables with mean $\mu$ and finite variance $\sigma^2$, define

$$\bar{X} = \frac{1}{T}\sum_{i=1}^{T} X_i,$$

$$\omega = \sqrt{T}\frac{\left(\bar{X} - \mu\right)}{\sigma}.$$

$\omega$ converges in distribution to a standard normal.

2.4.1.4 *Slutsky's Theorem.* For any random variable $X_T$, such that $p\lim X_T = a$, where $a$ is a constant, given a function $g(\cdot)$ continuous at $a$, $p\lim g(X_T) = g(a)$.

2.4.1.5 *Cramer's Theorem.* Given two random variables $X_T$ and $Y_T$, such that $Y_T$ converges in distribution to $Y$ and $X_T$ converges in probability to a constant $a$, the following relationships hold:

$X_T + Y_T$ converges in distribution to $(a + Y)$;
$Y_T/a_T$ converges in distribution to $(Y/a)$;
$Y_T \cdot a_T$ converges in distribution to $(Y \cdot a)$.

Note that all theorems introduced so far extend to vectors of random variables.

[1] For a formal treatment of these topics, see White (1984).

2.4.1.6 *Mann–Wald Theorem.* Consider a vector $\mathbf{z}_t$ $(k \times 1)$ of random variables which satisfies the following property:

$$p \lim T^{-1} \sum_{t=1}^{T} \mathbf{z}_t \mathbf{z}_t' = \mathbf{Q},$$

where $\mathbf{Q}$ is a positive definite matrix. Consider also a sequence $\epsilon_t$ of random variables, identically and independently distributed with zero mean and finite variance, $\sigma^2$, for which finite moments of each order are defined. If $E(\mathbf{z}_t \epsilon_t) = 0$, then

$$p \lim T^{-1} \sum_{t=1}^{T} \mathbf{z}_t \epsilon_t = \mathbf{0}, \sqrt{\frac{1}{T}} \sum_{t=1}^{T} \mathbf{z}_t \epsilon_t \xrightarrow{d} N\left(0, \sigma^2 \mathbf{Q}\right).$$

2.4.2 *Application to models for stationary time-series*

Consider the following time-series model:

$$y_t = \alpha y_{t-1} + \beta x_t + \epsilon_t,$$

where $x_t$ is a stationary variable and $|\alpha| < 1$. As already shown, $E(y_t \epsilon_{t-i}) \neq 0$ and the OLS estimator of $\alpha$ is biased.

Re-write the model as:

$$\begin{aligned} y_t &= \mathbf{z}_t \gamma + \epsilon_t, \\ \mathbf{z}_t &= \begin{bmatrix} y_{t-1} & x_t \end{bmatrix}, \\ \gamma &= \begin{bmatrix} \alpha \\ \beta \end{bmatrix}. \end{aligned}$$

By applying the Mann–Wald result, we can derive the asymptotic distribution of the OLS estimator of $\gamma$, $\widehat{\gamma}$:

$$\widehat{\gamma} \xrightarrow{d} N\left[\gamma, \sigma^2 \mathbf{Q}^{-1}\right],$$

and all the finite sample results available for cross-section can be extended to stationary time-series just by considering large-sample theory.

## 2.5 Stochastic trends and spurious regressions

From what we have discussed so far, it should be clear that econometric analysis depends on the variances and covariances among variables. In the case of independent sampling (cross-section) we can use finite sample moments for estimation and inference, and in the case of stationary time-series the consideration of moments in large samples can solve the problems peculiar to time-series in small samples. Within this framework non-stationarity causes problems: we know that unconditional moments are not defined for non-stationary time-series. Consider, for the sake of illustration, an OLS regression of an I(0) variable $y_t$ on an

I(1) variable $x_t$. The OLS estimator of the regression $y_t$ on $x_t$ converges to zero as the sample size increases. The variance of $x_t$, being divergent, dominates the covariance between the two variables. In general, asymptotic theory is not applicable to non-stationary time-series (see, for example, Hatanaka 1996; Maddala and Kim 1998). So, unless all the trends observed in time-series are deterministic, the solution of reverting to asymptotic theory is not directly accessible.

To give an intuition of the importance of non-stationarity in time-series and to illustrate the problems related to non-stationarity, consider the results of a 'crazy' regression in Table 2.2, obtained by relating the logarithm of consumption in the US to the logarithm of personal disposable income in the UK:

TABLE 2.2. Regressing US consumption on UK disposable income

SAMPLE 1960:1 1998:1

| Variable | Coefficient | Std. Error | t-Statistic | Prob. |
|---|---|---|---|---|
| C | -5.57 | 0.17 | -32.80 | 0.0000 |
| LYUK | 1.20 | 0.015 | 78.99 | 0.0000 |

$R^2$ 0.976, S.E. of regression 0.052, DW stat 0.137

Note that the regression features an extremely high $R^2$ and the UK disposable income is significant in explaining US consumption. We have a case of a spurious regression, which witnesses the relevance of non-stationarity in economic time-series. To elaborate on this point, consider the two simple univariate time-series models for LYUS and LYUK shown in Table 2.3.

TABLE 2.3. Univariate models for US consumption and UK disposable income

SAMPLE 1960:1 1998:1

| Variable | Coefficient | Std. Error | t-Statistic | Prob. |
|---|---|---|---|---|
| Dependent variable LCUS | | | | |
| C | 0.038 | 0.008 | 4.60 | 0.0000 |
| LCUS(-1) | 0.996 | 0.001 | 922.1 | 0.0000 |
| $R^2$ 0.99, S.E. of regr 0.0045, DW stat 1.392. | | | | |
| Dependent variable LYUK | | | | |
| C | 0.038 | 0.051 | 0.74 | 0.45 |
| LYUK(-1) | 0.997 | 0.004 | 214.14 | 0.0000 |
| $R^2$ 0.996, S.E. of regr 0.016, DW stat 2.31. | | | | |

Despite the simplicity of the two time-series models for LYUS and LYUK, we note that they can both be approximated by random walk models:

$$\begin{aligned}\mathrm{LCUS}_t &= a_0 + \mathrm{LCUS}_{t-1} + \epsilon_{1t},\\ \mathrm{LYUK}_t &= b_0 + \mathrm{LYUK}_{t-1} + \epsilon_{2t},\\ \epsilon_{1t} &\sim n.i.d.\left(0, \sigma^2_{\epsilon_1}\right),\\ \epsilon_{2t} &\sim n.i.d.\left(0, \sigma^2_{\epsilon_2}\right).\end{aligned}$$

As we already know, recursive substitution yields:

$$\mathrm{LCUS}_t = \mathrm{LCUS}_0 + a_0 t + \sum_{i=0}^{t-1} \epsilon_{1t-i},$$

$$\mathrm{LYUK}_t = \mathrm{LYUK}_0 + b_0 t + \sum_{i=0}^{t-1} \epsilon_{2t-i}.$$

When the following model is estimated:

$$\mathrm{LCUS}_t = \widehat{\alpha} + \widehat{\beta}\mathrm{LYUK}_t + \widehat{\epsilon}_t,$$

the coefficient $\widehat{\beta}$ is significant as both series have a deterministic trend. However, to have a non-spurious relation, we require that the regression also removes the stochastic trend from the dependent variables, leaving stationary residuals. Otherwise, the correlation we observe can be labelled as spurious. We report in Figure 2.6 the residuals from the OLS regression of LCUS on LYUK.

Visual impression confirms the intuition that the regression has delivered a spurious relation, failing to remove the stochastic trend from the non-stationary dependent variable. The reported Durbin–Watson statistic of 0.14 gives a more formal background to the visual impression. The Durbin–Watson statistic, originally designed to test for the presence of first-order autocorrelation in the residuals, can be re-calibrated to test for stationarity:

$$\mathrm{DW} = \frac{\sum_{i=2}^{T} \left(\widehat{\epsilon}_t - \widehat{\epsilon}_{t-1}\right)^2}{\sum_{i=2}^{T} \widehat{\epsilon}_t} \simeq 2\left(1 - \widehat{\rho}\right),$$

where $\widehat{\rho}$ is the OLS coefficient from the regression of $\widehat{\epsilon}_t$ on $\widehat{\epsilon}_{t-1}$. The test was originally tabulated to test the hypothesis $H_0$: $\rho = 0$; however, critical values for the null of non-stationarity $H_0$: $\rho = 1$ have been provided by Sargan and Bhargava (1983). According to such critical values, the null of non-stationarity cannot be rejected by an observed value of 0.14 for the Durbin–Watson statistic.

From the econometric point of view non-stationarity of time-series is problematic in that it might generate a spurious regression and it does not allow the use

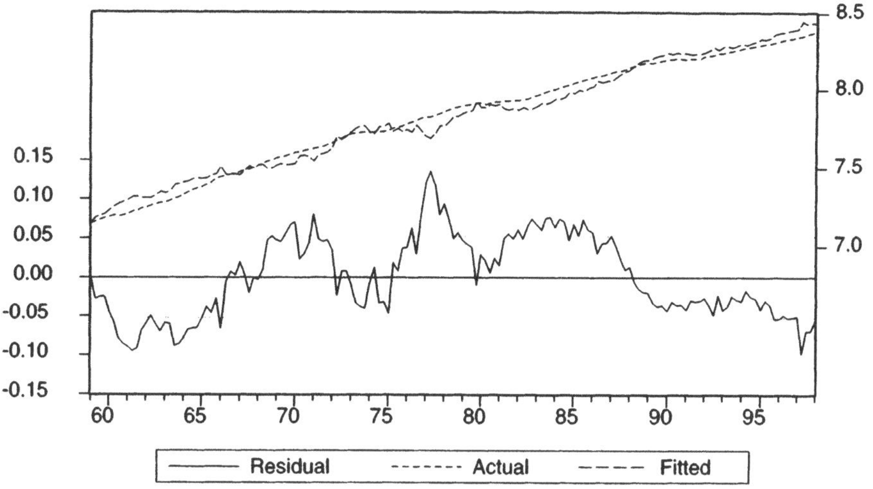


FIG. 2.6. A spurious regression

of standard large-sample theory for valid estimation and inference in the linear model. From the economic point of view the presence of unit root means that the effects of a shock persist forever and that cyclical fluctuations cannot be studied separately from long-run growth components, as long-run trends are not fixed. Pioneering work by Nelson and Plosser(1982) have renewed the attention of the profession for these issues and after their work many tests have been proposed to discriminate between stochastic and deterministic trends. The Dickey–Fuller (DF) and Augmented Dickey-Fuller (ADF) tests (1981) have enjoyed a remarkable empirical success. These are tests for the null hypothesis of non-stationarity of a generic time-series $x_t$, based on the following auxiliary regression:

$$x_t = \widehat{\mu} + \widehat{\gamma}t + \widehat{\delta}x_{t-1} + \sum_{i=0}^{k}\widehat{\varphi}_i \Delta x_{t-i-1} + \widehat{\epsilon}_t \qquad (2.7)$$

under the unit-root null hypothesis $\widehat{\delta} = 1$, therefore the test statistic is simply the t test: $t \equiv \left(\widehat{\delta} - 1\right)/SE\left(\widehat{\delta}\right)$, where $SE\left(\widehat{\delta}\right)$ is the standard error of the estimated coefficient. The ADF statistic is obtained by selecting an appropriate value for k in (2.7) ,while the DF statistic is obtained by setting k=0. Note that this statistic does not have the usual Student-t distribution, but it is skewed toward negative values. Dickey–Fuller(1981) calculate the appropriate asymptotic critical values, which are affected by the specification of the deterministic component of (2.7). The ADF tests offer a solution to the dynamic mis-specification of the simple regressions behind DF and CRDW tests; alternative solutions generate different tests for the same null hypothesis (Phillips-Perron 1988). It has been proved that the power of all these tests for unit-root against plausible deterministic trends alternative is very limited (DeJong and Whiteman 1991). Rudebusch (1993) analyses the case of the US real GNP to conclude that

> ...The appropriate conclusion from unit-root test on this data sample is that the existence of a unit-root is uncertain...

The low power problem becomes even more complicated when deterministic trends with structural breaks are considered, as in Zivot and Andrews (1992). Interestingly, the great majority of the available tests concentrate on the null of non-stationarity, there are some exceptions, such as the procedure proposed by Kiwiatkoski et al.(1992),but there are not many studies in the empirical literature reporting simultaneously tests for the null of non-stationarity and tests for the null of stationarity. Maddala and Kim (1998) conclude their book on unit roots, cointegration and structural change with a chapter on 'Future directions'; the last section of this chapter, entitled 'What is not needed', contains the following statement:

> ... what we do not need is more unit root test (each of which uses the Nelson–Plosser data as a Guinea pig)...

We agree with such a view and we prefer to concentrate on multivariate modelling of non-stationary time-series and to de-emphasize the debate on deterministic versus stochastic trends within the context of univariate models.

### 2.5.1 *Non-stationarity and the likelihood function*

Before considering solutions to the problems generated by non-stationarity it is instructive to illustrate such problems from a different perspective. Consider a vector $\mathbf{x}_t$ containing observations on time-series variables at time $t$. A sample of $T$ time-series observations on all the variables is represented as:

$$\mathbf{X}_T^1 = \begin{bmatrix} \mathbf{x}_1 \\ . \\ . \\ . \\ \mathbf{x}_T \end{bmatrix}.$$

In general, estimation is performed by considering the joint sample density function, known also as the likelihood function, which can be expressed as $D\left(\mathbf{X}_T^1 \mid \mathbf{X}_0, \boldsymbol{\theta}\right)$. The likelihood function is defined on the parameter space $\Theta$, given the observation of the observed sample $\mathbf{X}_T^1$ and of a set of initial conditions $\mathbf{X}_0$. One can interpret such initial conditions as the pre-sample observations on the relevant variables (which are usually unavailable). In case of independent observations the likelihood function can be written as the product of the density functions for each observation. However, this is not the relevant case for time-series, as time-series observations are in general sequentially correlated. In the case of time-series, the sample density is constructed using the concept of sequential conditioning. The likelihood function, conditioned with respect to initial conditions, can always be written as the product of a marginal density and a conditional density:

$$D\left(\mathbf{X}_T^1 \mid \mathbf{X}_0, \boldsymbol{\theta}\right) = D\left(\mathbf{x}_1 \mid \mathbf{X}_0, \boldsymbol{\theta}\right) D\left(\mathbf{X}_T^2 \mid \mathbf{X}_1, \boldsymbol{\theta}\right).$$

Obviously,

$$D\left(\mathbf{X}_T^2 \mid \mathbf{X}_0, \boldsymbol{\theta}\right) = D\left(\mathbf{x}_2 \mid \mathbf{X}_1, \boldsymbol{\theta}\right) D\left(\mathbf{X}_T^3 \mid \mathbf{X}_2, \boldsymbol{\theta}\right),$$

and, by recursive substitution:

$$D\left(\mathbf{X}_T^1 \mid \mathbf{X}_0, \boldsymbol{\theta}\right) = \prod_{t=1}^{T} D\left(\mathbf{x}_t \mid \mathbf{X}_{t-1}, \boldsymbol{\theta}\right).$$

Having obtained $D\left(\mathbf{X}_T^1 \mid \mathbf{X}_0, \boldsymbol{\theta}\right)$, we can in theory derive $D\left(\mathbf{X}_T^1, \boldsymbol{\theta}\right)$ by integrating with respect to $X_0$ the density conditional on pre-sample observations. In practice this could be intractable analytically, as $D\left(X_0\right)$ is not known. The hypothesis of stationarity becomes crucial at this stage, as stationarity restricts the memory of time-series and limits the effects of pre-sample observations to the first observations in the sample. This is why, in the case of stationary processes, one can simply ignore initial conditions. Clearly, the larger the sample, the better, as the weight of lost information becomes smaller. Moreover, note that even by omitting initial conditions, we have:

$$D\left(\mathbf{X}_T^1 \mid \mathbf{X}_0, \boldsymbol{\theta}\right) = D\left(\mathbf{x}_1 \mid \mathbf{X}_0, \boldsymbol{\theta}\right) \prod_{t=2}^{T} D\left(\mathbf{x}_t \mid \mathbf{X}_{t-1}, \boldsymbol{\theta}\right).$$

Therefore, the likelihood function is separated in the product on $T-1$ conditional distributions and one unconditional distribution. In the case of non-stationarity, the unconditional distribution is undefined. On the other hand, in the case of stationarity, the DGP is completely described by the conditional density function $D\left(\mathbf{x}_t \mid \mathbf{X}_{t-1}, \boldsymbol{\theta}\right)$.

2.5.1.1 *An illustration: the first-order autoregressive process.* To give more empirical content to our case, let us consider again the case of the univariate first-order autoregressive process,

$$x_t \mid \mathbf{X}_{t-1} \sim N\left(\lambda x_{t-1}, \sigma^2\right), \tag{2.8}$$

$$D\left(\mathbf{X}_T^1 \mid \lambda, \sigma^2\right) = D\left(x_1 \mid \lambda, \sigma^2\right) \prod_{t=2}^{T} D\left(x_t \mid \mathbf{X}_{t-1}, \lambda, \sigma^2\right). \tag{2.9}$$

From (2.9), the likelihood function clearly involves $T-1$ conditional densities and one unconditional density. The conditional densities are given by (2.8), the unconditional density can be derived only in the case of stationarity:

$$x_t = \lambda x_{t-1} + u_t,$$
$$u_t \sim N.I.D\left(0, \sigma^2\right).$$

We can obtain by recursive substitution:

$$x_t = u_t + \lambda u_{t-1} + ... + \lambda^{n-1} u_1 + \lambda^n x_0.$$

Only if $|\lambda| < 1$, the effect of the initial condition disappears and we can write the unconditional density of $x_t$ as:

$$D\left(x_t \mid \lambda, \sigma^2\right) = N\left(0, \frac{\sigma^2}{1-\lambda^2}\right).$$

Under stationarity we can derive the exact likelihood function:

$$D\left(\mathbf{X}_T^1 \mid \lambda, \sigma^2\right) = (2\pi)^{-\frac{T}{2}} \sigma^{-T} \left(1-\lambda^2\right)^{\frac{1}{2}} \qquad (2.10)$$
$$\exp\left[-\frac{1}{2\sigma^2}\left(\left(1-\lambda^2\right) x_1^2 + \sum_{t=2}^{T} \left(x_t - \lambda x_{t-1}\right)^2\right)\right],$$

and estimates of the parameters of interest are derived by maximizing this function. Note that $\widehat{\lambda}$ cannot be derived analytically, using the exact likelihood function; but it requires conditioning the likelihood and operating a grid search. Note also that, in large samples, using the approximate likelihood function by dropping the first observation works only under the hypothesis of stationarity. When the first observation is dropped and the approximate likelihood function is considered, one can show that the Maximum Likelihood (ML) estimate of $\lambda$ coincides with the OLS estimate.

## 2.6 Univariate decompositions of time-series

The general solution proposed to the problem introduced in the previous section is the search for a stationary representation of non-stationary time-series. This has been done both in univariate and multivariate frameworks. We discuss briefly methodologies used in a univariate framework, to move swiftly to decompositions in a multivariate framework, which are at the heart of our discussion of modern macroeconometrics.

Beveridge and Nelson (1981) provide an elegant way of decomposing a non-stationary time-series into a permanent and a temporary (cyclical) component by applying ARIMA methods. For any non-stationary time-series $x_t$ integrated of the first order, the Wold decomposition theorem could be applied to its first difference, to deliver the following representation:

$$\Delta x_t = \mu + C(L)\,\epsilon_t,$$
$$\epsilon_t \sim n.i.d.\left(0, \sigma_\epsilon^2\right),$$

where $C(L)$ is a polynomial of order $q$ in the lag operator. Consider now the polynomial $D(L)$, defined as:

$$D(L) = C(L) - C(1). \tag{2.11}$$

Given that $C(1)$ is a constant, also $D(L)$ will be of order $q$. Clearly,

$$D(1) = 0,$$

therefore, 1 is a root of $D(L)$, and

$$D(L) = C^*(L)(1 - L), \tag{2.12}$$

where $C^*(L)$ is a polynomial of order $q - 1$.

By equating (2.11) to (2.12), we have:

$$C(L) = C^*(L)(1 - L) + C(1),$$

and

$$\Delta x_t = \mu + C^*(L)\,\Delta\epsilon_t + C(1)\,\epsilon_t. \tag{2.13}$$

By integrating (2.13), we finally have:

$$x_t = C^*(L)\,\epsilon_t + \mu t + C(1)\,z_t$$
$$= C_t + TR_t,$$

where $z_t$ is a process for which $\Delta z_t = \epsilon_t$. $C_t$ is the cyclical component and $TR_t$ is the trend component made of a deterministic and a stochastic trend. Note that the trend component can be represented as:

$$TR_t = TR_{t-1} + \mu + C(1)\,\epsilon_t.$$

2.6.1 *Beveridge–Nelson decomposition of an IMA(1,1) process*

Consider the process:

$$\Delta x_t = \epsilon_t + \theta\epsilon_{t-1}, \quad 0 < \theta < 1.$$

In this case:

$$C(L) = 1 + \theta L,$$
$$C(1) = 1 + \theta,$$
$$C^*(L) = \frac{C(L) - C(1)}{1 - L} = -\theta.$$

The Beveridge and Nelson decomposition gives the following result:

$$x_t = C_t + TR_t$$
$$= -\theta\epsilon_t + (1 + \theta)\,z_t.$$

### 2.6.2 *Beveridge–Nelson decomposition of an ARIMA(1,1) process*

Consider the process:

$$\Delta x_t = \rho \Delta x_{t-1} + \epsilon_t + \theta \epsilon_{t-1}.$$

Here:

$$C(L) = \frac{1+\theta L}{1-\rho L},$$
$$C(1) = \frac{1+\theta}{1-\rho},$$
$$C^*(L) = \frac{C(L)-C(1)}{1-L} = -\frac{\theta+\rho}{(1-\rho)(1-\rho L)},$$

and the Beveridge and Nelson decomposition yields:

$$x_t = C_t + TR_t = -\frac{\theta+\rho}{(1-\rho)(1-\rho L)}\epsilon_t + \frac{1+\theta}{1-\rho}z_t.$$

### 2.6.3 *Deriving the Beveridge–Nelson decomposition in practice*

The practical derivation of a Beveridge and Nelson decomposition for any ARIMA process is easily derived by applying a methodology suggested by Cuddington and Winters (1987). For any I(1) process, the stochastic trend can be represented as:

$$TR_t = TR_{t-1} + \mu + C(1)\epsilon_t. \tag{2.14}$$

The decomposition can then be applied in the following steps:

1. identify the appropriate ARIMA model and estimate $\epsilon_t$ and all the parameters in $\mu$ and $C(1)$;
2. given an initial value for $TR_0$, use (2.14) to generate the permanent component of the time-series;
3. generate the cyclical component as the difference between the observed value in each period and the permanent component.

The above procedure gives the permanent component up to a constant. If the precision of this procedure is unsatisfactory, one can use further conditions to identify the decomposition more precisely. For example, one can impose the condition that the sample mean of the cyclical component is zero, to pin down the constant in the permanent component.

To illustrate how the procedure works in practice, we have simulated an ARIMA(1,1,1) model in E-Views for a sample of 200 observations, by running the following program:

```
smpl 1 2
genr x=0
```

```
smpl 1 200
genr u=nrnd
smpl 3 200
series x=x(-1)+0.6*x(-1)-0.6*x(-2)+u+0.5*u(-1)
```

From the previous section we know the exact Beveridge and Nelson decomposition of our $x_t$:

$$\begin{aligned} x_t &= C_t + TR_t \\ &= -\frac{1.1}{(1-0.6)(1-0.6L)}\epsilon_t + \frac{1.5}{0.4}z_t, \\ TR_t &= TR_{t-1} + \frac{1.5}{0.4}\epsilon_t. \end{aligned}$$

We can, therefore, generate the permanent component of X and the transitory component as follows:

```
smpl 1 2
genr p=0
smpl 3 200
series TR= TR(-1)+(1.5/0.4)*u
genr CYCLE=X-TR
```

Figure 2.7 reports the series X, TR and CYCLE.

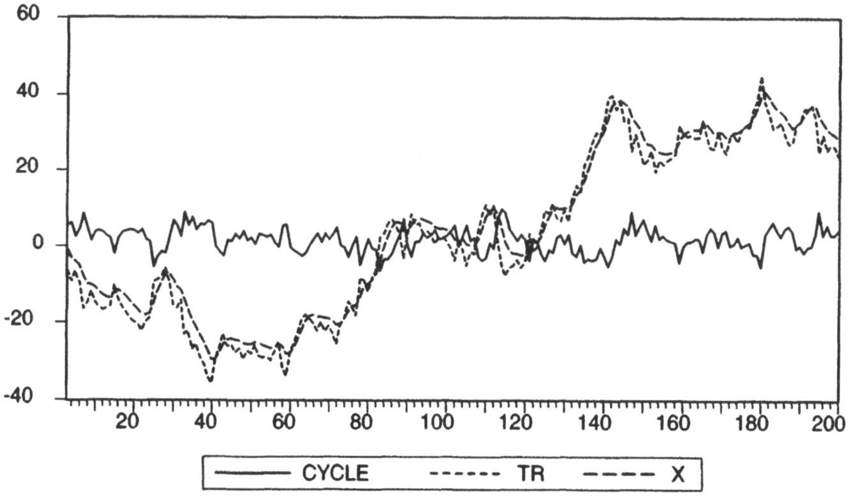


FIG. 2.7. A Beveridge–Nelson decomposition of an ARIMA(1,1,1) process

This is exactly the procedure that we follow in practice, except that we estimate parameters rather than impute them from a known DGP.

### 2.6.4 *Assessing the Beveridge–Nelson decomposition*

The properties of the permanent and temporary components of an integrated time-series delivered by the Beveridge–Nelson decomposition are worth some comments. The innovations in the permanent and the transitory components are perfectly negatively correlated; moreover, the trend component is more volatile than the actual time-series as the negative correlation between the permanent and the transitory components acts to smooth the original time-series. These results are easily seen for the simplest case we have already discussed. For example, in the case of the IMA(1,1) process, the correlation between the innovations in the permanent and transitory components is minus one and the variance of the innovation in the trend component is $(1.5/0.4)^2 \sigma_\epsilon^2 > \sigma_\epsilon^2$. Note that in general the variance of innovations might have an economic interpretation and economic theory might suggest different patterns of correlations between innovations from a perfectly negative correlation. As we shall see in one of the next chapters, an interesting pattern is the absence of correlation between the innovations in the cycle and the trend components of an integrated time-series. In general, different restrictions on the correlation between the trend and the cycle components lead to the identification of different stochastic trends for integrated time-series. As a consequence, the Beveridge–Nelson decomposition is not unique. In general, neither are all univariate decompositions. To see this point more explicitly we can compare the Beveridge–Nelson trend with the trend extracted using an alternative technique which has been recently very successful in time-series analysis: the Hodrick–Prescott filter.

Hodrick and Prescott proposed their method to analyse postwar US business cycles in a working paper circulated in the early 1980s and published in 1997. The Hodrick–Prescott (HP) filter computes the permanent component $TR_t$ of a series $x_t$ by minimizing the variance of $x_t$ around $TR_t$, subject to a penalty that constrains the second difference of $TR_t$. That is, the Hodrick–Prescott filter is derived by minimizing the following expression:

$$\sum_{t=1}^{T} (x_t - TR_t)^2 + \lambda \sum_{t=2}^{T-1} \left[ (TR_{t+1} - TR_t)^2 - (TR_t - TR_{t-1})^2 \right].$$

The penalty parameter $\lambda$ controls the smoothness of the series, by controlling the ratio of the variance of the cyclical component and the variance of the series. The larger the $\lambda$, the smoother the $TR_t$ approaches a linear trend. In practical applications $\lambda$ is set to 100 for annual data, 1600 for quarterly data and 14400 for monthly data.

In Figure 2.8 we report the Beveridge–Nelson trend and the Hodrick–Prescott trend (with $\lambda = 100$) for the data generated in the previous section.

Note that the Beveridge–Nelson trend is more volatile than the Hodrick–Prescott trend. It is possible to increase the volatility of the Hodrick–Prescott trend by reducing the parameter $\lambda$; however, the Hodrick–Prescott filter reaches at most

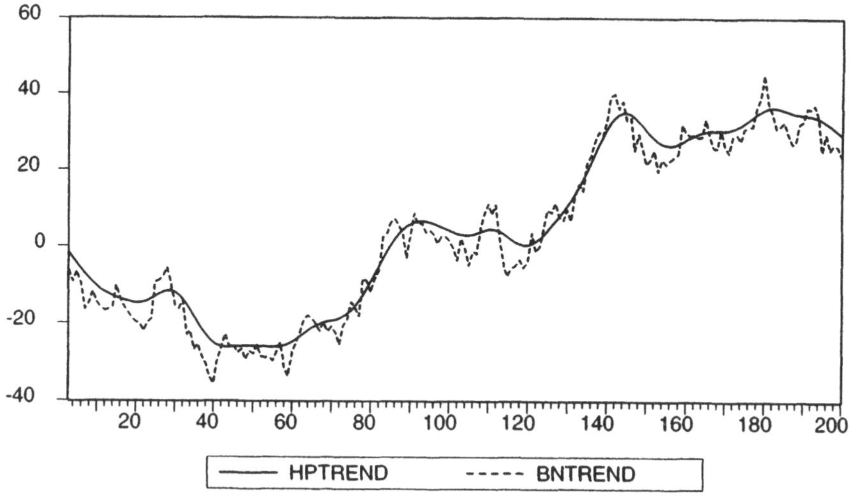


FIG. 2.8. Trend components: Hodrick–Prescott versus Beveridge–Nelson

the volatility of the actual time-series, which, as we already know, is smaller than the volatility of the Beveridge–Nelson trend.

The Hodrick–Prescott filter has the advantage of removing the same trend from all time-series; this might be desirable as some theoretical models, as, for example, real business cycle models, which indicate that macroeconomic variables share the same stochastic trend. However, Harvey and Jaeger (1993) showed that the use of such a filter can lead to the identification of spurious cyclical behaviour. The authors predicate a different approach to modelling time-series, known as structural time-series modelling, which we do not consider in our analysis, as it is less closely related to theoretical macroeconomic models, but certainly merits some attention (Harvey and Koopman 1996; Maravall 1995).

The comparison between the Hodrick–Prescott and the Beveridge–Nelson trend reinforces the argument of non-uniqueness of univariate decomposition made before. Moreover, we are left with the problem of how to use the filtered series in applied macroeconometrics and how to relate them to theoretical models. The empirical counterparts of theoretical macroeconomic models are multivariate time-series. Theoretical models often predict that different time-series share the same stochastic trend. The natural question at this point is if the problem of non-stationarity in time-series can be resolved by considering multivariate models. In this context, stationarity is obtained by considering combinations of non-stationary time-series sharing the same stochastic trend. If possible, it would justify the identification of trends by relating them to macroeconomic theory. We consider this possibility in the next sections.

## 2.7 Multivariate decompositions and dynamic models

Let us reconsider our spurious regression for US consumption in the context of a dynamic model. We augment the static regression to consider consumption and income lagged up to one year, i.e. we consider four lags of each variable. Results in Table 2.4, witness that the spurious regression disappears: contemporaneous and lagged US disposable income is significant in explaining US consumption, unlike contemporaneous and lagged UK disposable income.

TABLE 2.4. A dynamic model for US consumption

| Dependent variable $LCUS_t$, regression by OLS, 1960:1-1998:1 | | | | |
|---|---|---|---|---|
| | Model with US income | | Model with UK income | |
| | Coefficient | S.E. | Coefficient | S.E |
| c | 0.367 | 0.106 | 0.333 | 0.150 |
| $LCUS_{t-1}$ | 0.987 | 0.087 | 1.197 | 0.083 |
| $LCUS_{t-2}$ | -0.006 | 0.120 | -0.156 | 0.131 |
| $LCUS_{t-3}$ | 0.012 | 0.121 | 0.142 | 0.130 |
| $LCUS_{t-4}$ | -0.172 | 0.085 | -0.196 | 0.082 |
| LYUS | 0.258 | 0.037 | | |
| $LYUS_{t-1}$ | -0.126 | 0.049 | | |
| $LYUS_{t-2}$ | -0.068 | 0.050 | | |
| $LYUS_{t-3}$ | 0.021 | 0.049 | | |
| $LYUS_{t-4}$ | 0.034 | 0.042 | | |
| LYUK | | | 0.009 | 0.020 |
| $LYUK_{t-1}$ | | | 0.018 | 0.028 |
| $LYUK_{t-2}$ | | | -0.034 | 0.028 |
| $LYUK_{t-3}$ | | | -0.0163 | 0.028 |
| $LYUK_{t-4}$ | | | 0.0015 | 0.0229 |
| Trend | 0.00039 | 0.0001 | 0.00023 | 0.0001 |
| $R^2$ | 0.99 | | 0.99 | |
| S.E. | 0.0037 | | 0.0042 | |
| F-test on income | F(5,155)=10.324 | | F(5,155)=1.239 | |

This is an interesting result which leads us to think that, in case the problems related to non-stationarity can be solved, dynamic multivariate time-series models are the right foundation for macroeconometrics.

### 2.7.1 *Cointegration and error correction models*

To explain why the spurious results disappear when dynamic models are estimated, let us consider a simplified version of the dynamic specification estimated for consumption:

$$c_t = a_0 + a_1 c_{t-1} + a_2 y_t + a_3 y_{t-1} + \epsilon_t. \tag{2.15}$$

This specification has interesting dynamic properties which are worth discussing. First, note that the short-run elasticity of consumption with respect to income is different from the long-run elasticity. The short-run elasticity is $a_2$ while the long-run elasticity is $(a_2 + a_3) / (1 - a_1)$. The latter is found by setting all variables in the dynamic model (2.15) to their steady-state value $c_{t+i} = \bar{c}$, $y_{t+i} = \bar{y}$. To see this point immediately, consider the following re-parameterization of (2.15):

$$\Delta c_t = a_0 + a_2 \Delta y_t - \alpha (c_{t-1} - \beta_1 y_{t-1}) + \epsilon_t, \tag{2.16}$$
$$\alpha = (1 - a_1), \quad \beta_1 = \frac{a_2 + a_3}{1 - a_1}.$$

The estimated dynamic model includes both first differences and levels. The presence of the level variables generates a long-run solution, derived by setting all first differences either to zero (steady state with no deterministic trend) or a constant (steady state). Note the role of the terms in level: we can interpret $\beta_1 y_{t-1}$ as the long-run equilibrium level $c^*$ for the log of real consumption $c$. When $\alpha < 0$, consumption increases at time $t$ whenever $c_{t-1} < c^*_{t-1}$, and decreases whenever $c_{t-1} > c^*_{t-1}$. The system equilibrates in the presence of disequilibrium (i.e. a discrepancy between $c$ and $c^*$). Such error correction features guarantee that in the long-run the consumption will converge to its equilibrium value. For this reason the specification (2.16), with $\alpha < 0$, is termed the error correction model (ECM). Note that, in the case of an ECM representation, the difference between $c$ and $c^*$ is a stationary series. This defines cointegration. We say that two non-stationary variables integrated of order $d$ are cointegrated of order $b$, if there exists a linear combination of them which is integrated of order $d - b$. The case $d = 1$, $b = 1$ is interesting in that co-integration implies an ECM representation, which allows us to re-write a model in levels, involving non-stationary time-series, as a model involving only stationary variables. Such variables are stationary either because they are the first differences of non-stationary variables or because they are stationary linear combinations of non-stationary variables (cointegrating vectors).

The inclusion of both differences and levels in the estimated relationship is the key factor to the solution of the problems related to non-stationarity of the level of variables included in the specification. This solution to the non-stationarity problem also immediately reveals to the economist the long-run properties of the estimated model. To see this point practically, we can use E-Views to simulate the following bivariate model:

$$\Delta c_t = 0.25 \Delta y_t - 0.2 (c_{t-1} - y_{t-1}) + 0.003 u_{1t}, \tag{2.17}$$
$$\Delta y_t = 0.02 + 0.009 u_{2t},$$

where $u_{1t}$ and $u_{2t}$ are independently distributed standard normals, and the parameters are calibrated to reflect the long-run properties of the consumption function reported in Table 2.4. The volatility of the innovations are again calibrated to estimated processes on real data for the US economy; income is more volatile than consumption.

To show the properties of the model, we first generate samples for the two innovation processes; then we generate artificial data for consumption and income by constructing the above model and solving it dynamically. We do so for a sample of 100 observations. The simulated series in levels (LC and LY) are plotted in Figure 2.9 while Figure ?? plots the corresponding disequilibria (LC-LY).

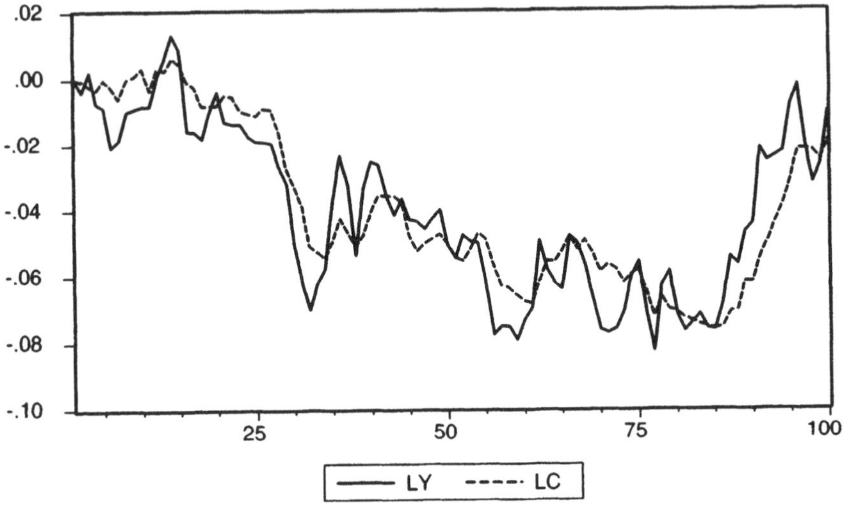


FIG. 2.9. Two cointegrated series

Note that the levels of LC and LY share a stochastic trend, which disappears from the series (LC-LY). The parameter $\alpha$ in the ECM specification determines the speed of adjustment in the presence of disequilibrium. To illustrate the role of this parameter we report the two series (LC-LY) generated by taking the same innovations for the sample 1:200. The innovations are drawn from an independent normal for all observations, except for observation 101, where the residuals in the income process are augmented by 0.036. This is a shock four standard deviations away from the mean of the distribution. We can then visually inspect the behaviour of the simulated series in the presence of an outlier. The process (2.17) is used to generate the first time-series of disequilibria (LC-LY), while the second time-series (LC_1-LY_1) is generated by keeping all the parameters unchanged with the exception of $\alpha$, which is tripled from 0.2 to 0.6. The resulting observations for disequilibria are reported in Figure 2.11.

The disequilibria from the second simulation are less persistent to witness that the second system features a faster speed of adjustment in the presence

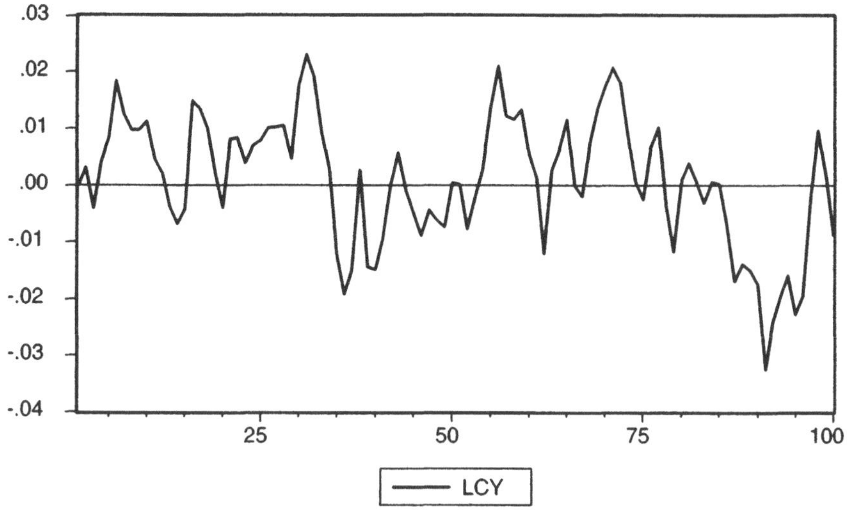


FIG. 2.10. Disequilibrium

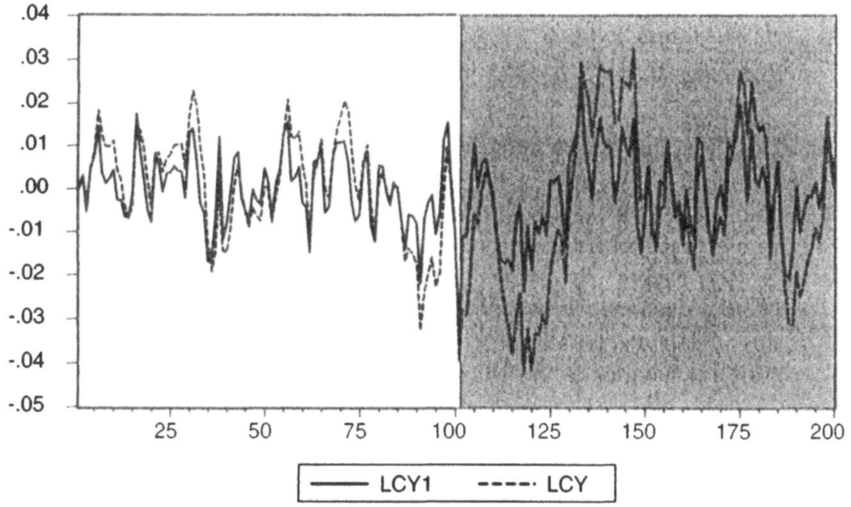


FIG. 2.11. Speed of adjustments and disequilibrium

of disequilibrium. All the simulated series are contained in the E-Views workfile ecm.wf1, with which the reader can experiment to convince herself of the properties of error correction models.

As an application of further interest, let us reconsider the static regression in the light of our discussion of dynamic models.

Given the following DGP:

$$\begin{aligned} y_t &= a_1 y_{t-1} + a_2 x_t + a_3 x_{t-1} + u_{1t}, \\ x_t &= b_1 x_{t-1} + u_{2t}, \\ \begin{pmatrix} u_{1t} \\ u_{2t} \end{pmatrix} &\sim N.I.D. \left( \begin{pmatrix} 0 \\ 0 \end{pmatrix}, \begin{pmatrix} \sigma_{11} & 0 \\ 0 & \sigma_{22} \end{pmatrix} \right), \end{aligned} \tag{2.18}$$

a static model is estimated by OLS:

$$\begin{aligned} y_t &= \gamma x_t + \varepsilon_t, \\ \widehat{\gamma} &= \frac{\sum x_t y_t}{\sum x_t^2}. \end{aligned}$$

Assess the results of running the static model by taking $p\lim \widehat{\gamma}$:

$$p\lim \widehat{\gamma} = p\lim \left[ a_1 \frac{\sum x_t y_{t-1}/T}{\sum x_t^2/T} + a_2 + a_3 \frac{\sum x_t x_{t-1}/T}{\sum x_t^2/T} + \frac{\sum x_t u_{1t}/T}{\sum x_t^2/T} \right].$$

Under the hypothesis that (2.18) is stationary ($|b_1| < 1$), we can substitute for $x_t$ in terms of $x_{t-1}$ and $u_{2t}$ and apply Slutsky's and Cramer's theorems to derive the following result:

$$\begin{aligned} p\lim \widehat{\gamma} &= \frac{a_2 + a_3 b_1}{1 - a_1 b_1}, \\ a_2 \leq p\lim \widehat{\gamma} &\leq \frac{a_2 + a_3}{1 - a_1}. \end{aligned}$$

Note that as $b_1$ approaches zero the elasticity of $y$ with respect to $x$ delivered by the static regression goes asymptotically to the true short-run elasticity, while as $b_1$ approaches one, such elasticity converges to the long-run elasticity. Technically speaking, we cannot show what happens when $b_1$ equals one, because this violates the stationarity conditions which we have used to derive the asymptotic behaviour of the OLS estimator. However, confirming the above intuition, Stock (1987) has shown that the OLS estimator of the parameters determining the long-run relationship of non-stationary cointegrated series is super-consistent. It converges towards the true value at speed of order $T$, much higher than the speed of order $\sqrt{T}$, with which the OLS estimator converges to its true value in regression between stationary time-series. This result provides the background to a two-step research strategy, according to which the cointegrating relations are estimated first in the static model and then used to estimate a dynamic ECM model, involving only stationary variables. This strategy is less efficient than the simultaneous estimation of short-run and long-run dynamics. The static regression delivers super-consistent estimates of the cointegrating parameters despite being mis-specified, because the omitted variables are the stationary variables determining the short-run dynamics, which, in large samples, should not affect the estimation of cointegrating parameters. Research using Monte-Carlo simulation shows that the dimension of the samples required to appeal to the super-consistency theorem is much higher than that of the samples usually available for time-series modelling (see, for example, Banerjee et al. 1986, Banerjee and Hendry 1992, Banerjee et al. 1993). Moreover, the empirical counterparts of macroeconomic models are usually dynamic multivariate time-series models. Therefore, one pays a price considering static univariate models as a basis for empirical work. We devote more attention to this issue in the next section.

### 2.7.2 *Cointegration in a multivariate framework*

So far we have stressed the importance of the magnitude of the adjustment parameter $\alpha$ as the relevant discriminant to decide on cointegration, but we have not yet provided a statistical framework to test such a hypothesis. We also mentioned the importance of dimensionality of the system in empirical work. In this section we shall elaborate on these points and illustrate Johansen's approach (1988; 1995) to cointegration in a multivariate framework.

Until now we have considered cointegration in a bivariate context. Things differ, though, in the multivariate case. In general, between $n$ non-stationary series we can have up to $n-1$ cointegrating vectors and the single equation dynamic modelling can cause serious troubles when there are multiple cointegrating vectors. To illustrate the problem, let us consider the case of an econometrician who uses cointegration techniques to investigate money demand. Following the standard economic background to empirical investigations of money demand (see, for example, Hendry and Ericsson 1991) the chosen dataset includes money, $m$, a price index, $p$, real income, $y$, the own interest rate on money, $R^m$, and the opportunity cost of holding money, $R^b$. All variables are in logarithms, with the exception of interest rates. The investigator specifies a dynamic single-equation model for real money towards the identification of a money demand equation, which takes the following shape:

$$
\begin{aligned}
(m-p)_t &= a_0 + a_1 (m-p)_{t-1} + a_2 y_{t-1} + a_3 y_{t-2} \\
&\quad + a_4 R^m_{t-1} + a_5 R^m_{t-2} + a_6 R^b_{t-1} + a_7 R^b_{t-2} + u_t.
\end{aligned}
\tag{2.19}
$$

This statistical model fits the data well. As it is found that $a_1 < 1$, the investigation leads to the identification of a long-run equilibrium money demand, which results clearly from the ECM reparameterization of the dynamic model (2.19):

$$
\begin{aligned}
\Delta (m-p)_t &= a_0 - a_3 \Delta y_{t-1} - a_5 \Delta R^m_{t-1} - a_6 \Delta R^b_{t-1} \\
&\quad + (a_1 - 1)\left[(m-p)_{t-1} - (m-p)^*_{t-1}\right] + u_t \\
(m-p)^*_{t-1} &= \frac{a_2 + a_3}{1-a_1} y_{t-1} + \frac{a_4 + a_5}{1-a_1} R^m_{t-1} + \frac{a_6 + a_7}{1-a_1} R^b_{t-1}.
\end{aligned}
\tag{2.20}
$$

However, the good fit of the statistical model might be combined with an incorrect identification of the long-run solution. Think, for example, of the case in which the non-stationary vector containing the five variables of interest admits two cointegration relationships: $(m-p-y)$ and $\left(R^m - \beta_{22}R^b\right)$. The first is generated by the stationarity of the velocity of circulation of money and the second one by the behaviour of the banking sector, which sets the interest rate on money as a mark-down on the opportunity cost of holding money. In the short run, money reacts to disequilibria with respect to both long-run solutions. Hence money demand is correctly parameterized as:

$$\Delta(m-p)_t = \pi_0 + \pi_1 \Delta y_{t-1} + \pi_2 \Delta R^m_{t-1} + \pi_3 \Delta R^b_{t-1} \qquad (2.21)$$
$$-\alpha_1 (m_{t-1} - p_{t-1} - y_{t-1}) + \alpha_2 \left(R^m_{t-1} - \beta_{22} R^b_{t-1}\right) + u_t.$$

Note that, in the case of a unit long run elasticity of money with respect to income $\left(\frac{a_2+a_3}{1-a_1} = 1\right)$, the statistical specification of (2.16) and (2.21) is identical: the residuals $u_t$ are the same; however identification is very different. While (2.21) represents the correct specification, (2.16) identifies as long-run elasticities what are in fact mixtures of cointegrating parameters and parameters determining the speed of adjustment with respect to disequilibria in the true model. The single-equation approach leads to a belief that the long-run elasticity of money demand with respect to the opportunity cost of holding money is $(a_6 + a_7)/(1-a_1)$, while in fact such an estimated coefficient is a convolution of the parameter $\alpha_2$, determining the speed with which money demand reacts to a misalignment of interest rates with respect to their equilibrium value, and the parameter $c$, determining the mark-down of the own interest rate on money with respect to the interest rate on the opportunity cost of holding money. This identification has serious consequences in the intepretation of estimated parameters. When the above problem occurs a structural instability in the short-term adjustment parameter $\beta_{22}$ would mislead the researcher into the belief that the long-run money demand is unstable.

The solution of this identification problem requires a framework to allow the researcher to find the number of cointegrating vectors among a set of variables and to identify them. The procedure proposed by Johansen (1988; 1992) within the framework of the vector autoregressive model achieves both results.

### 2.7.3 *The Johansen procedure*

Consider the multivariate generalization of the single-equation dynamic model discussed above, i.e. a vector autoregressive model (VAR) for the vector of, possibly non-stationary, $m$-variables $\mathbf{y}$:

$$\mathbf{y}_t = \mathbf{A}_1 \mathbf{y}_{t-1} + \mathbf{A}_2 \mathbf{y}_{t-2} + \ldots + \mathbf{A}_n \mathbf{y}_{t-n} + \mathbf{u}_t. \qquad (2.22)$$

By proceeding in the same way we did for the simple single-equation dynamic model, we can reparameterize the VAR in levels as a model involving levels and the first differences of variables.

Start by subtracting $\mathbf{y}_{t-1}$ from both sides of the VAR to obtain:

$$\Delta \mathbf{y}_t = (\mathbf{A}_1 - \mathbf{I})\,\mathbf{y}_{t-1} + \mathbf{A}_2\mathbf{y}_{t-2} + \ldots + \mathbf{A}_n\mathbf{y}_{t-n} + \mathbf{u}_t. \tag{2.23}$$

Subtract $(\mathbf{A}_1 - \mathbf{I})\,\mathbf{y}_{t-2}$ from both sides:

$$\Delta \mathbf{y}_t = (\mathbf{A}_1 - \mathbf{I})\,\Delta\mathbf{y}_{t-1} + (\mathbf{A}_1 + \mathbf{A}_2 - \mathbf{I})\,\mathbf{y}_{t-2} + \ldots + \mathbf{A}_n\mathbf{y}_{t-n} + \mathbf{u}_t. \tag{2.24}$$

By repeating this procedure until $n-1$, we end up with the following specification:

$$\begin{aligned}\Delta \mathbf{y}_t &= \Pi_1\Delta\mathbf{y}_{t-1} + \Pi_1\Delta\mathbf{y}_{t-2} + \ldots + \Pi\mathbf{y}_{t-n} + \mathbf{u}_t \\ &= \sum_{i=1}^{n-1}\Pi_i\Delta\mathbf{y}_{t-i} + \Pi\mathbf{y}_{t-n} + \mathbf{u}_t,\end{aligned} \tag{2.25}$$

where:

$$\Pi_i = -\left(I - \sum_{j=1}^{i}\mathbf{A}_j\right),$$

$$\Pi = -\left(I - \sum_{i=1}^{n}\mathbf{A}_i\right).$$

Clearly the long-run properties of the system are described by the properties of the matrix $\Pi$. There are three cases of interest:

1. rank $(\Pi) = 0$. The system is non-stationary, with no cointegration between the variables considered. This is the only case in which non-stationarity is correctly removed simply by taking the first differences of the variables;
2. rank $(\Pi) = m$, full. The system is stationary;
3. rank $(\Pi) = k < m$. The system is non-stationary but there are $k$ cointegrating relationships among the considered variables. In this case $\Pi = \boldsymbol{\alpha}\boldsymbol{\beta}'$, where $\alpha$ is an $(m \times k)$ matrix of weights and $\boldsymbol{\beta}$ is an $(m \times k)$ matrix of parameters determining the cointegrating relationships.

Therefore, the rank of $\Pi$ is crucial in determining the number of cointegrating vectors. The Johansen procedure is based on the fact that the rank of a matrix equals the number of its characteristic roots that differ from zero. Here is the intuition on how the tests can be constructed. Having obtained estimates for the parameters in the $\Pi$ matrix, we associate with them estimates for the $m$ characteristic roots and we order them as follows $\lambda_1 > \lambda_2 > \ldots > \lambda_m$. If the variables are not cointegrated, then the rank of $\Pi$ is zero and all the characteristic roots equal zero. In this case each of the expression $\ln(1-\lambda_i)$ equals zero, too. If, instead, the rank of $\Pi$ is one, and $0 < \lambda_1 < 1$, then $\ln(1-\lambda_1)$ is negative and $\ln(1-\lambda_2) = \ln(1-\lambda_3) = \ldots = \ln(1-\lambda_m) = 0$. Johansen derives a test on the number of characteristic roots that are different from zero by considering the two following statistics:

$$\lambda_{\text{trace}}(k) = -T \sum_{i=k+1}^{m} \ln\left(1 - \widehat{\lambda}_i\right),$$
$$\lambda_{\max}(k, k+1) = -T \ln\left(1 - \widehat{\lambda}_{k+1}\right),$$

where $T$ is the number of observations used to estimate the VAR. The first statistic tests the null of at most $k$ cointegrating vectors against a generic alternative. The test should be run in sequence starting from the null of at most zero cointegrating vectors up to the case of at most $m$ cointegrating vectors. The second statistic tests the null of at most $k$ cointegrating vectors against the alternative of at most $k+1$ cointegrating vectors. Both statistics are small under the null hypothesis. Critical values are tabulated by Johansen and they depend on the number of non-stationary components under the null and on the specification of the deterministic component of the VAR. Johansen (1994) has shown in the past some preference for the trace test, based on the argument that the maximum eigenvalue test does not give rise to a coherent testing strategy.

To illustrate briefly the intuition behind the procedure, consider the VAR representation of our simple dynamic model (2.18), introduced in one of the previous sections, for the two variables, $x$ and $y$:

$$\begin{pmatrix} y_t \\ x_t \end{pmatrix} = \begin{pmatrix} a_{11} & a_{12} \\ 0 & 1 \end{pmatrix} \begin{pmatrix} y_{t-1} \\ x_{t-1} \end{pmatrix} + \begin{pmatrix} u_{1t} \\ u_{2t} \end{pmatrix}. \tag{2.26}$$

System (2.26) can be reparameterized as follows in terms of the VECM representation:

$$\begin{pmatrix} \Delta y_t \\ \Delta x_t \end{pmatrix} = \begin{pmatrix} a_{11}-1 & a_{12} \\ 0 & 0 \end{pmatrix} \begin{pmatrix} y_{t-1} \\ x_{t-1} \end{pmatrix} + \begin{pmatrix} u_{1t} \\ u_{2t} \end{pmatrix}, \tag{2.27}$$

from which, clearly,

$$\Pi = \begin{pmatrix} a_{11}-1 & a_{12} \\ 0 & 0 \end{pmatrix}, \quad \alpha = \begin{pmatrix} a_{11}-1 \\ 0 \end{pmatrix}, \quad \beta' = \left(1 \;\; -\tfrac{a_{12}}{1-a_{11}}\right).$$

To expand this intuition, let us reconsider our example on money demand from the previous section.

The baseline VAR can be specified as:

$$\begin{bmatrix} (m-p)_t \\ y_t \\ R_t^m \\ R_t^b \end{bmatrix} = A_0 + A_1 \begin{bmatrix} (m-p)_{t-1} \\ y_{t-1} \\ R_{t-1}^m \\ R_{t-1}^b \end{bmatrix} + A_2 \begin{bmatrix} (m-p)_{t-2} \\ y_{t-2} \\ R_{t-2}^m \\ R_{t-2}^b \end{bmatrix} + \begin{bmatrix} u_{1t} \\ u_{2t} \\ u_{3t} \\ u_{4t} \end{bmatrix},$$

which could then be reparameterized in VECM form:

$$\begin{bmatrix} \Delta (m-p)_t \\ \Delta y_t \\ \Delta R_t^m \\ \Delta R_t^b \end{bmatrix} = \Pi_0 + \Pi \begin{bmatrix} (m-p)_{t-1} \\ y_{t-1} \\ R_{t-1}^m \\ R_{t-1}^b \end{bmatrix} + \Pi_1 \begin{bmatrix} \Delta (m-p)_{t-1} \\ \Delta y_{t-1} \\ \Delta R_{t-1}^m \\ \Delta R_{t-1}^b \end{bmatrix} + \begin{bmatrix} u_{1t} \\ u_{2t} \\ u_{3t} \\ u_{4t} \end{bmatrix}.$$

Since we know that there are two cointegrating vectors, we have:

$$\Pi = \alpha\beta',$$
$$\text{rank } \Pi = 2,$$
$$\beta' = \begin{bmatrix} 1 & -1 & 0 & 0 \\ 0 & 0 & 1 & -\beta_{22} \end{bmatrix}.$$

As we have analysed only one equation in our previous discussion of the system, the only constraints we have on the specification for $\alpha$ are $\alpha_{11} < 0, \alpha_{12} > 0$. A possible specification for $\alpha$ is then:

$$\alpha = \begin{bmatrix} \alpha_{11} & \alpha_{12} \\ 0 & 0 \\ 0 & \alpha_{32} \\ 0 & 0 \end{bmatrix}.$$

With the above specification for the loadings, money demand adjusts both in presence of misalignment of velocity with respect to the equilibrium velocity and of misalignements of interest rates with respect to their equilibrium spread. In particular money demand increases when velocity is 'too high' and the opportunity cost of holding money is 'too low'. In the case of disequilibrium in interest rates it is the interest on money which adjusts, while the dynamics of interest rates, on the alternative of money in agents'portfolio does not react to disequilibria.

$$\begin{bmatrix} \alpha_{11} & \alpha_{12} \\ 0 & 0 \\ 0 & \alpha_{32} \\ 0 & 0 \end{bmatrix} \begin{bmatrix} 1 & -1 & 0 & 0 \\ 0 & 0 & 1 & -\beta_{22} \end{bmatrix} = \begin{bmatrix} \alpha_{11} & -\alpha_{11} & \alpha_{12} & -\alpha_{12}\beta_{22} \\ 0 & 0 & 0 & 0 \\ 0 & 0 & \alpha_{32} & -\alpha_{32}\beta_{22} \\ 0 & 0 & 0 & 0 \end{bmatrix}.$$

### 2.7.4 *Identification of multiple cointegrating vectors*

The Johansen procedure allows us to identify the number of cointegrating vectors. However, in the case of existence of multiple cointegrating vectors, an interesting identification problem arises: $\alpha$ and $\beta$ are only determined up to the space spanned by them. Thus, for any non-singular matrix $\xi$ conformable by product:

$$\Pi = \alpha\beta' = \alpha\xi^{-1}\xi\beta'.$$

In other words $\beta$ and $\beta'\xi$ are two observationally equivalent bases of the cointegrating space. The obvious implication is that before solving such an identification problem no meaningful economic interpretation of coefficients in cointegrating vectors can be proposed. The solution is imposing a sufficient number of restrictions on parameters such that the matrix satisfying such constraints in the cointegrating space is unique. Such a criterion is derived by Johansen (1992) and discussed in the works of Johansen and Juselius (1990), Giannini (1992) and Hamilton (1994). Given the matrix of cointegrating vectors $\boldsymbol{\beta}$, we can formulate linear constraints on the different cointegrating vectors using the $R_i$ matrices of dimensions $r_i \times n$. Let us consider the columns of $\boldsymbol{\beta}$, i.e. the parameters in each cointegrating vector, ignoring the normalization constraint to one of one variable in each cointegrating vector. Any structure of linear constraints can be represented as

$$\mathbf{R}_i\boldsymbol{\beta}_i = 0,$$
$$R_i\,(r_i \times n)\,, \quad \boldsymbol{\beta}_i(n \times 1), \quad \text{rank } R_i = r_i.$$

The same constraints can be expressed in explicit forms as

$$\boldsymbol{\beta}_i = \mathbf{S}_i\theta_i,$$

where $S_i\,(n \times (n - r_i))$, $\boldsymbol{\beta}_i(n \times 1)$, $\theta_i\,((n - r_i) \times 1)$, rank $S_i = n - r_i$, $\mathbf{R}_i\mathbf{S}_i = 0$.

A necessary and sufficient condition for identification of parameters in the $i$-th cointegrating vector is:

$$\text{rank } (\mathbf{R}_i\boldsymbol{\beta}) = r - 1. \tag{2.28}$$

When (2.28) is satisfied, it is not possible to replicate the $i$-th cointegrating vector by taking linear combinations of the parameters in the other cointegrating vectors. In this case, the matrix obtained by applying to the cointegrating space the restrictions of the $i$-th cointegrating vector has rank $r - 1$.

A necessary condition for identification is immediately derived in that $\mathbf{R}_i\boldsymbol{\beta}$ must have enough rows to satisfy condition (2.28); therefore, a necessary condition is that each cointegrating vector has at least $r - 1$ restrictions.

A sufficient condition for identification is provided by Johansen by considering the implicit and explicit form of expressing constraints:

**Theorem 2.1** *The i-th cointegrating vector is identified by the constraints* $\mathbf{S}_1$, $\mathbf{S}_2$, ... , $\mathbf{S}_r$, *if for each k=1,...,r-1 and for each set of indices* $1 < j_1 < ... < j_k < r$ *not containing i, we have that rank* $[R_iS_{j_1}, ..., R_iS_{j_k}] > k$

Given identification of the system, we can distinguish the case of just-identification and over-identification. In case of over-identification, the over-identifying restrictions are testable.

To illustrate the procedure let us reconsider our example on money demand. Adopting the following vectorial representation of the series: $(m-p\ y\ R^m\ R^b)'$, and leaving aside normalizations, the matrix $\boldsymbol{\beta}$ can be represented as:

$$\begin{pmatrix} \beta_{11} & 0 \\ -\beta_{11} & 0 \\ 0 & \beta_{32} \\ 0 & -\beta_{42} \end{pmatrix}.$$

Given the following general representation of the matrix $\boldsymbol{\beta}$:

$$\begin{pmatrix} \beta_{11} & \beta_{12} \\ \beta_{21} & \beta_{22} \\ \beta_{31} & \beta_{32} \\ \beta_{41} & \beta_{42} \end{pmatrix},$$

our constraints imply the following specification for the matrices $R_i$ and $S_i$:

$$R_1 = \begin{pmatrix} 1\,1\,0\,0 \\ 0\,0\,1\,0 \\ 0\,0\,0\,1 \end{pmatrix}, \quad S_1 = \begin{pmatrix} 1 \\ -1 \\ 0 \\ 0 \end{pmatrix},$$

$$R_2 = \begin{pmatrix} 1\,0\,0\,0 \\ 0\,1\,0\,0 \end{pmatrix}, \quad S_2 = \begin{pmatrix} 0\,0 \\ 0\,0 \\ 1\,0 \\ 0\,1 \end{pmatrix}.$$

The necessary conditions for identification are obviously satisfied, while the sufficient conditions for identification requires that rank $(R_1S_2) \geq 1$, and rank $(R_2S_1) \geq 1$. They also satisfy

$$R_1S_2 = \begin{pmatrix} 0\,0 \\ 1\,0 \\ 0\,1 \end{pmatrix}, \quad R_2S_1 = \begin{pmatrix} 1 \\ -1 \end{pmatrix}.$$

### 2.7.5 *Hypothesis testing with multiple cointegrating vectors*

The Johansen procedure allows for testing the validity of restricted forms of cointegrating vectors. More precisely, the validity of restrictions (over-identifying restrictions) in addition to those necessary to identify the long-run equilibria can be tested. The intuition behind the construction of all tests is that when there are $r$ cointegrating vectors, only these $r$ linear combination of variables are stationary; therefore, the test statistics involve comparing the number of cointegrating vectors under the null and the alternative hypotheses. Following this intuition, we understand why only the over-identifying restrictions can be tested. Just-identified models feature the same long-run matrix $\Pi$, and therefore, the same eigenvalues of $\Pi$. Consider the case of testing restrictions on a set of $r$ identified cointegrating vectors stacked in the matrix $\boldsymbol{\beta}$. The test statistic involves comparing the number of cointegrating vectors under the null and the alternative hypothesis. Let $\widehat{\lambda}_1, \widehat{\lambda}_2, \ldots, \widehat{\lambda}_r$ be the ordered eigenvalues of the $\Pi$ matrix in the unrestricted model, and $\widehat{\lambda}_1^*, \widehat{\lambda}_2^*, \ldots, \widehat{\lambda}_r^*$ the ordered eigenvalues of the $\Pi$ matrix in the restricted model. Restrictions on $\boldsymbol{\beta}$ are testable by forming the following test statistic:

$$T\sum_{i=1}^{r}\left[\ln\left(1-\widehat{\lambda}_i^*\right)-\ln\left(1-\widehat{\lambda}_i\right)\right]. \tag{2.29}$$

Johansen (1992) shows that the statistic (2.29) has a $\chi^2$-distribution with degrees of freedom equal to the number of over-identifying restrictions. Note that small values of $\widehat{\lambda}_i^*$ with respect to $\widehat{\lambda}_i$ imply a reduction of the rank of $\Pi$ when the restrictions are imposed and hence the rejection of the null hypothesis. This testing procedure can be extended to tests on restrictions on the matrix of weights $\boldsymbol{\alpha}$ or on the deterministic components (constant and trends) of the cointegrating vectors.

### 2.7.6 *Cointegration and common stochastic trends*

Having discussed the VECM representation for a vector of $m$ non-stationary variables admitting $k$ cointegrating relationships, let us compare it with the multivariate extension of the Beveridge–Nelson decomposition. Consider the simple case of an I(1) vector $\mathbf{y}_t$ featuring first-order dynamics and no deterministic component:

$$\Delta\mathbf{y}_t = \boldsymbol{\alpha}\boldsymbol{\beta}'\mathbf{y}_{t-1} + \mathbf{u}_t, \tag{2.30}$$

where $\alpha$ is the $(m \times k)$ matrix of loadings and $\boldsymbol{\beta}$ is the $(m \times k)$ matrix of parameters in the cointegrating relationships. As $\mathbf{y}_t$ is I(1), we can apply the Wold decomposition theorem to $\Delta\mathbf{y}_t$ to obtain the following representation:

$$\Delta\mathbf{y}_t = \mathbf{C}(L)\,\mathbf{u}_t,$$

from which, by applying the algebra illustrated in our discussion of the univariate Beveridge–Nelson decomposition, we can derive the following stochastic trends representation:

$$\mathbf{y}_t = \mathbf{C}^*(L)\,\mathbf{u}_t + \mathbf{C}(1)\,\mathbf{z}_t,$$

where $\mathbf{z}_t$ is a process for which $\Delta\mathbf{z}_t = \mathbf{u}_t$. The existence of cointegration imposes restrictions on the $\mathbf{C}$ matrices. The stochastic trends must cancel out when the

$k$ stationary linear combinations of the variables in $\mathbf{y}_t$ are considered. In other words we must have:

$$\boldsymbol{\beta}'\mathbf{C}(1) = 0.$$

By investigating further the relation between the VECM and the stochastic trend representations, we can give a more precise parameterization of the matrix $\mathbf{C}(1)$.

Note first that equation (2.21) is equivalent to:

$$\mathbf{y}_t = \left(I_m + \boldsymbol{\alpha}\boldsymbol{\beta}'\right)\mathbf{y}_{t-1} + \mathbf{u}_t. \tag{2.31}$$

Pre-multiplying this system by $\boldsymbol{\beta}'$ yields:

$$\begin{aligned}\boldsymbol{\beta}'\mathbf{y}_t &= \boldsymbol{\beta}'\left(I_m + \boldsymbol{\alpha}\boldsymbol{\beta}'\right)\mathbf{y}_{t-1} + \boldsymbol{\beta}'\mathbf{u}_t \\ &= \left(I_k + \boldsymbol{\alpha}\boldsymbol{\beta}'\right)\boldsymbol{\beta}'\mathbf{y}_{t-1} + \boldsymbol{\beta}'\mathbf{u}_t.\end{aligned}$$

Solving this model recursively, we obtain the MA representation for the $k$ cointegrating relationships:

$$\boldsymbol{\beta}'\mathbf{y}_t = \sum_{i=0}^{\infty}\left(I_k + \boldsymbol{\alpha}\boldsymbol{\beta}'\right)^i\boldsymbol{\beta}'\mathbf{u}_{t-i}. \tag{2.32}$$

By substituting (2.32) in (2.21) we have the MA representation for $\Delta\mathbf{y}_t$,

$$\Delta\mathbf{y}_t = \sum_{i=1}^{\infty}\boldsymbol{\alpha}\left(I_k + \boldsymbol{\alpha}\boldsymbol{\beta}'\right)^{i-1}\boldsymbol{\beta}'\mathbf{u}_{t-i} + \mathbf{u}_t,$$

from which we have

$$\mathbf{C}(1) = I_n - \boldsymbol{\alpha}\left(\boldsymbol{\beta}'\boldsymbol{\alpha}\right)^{-1}\boldsymbol{\beta}'. \tag{2.33}$$

Now note the beautiful relation (see Johansen 1995: 40),

$$I_n = \beta_\perp\left(\alpha'_\perp\beta_\perp\right)^{-1}\alpha'_\perp + \alpha\left(\beta'\alpha\right)^{-1}\beta', \tag{2.34}$$

where $\beta_\perp, \alpha_\perp$ are $((m \times (m-k))$ matrices of rank $m-k$ such that $\alpha'_\perp\alpha = 0$, $\beta'_\perp\beta = 0$.

Using (2.34) in (2.33), we have

$$\mathbf{C}(1) = \beta_\perp\left(\alpha'_\perp\beta_\perp\right)^{-1}\alpha'_\perp,$$

and

$$\mathbf{y}_t = \mathbf{C}^*(L)\,\mathbf{u}_t + \beta_\perp\left(\alpha'_\perp\beta_\perp\right)^{-1}\left(\alpha'_\perp\mathbf{z}_t\right),$$

which shows that a system of $m$ variables with $k$ cointegrating relationships features $(m-k)$ linearly independent common trends (**TR**). The common trends are given by $(\alpha'_{\perp}\mathbf{z}_t)$, while the coefficients on these trends are $\beta_{\perp}(\alpha'_{\perp}\beta_{\perp})^{-1}$. Note also that stochastic trends depend on a set of initial conditions and cumulated disturbances,

$$\mathbf{TR}_t = \mathbf{TR}_{t-1} + C(1)\,\mathbf{u}_t.$$

Our brief discussion should have made clear that the VECM model and the MA model are complementary. As a consequence, the identification problem relevant for the vector of parameters in the cointegrating vectors $\beta$ is also relevant for the vector of parameters determining the stochastic trends $\boldsymbol{\alpha}_{\perp}$. However, there is one aspect in which the two concepts are different. In theory, identified cointegrating relationships on a given set of variables should be robust to augmentation of the information set by adding new variables which should have a zero coefficient in the cointegrating vectors of the VECM representation of the larger information set. This is not true for the stochastic trends. Consider the case of augmenting an information set consiting of $m$ variables admitting $k$ cointegrating vectors to $m+n$ variables. The number of cointegrating vectors is constant while the number of stochastic trends increases by $n$; moreover, an unanticipated shock in the small system need not be unanticipated in the larger system. Note that we have added 'in theory' to our statement. In practice, given the size of available samples, application of the procedure to analyse cointegration in a larger set of variables might lead the identification of different cointegrating relationships from those obtained on a smaller set of variables.

### 2.7.7 *VECM and common trends representations*

The joint behaviour of consumption and income under the permanent income hypothesis (PIH) is a good empirical example to illustrate VECM and common trend representations. Let $y_t$, $y_t^p$ and $c_t$ denote, respectively, the logarithms of aggregate disposable income, permanent income, and consumption. Under PIH the joint distribution of consumption and income can be characterized as follows:

$$\begin{aligned} y_t &= y_t^p + v_t, \\ y_t^p &= \mu_y + y_{t-1}^p + u_t, \\ c_t &= y_t^p. \end{aligned}$$

Permanent income is the stochastic trend of income, which is made of the permanent component and of a transitory component, $v_t$ and $u_t$ are the shocks to the transitory and the permanent component of income; naturally, they are orthogonal and normally and independently distributed. Consumption and income are cointegrated, in fact they share the single unobservable common stochastic trend in this system.

By eliminating the unobservable stochastic trend from the system, we have a bi-variate structural representation:

$$\begin{aligned} y_t &= c_t + v_t, \\ c_t &= \mu_y + c_{t-1} + u_t. \end{aligned} \tag{2.35}$$

We obtain the VAR(1) representation by substituting for $c_t$ in the first equation from the second equation of (2.35):

$$\begin{pmatrix} y_t \\ c_t \end{pmatrix} = \begin{pmatrix} \mu_y \\ \mu_y \end{pmatrix} + \begin{pmatrix} 0 & 1 \\ 0 & 1 \end{pmatrix} \begin{pmatrix} y_{t-1} \\ c_{t-1} \end{pmatrix} + \begin{pmatrix} w_t \\ u_t \end{pmatrix},$$
$$w_t = u_t + v_t,$$

from which we obtain the VECM representation:

$$\begin{pmatrix} \Delta y_t \\ \Delta c_t \end{pmatrix} = \begin{pmatrix} \mu_y \\ \mu_y \end{pmatrix} + \begin{pmatrix} -1 & 1 \\ 0 & 0 \end{pmatrix} \begin{pmatrix} y_{t-1} \\ c_{t-1} \end{pmatrix} + \begin{pmatrix} w_t \\ u_t \end{pmatrix},$$

where

$$\begin{aligned} \Pi &= \begin{pmatrix} -1 & 1 \\ 0 & 0 \end{pmatrix} \\ &= \begin{pmatrix} 1 \\ 0 \end{pmatrix} \begin{pmatrix} -1 & 1 \end{pmatrix} \\ &= \alpha\beta'. \end{aligned}$$

The common trend representation is derived by considering that, as $y_t - c_t = v_t$, the MA representation for consumption and income growth is:

$$\begin{pmatrix} \Delta y_t \\ \Delta c_t \end{pmatrix} = \begin{pmatrix} \mu_y \\ \mu_y \end{pmatrix} + \begin{pmatrix} 1 & 0 \\ 0 & 1 \end{pmatrix} \begin{pmatrix} w_t \\ u_t \end{pmatrix} + \begin{pmatrix} -1 & 1 \\ 0 & 0 \end{pmatrix} \begin{pmatrix} w_{t-1} \\ u_{t-1} \end{pmatrix},$$

from which:

$$\begin{pmatrix} y_t \\ c_t \end{pmatrix} = \begin{pmatrix} \mu_y \\ \mu_y \end{pmatrix} t + \mathbf{C}^* (L) \begin{pmatrix} w_t \\ u_t \end{pmatrix} + C(1)\mathbf{z}_t,$$

and

$$C(1) = \beta_\perp \left(\alpha'_\perp \beta_\perp\right)^{-1} \alpha'_\perp,$$
$$\begin{pmatrix} 0 & 1 \\ 0 & 1 \end{pmatrix} = \begin{pmatrix} 1 \\ 1 \end{pmatrix} \left[ \begin{pmatrix} 0 & 1 \end{pmatrix} \begin{pmatrix} 1 \\ 1 \end{pmatrix} \right]^{-1} \begin{pmatrix} 0 & 1 \end{pmatrix}.$$

Since in this application $\left(\alpha'_\perp \beta_\perp\right)^{-1} = 1$, consumption and income have a single common stochastic trend. Such trend can be represented as

$$\alpha'_\perp \left( \begin{pmatrix} \mu_y \\ \mu_y \end{pmatrix} t + \begin{pmatrix} \sum_{i=1}^{t} w_t \\ \sum_{i=1}^{t} u_t \end{pmatrix} \right),$$

and only shocks to the permanent component of income enter the trend.

## 2.8 Multivariate cointegration: an application to US data

To illustrate empirically how cointegration analysis is performed, let us consider monthly data from the US economy for the variables in basic macroeconomic models: the logarithm of the real M2 $(m - p)$, seasonally adjusted, CPI inflation $(\pi)$, the logarithm of monthly real GDP $(y)$, the nominal own return on M2 $(R^m)$, and the nominal opportunity cost of holding money as measured by the interest rate on three-month Treasury Bills $(R^b)$. All series except $R^m$ come from the article by Leeper, Sims and Zha (1996). $R^m$ has been retrieved by the St. Louis Fed website at http://www.stls.frb.org/fred/. They are available in the file lszusa.xls. We shall perform cointegration analysis using the package Pc-Fiml by Doornik and Hendry (1994), alternative menu-driven packages are available in RATS (see Mosconi 1998, Hansen and Juselius 1995), E-Views does not allow all the steps of analysis to be performed in that specification and testing of the long-run restrictions is not (yet) available.

### 2.8.1 *Specification of the VAR model*

The first step of the empirical analysis is the specification of the VAR model. The specification of the VAR requires the consideration of two issues: the set of variables included in the VAR and the lag length. These are crucial issues, since mis-specification of the VAR leads to incorrect inference. In general the set of variables to be included in the VAR is determined by the economic problem at hand; however, this criterion does not rule out the possibility of mis-specification. Consider the case of the set of variables chosen for our example, they include all the variables used in a simple IS-LM model of a closed economy, but nothing guarantees that the US economy is correctly described by such model. Suppose that the central bank targets expected inflation by using short-term interest rates as an instrument. The model is mis-specified if it omits any leading indicator for inflation monitored by central bank. An obvious candidate is the commodity price index but there might be more, such as long-term interest rates or other asset prices. In the absence of an obvious baseline model, the behaviour of residuals serves as an indicator of mis-specification. In a correctly specified model residuals should be random normal variables with zero mean and a constant variance-covariance matrix. One can take the departure of fitted residuals from those hypotheses, as an indicator of mis-specification. However, even when all the relevant variables have been included, the model can still be mis-specified because of omitted relevant dynamics. The selection of the order of the VAR is an important step in the specification. Sims (1980) suggests a statistic to test the validity of restrictions imposed on a general model:

$$(T - k) \left[ \log |\Sigma_r| - \log |\Sigma_{unr}| \right],$$

where $T$ is the sample size, $k$ is the number of parameters estimated in each equation of the VAR, $|\Sigma_r|$ is the determinant of the variance-covariance matrix of the residuals in the fitted restricted model, $|\Sigma_{unr}|$ is the determinant of the variance-covariance matrix of the residuals in the fitted general unrestricted model. The statistic has a $\chi^2$-distribution with degrees of freedom equal to the number of restrictions in the system. The term $(T - k)$ includes a small sample correction, and as $T$ becomes larger the correction for a small sample $(T - k)/T$ converges towards unity. Obviously, the selection of variables and the selection of the lag length are not independent processes; in fact, a longer lag length might be the consequence of the omission of a relevant variable from the VAR. In practice we start from a baseline VAR including the set of variables suggested by the theory and a sufficiently long lag, then check the behaviour of residuals. When well-behaved residuals are obtained, we reduce the lag length by testing the validity of the implied restrictions.

Our general baseline model is a VAR estimated over the sample 1960:1-1979:6. It includes fifteen lags of each of the five variables, a constant, and a trend:

$$\begin{pmatrix} y_t \\ \pi_t \\ (m-p)_t \\ R_t^m \\ R_t^b \end{pmatrix} = \mathbf{a}_o + \mathbf{a}_1 t + \sum_{i=1}^{14} A_i L^i \begin{pmatrix} y_t \\ \pi_t \\ (m-p)_t \\ R_t^m \\ R_t^b \end{pmatrix} + \mathbf{u}_t. \tag{2.36}$$

We have chosen to close our estimation period at 1979, because from the second part of 1979 to 1982 the Fed had changed its operating procedure from an interest rate targeting regime to a reserves targeting regime. As a consequence, the parameters in the Fed's reaction function must have changed. Estimating cointegrating models using data from a single regime is crucial, since structural instability might be dangerous in cointegrated models. The intuition is simple: in the presence of parameters' instability a cointegrated model is likely to push the system towards the 'wrong' long-term equilibria with very serious consequences for forecasting and policy simulation. Checking residuals' behaviour is also important in this respect, as pathologic behaviour of residuals is a clear symptom of parameters' instability.

The estimation of our baseline model delivers the set of residuals reported in Figure 2.12.

The residuals are normalized; hence, the residuals with absolute values higher than 1.96 occur with a probability of one percent under the null of normality. We notice many outliers. In fact, when a formal test of normality of residuals is performed the null is strongly rejected[2]. This is worrying, since non-normality might signal mis-specification, and also since departure from normality might induce misleading inference in the application of the Johansen procedure. Interestingly, most outliers occur on the occasions of the oil price crises. So, probably, a commodity price index is a relevant omitted variable causing non-normality in the residuals. However, the inclusion of a commodity price

[2] We discuss tests for normality later in the book.

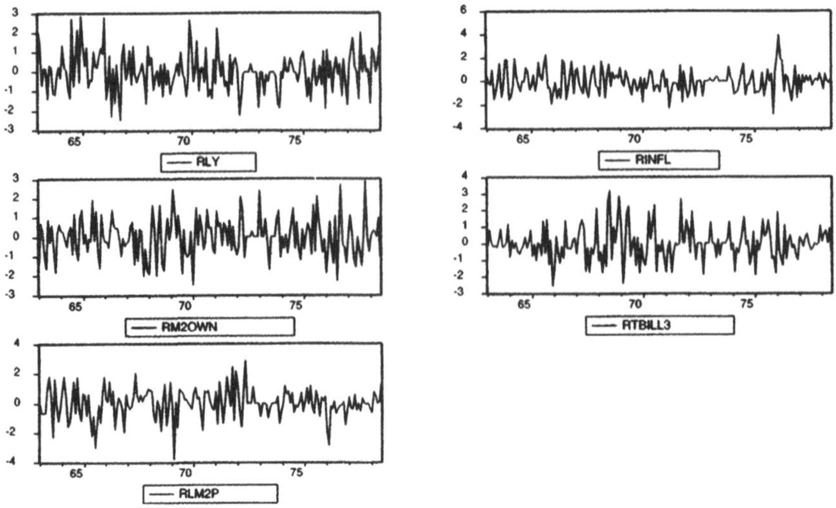


FIG. 2.12. VAR residuals with outliers

index as a further endogenous variable in our system simply shifts the outlier problem from our equation for interest rates to the commodity price index. No variable included in this system has a high explanatory potential for a commodity price index. Thus we include in the system contemporaneous and lagged (up to the sixth lag) commodity price inflation. We consider it as a stationary exogenous variable, the choice that we discuss later on. We also include dummies for exceptional periods during the oil price crises as exogenous variables. In general, dumMMYY is a variable taking value 1 in the MM month of the year YY and zero anywhere else. We include the following dummy variables: dum7306, dum7307, dum7308, dum7310, dum7311, dum7312, dum7402, dum7403, dum7407, dum7408, dum7409, dum7501, dum7505, dum7806, dum7808, dum7811, dum7904. Note that the inclusion of dummies and exogenous variables in the specification modifies the deterministic nucleus of our model and, thus, appropriate critical values for the tests should be re-computed (see Johansen and Nielsen 1993 and Osterwald–Lenum 1992). We do not take this step explicitly; instead, we report the critical values (obtained by using tools in version nine of Pc-Fiml) in Table 2.7.

The inclusion of the dummies in the system delivers a new set of residuals, shown in Figure 2.13, which are virtually free from outliers and show no departure from the hypothesis of normality.

We proceed then to assess the possibility of simplification of the system. The progressive simplification strategy, based on the likelihood ratio tests discussed above, leads us to a specification with six lags.

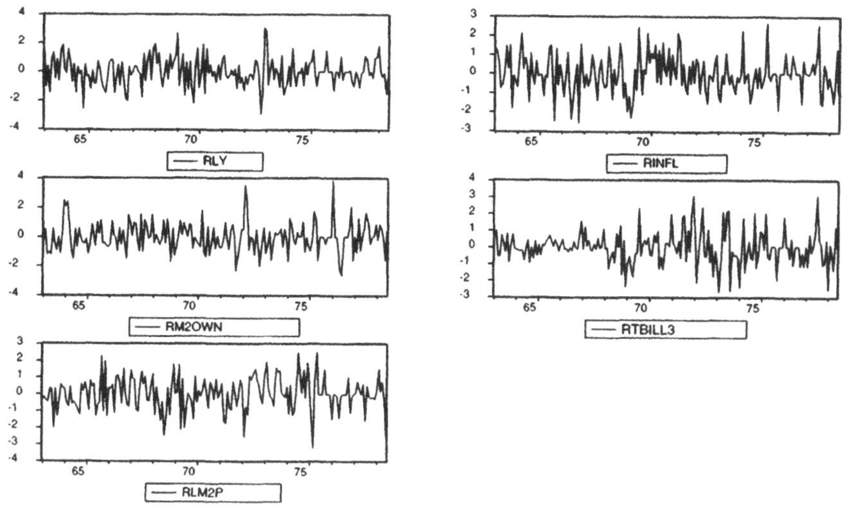


FIG. 2.13. VAR residuals without outliers

### 2.8.2 *Selection of the deterministic components in the VECM specification*

The choice of the determistic components in the VAR requires attention, since it affects the distribution of the relevant statistics to perform cointegration analysis. Given the following general VECM model:

$$\Delta \mathbf{y}_t = \mu_0 + \mu_1 t + \Pi_1 \Delta \mathbf{y}_{t-1} + \Pi_1 \Delta \mathbf{y}_{t-2} + \ldots + \Pi \mathbf{y}_{t-n} + \mathbf{u}_t,$$

five possible specifications for the deterministic components are considered in the literature:

1. $\mu_0 = 0$, $\mu_1 = 0$, which determines a zero mean in the I(0) components and a non-zero mean in the I(1) components;
2. $\mu_0 = \alpha\beta_1$, $\mu_1 = 0$ which restricts the constant to belong to the cointegrating space, inducing a non-zero mean both in the I(0) and the I(1) components;
3. $\mu_0 = unrestricted$, $\mu_1 = 0$ which generates a zero mean in the I(0) components and a linear trend in the I(1) component;
4. $\mu_0 = unrestricted$, $\mu_1 = \alpha\beta_1$ which generates a linear trend both in the I(0) and the I(1) components;
5. $\mu_0 = unrestricted$, $\mu_1 = unrestricted$, which generates a linear trend in the I(0) components and a quadratic trend in the I(1) components.

Different critical values have been tabulated for each specification (see Johansen 1996) and are automatically available in all packages performing the Johansen procedure. Note that the inclusion of intervention dummies also modifies the deterministic components of the VAR, which in principle requires an *ad hoc* tabulation of the relevant critical values.

In our application we choose specification 4 as some of our series show trends in levels and, as already stated, we ignore the modification of the relevant distribution generated by the inclusion of dummies.

### 2.8.3 *Test for the rank of* Π

Having specified the VAR and the deterministic components, we estimate the Π matrix and start our analysis of the long-run properties of the system. We apply the Johansen procedure to identify the rank of the matrix Π in the following reparameterization of our model:

$$\begin{bmatrix} \Delta y_t \\ \Delta \pi_t \\ \Delta R_t^m \\ \Delta R_t^b \\ \Delta (m-p)_t \end{bmatrix} = \begin{bmatrix} d_{0,11} \\ d_{0,21} \\ d_{0,31} \\ d_{0,41} \\ d_{0,51} \end{bmatrix} + \sum_{i=0}^{6} F_i \Delta_{12} LPCM_{t-i} + \mathbf{g}'\mathbf{DUM}_t$$

$$+ \sum_{i=1}^{5} D_i \begin{bmatrix} \Delta y_{t-i} \\ \Delta \pi_{t-i} \\ \Delta R_{t-i}^m \\ \Delta R_{t-i}^b \\ \Delta (m-p)_{t-i} \end{bmatrix} + \Pi \begin{bmatrix} y_{t-6} \\ \pi_{t-6} \\ R_{t-6}^m \\ R_{t-6}^b \\ (m-p)_{t-6} \end{bmatrix} + \begin{bmatrix} u_{1t} \\ u_{2t} \\ u_{3t} \\ u_{4t} \\ u_{5t} \end{bmatrix}.$$

The results of the Johansen procedure are reported in Table 2.5, where 'Eigenval' is the maximum eigenvalue test, 'C.Eigenval' is the maximum eigenvalue test corrected for a small sample, i.e. using $T-k$ instead of $T$, 'Trace' is the trace test, 'C.Trace' is the trace test corrected for a small sample and 95% are the critical values tabulated for our specification of the deterministic components.

TABLE 2.5. Analysis of the Π matrix in the estimated VAR model

| Eigenvalue | $H_0$: rank $= p$ | Eigenval | C.Eigenval | 95% | Trace | C.Trace | 95% |
|---|---|---|---|---|---|---|---|
| 0.185 | $p = 0$ | 45.74 | 39.61 | 37.5 | 134.1 | 116.1 | 87.3 |
| 0.148 | $p \leq 1$ | 35.93 | 31.11 | 31.5 | 88.36 | 76.53 | 63 |
| 0.133 | $p \leq 2$ | 32.14 | 27.84 | 25.5 | 52.44 | 45.41 | 42.4 |
| 0.083 | $p \leq 3$ | 19.56 | 16.94 | 19 | 20.3 | 17.58 | 25.3 |
| 0.0033 | $p \leq 4$ | 0.74 | 0.64 | 12.3 | 0.74 | 0.64 | 12.3 |

Table 2.5 poses an interesting problem to the applied researcher, as the trace statistic and the maximum eigenvalue statistic deliver different results, with more relevant differences in the case of the adoption of a small sample correction for the statistics. We opt for rejecting the null of at most one cointegrating vector and do not reject the null of at most two. Of course, such choice is debatable.

Note that, before any identifying restrictions are introduced, most available cointegrating packages deliver some point estimates of the $\alpha$ and $\beta$ matrices shown in Table 2.6.

TABLE 2.6. Cointegrating vectors: the Johansen interpretation

Standardized $\beta'$

| $y$ | $\pi$ | $m-p$ | $R^m$ | $R^b$ | $Trend$ |
|---|---|---|---|---|---|
| 1 | 0.078 | -0.40 | 3.55 | -3.96 | -0.18 |
| 1.08 | 1 | -0.61 | -1.20 | -1.08 | -0.15 |

Standardized $\alpha$

| | | |
|---|---|---|
| $y$ | -0.02 | -0.013 |
| $\pi$ | 0.02 | -0.005 |
| $m-p$ | 0.047 | -0.018 |
| $R^m$ | -0.00008 | -0.002 |
| $R^b$ | 0.03 | 0.01 |

These estimates are obtained by imposing a default identification which delivers cointegrating vectors orthogonal to each other. In some context, for example a demand and supply system, this assumption might be the economic case of interest. However, this is different in general and in our specific example. In the next section we evaluate the potential of a different identification of economic interest by checking the validity of over-identifying restrictions.

### 2.8.4 *Specification and testing of the long-run restrictions*

We consider two different proposals. In the first one we identify a traditional money demand and a relation between the own interest rate on money and the opportunity cost of holding money. As an alternative, we identify an interest rate reaction function in which the nominal interest rate responds to inflation, output, and a linear trend, along with a relation between interest rates and inflation. We have selected these two specifications because, as we shall see, they form the basis for two alternative targeting strategies: inflation targeting via the control of money growth and inflation targeting via the control of interest rates.

We can parameterize the restrictions implied by the first identification scheme as follows:

$$\Pi = \boldsymbol{\alpha}\boldsymbol{\beta}',$$

$$\boldsymbol{\alpha} = \begin{pmatrix} \alpha_{11} & \alpha_{12} \\ \alpha_{21} & \alpha_{22} \\ \alpha_{31} & \alpha_{32} \\ \alpha_{41} & \alpha_{42} \\ \alpha_{51} & \alpha_{52} \\ \alpha_{61} & \alpha_{62} \end{pmatrix},$$

$$\boldsymbol{\beta}' = \begin{pmatrix} \beta_{11} & 0 & 1 & \beta_{41} & \beta_{51} & \beta_{61} \\ 0 & \beta_{22} & 0 & \beta_{42} & 1 & 0 \end{pmatrix}.$$

The results, reported in Table 2.7, show that the two over-identifying restrictions are not rejected. The first cointegrating vector is consistent with a money demand function as far as the semi-elasticities with respect to interest rates are concerned, the elasticity with respect to income is somewhat high, although it is compensated by a deterministic trend with the opposite sign. However, looking at the weights on the cointegrating vectors we note that real money reacts very little to disequilibrium in the first cointegrating relationship. The only strongly significant weight is the one describing the reaction of real income to disequilibrium in the second cointegrating relationship.

TABLE 2.7. A scheme of over-identified cointegrating vectors

| Standardized $\beta'$ | | | | | |
|---|---|---|---|---|---|
| $y$ | $\pi$ | $m-p$ | $R^m$ | $R^b$ | $Trend$ |
| −2.20 (0.17) | 0 | 1 | −7.29 (2.16) | 7.51 (0.96) | 0.38 (0.06) |
| 0 | 1.08 (0.22) | 0 | −3.16 (0.59) | 1 | 0 |

| Standardized $\alpha$ | | |
|---|---|---|
| $y$ | 0.064 (0.015) | −0.17 (0.036) |
| $\pi$ | −0.0016 (0.009) | −0.034 (0.021) |
| $m-p$ | −0.019 (0.009) | −0.014 (0.023) |
| $R^m$ | −0.0006 (0.0001) | 0.002 (0.003) |
| $R^b$ | −0.023 (0.008) | 0.03 (0.02) |

LR test, rank=2: $\chi^2(2) = 1.03$ [0.59]

Let us consider the second alternative and parameterize restrictions as follows:

$$\Pi = \alpha\beta',$$

$$\alpha = \begin{pmatrix} \alpha_{11} & \alpha_{12} \\ \alpha_{21} & \alpha_{22} \\ \alpha_{31} & \alpha_{32} \\ \alpha_{41} & \alpha_{42} \\ \alpha_{51} & \alpha_{52} \\ \alpha_{61} & \alpha_{62} \end{pmatrix},$$

$$\beta' = \begin{pmatrix} \beta_{11} & -1 & 0 & 0 & 1 & \beta_{61} \\ 0 & \beta_{22} & 0 & \beta_{42} & 1 & 0 \end{pmatrix}.$$

The results, reported in Table 2.8, show the plausibility of the interpretation of the first cointegrating relation as a reaction function for the monetary policy-maker. Policy rates react to inflation, with a coefficient which can be restricted to one, and to deviation of output from the deterministic trend (a non-stationary variable in our specification). The estimated weights sufficiently support the identification of this relationship as an equilibrium for the policy rates. The second cointegrating vector does not differ significantly from the one obtained within the first identification scheme.

TABLE 2.8. A scheme of over-identified cointegrating vectors

| Standardized $\beta'$ | | | | | |
|---|---|---|---|---|---|
| $y$ | $\pi$ | $m-p$ | $R^m$ | $R^b$ | $Trend$ |
| −0.22 (0.03) | −1 | 0 | 0 | 1 (0.68) | 0.08 (0.009) |
| 0 | −0.96 (0.17) | 0 | 2.75 (0.47) | 1 | 0 |

| Standardized $\alpha$ | | |
|---|---|---|
| $y$ | 0.13213 (0.069) | −0.002 (0.039) |
| $\pi$ | 0.047 (0.038) | −0.017 (0.022) |
| $m-p$ | −0.09 (0.042) | −0.09 (0.034) |
| $R^m$ | 0.007 (0.005) | 0.003 (0.0029) |
| $R^b$ | −0.13 (0.036) | −0.062 (0.021) |

LR test, rank=2: $\chi^2(4) = 6.1$ [0.19]

We conclude our analysis of these two alternative identification schemes by stressing that statistical criteria do not lead to an unequivocal identification, then the choice between the two alternatives is very likely to rely on economic criteria.

## 2.9 Multivariate decompositions: some considerations

The purpose of our illustration of the Johansen procedure in the previous section was to show that the identification of cointegrating vectors involves a multi-step process. The outcome of many of these steps is not clear-cut, and, therefore, the final product might be across researchers. The presence of structural breaks, paired with the specification issues, and the size of available samples, have an important impact on the empirical application of the procedure. Alternative methods to this procedure have been proposed in the literature; see, for example, Horvath and Watson (1995), Phillips (1991), Reimers (1992) and Saikkonen (1993). However, one should remember that the specification of a dynamic model in levels has proved sufficient to remove the spurious regression problem and that the VECM representation of a VAR model in levels is just a reparameterization, before the rank reduction restrictions are imposed. Sims, Stock and Watson (1990), argue that a VAR model in levels in the presence of cointegration is over-parameterized and, therefore, leads to inefficient but consistent estimates of the parameters of interest. The loss of efficiency has to be weighted against the risk of inconsistency of estimates which occurs when the wrong cointegrating restrictions are imposed. Imposing the wrong cointegrating parameters will make the system converge to the wrong long-run equilibria but will also bias the short-run dynamics, as the system is pulled in the wrong direction. For this reason the recent research has taken a defined line and VARs in levels rather than cointegrated VARs are used when the issue of economic interest is related to the short-run rather than to the long-run. A standard example is the analysis of the monetary transmission mechanism. Sims, Stock, and Watson (1990) go much deeper in these issues. They show that standard distributions can be applied when doing an inference in a VAR model which involves variables admitting stationary linear combinations, reverting to non-standard distributions only when the subsets of variables on which inference is performed do not admit any stationary linear combination.

As a matter of fact cointegrated VARs are mainly data-driven specifications. The macro-model for the relevant DGP is not fully specified, as is clearly the case with the example discussed in this chapter where we started off our investigation by a model centred on money and we end up specifying a long-run structure where the quantity of money, being fully demand determined, plays no role in the monetary transmission mechanism. It is not easy to interpret the results from a simultaneous model, when we have (loose) theories generating only a subset of the equations. Moreover, there are difficulties with an approach aimed at discriminating between theories on the basis of the outcome of test statistics, based on a number of joint hypotheses, some of which are clearly independent from the theories tested. There are also issues with the critical values for the testing procedures in the Johansen framework:

1. they depend crucially on the specification of the deterministic nucleus of the VAR, so the inclusion of dummies for outliers introduces modifications in the relevant critical values. A solution to this problem is available, see Johansen and Nielsen (1993);
2. recent work by Johansen (1999), has shown that it is important to implement small sample corrections for the asymptotic critical values, when applicable.

Taking these two aspects together, it is likely that a re-assessment of all the empirical evidence proposed in the 1990s without implementing the appropriate corrections is necessary. So what do we make of all the sentences issued on theories using the wrong critical values?

Note also that cointegration analysis is based on a multi-step framework: specification of the VAR and its deterministic component, identification of the number of cointegrating vectors, identification of the parameters in cointegrating vectors, tests on the speed of adjustment with respect to disequilibria. The results of the final test depend on the outcome of the previous stages in the empirical analysis, but the outcome of each step is not so easily and uniquely established empirically.

Of course there is something to be said for a methodology aimed at exploiting cointegration to deliver a stationary representation of a non-stationary vector autoregressive process in which short-run and long-run dynamics are naturally separated and sound statistical inference can be applied. However, the practical implementation of such methodology requires the researcher to deal with specification and identification problems which are not easily, and above all not uniquely, solved.

## 2.10 References

Amisano, G., and Giannini, C. (1997). *Topics in Structural VAR Econometrics.* 2nd edn, New York: Springer Verlag.

Banerjee, A., Dolado, J. J., Hendry, D. F. and Smith, G. W. (1986). 'Exploring Equilibrium Relationships in Econometrics through Static Models: some Monte Carlo Evidence'. *Oxford Bulletin of Economics and Statistics*, August.

Banerjee, A., Dolado, J. J., Galbraith, J. W. and Hendry, D. F. (1993). *Cointegration, Error Correction, and the Econometric Analysis of Non-Stationary Data.* Oxford University Press.

Banerjee, A., and Hendry, D. F. (1992). 'Testing Integration and Cointegration'. *Oxford Bulletin of Economics and Statistics*, 54, Special Issue.

Beveridge, S., and Nelson, C. (1981). 'A New Approach to the Decomposition of Economic Time Series into Permanent and Transitory Components with Particular Attention to the Measurement of Business Cycle'. *Journal of Monetary Economics*, 151-174.

Bhargava, A. (1986). 'On the Theory of Testing for Unit Roots in Observed Time Series'. *Review of Economic Studies*, 53: 369-384.

Cuddington, J. T., and Winters, L. A. (1987). 'The Beveridge-Nelson decomposition of economic time-series. A quick computational method'. *Journal of Monetary Economics*, 19: 125-127.

DeJong, D. N., and Whiteman, C. H. (1991). 'Reconsidering Trends and random walks in macroeconomic time-series'. *Journal of Monetary Economics*, 28: 221-254.

Dickey, D. A., and Fuller, W. A. (1981). 'Likelihood Ratio Statistics for Autoregressive Time Series with a Unit Root'. *Econometrica*, 49:1057-1072.

Doornik, J., and Hendry, D. F. (1994). *PcFiml 8.0. Interactive Econometric Modelling of Dynamic Systems.* London: International Thomson Publishing.

Enders, W. (1995). *Applied Econometric Time Series.* New York: Wiley Series in Probability and Mathematical Statistics.

Engle, R. F., and Granger, C. W. J. (1987). 'Cointegration and Error Correction: Representation, Estimation and Testing'. *Econometrica*, 55: 251-276.

Engle, R. F., Granger, C. W. J., and Hallman, J. J. (1987). 'Combining Short and Long Run Forecasts: an Application of Seasonal Cointegration to Monthly Electricity Sales Forecasting'. Unpublished paper, University of California San Diego.

Fuller, W. A. (1976). *Introduction to Statistical Time Series.* New York: J. Wiley and Sons.

Giannini, C. (1992). 'Topics in Structural VAR Econometrics'. *Lecture Notes in Economics and Mathematical Systems*, Springer-Verlag.

Giannini, C., Lanzarotti, S., and Seghelini, M. (1994). 'A Traditional Interpretation of Macroeconomi Fluctuations: the Case of Italy'. *European Journal of Political Economy.*

Gonzalo, J. (1994). 'Five Alternative Methods of Estimating Long-run Equilibrium Relationships'. *Journal of Econometrics*, 60: 203-233.

Granger, C. W. J. (1986). 'Developments in the Study of Cointegrated Economic Variables'. *Oxford Bulletin of Economic and Statistics*, 48: 213-228.

Granger, C. W. J., and Newbold, P. (1974). 'Spurious Regressions in Econometrics'. *Journal of Econometrics*, 2: 111-120.

Hamilton, J. (1994). *Time-Series Analysis.* Princeton: Princeton University Press.

Hansen, H., and Juselius, K. (1995). *CATS in RATS. Cointegration Analysis of Time Series.* Evanston: Estima.

Harvey, A. C., and Jaeger, A. (1993). 'Detrending, Stylized Facts and the Business Cycles'. *Journal of Applied Econometrics.*

Harvey, A. C., and Koopman, S. J.(1996) 'Multivariate Structural Time Series Models' in C. Heij et al. (eds.), *Systematic Dynamics in Economic and Financial Models.* New York: John Wiley.

Hatanaka, M. (1987). *Time-Series-based-econometrics.* Oxford: Oxford University Press.

Hendry, D. F. (1987) 'Econometric Modelling with Cointegrated Variables'. *Oxford Bulletin of Economic and Statistics*, 48: 201-212.

Hendry, D. F. (1995). *Dynamic Econometrics.* Oxford: Oxford University Press.

Hendry, D. F., and Ericsson, N. (1991). 'Modeling the demand for narrow money in the United Kingdom and the United States'. *European Economic Review*, 35: 833-886.

Hodrick, R. J., and Prescott, E. C. (1997). 'Postwar U.S. Business Cycles: An Empirical Investigation'. *Journal of Money, Credit, and Banking*, 29: 116.

Horvath, M. T. K., and Watson, M. W. (1995). 'Testing for cointegration when some of the cointegrating vectors are known'. *Econometric Theory*, 11: 984-1014.

Johansen, S. (1988). 'Statistical Analysis of Cointegration Vectors'. *Journal of Economics Dynamics and Control*, March.

Johansen, S. (1989). 'Likelihood-based Inference on Cointegration: Theory and Applications'. Mimeo, University of Copenhagen.

Johansen, S. (1992). *Identifying Restrictions of Linear Equations.* University of Copenaghen, Institute of Mathematical Statistics.

Johansen, S. (1994). 'The role of the Constant and Linear Terms in Cointegration Analysis of Nonstationary Variables'. *Econometric Reviews*, 13: 205-229.

Johansen, S. (1995). *Likelihood Based Inference on Cointegration in the Vector Autoregressive Model.* Oxford: Oxford University Press.

Johansen, S., and Bartlett, A. (1999). 'Correction Factor for Tests on the Cointegrating Relationships'. Available at http://www.iue.it/Personal/Johansen/Welcome.html.

Johansen, S., and Juselius, K. (1990). 'Maximum Likelihood Estimation and Inference on Cointegration with Applications to the Demand for Money'. *Oxford Bulletin of Economics and Statistics*, May.

Johansen, S., and Nielsen, B. G. (1993). 'Asymptotics for the cointegration rank test tests in the presence of intervantion dummies'. *Manual for the simulation program DisCo.* Manual and program are available at the URL http://www.nuff.ox.ac.uk/users/nielsen/disco.html.

King, R. G., Plosser, C. I., Stock, J. H., and Watson, M. W. (1991). 'Stochastic trends and economic fluctuations'. *American Economic Review*, 81, 4: 820-840.

Kiwiatkowski, D., Phillips, P. C. B., Schmidt, P., and Shin, Y. (1992). 'Testing the Null Hypothesis of Stationarity against the alternative of a Unit Root: How Sure Are We That Economic Time Series Have a Unit Root?'. *Journal of Econometrics*, 54: 159-178.

Leeper, E. M., Sims, C. A., and Zha, T. (1996). 'What does monetary policy do?'. *Brookings Paper on Economic Activity*, 2: 1-79.

Maddala, G. S., and Kim, I. M. (1998). *Unit roots, Cointegration and Structural Change.* Cambridge: Cambridge University Press.

Maravall, A. (1995) 'Unobserved Components in Economic Time Series' in M. H. Pesaran and M. Wickens (eds.), *Handbook of Applied Econometrics. Macroeconomics*, Oxford: Basil Blackwell.

Mellander, E., Vredin, A., and Warne, A. (1992). 'Stochastic trends and economic fluctuations in a small open economy'. *Journal of Applied Econometrics*, 7: 369-394.

Mosconi, R. (1998). *Malcolm. The theory and practice of cointegration analysis in RATS.* Venezia: Cafoscarina.

Nelson, C. R., and Plosser, C. I. (1982). 'Trends versus Random Walks in economic time-series. Some evidence and implications'. *Journal of Monetary Economics*, 10: 139-162.

Osterwald-Lenum, M. (1992). 'A note with quantiles of the asymptotic distribution of the maximum likelihood cointegration rank test statistics'. *Oxford Bulletin of Economics and Statistics*, 54: 461-472.

Perron, P. (1987). 'The Great Crash, the Oil Price Shock and the Unit Root Hypothesis'. Research Paper, Department of Economics, University of Montreal, Quebec, Canada.

Phillips, P. C. B. (1991). 'Optimal Inference in Cointegrated Systems'. *Econometrica*, 59: 283-306.

Phillips, P. C. B., and Perron, P. (1988). 'Testing for a unit root in time-series regression'. *Biometrika*, 75: 335-346.

Reimers, H. E. (1992). 'Comparison of test for multivariate cointegration'. *Statistical Papers*, 33: 335-359.

Rudebusch, G. D. (1993). 'The Uncertain Unit Root in Real GNP'. *The American Economic Review*, 83: 264-272.

Saikkonen, P. (1993). 'Estimation of cointegration Vectors with Linear Restrictions'. *Econometric Theory*, 9: 19-35.

Salmon, M. (1982). 'Error Correction Mechanisms'. *The Economic Journal*, 92: 615-629.

Sargan, D. (1964). 'Wages and Prices in the United Kingdom: A Study in Econometric Methodology'. In P. E. Hart, G. Mills and J. K. Whitaker (eds.), *Econometric Analysis of National Economic Planning*. London: Butterworth, 25-63.

Sargan, J. D., and Barghava, A. (1983). 'Testing Residuals from Least Squares Regression for Being Generated by Gaussian Random Walk'. *Econometrica*, 51: 153-174.

Sims, C. (1980). 'Macroeconomics and Reality'. *Econometrica*, 48:1-49.

Sims, C., Stock, J. and Watson, M. (1990). 'Inference in Linear Time Series Models with Some Unit Roots'. *Econometrica*, 58, 1: 113-144.

Spanos, A. (1986). *Statistical Foundations of Econometric Modelling*. Cambridge: Cambridge University Press.

Stock, J. H. (1987). 'Asymptotic Properties of the Least Squares Estimator of Cointegrating Vectors'. *Econometrica*, 55: 1035-1056.

Stock, J. H., and West, K. D. (1987). *Integrated Regressors and the Test of the Permanent Income Hypothesis*. Princeton University, Woodrow Wilson School D.P. 127.

White, H. (1984). *Asymptotic Theory for Econometricians*. London: Academic Press.

Zivot, E. and Andrews, D. W. K. (1992). 'Further Evidence on the Great Crash, the Oil-Price Shock and the Unit Root Hypothesis'. *Journal of Business Economics and Statistics*, 10: 251-270.

# 3

# IDENTIFICATION PROBLEM IN MACROECONOMETRICS

## 3.1 Introduction

VAR in levels and VECM representations specify the probabilistic structure of the data. Consider the case of an empirical investigation of the monetary transmission mechanism to evaluate the impact of monetary policy on macroeconomic variables. Let's partition the vector of $n$ variables of interest into two subsets: $\mathbf{Y}$, which represents the vector of macroeconomic variables of interest and $\mathbf{M}$, the vector of monetary variables determined by the interaction between the monetary policy maker and the economy. As we have seen that the VECM is obtained by imposing restrictions on the VAR, consider the general unrestricted system:

$$\begin{pmatrix} \mathbf{Y}_t \\ \mathbf{M}_t \end{pmatrix} = D_1(L) \begin{pmatrix} \mathbf{Y}_{t-1} \\ \mathbf{M}_{t-1} \end{pmatrix} + \mathbf{u}_t, \tag{3.1}$$

$$\mathbf{u}_t = \begin{pmatrix} \mathbf{u}_t^Y \\ \mathbf{u}_t^M \end{pmatrix},$$

$$u_t \mid I_{t-1} \sim n.i.d. \left(\mathbf{0}, \sum\right),$$

$$\begin{pmatrix} \mathbf{Y}_t \\ \mathbf{M}_t \end{pmatrix} \mid I_{t-1} \Bigg) \sim \left(D_1(L) \begin{pmatrix} \mathbf{Y}_{t-1} \\ \mathbf{M}_{t-1} \end{pmatrix}, \sum\right).$$

This system specifies the statistical distribution for the vector of variables of interest conditional upon the information set available at time $t-1$. In the case of the VECM specification, after the solution of the identification problems of cointegrating vectors, the information set available at $t-1$ contains $n$ lagged endogenous variables and $r$ cointegrating vectors. We face an identification problem, since there is more than one structure of economic interest which can give rise to the same statistical model for our vector of variables.

For any given structure,

$$\mathbf{A} \begin{pmatrix} \mathbf{Y}_t \\ \mathbf{M}_t \end{pmatrix} = \mathbf{C}_1(L) \begin{pmatrix} \mathbf{Y}_{t-1} \\ \mathbf{M}_{t-1} \end{pmatrix} + \mathbf{B} \begin{pmatrix} \boldsymbol{\nu}_t^Y \\ \boldsymbol{\nu}_t^M \end{pmatrix}, \tag{3.2}$$

$$\left(\begin{matrix} \boldsymbol{\nu}_t^Y \\ \boldsymbol{\nu}_t^M \end{matrix} \mid I_{t-1}\right) \sim (\mathbf{0}, \mathbf{I}),$$

which give rise to the observed reduced form (3.1) when the following restrictions are satisfied:

$$\mathbf{A}^{-1}\mathbf{C}_1(L) = D_1(L), \quad \mathbf{A} \begin{pmatrix} \mathbf{u}_t^Y \\ \mathbf{u}_t^M \end{pmatrix} = \mathbf{B} \begin{pmatrix} \boldsymbol{\nu}_t^Y \\ \boldsymbol{\nu}_t^M \end{pmatrix}.$$

There exists a whole class of structures which produce the same statistical model (3.1) under the same class of restrictions:

$$F\mathbf{A}\begin{pmatrix}\mathbf{Y}_t\\ \mathbf{M}_t\end{pmatrix} = F\mathbf{C}_1(L)\begin{pmatrix}\mathbf{Y}_{t-1}\\ \mathbf{M}_{t-1}\end{pmatrix} + F\mathbf{B}\begin{pmatrix}\nu_t^Y\\ \nu_t^M\end{pmatrix}, \tag{3.3}$$

where $F$ is an admissible matrix, i.e. it is conformable by product with $\mathbf{A}$, $\mathbf{C}_1(L)$, and $\mathbf{B}$, and $F\mathbf{A}$, $F\mathbf{C}_1(L)$, $F\mathbf{B}$ feature the same restrictions with $\mathbf{A}$, $\mathbf{C}_1(L)$, $\mathbf{B}$.

### 3.1.1 *Identifiability*

A model is identifiable if all its possible structures are identifiable, i.e. each structure is associated with a different distribution. This happens when the only admissible $F$ matrix is identity.

Let us show this by considering identification of the first equation. To achieve identification some restrictions must be imposed, as the number of parameters in the reduced form (3.1) is smaller than the number of parameters in the structure (3.2). For the sake of exposition we start with zero restrictions on the matrices $\mathbf{A}$ and $\mathbf{C}_1$, determining the first moments of the conditional distributions of the vector of variables of interest and concentrate on a first-order autoregressive representation:

$$\mathbf{A}\begin{pmatrix}\mathbf{Y}_t\\ \mathbf{M}_t\end{pmatrix} = \mathbf{C}_1\begin{pmatrix}\mathbf{Y}_{t-1}\\ \mathbf{M}_{t-1}\end{pmatrix} + \begin{pmatrix}\epsilon_t^Y\\ \epsilon_t^M\end{pmatrix}, \tag{3.4}$$
$$\begin{pmatrix}\epsilon_t^Y\\ \epsilon_t^M\end{pmatrix} = \mathbf{B}\begin{pmatrix}\nu_t^Y\\ \nu_t^M\end{pmatrix}.$$

Zero restrictions on the first equations can be represented as

$$\begin{matrix}1\\ n-1\end{matrix}\begin{bmatrix}1, a_1' & 0\\ A_1^* & A_1\end{bmatrix}, \quad \begin{bmatrix}c_1' & 0\\ C_1^* & C_1\end{bmatrix},$$

so $(n-n_1)$ endogenous variables and $(n-k_1)$ exogenous variables are restricted to zero. $A_1^*$ is a $((n-1)\times n_1)$ matrix containing the coefficients with which the $n_1$ variables contemporaneously entering the first equation enter the remaining $n-1$ equations in the system. $A_1$ is a $((n-1)\times(n-n_1))$ matrix containing the coefficients with which the $n-n_1$ variables not contemporaneously entering the first equation enter the remaining $n-1$ equations in the system. Analogously, $C_1^*$ is a $((n-1)\times k_1)$ matrix containing the coefficients with which the $k_1$ variables entering with a lag in the first equation enter in the remaining $n-1$ equations; and $C_1$ is a $((n-1)\times(n-k_1))$ matrix containing the coefficients with which the $n-n_1$ variables not entering with a lag in the first equation enter as lagged variables in the remaining $n-1$ equations. Represent the first row of $F$ as $\begin{pmatrix}1 & f'\end{pmatrix}$. Admissibility implies

$$f'(A_1 \mid C_1) = 0.$$

Only when these conditions are satisfied, the first rows of $F\mathbf{A}$, and $F\mathbf{C}_1$ feature the same restrictions with $\mathbf{A}$, and $\mathbf{C}_1$.

Identification implies that the only solution is $f\prime = 0$, as the first row of an $(n \times n)$ identity matrix have unity as the first element and zeros as the remaining $(n - 1)$ elements. Therefore, the condition for identification is

$$\text{rank } (A_1 \mid C_1) = n - 1.$$

This is a necessary and sufficient condition for identification. As $(A_1 \mid B_1)$ has $(n - 1)$ rows and $(n - n_1) + (n - k_1)$ columns, a necessary condition for identification is that the number of columns is sufficiently large to let the rank equal $n - 1$:

$$n - k_1 \geq n_1 - 1.$$

Therefore, for the first equation to be identified, we need that the number of omitted lagged variables must be greater than the number of included contemporaneous variables minus one (the one variable with respect to which the equation is normalized). The model is not identified when $n - k_1 < n_1 - 1$, is just-identified when $n - k_1 = n_1 - 1$, the model is over-identified, with $n + 1 - (n_1 + k_1)$ over-identifying restrictions, when $n - k_1 > n_1 - 1$.

This discussion of identifiability can be generalized to non-zero restrictions by considering the following representation:

$$\begin{pmatrix} \mathbf{Y}_t \\ \mathbf{M}_t \\ \mathbf{Y}_{t-1} \\ \mathbf{M}_{t-1} \end{pmatrix} = \mathbf{w}_t, \qquad (\mathbf{A} \mid -\mathbf{C}_1) = \mathbf{D}, \qquad \boldsymbol{\epsilon}_t = \begin{pmatrix} \boldsymbol{\epsilon}_t^Y \\ \boldsymbol{\epsilon}_t^M \end{pmatrix}.$$

The system becomes:

$$\mathbf{D}\mathbf{w}_t = \boldsymbol{\epsilon}_t, \tag{3.5}$$

$$\mathbf{D} = \begin{pmatrix} \mathbf{D}_1' \\ . \\ \mathbf{D}_n' \end{pmatrix}.$$

General restriction on the $i$-th equation can be represented as:

$$\mathbf{R}_i \mathbf{D}_i = 0,$$

where $\mathbf{R}_i$ is the $(k_i \times (n + n))$ matrix imposing $k_i$ restrictions on the $2n$ elements of the $i$-th equation in the system.

A necessary and sufficient condition for identification is then:

$$\text{rank } \mathbf{R}_i \, (\mathbf{D}_1 \mid \mathbf{D}_2 ... \mid \mathbf{D}_n) = n - 1,$$

which shows the equivalence between the conditions for short-run identification and those required to achieve long-run identification of cointegrating parameters.

We end this section by noting that the short-run and long-run identifications in a VECM are two completely separated problems. Consider the simplest VECM representation of a first order VAR:

$$\begin{aligned}\Delta \mathbf{y}_t &= (\mathbf{A}_1 - \mathbf{I})\,\mathbf{y}_{t-1} + \mathbf{u}_t \\ &= \Pi \mathbf{y}_{t-1} + \mathbf{u}_t.\end{aligned}$$

When the long-run identification problem is solved, we reduce $\Pi$ to $\boldsymbol{\alpha\beta}'$ and re-write the VECM as:

$$\begin{aligned}\Delta \mathbf{y}_t &= \boldsymbol{\alpha} \mathbf{z}_{t-1} + \mathbf{u}_t, \\ \mathbf{z}_{t-1} &= \boldsymbol{\beta}' \mathbf{y}_{t-1},\end{aligned}$$

which makes clear that the identification of parameters in the structural form:

$$\mathbf{A}\Delta \mathbf{y}_t = \mathbf{A}\boldsymbol{\alpha} \mathbf{z}_{t-1} + \mathbf{A}\mathbf{u}_t.$$

is independent from the identification of parameters in the matrix $\boldsymbol{\beta}$.

## 3.2 Identification in the Cowles Commission approach

The traditional approach, to econometric modelling of the monetary transmission mechanism, usually referred to as the 'Cowles Commission' approach, aims at the quantitative evaluation of the effects of modification in the exogenous variables in the system on the endogenous ones in the system. Variables controlled by the monetary policy-maker (the instruments of monetary policy) are taken as exogenous, while macroeconomic variables, which represent the final goals of the policy-maker, are assumed to be endogenous. The policy experiment of interest usually consists of modifying such exogenous variables to assess the impact on the macroeconomic variables of interest. Leaving aside the deterministic component, the Cowles Commission specification modifies the general dynamic model of the previous section, as follows:

$$\mathbf{A}\begin{pmatrix}\mathbf{Y}_{t-1}\\ \mathbf{M}_{t-1}\end{pmatrix} = \mathbf{C}_1(L)\begin{pmatrix}\mathbf{Y}_{t-1}\\ \mathbf{M}_{t-1}\end{pmatrix} + \mathbf{C}_2(L)\begin{pmatrix}\bar{M}_t\end{pmatrix} + \begin{pmatrix}\epsilon_t^Y\\ \epsilon_t^M\end{pmatrix}, \tag{3.6}$$

where $\mathbf{Y}$ represents the vector of macroeconomic variables of interest, while $\mathbf{M}$ is the vector of monetary variables determined by the interaction between the monetary policy-maker and the economy. $\bar{M}$ represents a sub-vector of the monetary variables, which are assumed to be exogenous, since they are directly and fully controlled by the monetary policy-maker. The process generating these variables does not contain any interaction with the other variables in the system. $\mathbf{C}_1(L)$, and $\mathbf{C}_2(L)$ are polynomials in the lag operator $L$, taking the general form $\mathbf{C}_i(L) = c_0 + c_1 L + c_2 L^2 + ... + c_n L^n$.

The general conditions for identification derived in the previous section are applicable to the above specification. Treating some variables as exogenous aids identification in that exogenous variables are considered as the lagged endogenous variables from the point of view of identification. The general conditions for identification are:

$$\text{rank}\ \mathbf{R}_i\left(\mathbf{D}_1 \mid \mathbf{D}_2 \mid \ldots \mid \mathbf{D}_n\right) = n - 1.$$

Note that the inclusion of exogenous variables increases the columns of the matrix $\mathbf{R}_i\left(\mathbf{D}_1 \mid \mathbf{D}_2 \mid \ldots \mid \mathbf{D}_n\right)$ and, therefore, the chances for the model to be identified.

### 3.2.1 *An illustration: identifying the IS-LM-AD-AS model*

Let us consider the simplest macroeconomic model for a closed economy to illustrate how conditions for identification are checked. The model consists of four equations:

$$
\begin{aligned}
y_t &= c_{11} + y_t^* - a_{13}(R_t - \pi_t^e) + \epsilon_{1t}, && (3.7)\\
\pi_t &= \pi_t^e + a_{21}\left(y_t - y_t^*\right) + \epsilon_{2t}, && (3.8)\\
m_t - p_t &= c_{13} + a_{31} y_t - a_{33} R_t + \epsilon_{3t}, && (3.9)\\
\pi_t^e &= \beta \pi_{t-1} + (1-\beta)\, \pi_t + \epsilon_{4t}. && (3.10)
\end{aligned}
$$

Equation (3.9) describes an LM equation, which, for $a_1 = 1$, relates the nominal interest rate to (the logarithm of) money circulation velocity. Equation (3.7) describes an IS curve in a closed economy and shows immediately that a monetary policy authority can influence the level of activity only if, by controlling the nominal interest rate, it manages to influence the real interest rate. Equation (3.8) is an expectations-augmented Phillips curve, according to which actual inflation is determined by expected inflation and deviations of output from its potential level $y^*$, which we take as a deterministic trend. Equation (3.10) describes the mechanism of expectation formation. The extreme case of price-stockiness is obtained by setting $\beta = 1$, while the case of rational expectations-perfect price flexibility is obtained by setting $\beta = 0$.

Note that the model has no equation for money. Money supply is not modelled, as it is considered exogenous, i.e. fully controlled by the monetary authority. The econometrician's task is the estimation of the unknown parameters to simulate the impact of a different path for the exogenous variables controlled by the monetary authority. The model uses four equations to determine four endogenous variables, $\pi_t$, $\pi_t^e$, $R_t$, and $y_t$ for given values of the two exogenous variables, $y^*$, and $m_t$. The exogeneity status is attributed to $y_t^*$ and $m_t$, either because they describe the available technology and demography or because they are fully controlled by the policy-maker.

Consider the extreme case of price-stickiness, given by $\beta = 1$, and use equation (3.10) to eliminate expected inflation from the model. Then the IS-LM-AD-AS model becomes a special case of our general specification (3.6):

$$\mathbf{A}\begin{bmatrix} y_t \\ p_t \\ R_t \\ m_t \\ y_t^* \end{bmatrix} = \mathbf{C}_0 \begin{bmatrix} 1 \\ t \end{bmatrix} + \mathbf{C}_1 \begin{bmatrix} y_{t-1} \\ p_{t-1} \\ m_{t-1} \end{bmatrix} + \mathbf{C}_2 \left[ p_{t-2} \right] + \begin{bmatrix} \epsilon_{1t} \\ \epsilon_{2t} \\ \epsilon_{3t} \\ \epsilon_{4t} \\ \epsilon_{5t} \end{bmatrix}, \tag{3.11}$$

where

$$\mathbf{A} = \begin{bmatrix} 1 & 0 & a_{13} & 0 & -1 \\ -a_{21} & 1 & 0 & 0 & a_{21} \\ -\frac{a_{31}}{a_{33}} & -\frac{1}{a_{33}} & 1 & \frac{1}{a_{33}} & 0 \\ 0 & 0 & 0 & 1 & 0 \\ 0 & 0 & 0 & 0 & 1 \end{bmatrix},$$

$$\mathbf{C}_0 = \begin{bmatrix} c_{0,11} & 0 \\ c_{0,21} & 0 \\ c_{0,31} & 0 \\ c_{0,41} & 0 \\ c_{0,51} & c_{0,52} \end{bmatrix}, \quad \mathbf{C}_1 = \begin{bmatrix} 0 & a_{13} & 0 \\ 0 & 2 & 0 \\ 0 & 0 & 0 \\ 0 & 0 & 1 \\ 0 & 0 & 0 \end{bmatrix}, \quad \mathbf{C}_2 = \begin{bmatrix} -a_{13} \\ -1 \\ 0 \\ 0 \\ 0 \end{bmatrix}.$$

Note that $y_t^*$ is a deterministic trend and money is exogenous in that its rate of growth is fixed to $c_{0,41}$. The effect of monetary policy on macroeconomic variables is evaluated by assessing the impact on the system of modifications in this parameter. To apply to this specific case our general discussion of identifiability consider using the representation (3.5):

$$\mathbf{w}_t = \begin{bmatrix} y_t \\ p_t \\ R_t \\ m_t \\ y_t^* \\ 1 \\ t \\ y_{t-1} \\ p_{t-1} \\ m_{t-1} \\ p_{t-2} \end{bmatrix},$$

$$\mathbf{D} = \begin{bmatrix} \mathbf{D}_1' \\ \mathbf{D}_2' \\ \mathbf{D}_3' \\ \mathbf{D}_4' \\ \mathbf{D}_5' \end{bmatrix} = \begin{bmatrix} 1 & 0 & a_{13} & 0 & -1 & c_{0,11} & 0 & 0 & a_{13} & 0 & -a_{13} \\ -a_{21} & 1 & 0 & 0 & a_{21} & c_{0,21} & 0 & 0 & 2 & 0 & -1 \\ -\frac{a_{31}}{a_{33}} & -\frac{1}{a_{33}} & 1 & \frac{1}{a_{33}} & 0 & c_{0,31} & 0 & 0 & 0 & 0 & 0 \\ 0 & 0 & 0 & 1 & 0 & c_{0,41} & 0 & 0 & 0 & 1 & 0 \\ 0 & 0 & 0 & 0 & 1 & c_{0,51} & c_{0,52} & 0 & 0 & 0 & 0 \end{bmatrix}.$$

The restrictions in the first equation are imposed by the following matrix:

$$R_1 = \begin{bmatrix} 0&1&0&0&0&0&0&0&0&0&0 \\ 0&0&0&1&0&0&0&0&0&0&0 \\ 1&0&0&0&1&0&0&0&0&0&0 \\ 0&0&0&0&0&0&1&0&0&0&0 \\ 0&0&0&0&0&0&0&1&0&0&0 \\ 0&0&1&0&0&0&0&0&-1&0&0 \\ 0&0&1&0&0&0&0&0&0&0&1 \\ 0&0&0&0&0&0&0&0&0&0&1 \end{bmatrix}.$$

The first equation is then over-identified with $(8-4)$ over-identifying restrictions when the following rank condition is satisfied:

$$\text{rank } \mathbf{R}_1 (\mathbf{D}_1 \mid \mathbf{D}_2 \mid \ldots \mid \mathbf{D}_5) = 4.$$

By applying the procedure to all the equations in the system, one can show that the second equation is over-identified with four over-identifying restrictions, the third equation is over-identified with two, the fourth equation with five, and the fifth equation with four. We conclude that the model is identified and imposes a total of nineteen over-identifying restrictions.

## 3.3 Great critiques

The Cowles Commission approach to the identification of structural econometric models broke down in the 1970s when some authors discovered that this type of model

...did not represent the data, ... did not represent the theory... were ineffective for practical purposes of forecasting and policy evaluation... (Pesaran and Smith 1995).

Different explanations of the failure of the Cowles Commission approach gave rise to the different prominent methods of empirical research: the LSE (London School of Economics) approach, the VAR approach, and the intertemporal optimization-Real Business Cycle approach. We shall discuss and illustrate the empirical research strategy of these three alternative approaches by interpreting them as different proposals to solve problems observed in the Cowles Commission approach.

The LSE approach was initiated by Denis Sargan but owes its diffusion to a number of Sargan's students and is extremely well described in the book by David Hendry (1995). This approach to macroeconometric modelling explains the ineffectiveness of the Cowles Commission models for the practical purposes of forecasting and policy as due to their incapability of representing the data. The root of the failure of the traditional approach lies in the little attention paid to the statistical model implicit in the estimated structure. Regarding our simple example of the IS-LM-AD-AS model, the identified structure is estimated without checking that the implicit statistical model is an accurate description of the data. Spanos (1990) considers the case of a simple demand and supply model to show how the reduced form is ignored in the traditional approach. Most of the widely used estimators allow the derivation of numerical values for the structural parameters without even seeing the statistical models represented by the reduced form. There are several possible causes for the inadequacy of statistical models implicit in structural econometric models: omission of relevant variables, or of the relevant dynamics for the included variables (note, for example, that the estimated money demand in our simple example is a simple, static equation), or invalid assumptions of exogeneity. The LSE solution to the specification problem is the theory of reduction. Any econometric model is interpreted as a simplified representation of the unobservable data generating process (DGP). For the representation to be valid or 'congruent', to use Hendry's own terminology, the information lost in moving from the DGP to its representation, given by the adopted specification, must be irrelevant to the problem at hand. Adequacy of the statistical model is evaluated by analysing the reduced form. Therefore, the prominence of the structural model, with respect to the reduced form representation in the Cowles Commission approach to identification and specification is reversed. The LSE approach starts its specification and identification procedure with a general dynamic reduced form model. The congruency of such a model cannot be directly assessed against the true DGP, which is unobservable. However, a series of diagnostic tests is proposed as criteria for evaluating the congruency of the baseline model. The general principle guiding the application of such criteria is that congruent models should feature true random residuals; hence, any departure of the vector of residuals from a random normal multivariate distribution should signal a mis-specification. Once the baseline model.has been validated, the reduction process begins by simplifying the dynamics and reducing the dimensionality of the model by omitting the equations for those variables for which the null hypothesis of exogeneity is not rejected. The concept of exogeneity is refined within the LSE approach and is decomposed into different categories, determined by the purpose of the estimation of the econometric model. A further stage in the simplification process can be the imposition of the rank reduction restrictions in the matrix determining the long-run equilibria of the system and the identification of cointegrating vectors. The product of this stage is a statistical model for the data, possibly discriminating between short-run dynamics and the long-run equilibria. Only after this validation procedure is the structural model identified and estimated. A just-identified specification does not require any further testing, as its implicit reduced form does not impose any further restrictions on the baseline statistical model. The validity of over-identified specification is instead tested by evaluating the validity of the restrictions implicitly imposed on the general reduced form. After this last diagnostic for the validity of the reduction process has been performed, the structural model is used for the practical purposes of forecasting and policy evaluation.

While the LSE approach finds its explanation of the failure of Cowles Commission models in their incapability of representing the data, different approaches initiated by the two famous critiques of Lucas (1976) and Sims (1980), relate their explanations to the incapability of the traditional models to represent the theory. The general class of theoretical models of reference for these two critiques are forward-looking intertemporal optimization models. Lucas attacks the identification scheme proposed by the Cowles Commission by pointing out that these models do not take expectations into account explicitly and, therefore, the identified parameters within the Cowles Commission approach are a mixture of 'deep parameters' describing preference and technology into the economy, and expectational parameters which, by their nature, are not stable across different policy regimes. The main consequence of such instability is that traditional structural macro-models are useless for the purpose of policy simulation. To show this, let us reconsider the case of our simple model of the monetary transmission mechanism estimated for simulating the impact of different monetary policies on macroeconomic variables.

Assume the following DGP in which expected monetary policy matters for the determination of macroeconomic variables in the economy:

$$\begin{pmatrix} \mathbf{Y}_t \\ \mathbf{M}_t \end{pmatrix} = D_1(L) \begin{pmatrix} \mathbf{Y}_{t-1} \\ \mathbf{M}_{t-1} \end{pmatrix} + D_2 \left( \bar{M}^e_{t+1} \right) + \begin{pmatrix} \mathbf{u}^Y_t \\ \mathbf{u}^M_t \end{pmatrix}. \tag{3.12}$$

A Cowles Commission model is estimated without explicitly including expectations over a sample featuring the following money supply rule:

$$M_{t+1} = a_0 + M_t. \tag{3.13}$$

The fitted model will, therefore, have the following specification:

$$\begin{pmatrix} \mathbf{Y}_t \\ \mathbf{M}_t \end{pmatrix} = D_1(L) \begin{pmatrix} \mathbf{Y}_{t-1} \\ \mathbf{M}_{t-1} \end{pmatrix} + D_2 a_0 + D_2 \left( M_t \right) + \begin{pmatrix} \mathbf{u}^Y_t \\ \mathbf{u}^M_t \end{pmatrix}. \tag{3.14}$$

Equation (3.14) is not the correct model to simulate the impact of any rule different from (3.13). Consider the case of

$$M_{t+1} = a_1 + M_t.$$

The correct model, in terms of observable variables, for simulating the effect of the new policy would be:

$$\begin{pmatrix} \mathbf{Y}_t \\ \mathbf{M}_t \end{pmatrix} = D_1(L) \begin{pmatrix} \mathbf{Y}_{t-1} \\ \mathbf{M}_{t-1} \end{pmatrix} + D_2 a_1 + D_2 \left( M_t \right) + \begin{pmatrix} \mathbf{u}^Y_t \\ \mathbf{u}^M_t \end{pmatrix}, \tag{3.15}$$

and a simulation based on (3.14) would give the wrong prediction on the effect of monetary policy.

The Sims (1980) critique runs parallel to that of Lucas but concentrates on the status of exogeneity arbitrarily attributed to some variables to achieve identification within structural Cowles Commission models. Sims argues that no variable can be deemed as exogenous in a world of forward-looking agents whose behaviour depends on the solution of an intertemporal optimization model. Again with reference to our example, reconsider the case for exogeneity of the money supply. If the monetary authority uses the money supply as an instrument to achieve given targets for the macroeconomic variables, then the money supply would naturally react not only to the output and inflation, but also to leading indicators for these variables. Assuming the money supply is exogenous, the estimated model completely omits an extremely relevant feedback and loses an important feature of the data. Moreover, by assuming incorrectly exogeneity, the model might induce a spurious statistic efficacy of monetary policy in the determination of macroeconomic variables. Endogeneity of money does generate correlations between macroeconomic and monetary variables, which, by invalidly assuming money as exogenous, can be interpreted as a causal relation running from money to the macroeconomic variables.

We consider a deeper illustration of the different approaches to identification in response to the problems with the Cowles Commission approach, and we shall then devote the rest of the book to the analysis of how such different approaches are put to work to construct macroeconometric models.

## 3.4 Identification in LSE methodology

To illustrate the LSE approach to identification, re-consider the Cowles Commission specification of the IS-LM-AS model. The Cowles Commission's strategy involves direct specification of an identified structure of interest such as (3.11). The LSE research strategy begins from the specification of a general statistical model, i.e. a reduced form. There are no specific rules in the choice of the baseline specification, the only constraint being that such specification should be sufficiently general to deliver a congruent representation of the underlying unknown data generating process. A possible baseline specification can be the following:

$$\begin{bmatrix} y_t \\ p_t \\ R_t \\ m_t \\ y_t^* \end{bmatrix} = \begin{bmatrix} d_{0,11} & d_{0,12} \\ d_{0,21} & d_{0,22} \\ d_{0,31} & d_{0,32} \\ d_{0,41} & d_{0,42} \\ d_{0,51} & d_{0,52} \end{bmatrix} \begin{bmatrix} 1 \\ t \end{bmatrix}$$
$$+ \begin{bmatrix} d_{1,11} & d_{1,12} & d_{1,13} & d_{1,14} & d_{1,15} \\ d_{1,21} & d_{1,22} & d_{1,23} & d_{1,24} & d_{1,25} \\ d_{1,31} & d_{1,32} & d_{1,33} & d_{1,34} & d_{1,35} \\ d_{1,41} & d_{1,42} & d_{1,43} & d_{1,44} & d_{1,45} \\ d_{1,51} & d_{1,52} & d_{1,53} & d_{1,54} & d_{1,55} \end{bmatrix} \begin{bmatrix} y_{t-1} \\ p_{t-1} \\ R_{t-1} \\ m_{t-1} \\ y_{t-1}^* \end{bmatrix} \tag{3.16}$$
$$+ \begin{bmatrix} d_{2,11} & d_{2,12} & d_{2,13} & d_{2,14} & d_{2,15} \\ d_{2,21} & d_{2,22} & d_{2,23} & d_{2,24} & d_{2,25} \\ d_{2,31} & d_{2,32} & d_{2,33} & d_{2,34} & d_{2,35} \\ d_{2,41} & d_{2,42} & d_{2,43} & d_{2,44} & d_{2,45} \\ d_{2,51} & d_{2,52} & d_{2,53} & d_{2,54} & d_{2,55} \end{bmatrix} \begin{bmatrix} y_{t-2} \\ p_{t-2} \\ R_{t-2} \\ m_{t-2} \\ y_{t-2}^* \end{bmatrix} + \begin{bmatrix} u_{1t} \\ u_{2t} \\ u_{3t} \\ u_{4t} \\ u_{5t} \end{bmatrix}.$$

Note that this model is much more general than the Cowles Commission specification, as far as the dynamics of all variables is concerned; moreover, no a priori restriction on the nature of the trend is imposed. The first step of the model validation procedure consists of the evaluation of the lag truncation: is the chosen length of the polynomial in the lag operator ($L = 2$, in our case) long enough to capture the dynamics in the data? If the answer is yes, then we take the next step of the specification strategy: to identify the long-run structure and re-specify the reduced form as a VECM. As we have already pointed out, this step can be skipped at only the risk of loss in efficiency. To keep the LSE specification more directly comparable with the Cowles Commission IS-LM-AS model, we do run this risk and keep the reduced form in levels. The last step of the LSE identification strategy is the specification of structural models. Just-identified models impose no further restrictions on the validated reduced form, while over-identified structures do impose testable restrictions on the reduced form. Testing such restrictions is the final model evaluation criteria. The validity of the over-identifying restrictions can be checked by comparing the reduced form implicit in the structural model (3.11) with the general reduced form (3.16). We find the reduced form implicit in the structural model (3.11), pre-multiplying the model by:

$$\begin{bmatrix} 1 & 0 & a_{13} & 0 & -1 \\ -a_{21} & 1 & 0 & 0 & a_{21} \\ -\frac{a_{31}}{a_{33}} & -\frac{1}{a_{33}} & 1 & \frac{1}{a_{33}} & 0 \\ 0 & 0 & 0 & 1 & 0 \\ 0 & 0 & 0 & 0 & 1 \end{bmatrix}^{-1} = \mathbf{A}^{-1}$$

$$\begin{bmatrix} y_t \\ p_t \\ R_t \\ m_t \\ y_t^* \end{bmatrix} = \mathbf{A}^{-1} \begin{bmatrix} c_{0,11} & 0 \\ c_{0,21} & 0 \\ c_{0,31} & 0 \\ c_{0,41} & 0 \\ c_{0,51} & c_{0,52} \end{bmatrix} \begin{bmatrix} 1 \\ t \end{bmatrix} + \mathbf{A}^{-1} \begin{bmatrix} 0 & a_{13} & 0 & 0 & 0 \\ 0 & 2 & 0 & 0 & 0 \\ 0 & 0 & 0 & 0 & 0 \\ 0 & 0 & 0 & 1 & 0 \\ 0 & 0 & 0 & 0 & 0 \end{bmatrix} \begin{bmatrix} y_{t-1} \\ p_{t-1} \\ R_{t-1} \\ m_{t-1} \\ y_{t-1}^* \end{bmatrix} \tag{3.17}$$
$$+\mathbf{A}^{-1} \begin{bmatrix} 0 & -a_{13} & 0 & 0 & 0 \\ 0 & -1 & 0 & 0 & 0 \\ 0 & 0 & 0 & 0 & 0 \\ 0 & 0 & 0 & 0 & 0 \\ 0 & 0 & 0 & 0 & 0 \end{bmatrix} \begin{bmatrix} y_{t-2} \\ p_{t-2} \\ R_{t-2} \\ m_{t-2} \\ y_{t-2}^* \end{bmatrix} + \mathbf{A}^{-1} \begin{bmatrix} \epsilon_{1t} \\ \epsilon_{2t} \\ \epsilon_{3t} \\ \epsilon_{4t} \\ \epsilon_{5t} \end{bmatrix}$$

Note that (3.17) imposes more than nineteen restrictions on (3.16); in fact, it imposes nineteen over-identifying restrictions on (3.16) in addition to those necessary to determine the chosen specification for $m_t$ and $y_t^*$. The LSE methodology finds the roots of the failure of Cowles Commission models in choosing a specification rather than accepting a general baseline one.

## 3.5 Identification in VAR methodology

We have seen that the LSE methodology has interpreted the failure of the traditional approach as a result of a specification strategy leading to mis-specified and ill-identified models. The LSE methodology, however, leaves unquestioned the potential of macroeconometric modelling for simulation and econometric policy evaluation. The VAR approach shares with the LSE approach the diagnosis of the problem of Cowles Commission models but also questions the potential. VAR models differ from structural LSE models in the purpose of their specification and estimation. In the traditional approach, the typical question asked within a macroeconometric framework is 'What is the optimal response by the monetary authority to movements in macroeconomic variables for achieving given targets for the same variables?'. After the Lucas critique, questions like 'How should a central bank respond to shocks in macroeconomic variables?' are answered within the framework of quantitative monetary general equilibrium models of the business cycle. Thus, the answer is based on a theoretical model rather than on an empirical *ad hoc* macroeconometric one. Within this framework, there is a new role for empirical analysis, i.e. to provide the evidence on the stylized facts to be included in the theoretical model adopted for policy analysis and to decide between competing general equilibrium monetary models. The operationalization of this research program is well described in a recent paper by Christiano, Eichenbaum, and Evans (1998). There are three relevant steps:

1. monetary policy shocks are identified in actual economies;
2. then, the response of relevant economic variables to monetary shocks is described;
3. finally, the same experiment is performed in the model economies to compare actual and model-based responses as an evaluation tool and a selection criterion for theoretical models.

To pin down more precisely the symmetries and differences between LSE-type structural models and VAR models, consider again the case of the monetary transmission mechanism (MTM). The two types of models have a common structure, which we have represented as follows:

$$\mathbf{A}\begin{pmatrix}\mathbf{Y}_t\\ \mathbf{M}_t\end{pmatrix} = \mathbf{C}(L)\begin{pmatrix}\mathbf{Y}_{t-1}\\ \mathbf{M}_{t-1}\end{pmatrix} + \mathbf{B}\begin{pmatrix}\nu_t^Y\\ \nu_t^M\end{pmatrix}. \tag{3.18}$$

The main difference between the two approaches lies in the aim for which models are estimated.

Traditional Cowles Commission structural models are designed to identify the impact of policy variables on macroeconomic quantities in order to determine the value to assign to the monetary instruments, $\mathbf{M}$, to achieve a given target for the macroeconomic variables, $\mathbf{Y}$, assuming exogeneity of the policy variables in $\mathbf{M}$ on the ground that these are the instruments controlled by the policy-maker. Identification in traditional structural models is obtained without assuming the orthogonality of structural disturbances. Remember that we have labelled the vector $\epsilon$ as structural disturbance in traditional models and LSE models, where

$$\begin{pmatrix}\epsilon_t^Y\\ \epsilon_t^M\end{pmatrix} = \mathbf{B}\begin{pmatrix}\nu_t^Y\\ \nu_t^M\end{pmatrix}.$$

As we shall see, the impact of monetary policy is described by dynamic multipliers, which describe the response of macroeconomic variables to a modification in the exogenous monetary instruments. Dynamic multipliers are traditionally computed without separating the changes in the monetary variables into the expected and unexpected components.

The assumed exogeneity of the monetary variables makes the model invalid for policy analysis, if monetary policy reacts endogenously to the macroeconomic variables. The LSE methodology would recognize the problem of the invalid exogeneity assumption for **M**, and then proceed to the identification of an alternative enlarged model (presumably such identification will be obtained through the imposition of a priori restrictions on the dynamics of the lagged variables). However, the new model would still be used for simulation and econometric policy evaluation, whenever the appropriate concept of exogeneity (respectively, as we shall see, strong exogeneity and superexogeneity) is satisfied by the adopted specification.

The VAR modelling would reject the Cowles Commission identifying restrictions as 'incredible' for reasons not very different from the ones pinned down by the LSE approach. However, VAR models of the transmission mechanism are not estimated to yield advice on the best monetary policy; rather they are estimated to provide empirical evidence on the response of macroeconomic variables to monetary policy impulses in order to discriminate between alternative theoretical models of the economy. Monetary policy actions should be identified using restrictions independent from the competing models of the transmission mechanism under empirical investigation, taking into account the potential endogeneity of policy instruments.

In a couple of papers, Christiano, Eichenbaum, and Evans (1996a; 1996b) apply the VAR approach to derive 'stylized facts' on the effect of a contractionary policy shock, and conclude that plausible models of the monetary transmission mechanism should be consistent at least with the following evidence on price, output, and interest rates:

1. the aggregate price level initially responds very little;
2. interest rates initially rise;
3. aggregate output initially falls, then follows a $j$-shaped response with a zero long-run effect of the monetary impulse.

Such evidence leads to the dismissal of traditional real business cycle models, which are incompatible with the liquidity effect of monetary policy on interest rates, and of the Lucas (1972) model of money, in which the effect of monetary policy on output depends on 'price misperceptions'. The evidence seems more in line with alternative intepretations of the monetary transmission mechanism based on sticky prices models (Goodfriend and King 1997), limited participation models (Christiano and Eichenbaum 1992), or models with indeterminacy-sunspot equilibria (Farmer 1997).

Having stated the objective of VAR models, we are ready to assess how the technical opportunities for identification, estimation, and simulation are exploited to analyse the MTM, keeping in mind that VAR models concentrate on shocks.

First we identify the relevant shocks and describe the response of the system to shocks by analysing impulse responses (the propagation mechanism of the shocks), forecasting error variance decomposition, and historical decomposition.

Following Amisano and Giannini (1997), we represent the general structural model of interest as follows:

$$\mathbf{A}\begin{pmatrix}\mathbf{Y}_t\\ \mathbf{M}_t\end{pmatrix} = \mathbf{C}(L)\begin{pmatrix}\mathbf{Y}_{t-1}\\ \mathbf{M}_{t-1}\end{pmatrix} + \mathbf{B}\begin{pmatrix}\boldsymbol{\nu}_t^Y\\ \boldsymbol{\nu}_t^M\end{pmatrix} \tag{3.19}$$

where $\mathbf{Y}$ and $\mathbf{M}$ are vectors of macroeconomic (non-policy) variables (e.g. output and prices) and variables controlled by the monetary policy-maker (e.g. interest rates and monetary aggregates containing information on monetary policy actions), respectively; matrix $\mathbf{A}$ describes the contemporaneous relations among the variables; $\mathbf{C}(L)$ is a matrix finite-order lag polynomial; $\boldsymbol{\nu} \equiv \begin{pmatrix}\boldsymbol{\nu}^Y\\ \boldsymbol{\nu}^M\end{pmatrix}$ is a vector of structural disturbances to the non-policy and policy variables normally independently distributed with identity variance-covariance matrix; non-zero off-diagonal elements of $\mathbf{B}$ allow some shocks to affect directly more than one endogenous variable in the system.

The structural model (3.19) is not directly observable; however, a VAR can be estimated as the reduced form of the underlying structural model:

$$\begin{pmatrix}\mathbf{Y}_t\\ \mathbf{M}_t\end{pmatrix} = \mathbf{A}^{-1}\mathbf{C}(L)\begin{pmatrix}\mathbf{Y}_{t-1}\\ \mathbf{M}_{t-1}\end{pmatrix} + \begin{pmatrix}\mathbf{u}_t^Y\\ \mathbf{u}_t^M\end{pmatrix}, \tag{3.20}$$

where $\mathbf{u}$ denotes the VAR residual vector, normally independently distributed with full variance-covariance matrix $\Sigma$. The relation between the VAR residuals in $\mathbf{u}$ and the structural disturbances in $\boldsymbol{\nu}$ is therefore:

$$\mathbf{A}\begin{pmatrix}\mathbf{u}_t^Y\\ \mathbf{u}_t^M\end{pmatrix} = \mathbf{B}\begin{pmatrix}\boldsymbol{\nu}_t^Y\\ \boldsymbol{\nu}_t^M\end{pmatrix}. \tag{3.21}$$

Undoing the partitioning, we have

$$\mathbf{u}_t = \mathbf{A}^{-1}\mathbf{B}\boldsymbol{\nu}_t,$$

from which we derive the relation between the variance-covariance matrix of $\mathbf{u}_t$ (observed) and the variance-covariance matrix of $\boldsymbol{\nu}_t$ (unobserved) as follows:

$$E\left(\mathbf{u}_t\mathbf{u}_t'\right) = \mathbf{A}^{-1}\mathbf{B}E\left(\boldsymbol{v}_t\boldsymbol{v}_t'\right)\mathbf{B}'\mathbf{A}^{-1}.$$

Substituting population moments with sample moments we have:

$$\widehat{\Sigma} = \widehat{\mathbf{A}}^{-1}\widehat{\mathbf{B}}\mathbf{I}\widehat{\mathbf{B}}'\widehat{\mathbf{A}}^{-1}.$$

$\widehat{\Sigma}$ contains $n(n+1)/2$ different elements, which is the maximum number of identifiable parameters in matrices $\mathbf{A}$ and $\mathbf{B}$; therefore, identifying restrictions are imposed on these matrices. We analyse the different types of identifying restrictions in a chapter devoted to VAR models.

Once the shocks have been identified, the dynamic properties of the system can be described by analysing the response of all variables in the system to such shocks. Note that VAR models do not include expectations explicitly and might therefore be subject to the Lucas critique. The general defence of VAR modellers against the Lucas critique relies upon the fact that the disturbed variables are the shocks and, therefore, the estimated parameters are not modified for simulation purposes.

## 3.6 Identification in intertemporally optimized models

The natural outcome of the Lucas critique is intertemporally optimized models in which deep parameters, independent from a particular policy regime, are identified separately from expectational parameters, specific to policy regimes. The intertemporal optimization approach to macroeconomics leads naturally to a framework for identification and estimation of the deep parameters of interest. The first-order conditions for the solution of intertemporal optimization problems are orthogonality conditions, which can be exploited for identification and estimation of the structural parameters of interest. To illustrate this, consider the simplest version of the inflation targeting problem, described by Svensson (1997). The central bank faces the following intertemporal optimization problem:

$$\min \quad E_t \sum_{i=0}^{\infty} \delta^i L_{t+i}, \tag{3.22}$$

where:

$$L = \frac{1}{2}\left[(\pi_t - \pi^*)^2 + \lambda x_t^2\right], \tag{3.23}$$

where $E_t$ denotes expectations conditional upon the information set available at time $t$, $\delta$ is the relevant discount factor, $L$ is the loss function of the central bank. $\pi_t$ is inflation at time $t$, $\pi^*$ is the target level of inflation, $x$ represents deviations of output from its natural level, and $\lambda$ is a parameter which determines the degree of flexibility in inflation targeting. When $\lambda = 0$ the central bank is defined as a strict inflation targeter. As the monetary instrument is the policy rate, $i_t$, the structure of the economy must be described to obtain an explicit form for the policy rule. We consider the following specification for aggregate supply and demand in a closed economy[1]:

$$x_{t+1} = \beta_x x_t - \beta_r \left(i_t - E_t \pi_{t+1} - \bar{r}\right) + u_{t+1}^d, \tag{3.24}$$

[1]As we see in one of the next chapters these two functions are the outcome of the solutions of intertemporal optimization problems by agents in the private sector.

$$\pi_{t+1} = \pi_t + \alpha_x x_t + u^s_{t+1}. \tag{3.25}$$

Note that macroeconomic variables do not react contemporaneously to the instrument of monetary policy. This is the first identifying restriction for the relevant parameters in the model. As shown in the article by Svensson (1997), the first-order conditions for optimality may be written as:

$$\frac{dL}{di_t} = (E_t \pi_{t+2} - \pi^*) = -\frac{\lambda}{\delta \alpha_x k} E_t x_{t+1}, \tag{3.26}$$

$$k = 1 + \frac{\delta \lambda k}{\lambda + \delta \alpha_x^2 k}.$$

Equations (3.26) are orthogonality conditions involving all the deep parameters describing the structure of preferences of the central banker $\pi^*$, $\delta$, $\lambda$, and only one parameter coming from the structure of the economy, $\alpha_x$. Using (3.25) in (3.24) we obtain:

$$E_t \pi_{t+2} = E_t \pi_{t+1} + \alpha_x [\beta_x x_t - \beta_r (i_t - E_t \pi_{t+1} - \bar{r})], \tag{3.27}$$

and by substituting (3.27) in (3.26), we derive an interest rate rule:

$$i_t = \bar{r} + \pi^* + \left( \frac{1 + \alpha_x \beta_r}{\alpha_x \beta_r} \right) (E_t \pi_{t+1} - \pi^*) \tag{3.28}$$

$$+ \frac{\beta_x}{\beta_r} x_t + \frac{\lambda}{\delta \alpha_x k} \frac{1}{\alpha_x \beta_r} E_t x_{t+1}.$$

The parameters in the interest rate rule (3.28) are convolutions of the parameters describing the central bank's preferences $(\pi^*, \lambda, \delta)$ and of those describing the structure of the economy $(\alpha_x, \beta_r, \beta_x, \bar{r})$. Thus, it is impossible to assess from the estimation of the rule whether the responses of central banks to output and inflation are consistent with the parameters describing the impact of the policy instrument on these variables. Note, for example, that the estimation of an interest rate rule relating the policy rate to the output gap and to the deviation of expected inflation from its target does not help to distinguish a strict inflation targeter ($\lambda = 0$, in the terminology of Svensson) from a flexible inflation targeter ($\lambda > 0$).

There is only one empirical implication of the rule which can be confronted with the data independently from the identification of the parameters of interest, namely, whether the parameter describing the reaction of policy rates to a gap between expected and target inflation is larger than one. A monetary policy which accommodates changes in inflation, $\partial i_t / \partial E_t \pi_{t+1} \leq 1$, will not in general converge to the target rate $\pi^*$. This empirical prediction is the one which has attracted most of the discussion on estimated monetary policy rules (see Clarida, Galì, and Gertler 1998, 1999 ).

By comparing the first-order conditions for optimality, known as Euler equations, with the explicit interest rate rule, we note that the deep parameters of interest are much more easily identifiable from (3.26). While in our specific example (3.26) depends mainly on deep parameters describing taste and technology, there are macroeconomic applications in which the Euler equations depend only on these parameters. The identification and estimation strategy, naturally consistent with the intertemporal optimization approach, is then to derive first the Euler equations and use them to pin down the deep parameters of interest. This step is achieved by applying an estimation method directly based on orthogonality conditions, the generalized method of moments. Numerical values to the remaining parameters in the model are then attributed, not necessarily by estimation. Finally, the models are simulated and evaluated by comparing actual data with simulated data.

In the next chapters of the book we shall consider more deeply all the different approaches to macroeconometric modelling by considering a common macroeconomic issue: the analysis of the monetary transmission mechanism.

## 3.7 References

Amisano, G., and Giannini, C. (1996). *Topics in Structural VAR Econometrics.* 2nd edn. New York: Springer Verlag.

Christiano, L. J., and Eichenbaum, M. (1992). 'Liquidity Effects and the Monetary Transmission Mechanism'. *American Economic Review*, 82/2: 346-353

Christiano, L. J., Eichenbaum, M., and Evans, C. L. (1996a). 'The Effects of Monetary Policy Shocks: Evidence from the Flow of Funds'. *Review of Economics and Statistics*, 78: 16-34.

Christiano, L. J., Eichenbaum, M., and Evans, C. L. (1996b). 'Monetary Policy Shocks and their Consequences: Theory and Evidence'. Paper presented at ISOM.

Christiano, L. J., Eichenbaum, M., and Evans, C. L. (1998). 'Monetary Policy shocks: what have we learned and to what end'. NBER working paper No. 6400.

Clarida, R., Gali, J., and Gertler, M. (1998a). 'Monetary policy rules in practice: some international evidence'. *European Economic Review*, 42.

Clarida, R., Gali, J., and Gertler, M. (1998b). 'Monetary policy rules and macroeconomic stability: evidence and some theory'. NBER working paper No. 6442.

Clarida, R., Gali, J., and Gertler, M. (1999). 'The science of monetary policy: a new keynesian perspective'. *Journal of Economic Literature*, 37:1661-1707.

Farmer, R. E. A. (1997). 'Money in a Real Business Cycle Model'. Mimeo, Dept. of Economics, UCLA.

Giannini, C. (1992). 'Topics in Structural VAR Econometrics'. *Lecture Notes in Economics and Mathematical Systems*, Springer-Verlag.

Goodfriend, M., and King, R. (1997). 'The new neoclassical synthesis and the role of monetary policy'. NBER Macroeconomics Annual, MIT Press.

Hamilton, J. (1994). *Time-Series Analysis.* Princeton: Princeton University Press.

Hendry, D. F. (1995). *Dynamic Econometrics.* Oxford: Oxford University Press.

Lucas, R. E. Jr. (1972). 'Expectations and the Neutrality of Money'. *Journal of Economic Theory,* 4, April: 103-124.

Lucas, R. E. Jr. (1976). 'Econometric Policy Evaluation: A Critique'. In K. Brunner and A. Meltzer (eds.). *The Phillips curve and labor markets.* Amsterdam: North-Holland.

Johansen, S., and Juselius, K. (1994). 'Identification of the Long-run and the Short-Run Structure. An application to the IS-LM model'. *Journal of Econometrics,* 63: 7-36.

Pesaran, M. H., and Smith, R. (1994). 'Theory and Evidence in Economics'. *Journal of Econometrics.*

Sargan, D. (1964). 'Wages and Prices in the United Kingdom: A Study in Econometric Methodology'. In P. E. Hart, G. Mills and J. K. Whitaker (eds.). *Econometric Analysis of National Economic Planning.* London: Butterworth, 25-63.

Sims, C. A. (1980). 'Macroeconomics and Reality'. *Econometrica,* 48: 1-48.

Spanos, A. (1990). 'The Simultaneous Equations Models Revisited: Statistical Adequacy and Identification'. *Journal of Econometrics,* 44: 87-105.

Svensson, L. E. O. (1997). 'Inflation Forecast Targeting: Implementing and Monitoring Inflation Targets'. *European Economic Review,* 41: 1111-1146.

# 4

# COWLES COMMISSION APPROACH

## 4.1 Introduction

The traditional approach to econometric modelling of the monetary transmission mechanism, usually referred to as the Cowles Commission approach, aims at the quantitative evaluation of the effects of modification in the variables controlled by the monetary policy-maker (the instruments of monetary policy) on the macroeconomic variables which represent the final goals of the policy-maker. We can identify three stages in the traditional approach:

1. *specification and identification* of the theoretical model;
2. *estimation* of the relevant parameters, and assessment of the dynamic properties of the model, with particular emphasis on the long-run properties;
3. *simulation* of the effects of monetary policies.

We have already discussed the Cowles Commission approach to specification and identification in the previous chapters.

Before illustrating the approach at work, we devote the following sections to the discussion of estimation, simulation, and policy evaluation.

## 4.2 Estimation in the Cowles Commission approach

The crucial feature in the identification-specification stage, as shown by our IS-LM-AD-AS example, is that the specified empirical model is usually loosely related to theoretical models and that identification is achieved by imposing numerous a priori restrictions delivering exogeneity status to a number of variables. As a consequence, identification is easily achieved within Cowles Commission models, usually with a large number of over-identifying restrictions. We have also seen that criticisms of this approach attribute the roots of its failure to the imposition of too many restrictions and to its incapability of recovering the structural deep parameters of economic interest, describing preference of agents and the status of technology.

However, the traditional modelling was aware of the presence of some mis-specification in the estimated equations. The presence of such mis-specification resulted in a departure from the conditions which warrant that OLS estimators are best linear unbiased estimators (BLUE). The solution proposed was not re-specification but, instead, a modification of the estimation techniques. This is well reflected in the structure of the traditional textbooks: see, for example, Goldberger (1991), Johnston (1972), Pindyck and Rubinfield (1981) where the OLS estimator is introduced first and then different estimators are considered as solutions to different pathologies in the model residuals. Pathologies are identified as departures from the assumptions which guarantee that OLS estimators are BLUE. By now, it is well established that correcting the estimator is a strategy clearly inferior to improving the specification, i.e. correcting the model. Nevertheless, we devote some space to the discussion of alternative estimators, since they may serve as the last resort and be used when models cannot be improved due to the lack of necessary information.

### 4.2.1 *Heteroscedasticity, autocorrelation, and the GLS estimator*

Let us reconsider the single equation model of Chapter 1 and generalize it to the case in which the hypotheses of diagonality and constancy of the conditional variances-covariance matrix of the residuals do not hold:

$$\begin{aligned} \mathbf{y} &= \mathbf{X}\boldsymbol{\beta} + \boldsymbol{\epsilon}, \\ \boldsymbol{\epsilon} &\sim n.d.\left(\mathbf{0}, \boldsymbol{\sigma}^2 \Omega\right), \end{aligned} \tag{4.1}$$

where the vector $\mathbf{y}$ contains $T$ observations on the dependent variables, $\mathbf{X}$ contains $(T \times K)$ observations on the $K$ explanatory variables exogenous for the estimation of $(K \times 1)$ the vector $\boldsymbol{\beta}$, and $\Omega$ is a $(T \times T)$ symmetric and positive definite matrix. When the OLS method is applied to model (4.1), it delivers estimators which are consistent but not efficient; moreover, the traditional formula for the variance-covariance matrix of the OLS estimators, $\boldsymbol{\sigma}^2 \left(\mathbf{X}'\mathbf{X}\right)^{-1}$, is wrong and leads to an incorrect inference. Using the standard algebra of Chapter 1, one can show that the correct formula for the variance-covariance matrix of the OLS estimator is:

$$\boldsymbol{\sigma}^2 \left(\mathbf{X}'\mathbf{X}\right)^{-1} \mathbf{X}'\Omega\mathbf{X} \left(\mathbf{X}'\mathbf{X}\right)^{-1}.$$

To find a general solution to this problem, remember that the inverse of a symmetric definite positive matrix is also symmetric and definite positive and that for a given matrix $\Omega$, symmetric and definite positive, there always exists a $(T \times T)$ non-singular matrix $\mathbf{K}$, such that $\mathbf{K}'\mathbf{K} = \Omega^{-1}$ and $\mathbf{K}\Omega\mathbf{K}' = \mathbf{I}_T$.

To find the solution, consider the regression model obtained by pre-multiplying both the right-hand and the left-hand sides of (4.1) by $\mathbf{K}$:

$$\begin{aligned} \mathbf{K}\mathbf{y} &= \mathbf{K}\mathbf{X}\boldsymbol{\beta} + \mathbf{K}\boldsymbol{\epsilon}, \\ \mathbf{K}\boldsymbol{\epsilon} &\sim n.d.\left(\mathbf{0}, \boldsymbol{\sigma}^2 \mathbf{I}_T\right). \end{aligned} \tag{4.2}$$

The OLS estimator of the parameters of the transformed model (4.2) satisfies all the conditions for the applications of the Gauss–Markov theorem; therefore, the estimator

$$\begin{aligned} \widehat{\beta}_{GLS} &= \left(\mathbf{X}'\mathbf{K}'\mathbf{K}\mathbf{X}\right)^{-1} \mathbf{X}'\mathbf{K}'\mathbf{K}\mathbf{y} \\ &= \left(\mathbf{X}'\Omega^{-1}\mathbf{X}\right)^{-1} \mathbf{X}'\Omega^{-1}\mathbf{y}, \end{aligned}$$

known as the generalised least squares (GLS) estimator, is BLUE. The variance of the GLS estimator, conditional upon $\mathbf{X}$, becomes

$$Var\left(\widehat{\beta}_{GLS} \mid \mathbf{X}\right) = \sigma^2 \left(\mathbf{X}'\Omega^{-1}\mathbf{X}\right)^{-1}.$$

Note that, from the application of the Gauss–Markov theorem, it follows immediately that the variance of the GLS estimator is equal to the sum of the variance of any other linear estimator and a positive semidefinite matrix. Consider, for example, the variances of the OLS and the GLS estimators. Using the fact that if $\mathbf{A}$ and $\mathbf{B}$ are positive definite and $\mathbf{A}-\mathbf{B}$ is positive semidefinite, then $\mathbf{B}^{-1}-\mathbf{A}^{-1}$ is also positive semidefinite, we have:

$$\begin{aligned}
&\left(\mathbf{X}'\Omega^{-1}\mathbf{X}\right) - \left(\mathbf{X}'\mathbf{X}\right)\left(\mathbf{X}'\Omega\mathbf{X}\right)^{-1}\left(\mathbf{X}'\mathbf{X}\right) \\
&= \mathbf{X}'\mathbf{K}'\mathbf{K}\mathbf{X} - \left(\mathbf{X}'\mathbf{X}\right)\left(\mathbf{X}'\mathbf{K}^{-1}\left(\mathbf{K}'\right)^{-1}\mathbf{X}\right)^{-1}\left(\mathbf{X}'\mathbf{X}\right) \\
&= \mathbf{X}'\mathbf{K}'\left(\mathbf{I} - \left(\mathbf{K}'\right)^{-1}\mathbf{X}\left(\mathbf{X}'\mathbf{K}^{-1}\left(\mathbf{K}'\right)^{-1}\mathbf{X}\right)^{-1}\mathbf{X}'\mathbf{K}^{-1}\right)\mathbf{K}\mathbf{X} \\
&= \mathbf{X}'\mathbf{K}'\mathbf{M}_W'\mathbf{M}_W\mathbf{K}\mathbf{X},
\end{aligned}$$

where

$$\mathbf{M}_W = \left(\mathbf{I} - \mathbf{W}\left(\mathbf{W}'\mathbf{W}\right)^{-1}\mathbf{W}'\right), \tag{4.3}$$

$$\mathbf{W} = \left(\mathbf{K}'\right)^{-1}\mathbf{X}. \tag{4.4}$$

The applicability of the GLS estimator requires an empirical specification for the matrix $\mathbf{K}$. We consider here two specific applications where the appropriate choice of such a matrix leads to the solution of the problems in the OLS estimator generated, respectively, by the presence of first-order serial correlation and of heteroscedasticity in the residuals.

Consider first the case of first-order serial correlation in the residuals. We have the following model:

$$\begin{aligned}
y_t &= \mathbf{x}_t'\boldsymbol{\beta} + u_t, \\
u_t &= \rho u_{t-1} + \epsilon_t, \\
\epsilon_t &\sim n.i.d.\left(0, \sigma_\epsilon^2\right),
\end{aligned}$$

which, using our general notation, can be re-written as:

$$\mathbf{y} = \mathbf{X}\boldsymbol{\beta} + \boldsymbol{\epsilon}, \tag{4.5}$$

$$\boldsymbol{\epsilon} \sim n.d.\left(\mathbf{0}, \sigma^2\Omega\right),$$

$$\sigma^2 = \frac{\sigma_\epsilon^2}{1-\rho^2}, \tag{4.6}$$

$$\Omega = \begin{bmatrix} 1 & \rho & \rho^2 & . & . & \rho^{T-1} \\ \rho & 1 & \rho & . & . & \rho^{T-2} \\ \rho^2 & . & 1 & . & . & . \\ . & . & . & . & . & . \\ \rho^{T-2} & . & . & \rho & 1 & \rho \\ \rho^{T-1} & \rho^{T-2} & . & . & \rho & 1 \end{bmatrix}.$$

In this case, the knowledge of the parameter $\rho$ allows the empirical implementation of the GLS estimator. An intuitive procedure to implement the GLS estimator can then be the following:

1. estimate the vector $\boldsymbol{\beta}$ by OLS and save the vector of residuals $\widehat{u}_t$;
2. regress $\widehat{u}_t$ on $\widehat{u}_{t-1}$ to obtain an estimate $\widehat{\rho}$ of $\rho$;
3. construct the transformed model and regress $(y_t - \widehat{\rho} y_{t-1})$ on $(\mathbf{x}_t - \widehat{\rho}\mathbf{x}_{t-1})$ to obtain the GLS estimator of the vector of parameters of interest.

Note that the above procedure, known as the Cochrane–Orcutt procedure, can be repeated until convergence.

In the case of heteroscedasticity, our general model becomes

$$\mathbf{y} = \mathbf{X}\boldsymbol{\beta} + \boldsymbol{\epsilon},$$
$$\boldsymbol{\epsilon} \sim n.d.\,(\mathbf{0}, \Omega)\,,$$
$$\Omega = \begin{bmatrix} \sigma_1^2 & 0 & 0 & . & . & 0 \\ 0 & \sigma_2^2 & 0 & . & . & 0 \\ . & . & . & . & . & . \\ . & . & . & . & . & . \\ 0 & . & . & 0 & \sigma_{T-1}^2 & 0 \\ 0 & 0 & . & . & 0 & \sigma_T^2 \end{bmatrix}.$$

In this case, to construct the GLS estimator, we need to model heteroscedasticity choosing appropriately the $\mathbf{K}$ matrix. White (1980) proposes a specification based on the consideration that in the case of heteroscedasticity the variance-covariance matrix of the OLS estimator takes the form:

$$\boldsymbol{\sigma}^2 \left(\mathbf{X}'\mathbf{X}\right)^{-1} \mathbf{X}'\Omega\mathbf{X} \left(\mathbf{X}'\mathbf{X}\right)^{-1},$$

which can be used for inference, once an estimator for $\Omega$ is available. The following unbiased estimator of $\Omega$ is proposed:

$$\widehat{\Omega} = \begin{bmatrix} \widehat{u}_1^2 & 0 & 0 & . & . & 0 \\ 0 & \widehat{u}_2^2 & 0 & . & . & 0 \\ . & . & . & . & . & . \\ . & . & . & . & . & . \\ 0 & . & . & 0 & \widehat{u}_{T-1}^2 & 0 \\ 0 & 0 & . & . & 0 & \widehat{u}_T^2 \end{bmatrix}.$$

Alternative models for heteroscedasticity, known as ARCH (autoregressive conditional heteroscedasticity) processes, useful for high-frequency financial series, and based upon simultaneous modelling of the first two moments of time-series processes, have been proposed by Engle (1980) and Bollerslev (1986).

### 4.2.2 *Endogeneity*

The estimation of a simultaneous system needs the solution of a problem, independent of mis-specification, which has prompted most of the advances in estimation theory within the Cowles Commission approach: simultaneity.

To discuss simultaneity, we consider the following representation of a model of interest:

$$\begin{aligned} \mathbf{B}\mathbf{y}_t + \Gamma\mathbf{z}_t &= \mathbf{u}_t, \\ \mathbf{u}_t &\sim n.i.d.\,(\mathbf{0}, \Sigma)\,, \end{aligned} \tag{4.7}$$

where $\mathbf{y}_t$ is a $(G \times 1)$ vector of endogenous variables, $\mathbf{z}_t$ is a $(M \times 1)$ vector of exogenous variables, which are considered exogenous in that they are orthogonal to residuals. Therefore, in the case of a dynamic specification, the model contains all contemporaneous variables considered orthogonal to residuals, their lags, and the lags of the variables $\mathbf{y}_t$. $\mathbf{B}$ and $\Gamma$ are matrices of parameters, $(G \times G)$ and $(G \times M)$, respectively. Using matrix notation, we can represent (4.7) alternatively as:

$$\mathbf{B}\mathbf{y}' + \Gamma\mathbf{z}' = \mathbf{u}', \tag{4.8}$$

where $\mathbf{y}$ is a $(T \times G)$, $\mathbf{z}$ $(T \times M)$, and $\mathbf{u}$ $(T \times G)$ matrices.

To illustrate the problems with the OLS estimator generated by endogeneity, first consider the equation of the model, which we write as:

$$\mathbf{y}_1 = \mathbf{x}_1\boldsymbol{\delta}_1 + \mathbf{u}_1, \tag{4.9}$$

where $\mathbf{y}_1$ is a $(T \times 1)$ vector containing all the observations on the first endogenous variable in the model and $\mathbf{x}_1$ is a $(T \times (G_1 + M_1 - 1))$ matrix containing all observations on the $M_1$ exogenous variables included in the first equation and on the $G_1 - 1$ contemporaneous endogenous variables included in the first equation. Given that the matrix $\mathbf{x}_1$ contains some endogenous variables, in general we have:

$$p\,\lim \frac{1}{T}\mathbf{x}_1'\mathbf{u}_1 \neq 0, \tag{4.10}$$

and the OLS estimator of the parameters of interest is not consistent. Condition (4.10) is rationalized by referring to the reduced form of the system (4.7):

$$\begin{aligned} \mathbf{y}_t &= \mathbf{B}^{-1}\Gamma\mathbf{z}_t + \mathbf{B}^{-1}\mathbf{u}_t, \\ \mathbf{u}_t &\sim n.i.d.\,(\mathbf{0}, \Sigma)\,, \end{aligned} \tag{4.11}$$

which shows that, with the exception of special configurations for the matrices $\mathbf{B}$ and $\Sigma$, all endogenous variables are correlated with all residuals in $\mathbf{u}_1$.

### 4.2.3 *GIVE estimators*

The generalized instrumental variables estimator (GIVE) is derived by considering that, in the simultaneous model, condition (4.10) holds, but:

$$p \lim \frac{1}{T}\mathbf{z}'\mathbf{u}_1 = 0, \tag{4.12}$$

and, therefore, a consistent estimator of the parameters of interest can be derived by solving the following system of equations:

$$\begin{aligned} \mathbf{z}'\widehat{u}_1 &= 0, \\ \mathbf{z}'\left(\mathbf{y}_1 - \mathbf{x}_1\widehat{\boldsymbol{\delta}}_1\right) &= 0. \end{aligned} \tag{4.13}$$

System (4.13) contains a number of equations equal to the number of variables in $\mathbf{z}_1$, $M$, and the number of unknowns is equal to the number of parameters in the vector $\boldsymbol{\delta}_1, K_1 = G_1 + M_1 - 1$. There are three cases of interest:

1. $M < K_1$: the number of unknowns is larger than the number of equations and no estimators of the parameters of interest can be derived. Not surprisingly, the equation is not identified.
2. $M = K_1$: the number of uknowns equals the number of equations, the system is just identified, and (4.13) has a unique solution, which delivers an estimator of the parameters of interest:

$$\widehat{\boldsymbol{\delta}}_{1,IV} = \left(\mathbf{z}'\mathbf{x}_1\right)^{-1}\mathbf{z}'\mathbf{y}_1.$$

3. $M > K_1$: the number of equations is larger than the number of unknowns, the equation is over-identified and the estimator of parameters of interest is not unequivocally determined by the orthogonality condition (4.13).

An intuitive solution for the over-identification case is obtained by taking $K$ linear combinations of the $M_1$ orthogonality conditions. Define a matrix $\mathbf{L}$ of dimension $(K_1 \times M)$. Pre-multiplying the system (4.13) by $\mathbf{L}$, we have:

$$\begin{aligned} \mathbf{L}\mathbf{z}'\widehat{\mathbf{u}}_1 &= 0, \\ \mathbf{L}\mathbf{z}'\left(\mathbf{y}_1 - \mathbf{x}_1\widehat{\boldsymbol{\delta}}_1\right) &= 0. \end{aligned} \tag{4.14}$$

From (4.14) we derive the following estimator:

$$\widehat{\boldsymbol{\delta}}_1 = \left(\mathbf{L}\mathbf{z}'\mathbf{x}_1\right)^{-1}\mathbf{L}\mathbf{z}'\mathbf{y}_1. \tag{4.15}$$

From (4.15) it follows that

$$\widehat{\boldsymbol{\delta}}_1 - \boldsymbol{\delta}_1 = \left(\mathbf{L}\mathbf{z}'\mathbf{x}_1\right)^{-1}\mathbf{L}\mathbf{z}'\mathbf{u}_1, \tag{4.16}$$

and

$$\sqrt{T}\left(\widehat{\boldsymbol{\delta}}_1 - \boldsymbol{\delta}_1\right) = \left(\frac{1}{T}\mathbf{L}\mathbf{z}'\mathbf{x}_1\right)^{-1} \mathbf{L}\sqrt{T}\mathbf{z}_1'\mathbf{u}_1. \tag{4.17}$$

Given that consistency of the estimator is guaranteed by the hypothesis (4.12), and assuming that

$$p \lim \frac{1}{T}\mathbf{L}\mathbf{z}'\mathbf{x}_1 = \mathbf{L}\mathbf{M}_{zx_1}, \ \sqrt{T}\mathbf{z}'\mathbf{u}_1 \xrightarrow{L} N\left(0, \sigma_{11}\mathbf{M}_{zz}\right),$$

we can apply Cramer's theorem to conclude that:

$$\sqrt{T}\left(\widehat{\boldsymbol{\delta}}_1 - \boldsymbol{\delta}_1\right) \sim N\left(0, \sigma_{11}\left(\mathbf{L}\mathbf{M}_{zx_1}\right)^{-1}\mathbf{L}\mathbf{M}_{zz}\mathbf{L}'\left(\mathbf{M}_{x_1z}\mathbf{L}'\right)^{-1}\right). \tag{4.18}$$

Equation (4.18) characterizes completely the properties of the estimator; however, an empirical implementation requires the knowledge of the matrix $\mathbf{L}$. Note that the variance of the estimator depends on $\mathbf{L}$; hence, a natural criterion for choosing this matrix is the maximization of the efficiency of the estimator. Sargan (1988) shows that the variance of the estimator is minimized when $\mathbf{L} = \mathbf{M}_{x_1z}\mathbf{M}_{zz}^{-1}$, in which case we have:

$$\sqrt{T}\left(\widehat{\boldsymbol{\delta}}_1 - \boldsymbol{\delta}_1\right) \sim N\left(0, \sigma_{11}\left(\mathbf{M}_{x_1z}\mathbf{M}_{zz}^{-1}\mathbf{M}_{zx_1}\right)^{-1}\right). \tag{4.19}$$

The choice of $\mathbf{L}$ defines the following estimator:

$$\widehat{\boldsymbol{\delta}}_1 = \left(\mathbf{x}_1'\mathbf{z}\left(\mathbf{z}'\mathbf{z}\right)^{-1}\mathbf{z}'\mathbf{x}_1\right)^{-1}\mathbf{x}_1'\mathbf{z}\left(\mathbf{z}'\mathbf{z}\right)^{-1}\mathbf{z}'\mathbf{y}_1, \tag{4.20}$$

whose variance-covariance matrix can be estimated as follows:

$$s_1^2\left(\mathbf{x}_1'\mathbf{z}\left(\mathbf{z}'\mathbf{z}\right)^{-1}\mathbf{z}'\mathbf{x}_1\right)^{-1},$$

$$s_1^2 = \frac{1}{T}\left(\mathbf{y}_1 - \mathbf{x}_1\widehat{\boldsymbol{\delta}}_1\right)'\left(\mathbf{y}_1 - \mathbf{x}_1\widehat{\boldsymbol{\delta}}_1\right).$$

Equation (4.20) defines the generalized instrumental variables estimator (GIVE). Obviously, in the case of exact identification GIVE simplifies to $\left(\mathbf{z}'\mathbf{x}_1\right)^{-1}\mathbf{z}'\mathbf{y}_1$.

An equivalent estimator to GIVE is derived by the following two-step procedure:

1. regress, by OLS, $\mathbf{x}_1$ on $\mathbf{z}$ and construct fitted values $\widehat{\mathbf{x}}_1 = \mathbf{z}\left(\mathbf{z}'\mathbf{z}\right)^{-1}\mathbf{z}'\mathbf{x}_1 = \mathbf{z}\widehat{\mathbf{Q}}_1$;
2. regress by the OLS $\mathbf{y}_1$ on $\widehat{\mathbf{x}}_1$ to obtain:

$$\begin{aligned}\widehat{\boldsymbol{\delta}}_1 &= \left(\widehat{\mathbf{x}}_1'\widehat{\mathbf{x}}\right)^{-1}\widehat{\mathbf{x}}_1'\mathbf{y}_1 \\ &= \left(\mathbf{x}_1'\mathbf{z}\left(\mathbf{z}'\mathbf{z}\right)^{-1}\mathbf{z}'\mathbf{x}_1\right)^{-1}\mathbf{x}_1'\mathbf{z}\left(\mathbf{z}'\mathbf{z}\right)^{-1}\mathbf{z}'\mathbf{y}_1,\end{aligned}$$

which is known as the two-stage least squares (TSLS) estimator.

Note that to obtain a TSLS estimator as efficient as the GIVE estimator, it is important to avoid generating an estimate of the variance of the estimator using the residuals from the second stage:

$$\begin{aligned}\widehat{\mathbf{u}}_{1,\mathrm{TSLS}} &= \mathbf{y}_1 - \widehat{\mathbf{x}}_1\widehat{\boldsymbol{\delta}}_1 \\ &= \mathbf{y}_1 - \mathbf{x}_1\widehat{\boldsymbol{\delta}}_1 - (\widehat{\mathbf{x}}_1 - \mathbf{x}_1)\,\widehat{\boldsymbol{\delta}}_1 \\ &= \widehat{\mathbf{u}}_{1,\mathrm{GIVE}} - (\widehat{\mathbf{x}}_1 - \mathbf{x}_1)\,\widehat{\boldsymbol{\delta}}_1,\end{aligned}$$

which results in an upward biased estimator of the variance. The problem is easily solved, and in almost all econometric packages the TSLS and the GIVE estimators do not differ.

More interesting problems are generated by mis-specification. In general, a mis-specification arises when the instruments are correlated with residuals. The classical form of a mis-specification has omitted variables. Consider the following case where the data generating process is represented as

$$\mathbf{y}_1 = \mathbf{x}_1\boldsymbol{\delta}_1 + \mathbf{x}_1^*\boldsymbol{\delta}_1^* + \mathbf{u}_1,$$

and the following model is estimated:

$$\mathbf{y}_1 = \mathbf{x}_1\boldsymbol{\delta}_1 + \mathbf{v}_1.$$

The GIVE-TSLS estimator of $\boldsymbol{\delta}_1$ is:

$$\begin{aligned}\widehat{\boldsymbol{\delta}}_1 &= \left(\mathbf{x}_1'\mathbf{z}\,(\mathbf{z}'\mathbf{z})^{-1}\,\mathbf{z}'\mathbf{x}_1\right)^{-1}\mathbf{x}_1'\mathbf{z}\,(\mathbf{z}'\mathbf{z})^{-1}\,\mathbf{z}'\mathbf{y}_1 \\ &= \boldsymbol{\delta}_1 + \left(\mathbf{x}_1'\mathbf{z}\,(\mathbf{z}'\mathbf{z})^{-1}\,\mathbf{z}'\mathbf{x}_1\right)^{-1}\mathbf{x}_1'\mathbf{z}\,(\mathbf{z}'\mathbf{z})^{-1}\,\mathbf{z}'\,(\mathbf{x}_1^*\boldsymbol{\delta}_1^* + \mathbf{u}_1),\end{aligned}$$

which is not consistent whenever $\mathbf{x}_1^*$ is correlated with $\mathbf{z}$. In this case:

$$p\ \lim \frac{1}{T}\mathbf{z}'\mathbf{v}_1 \neq 0,$$

and the instruments in $\mathbf{z}$ cannot be considered as valid.

Sargan (1988) derived a statistic to test the null hypothesis of validity of instruments by showing that the quantity:

$$C = \frac{\widehat{\mathbf{u}}_1'\mathbf{z}\,(\mathbf{z}'\mathbf{z})^{-1}\,\mathbf{z}'\widehat{\mathbf{u}}_1}{s_1^2} = \frac{1}{T}\frac{\widehat{\mathbf{u}}_1'\mathbf{z}\,(\mathbf{z}'\mathbf{z})^{-1}\,\mathbf{z}'\widehat{\mathbf{u}}_1}{\left(\mathbf{y}_1 - \mathbf{x}_1\widehat{\boldsymbol{\delta}}_1\right)'\left(\mathbf{y}_1 - \mathbf{x}_1\widehat{\boldsymbol{\delta}}_1\right)},$$

is distributed as a $\chi^2$ with $M - K_1$ degrees of freedom under the null hypothesis of validity of instruments.

### 4.2.4 *Three-stage least squares (3SLS) and seemingly unrelated regressions estimators (SURE)*

The estimators we have considered so far solve the problems generated by simultaneity without reverting to the specification of the full structural model. For this reason GIVE-TSLS estimators are known as limited information estimators. To analyse full-information estimators, we need to introduce some new definitions.

For any two matrices $\mathbf{A}\,(m \times n)$ and $\mathbf{B}\,(p \times q)$, define as the Kronecker product, $\mathbf{A} \otimes \mathbf{B}$, the matrix $(mp \times nq)$ obtained by multiplying each element of $\mathbf{A}$ by $\mathbf{B}$. The following properties are related to the Kronecker product:

- $(\mathbf{A} \otimes \mathbf{B})(\mathbf{C} \otimes \mathbf{D}) = \mathbf{AC} \otimes \mathbf{BD}$, whenever the matrices $\mathbf{AC}$ and $\mathbf{BD}$ are defined;
- $(\mathbf{A} \otimes \mathbf{B})' = \mathbf{A}' \otimes \mathbf{B}'$;
- $(\mathbf{A} \otimes \mathbf{B})^{-1} = \mathbf{A}^{-1} \otimes \mathbf{B}^{-1}$, whenever the matrices $\mathbf{A}^{-1}$ and $\mathbf{B}^{-1}$ are defined.

Define vec$(\mathbf{A})$, the vectorization of $\mathbf{A}$, as the vector $(mn \times 1)$ obtained by stacking the $m$ transposed rows of $\mathbf{A}$:

$$\underset{(m\times n)}{\mathbf{A}} = \begin{pmatrix} a_{11} & \cdot\ \cdot & a_{1n} \\ \cdot & \cdot\ \cdot & \cdot \\ \cdot & \cdot\ \cdot & \cdot \\ a_{n1} & \cdot\ \cdot & a_{nn} \end{pmatrix},$$

$$vec\,(\mathbf{A}) = \begin{pmatrix} a_{11} \\ \cdot \\ \cdot \\ a_{1n} \\ a_{21} \\ \cdot \\ \cdot \\ a_{2n} \\ \cdot \\ \cdot \\ \cdot \\ a_{nn} \end{pmatrix}.$$

The vectorization and Kronecker product are linked by the following property:

$$vec\,(\mathbf{ABC}) = (\mathbf{A} \otimes \mathbf{C})'\,vec\,(\mathbf{B}).$$

To discuss the full-information estimation, consider that the $i$-th equations of our model can be represented as

$$\mathbf{y}_i = \mathbf{x}_i \boldsymbol{\delta}_i + \mathbf{u}_i,$$

where $\mathbf{y}_i$ is a $(T \times 1)$ vector containing $T$ observations on $i$-th endogenous variables, $\mathbf{x}_i$ is a $(T \times K_i)$ matrix, with $K_i = (G_i + M_i - 1)$ containing all the observations on the $G_i - 1$ endogenous and on the $M_i$ exogenous variables included in the $i$-th equation. We can give the following compact representation of the model:

$$\mathbf{y}^+ = \mathbf{x}^+\boldsymbol{\delta}^+ + \mathbf{u}^+, \tag{4.21}$$

where $\mathbf{y}^+$ is a $(GT \times 1)$ vector, $\mathbf{x}^+$ is a $\left(GT \times \sum_{i=1}^{G} K_i\right)$ matrix, $\boldsymbol{\delta}^+$ is a $\left(\sum_{i=1}^{G} K_i \times 1\right)$, $\mathbf{u}^+$ is a $(GT \times 1)$ vector:

$$\mathbf{y}^+ = \begin{pmatrix} \mathbf{y}_1 \\ \cdot \\ \cdot \\ \mathbf{y}_G \end{pmatrix}, \quad \mathbf{x}^+ = \begin{pmatrix} \mathbf{x}_1 & 0 & 0. & 0 \\ 0 & \mathbf{x}_2 & \cdot & \cdot \\ 0 & \cdot & \cdot & \cdot \\ 0 & \cdot & \cdot & \mathbf{x}_G \end{pmatrix},$$

$$\boldsymbol{\delta}^+ = \begin{pmatrix} \boldsymbol{\delta}_1 \\ \cdot \\ \cdot \\ \boldsymbol{\delta}_G \end{pmatrix}, \quad \mathbf{u}^+ = \begin{pmatrix} \mathbf{u}_1 \\ \cdot \\ \cdot \\ \mathbf{u}_G \end{pmatrix}.$$

The following properties hold for $\mathbf{u}^+$ :

$$E\left(\mathbf{u}^+\right) = 0,$$

$$E\left(\mathbf{u}^+\mathbf{u}^{+\prime}\right) = \begin{pmatrix} E\left(\mathbf{u}_1\mathbf{u}_1'\right) & E\left(\mathbf{u}_1\mathbf{u}_2'\right) & \cdot\,\cdot & E\left(\mathbf{u}_1\mathbf{u}_G'\right) \\ E\left(\mathbf{u}_2\mathbf{u}_1'\right) & E\left(\mathbf{u}_2\mathbf{u}_2'\right) & \cdot\,\cdot & \cdot \\ \cdot & \cdot & \cdot\,\cdot & \cdot \\ \cdot & \cdot & \cdot\,\cdot & \cdot \\ E\left(\mathbf{u}_G\mathbf{u}_1'\right) & \cdot & \cdot\,\cdot & E\left(\mathbf{u}_G\mathbf{u}_G'\right) \end{pmatrix},$$

where each block of the above matrix is $(T \times T)$.

Assuming that all residuals are contemporaneously but not serially correlated, with non-singular variance-covariance matrix $\Sigma$,[1] we have:

$$\begin{aligned} E\left(\mathbf{u}^+\mathbf{u}^{+\prime}\right) &= \Sigma \otimes I_T \\ &= \begin{pmatrix} \sigma_{11}I_T & \sigma_{12}I_T & \cdot\,\cdot & \sigma_{1G}I_T \\ \sigma_{21}I_T & \sigma_{22}I_T & \cdot\,\cdot & \cdot \\ \cdot & \cdot & \cdot\,\cdot & \cdot \\ \cdot & \cdot & \cdot\,\cdot & \cdot \\ \sigma_{G1}I_T & \cdot & \cdot\,\cdot & \sigma_{GG}I_T \end{pmatrix}. \end{aligned}$$

The problem to solve is the estimation of parameters in (4.21), taking into account simultaneity and the structure of correlations in $\Sigma$. These problems are solved in turn by the three-stage least squares (3SLS) estimator.

[1]The last assumption requires that all identities are excluded from the model.

4.2.4.1 *First stage: the diagonalization of* $\Sigma$. Consider the following decomposition for $\Sigma^{-1}$:

$$\Sigma^{-1} = \mathbf{HH}', \tag{4.22}$$

which always exists. From (4.22) we have:

$$\mathbf{H}\Sigma\mathbf{H}' = I_G.$$

By pre-multiplying (4.21) by $\mathbf{H}' \otimes I_T$, we obtain:

$$(\mathbf{H}' \otimes I_T)\,\mathbf{y}^+ = (\mathbf{H}' \otimes I_T)\,\mathbf{x}^+\boldsymbol{\delta}^+ + (\mathbf{H}' \otimes I_T)\,\mathbf{u}^+, \tag{4.23}$$

where residuals of (4.23) feature a diagonal variance-covariance matrix

$$\begin{aligned} E\left((\mathbf{H}' \otimes I_T)\,\mathbf{u}^+\mathbf{u}^{+\prime}\,(\mathbf{H}' \otimes I_T)'\right) &= (\mathbf{H}' \otimes I_T)\,(\Sigma \otimes I_T)\,(\mathbf{H}' \otimes I_T)' \\ &= (\mathbf{H}'\Sigma \otimes I_T)\,(\mathbf{H} \otimes I_T) \\ &= I_G \otimes I_T = I_{GT}. \end{aligned}$$

The completion of the first stage has left us with the following transformed model:

$$(\mathbf{H}' \otimes I_T)\,\mathbf{y}^+ = (\mathbf{H}' \otimes I_T)\,\mathbf{x}^+\boldsymbol{\delta}^+ + (\mathbf{H}' \otimes I_T)\,\mathbf{u}^+, \tag{4.24}$$

$$\mathbf{y}^* = \mathbf{x}^*\boldsymbol{\delta}^* + \mathbf{u}^*, \tag{4.25}$$

$$E\,(\mathbf{u}^*) = 0,\ E\,(\mathbf{u}^*\mathbf{u}^{*\prime}) = I_{GT}, \tag{4.26}$$

in which the variance-covariance matrix is diagonal, however, we still have simultaneity:

$$p\ \lim \frac{1}{T}\mathbf{x}^{*\prime}\mathbf{u}^* \neq 0.$$

4.2.4.2 *Second stage: choice of instruments.* To select instruments, remember that the reduced form of our original system can be represented as follows:

$$\mathbf{y}' = \mathbf{B}^{-1}\Gamma\mathbf{z}' + \mathbf{B}^{-1}\mathbf{u}'. \tag{4.27}$$

The vectorization of (4.27) delivers:

$$vec\,(\mathbf{y}') = vec\left(\mathbf{B}^{-1}\Gamma\mathbf{z}'\right) + vec\left(\mathbf{B}^{-1}\mathbf{u}'\right), \tag{4.28}$$

from which:

$$\begin{aligned} \mathbf{y}^+ &= vec\left(I_G\mathbf{B}^{-1}\Gamma\mathbf{z}'\right) + vec\left(\mathbf{B}^{-1}\mathbf{u}'\right) \\ &= (I_G \otimes \mathbf{z})\,vec\left(\mathbf{B}^{-1}\Gamma\mathbf{z}'\right) + vec\left(\mathbf{B}^{-1}\mathbf{u}'\right). \end{aligned} \tag{4.29}$$

Thus, the natural choice of instruments is $(I_G \otimes \mathbf{z})$.

4.2.4.3 *Third stage: applying the GIVE principle.* By applying the GIVE principle to (4.25), and choosing $\mathbf{z}^* = (I_G \otimes \mathbf{z})$ as instruments, we have:

$$\widehat{\boldsymbol{\delta}}_1^+ = \left(\mathbf{x}^{*\prime}\mathbf{z}^* \left(\mathbf{z}^{*\prime}\mathbf{z}^*\right)^{-1} \mathbf{z}^{*\prime}\mathbf{x}^*\right)^{-1} \mathbf{x}^{*\prime}\mathbf{z}^* \left(\mathbf{z}^{*\prime}\mathbf{z}^*\right)^{-1} \mathbf{z}^{*\prime}\mathbf{y}^*.$$

Remembering that

$$\begin{aligned}
\mathbf{x}^{*\prime}\mathbf{z}^* &= \mathbf{x}^{+\prime} (\mathbf{H} \otimes I_T) (I_G \otimes \mathbf{z}), \\
\mathbf{z}^{*\prime}\mathbf{z}^* &= (I_G \otimes \mathbf{z}') (I_G \otimes \mathbf{z}) = I_G \otimes \mathbf{z}'\mathbf{z}, \\
\mathbf{z}^{*\prime}\mathbf{y}^* &= (I_G \otimes \mathbf{z}') (\mathbf{H} \otimes I_T) \mathbf{y}^+ = (\mathbf{H}' \otimes \mathbf{z}') \mathbf{y}^+,
\end{aligned}$$

we can show the following results:

$$\begin{aligned}
\left(\mathbf{x}^{*\prime}\mathbf{z}^* \left(\mathbf{z}^{*\prime}\mathbf{z}^*\right)^{-1} \mathbf{z}^{*\prime}\mathbf{x}^*\right) &= \mathbf{x}^{+\prime} (\mathbf{H} \otimes \mathbf{z}) (I_G \otimes \mathbf{z}'\mathbf{z})^{-1} (\mathbf{H}' \otimes \mathbf{z}') \mathbf{x}^+ \\
&= \mathbf{x}^{+\prime} \left(\Sigma^{-1} \otimes \mathbf{z} (\mathbf{z}'\mathbf{z})^{-1} \mathbf{z}'\right) \mathbf{x}^+, \\
\left(\mathbf{x}^{*\prime}\mathbf{z}^* \left(\mathbf{z}^{*\prime}\mathbf{z}^*\right)^{-1} \mathbf{z}^{*\prime}\mathbf{y}^*\right) &= \mathbf{x}^{+\prime} (\mathbf{H} \otimes \mathbf{z}) (I_G \otimes \mathbf{z}'\mathbf{z})^{-1} (\mathbf{H}' \otimes \mathbf{z}') \mathbf{y}^+ \\
&= \mathbf{x}^{+\prime} \left(\Sigma^{-1} \otimes \mathbf{z} (\mathbf{z}'\mathbf{z})^{-1} \mathbf{z}'\right) \mathbf{y}^+ 1
\end{aligned}$$

and, finally, we have an expression for the 3SLS estimator

$$\widehat{\boldsymbol{\delta}}_1^+ = \left(\mathbf{x}^{+\prime} \left(\Sigma^{-1} \otimes \mathbf{z} (\mathbf{z}'\mathbf{z})^{-1} \mathbf{z}'\right) \mathbf{x}^+\right)^{-1} \mathbf{x}^{+\prime} \left(\Sigma^{-1} \otimes \mathbf{z} (\mathbf{z}'\mathbf{z})^{-1} \mathbf{z}'\right) \mathbf{y}^+.$$

The asymptotic distribution of the 3SLS can be written as:

$$\widehat{\boldsymbol{\delta}}_1^+ \sim N\left(\boldsymbol{\delta}^+, \left(\mathbf{x}^{+\prime} \left(\Sigma^{-1} \otimes \mathbf{z} (\mathbf{z}'\mathbf{z})^{-1} \mathbf{z}'\right) \mathbf{x}^+\right)^{-1}\right).$$

To make the estimator operational, we need an estimate of $\Sigma$. This can be obtained by using the sample correlations of the residuals from TSLS estimation.

To analyse the estimator more closely, we can re-write it in a more extensive format:

$$\mathbf{x}^{+\prime} \left(\Sigma^{-1} \otimes \mathbf{z} (\mathbf{z}'\mathbf{z})^{-1} \mathbf{z}'\right) \mathbf{x}^+ =$$

$$\begin{pmatrix} \mathbf{x}_1' & 0 & 0 & 0 \\ 0 & \mathbf{x}_2' & . & . \\ 0 & . & . & . \\ 0 & . & . & \mathbf{x}_G' \end{pmatrix} \begin{pmatrix} \sigma_{11}\mathbf{z} (\mathbf{z}'\mathbf{z})^{-1} \mathbf{z}' & .. & \sigma_{11}\mathbf{z} (\mathbf{z}'\mathbf{z})^{-1} \mathbf{z}' \\ . & .. & . \\ . & .. & . \\ \sigma_{G1}\mathbf{z} (\mathbf{z}'\mathbf{z})^{-1} \mathbf{z}' & .. & \sigma_{GG}\mathbf{z} (\mathbf{z}'\mathbf{z})^{-1} \mathbf{z}' \end{pmatrix} \begin{pmatrix} \mathbf{x}_1 & 0 & 0 & 0 \\ 0 & \mathbf{x}_2 & . & . \\ 0 & . & . & . \\ 0 & . & . & \mathbf{x}_G \end{pmatrix},$$

$$\mathbf{x}^{+\prime}\left(\Sigma^{-1}\otimes\mathbf{z}\left(\mathbf{z}'\mathbf{z}\right)^{-1}\mathbf{z}'\right)\mathbf{y}^{+}=\begin{pmatrix}\sum_{j=1}^{G}\sigma_{1j}\mathbf{x}_1'\mathbf{z}\left(\mathbf{z}'\mathbf{z}\right)^{-1}\mathbf{z}'\mathbf{y}_j\\ \vdots\\ \sum_{j=1}^{G}\sigma_{Gj}\mathbf{x}_G'\mathbf{z}\left(\mathbf{z}'\mathbf{z}\right)^{-1}\mathbf{z}'\mathbf{y}_j\end{pmatrix},$$

where $\sigma_{ij}$ represents the generic element $i$, $j$ of the matrix $\Sigma^{-1}$.

Let us consider some specific cases of the 3SLS estimator. Note first that the 3SLS estimator coincides with the TSLS when the matrix $\Sigma$ is diagonal. In this case, we have:

$$\begin{aligned}\widehat{\boldsymbol{\delta}}^{+}&=\left(\mathbf{x}^{+\prime}\left(\Sigma^{-1}\otimes\mathbf{z}\left(\mathbf{z}'\mathbf{z}\right)^{-1}\mathbf{z}'\right)\mathbf{x}^{+}\right)^{-1}\mathbf{x}^{+\prime}\left(\Sigma^{-1}\otimes\mathbf{z}\left(\mathbf{z}'\mathbf{z}\right)^{-1}\mathbf{z}'\right)\mathbf{y}^{+}\\&=\begin{pmatrix}\left(\mathbf{x}_1'\mathbf{z}\left(\mathbf{z}'\mathbf{z}\right)^{-1}\mathbf{z}'\mathbf{x}_1\right)^{-1}\mathbf{x}_1'\mathbf{z}\left(\mathbf{z}'\mathbf{z}\right)^{-1}\mathbf{z}'\mathbf{y}_1\\ \vdots\\ \left(\mathbf{x}_G'\mathbf{z}\left(\mathbf{z}'\mathbf{z}\right)^{-1}\mathbf{z}'\mathbf{x}_G\right)^{-1}\mathbf{x}_G'\mathbf{z}\left(\mathbf{z}'\mathbf{z}\right)^{-1}\mathbf{z}'\mathbf{y}_G\end{pmatrix}.\end{aligned}$$

This equivalence result holds also when all the equations in the system are exactly identified.

Another interesting case arises when the matrix $\mathbf{B}$ in our structural model (4.7) is diagonal:

$$\mathbf{y}^{+}=\mathbf{x}^{+}\boldsymbol{\delta}^{+}+\mathbf{u}^{+}, \tag{4.30}$$

$$E\left(\mathbf{u}^{+}\right)=0, \tag{4.31}$$

$$E\left(\mathbf{u}^{+}\mathbf{u}^{+\prime}\right)=\Sigma\otimes I_T, \tag{4.32}$$

$$p\lim\frac{1}{T}\mathbf{x}^{+\prime}\mathbf{u}^{+}=0. \tag{4.33}$$

The particular structure of $\mathbf{B}$ implies that all the simultaneity in the system comes from the correlation of residuals; therefore, after the implementation of the first stage of the 3SLS, the diagonalization of the variance-covariance matrix, a consistent estimator is derived by applying the OLS to the transformed model. The relevant estimator is then:

$$\begin{aligned}\widehat{\boldsymbol{\delta}}^{+}&=\left(\mathbf{x}^{*\prime}\mathbf{x}^{*}\right)^{-1}\mathbf{x}^{*\prime}\mathbf{y}^{*}\\&\left(\mathbf{x}^{+\prime}\left(\Sigma^{-1}\otimes\mathbf{I}_T\right)\mathbf{x}^{+}\right)^{-1}\mathbf{x}^{+\prime}\left(\Sigma^{-1}\otimes\mathbf{I}_T\right)\mathbf{y}^{+},\end{aligned}$$

which is known as the seemingly unrelated regression equations (SURE) or Zellner's estimator.

A further interesting specific case of the SURE estimator is obtained when each equation of the system contains the same set of regressors:

$$\mathbf{x}^{+}=\begin{pmatrix}\mathbf{x}_1 & 0 & 0. & 0\\ 0 & \mathbf{x}_2 & . & .\\ 0 & . & . & .\\ 0 & . & . & \mathbf{x}_G\end{pmatrix}$$

$$=\begin{pmatrix}\mathbf{x} & 0 & 0. & 0\\ 0 & \mathbf{x} & . & .\\ 0 & . & . & .\\ 0 & . & . & \mathbf{x}\end{pmatrix}=I\otimes\mathbf{x}.$$

By substituting for $\mathbf{x}^{+}$ in the expression for the Zellner estimator, we obtain:

$$\begin{aligned}\widehat{\delta}_1^{+}&=\left((I\otimes\mathbf{x})'\left(\Sigma^{-1}\otimes\mathbf{I}_T\right)(I\otimes\mathbf{x})\right)^{-1}(I\otimes\mathbf{x})'\left(\Sigma^{-1}\otimes\mathbf{I}_T\right)\mathbf{y}^{+}\\&=\left(I\Sigma^{-1}I\otimes\mathbf{x}'I_T\mathbf{x}\right)^{-1}\left(I\Sigma^{-1}\otimes\mathbf{x}'\mathbf{I}_T\right)\mathbf{y}^{+}\\&=\left(\Sigma\otimes(\mathbf{x}'\mathbf{x})^{-1}\right)\left(\Sigma^{-1}\otimes\mathbf{x}'\right)\mathbf{y}^{+}\\&=\left(I_G\otimes(\mathbf{x}'\mathbf{x})^{-1}\mathbf{x}'\right)\mathbf{y}^{+},\end{aligned}$$

which gives a compact representation of the OLS estimators applied equation by equation.

### 4.2.5 *FIML estimator*

Lastly, we give a brief description of the most general full-information estimator: the full information maximum likelihood (FIML) estimator. Considering the reduced form of our model (4.11) and taking logarithms, we can write the joint distribution of $\mathbf{y}_1,\dots,\mathbf{y}_T$, as follows:

$$\begin{aligned}\log L=&\frac{-GT}{2}\log(2\pi)-\frac{T}{2}\log\left|\mathbf{B}^{-1}\Sigma\mathbf{B}'^{-1}\right|\\&-\frac{1}{2}\sum_{t=1}^{T}\left(\mathbf{y}_t-\mathbf{B}^{-1}\Gamma\mathbf{x}_t\right)'\mathbf{B}'\Sigma^{-1}\mathbf{B}\left(\mathbf{y}_t-\mathbf{B}^{-1}\Gamma\mathbf{x}_t\right).\end{aligned}\tag{4.34}$$

Note that

$$\left(\mathbf{y}_t-\mathbf{B}^{-1}\Gamma\mathbf{x}_t\right)'\mathbf{B}'=\left(\mathbf{B}\mathbf{y}_t-\Gamma\mathbf{x}_t\right)',$$

and that from a standard result on determinants:

$$-\frac{T}{2}\log\left|\mathbf{B}^{-1}\Sigma\mathbf{B}'^{-1}\right|=T\left|\log\mathbf{B}\right|-\frac{T}{2}\log|\Sigma|.$$

Thus, we can re-write our log-likelihood function as:

$$\begin{aligned}\log L=&\frac{-GT}{2}\log(2\pi)+T\left|\log\mathbf{B}\right|-\frac{T}{2}\log|\Sigma|\\&-\frac{1}{2}\sum_{t=1}^{T}\left(\mathbf{B}\mathbf{y}_t-\Gamma\mathbf{x}_t\right)'\Sigma^{-1}\left(\mathbf{B}\mathbf{y}_t-\Gamma\mathbf{x}_t\right).\end{aligned}\tag{4.35}$$

The FIML estimator is derived by maximizing (4.35) with respect to $\mathbf{B}$, $\Gamma$, and $\Sigma$. A number of technical issues arise, since the problem is non-linear; for a good discussion of these problems and solutions, see Hendry (1996). The FIML is the most general system estimator, since all the others can be derived as its special cases; for a detailed derivation see Hendry (1976).

## 4.3 Simulation

Having identified the model and estimated the parameters of interest, we proceed to the simulation. For given values of the parameters and the exogenous variables, we recover values for the endogenous variables by finding the dynamic solution of the model. To illustrate how this result is accomplished, consider the following general representation of a model including $n$ endogenous variables $\mathbf{y} = (y_1, y_2, ..., y_n)$ and $k$ exogenous variables $\mathbf{x} = (x_1, x_2, ..., x_k)$:

$$\begin{aligned}
y_{1t} &= f_1\left(y_{1t}, ..., y_{nt}, A_1(L)\mathbf{y}_{t-1}, \mathbf{x}_t, B_1(L)\mathbf{x}_{t-1}\right), \\
y_{2t} &= f_2\left(y_{1t}, ..., y_{nt}, A_2(L)\mathbf{y}_{t-1}, \mathbf{x}_t, B_2(L)\mathbf{x}_{t-1}\right), \\
&\vdots \\
y_{kt} &= f_k\left(y_{1t}, ..., y_{nt}, A_k(L)\mathbf{y}_{t-1}, \mathbf{x}_t, B_k(L)\mathbf{x}_{t-1}\right), \\
&\vdots \\
y_{nt} &= f_n\left(y_{1t}, ..., y_{nt}, A_n(L)\mathbf{y}_{t-1}, \mathbf{x}_t, B_n(L)\mathbf{x}_{t-1}\right).
\end{aligned}$$

In the specifications discussed so far the functions $f_i$ are linear, however, a more general specification can fit within this framework.

Solving the model amounts to finding a fixed point, such that

$$\mathbf{y}_t = f\left(\mathbf{y}_t, \mathbf{A}(L)\mathbf{y}_{t-1}, \mathbf{x}_t, \mathbf{B}(L)\mathbf{x}_{t-1}\right).$$

A popular numerical method, implemented in numerous packages, for example E-Views, is the Gauss–Seidel method. The Gauss–Seidel method finds the fixed point by iteration using the updating rule:

$$\mathbf{y}_t^{i+1} = f\left(\mathbf{y}_t^i, \mathbf{A}(L)\mathbf{y}_{t-1}^{i+1}, \mathbf{x}_t, \mathbf{B}(L)\mathbf{x}_{t-1}\right).$$

The method solves the equations in the order that they appear in the model. So, if an endogenous variable that has already been solved appears later in some other equation, Gauss–Seidel uses the value as solved in that iteration. To illustrate this, the $k$-th variable in the $i$-th iteration is solved by

$$y_{kt}^i = f_k\left(y_{1t}^i, ..., y_{k-1t}^i, y_{kt}^i, y_{k+1t}^{i-1}, ..., y_{nt}^{i-1}, A_k(L)\mathbf{y}_{t-1}, \mathbf{x}_t, B_k(L)\mathbf{x}_{t-1}\right).$$

As a consequence, the ordering of the variables matters and equations with relatively few right-hand side endogenous variables should be listed early in the model. As the model is solved by setting disturbances to zero, we have a deterministic solution, and a stochastic solution is easily generated, solving the model by adding drawings from random variables and taking expected values afterwards.

## 4.4 Policy evaluation

Dynamic simulation is used to evaluate the effect of different policies, defined by specifying different patterns for the exogenous variables. Policy evaluation is implemented by examining how the predicted values of the endogenous variables change after some exogenous variables are modified. This implies simulating the model twice. First, a baseline, *control*, simulation is run. Such simulation can be run within the sample, in which case observed data are available for the exogenous variables, or outside the available sample, and values are assigned to the exogenous variables. In the case of out-of-sample simulation, which is equivalent to forecasting the endogenous variables for a given scenario for the exogenous variables, it is useful to assign values to the exogenous variables such that the baseline simulation path exhibits standard historical patterns for the endogenous variables. The results of such baseline simulation are then compared with those obtained from an alternative, *disturbed*, simulation, based on the modification of the relevant exogenous variables. Policy evaluation is usually based on *dynamic multipliers*.

Consider the case of the simulation of a model over a sample of size $T$, and index the generic observation in that sample by $t$. Denote the series of values attributed to the exogenous variable $x$ in the baseline simulation by $x_t^b$, and the series of alternative values attributed to the same variables in the disturbed simulation by $x_t^d = x_t^b + \delta$. Similarly, denote the solved value for the endogenous variable $y_n$ at time $t$ in the baseline simulation by $y_{nt}^b$ and the solved value for the endogenous variable $y_n$ at time $t$ in the disturbed simulation by $y_{nt}^d$.

The dynamic multiplier is defined as:

$$DM_t = \frac{\left(y_{nt}^d - y_{nt}^b\right)}{\left(x_t^d - x_t^b\right)} = \frac{\left(y_{nt}^d - y_{nt}^b\right)}{\delta}. \tag{4.36}$$

When the model is stable, long-run multipliers, obtained for large $t$, converge to fixed numbers. Note that in linear systems long-run multipliers are also obtained by giving a temporary (one period) impulse to the exogenous variable and then computing the cumulative response of the endogenous variables.

For illustration, assume that the estimation of a given sample, say 1960:1-1998:2, of a simple dynamic model for consumption and income, has delivered the following results, similar to those obtained in the dynamic model of US consumption discussed in Chapter 2:

$$\Delta c_t = 0.25 * \Delta y_t - 0.15 * (c_{t-1} - y_{t-1}),$$
$$\Delta y_t = 0.008.$$

Given the results of the estimation of the model over the sample 1960:1–1998:2, we aim at deriving the dynamic multiplier, describing the response of consumption to a 1% increase in income by simulating the model over the period 1998:2–2020:4.

The following E-Views program (run after having opened the file usuk.wf1) achieves the result:

```
SMPL 1998:4 1998:4
LCUS= 8.55
LYUS=8.55
SMPL 1999:1 2020:4
model consinc
consinc.append LCUS =LCUS(-1)-0.15*LCUS(-1)+0.15*LYUS(-1)
 +0.250*(LYUS-LYUS(-1))
consinc.append LYUS =0.008 +LYUS(-1)
COPY CONSINC M_TEMP
M_TEMP.APPEND ASSIGN @ALL _BL
M_TEMP.SOLVE
delete M_TEMP
SMPL 1999:1 2020:4
genr dum991=0
smpl 1999:1 1999:1
dum991=1
smpl 1999:1 2020:4
model consinc1
consinc1.append LCUS =LCUS(-1)-0.15*LCUS(-1)+0.15*LYUS(-1)
+0.250*(LYUS-LYUS(-1))
consinc1.append LYUS =0.008 +LYUS(-1)+0.01*dum991
COPY CONSINC1 M_TEMP
M_TEMP.APPEND ASSIGN @ALL _DS
M_TEMP.SOLVE
delete M_TEMP
SMPL 1999:1 2020:4
genr DM=100*(LCUS_DS-LCUS_BL)
plot DM
```

The program begins by setting consumption at its long-run solution. Then the relevant model is constructed by defining it as `consinc` and including the specification for the two equations. The model `consinc` is then copied into a temporary model, `m_temp`, which is solved dynamically for the sample 1998:2–2020:4, and the suffix `_BL` (for 'baseline') is attributed to the variables generated by the solution. In the following step the disturbed solution is generated by adding a 1% shock for one period (1998:1) to LYUS. Note that as LYUS has a unit root, the one-period shock has a permanent effect. The disturbed solution is then computed and the suffix `_DS` is attached to the generated variables. Lastly, the dynamic multiplier is computed by applying formula (4.36); we report it in Figure 4.1:

Having illustrated the basics with this simple case, we move to discussing a more articulate Cowles Commission model of the monetary transmission mech-

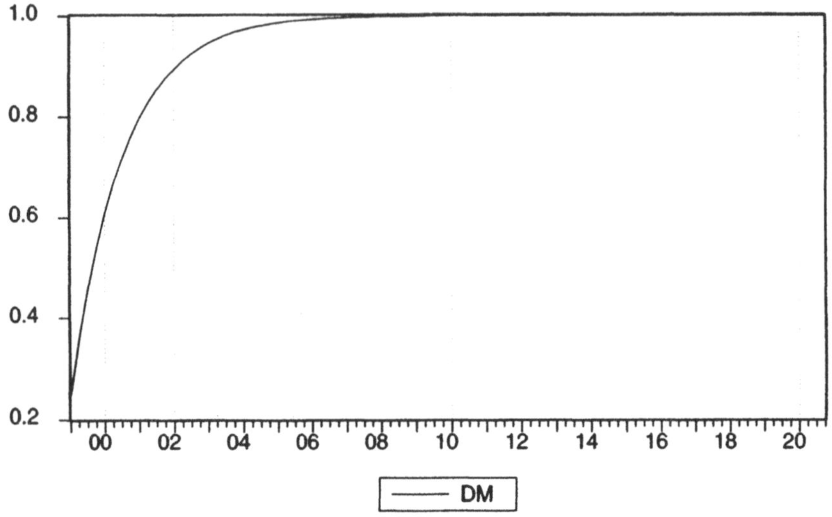


FIG. 4.1. Dynamic multiplier

anism by taking all the steps, from specification to simulation.

## 4.5 A model of the monetary transmission mechanism

### 4.5.1 *Specification of the theoretical model*

We consider the closed-economy IS-LM specification with autoregressive expectations:

$$y_t = c_{0,11} + y_t^* - a_{13}(R_t - \pi_t^e) + \epsilon_{1t}, \tag{4.37}$$
$$\pi_t = \pi_t^e + a_{21}(y_t - y_t^*) + \epsilon_{2t}, \tag{4.38}$$
$$m_t - p_t = c_{0,31} + a_{31} y_t - a_{33} R_t + \epsilon_{3t}, \tag{4.39}$$
$$\pi_t^e = \beta \pi_{t-1} + (1 - \beta)\pi_t + \epsilon_{4t}, \tag{4.40}$$
$$m_t = c_{0,41} + m_{t-1}, \tag{4.41}$$
$$y_t^* = c_{0,51} + c_{0,52} t + \epsilon_{5t}. \tag{4.42}$$

Note that money supply is not stochastic, as it is considered as fully controlled by the monetary authority. The econometrician's task is the estimation of the unknown parameters to simulate the impact of a different path for the exogenous variable controlled by the monetary authority. The model uses four equations to determine four endogenous variables, $\pi_t, \pi_t^e, R_t$, and $y_t$, for given values of the two exogenous variables, $y_t^*$ and $m_t$. The exogeneity status is attributed to $y_t^*$ and $m_t$, either because they describe the available technology and demography or because they are fully controlled by the policy-maker. Note that under the hypothesis of dynamic stability of the estimated model, the estimated values for the parameters determine only the short-run dynamics of output and inflation, since the long-run equilibrium solutions are determined almost independently (totally independently in the case $a_{31} = 1$) from the estimated parameters ($\pi = \Delta m - a_{31}\Delta y^*$, $y = y^*$).

### 4.5.2 *Estimation of the parameters of interest*

We consider a monthly dataset for the US economy (which we assume a relatively closed economy) to construct, estimate, and simulate a version of the macroeconomic model. The dataset, available in Excel format as lszusa.xls, contains the following variables[2] for the sample 1959:7–1996:3:

CPISA: Consumer price index adjusted for seasonality;

M1SA: M1 stock adjusted for seasonality;

M2SA: M2 stock adjusted for seasonality;

PCM: IMF index of commodity price in dollars;

RGDP: real US GDP at quarterly frequencies;

RGDPMON: real US GDP at quarterly frequencies (quarterly data interpolated by Chow-Lin(1971) procedure);

TBILL3: annually compounded nominal return on three-month TBills;

TBOND10: annually compounded redemption yield on 10-year TBonds.

Having imported the data from the Excel format into E-Views the following transformations are performed using the program lsz.prg:

```
genr lp=100*log(cpisa)
genr ly=100*log(rgdpmon)
genr infl=(lp-lp(-12))
genr rr=tbill3-infl(-1)
genr lm1=100*log(m1sa)
genr lm2=100*log(m2sa)
genr d12lm2=(lm2-lm2(-12))
genr d12lm1=(lm1-lm1(-12))
genr lyst=773.27+0.275*@TREND(1959:1)
genr vel=lp+ly-lm2
```

We initially deal with non-observable variables and we solve the problem of expected inflation by setting (arbitrarily) $\beta = 1$ in equation (4.40)and substituting lagged inflation for the expected. Then, we obtain an observable proxy for potential output fitting a simple deterministic trend for output.

[2]For a complete description of the dataset see Leeper, Sims, and Zha (1997).

TABLE 4.1. LYST=C(1)+C(2)*@TREND(1959:1)

| Coefficient | Estimate | Std. Error | t-Statistic | Prob. |
|---|---|---|---|---|
| C(1) | 773.2748 | 0.466437 | 1657.833 | 0.0000 |
| C(2) | 0.274909 | 0.002476 | 111.0279 | 0.0000 |

| | |
|---|---|
| $R^2$ 0.975006 | Mean dependent var 818.4973 |
| Adjusted $R^2$ 0.974927 | S.D. dependent var 25.59787 |
| S.E. of regression 4.053267 | Akaike info criterion 2.805316 |
| Sum squared resid 5191.555 | Schwarz criterion 2.828976 |
| Log likelihood -895.2677 | $F-$statistic 12327.19 |
| Durbin−Watson stat 0.018264 | Prob($F-$statistic) 0.000000 |

Note that from the estimated parameter values, we find that potential ouptut grows at annual rate of $(1 + 0.0027)^{12} - 1 = 0.0329\%$.

We proceed now to the estimation of all the structural relations included in the model. We begin with the money demand, which we simplify to a linear relation between the logarithm of velocity of circulation of money[3] and the short-term interest rate, which we take as a proxy of the opportunity cost of holding money.

TABLE 4.2. VEL =C(1)+C(2)*TBILL3

| Coefficient | Estimate | Std. Error | t-Statistic | Prob. |
|---|---|---|---|---|
| C(1) | 527.9095 | 0.431272 | 1224.075 | 0.0000 |
| C(2) | 1.781791 | 0.061783 | 28.83933 | 0.0000 |

| | |
|---|---|
| $R^2$ 0.724668 | Mean dependent var 539.0975 |
| Adjusted $R^2$ 0.723797 | S.D. dependent var 6.392876 |
| S.E. of regression 3.359777 | Akaike info criterion 2.430019 |
| Sum squared resid 3567.040 | Schwarz criterion 2.453679 |
| Log likelihood -835.5954 | $F$-statistic 831.7067 |
| Durbin−Watson stat 0.117228 | Prob($F$-statistic) 0.000000 |

Note that the semi-elasticity of the velocity circulation with respect to interest rate is 1.78, implying that an increase of 100 basis points in short-term rates is paired with a 178 points increase in velocity circulation. Note that this is not the elasticity, since the elasticity $\eta_{r,VEL} = \frac{\partial(p+y-m)}{\partial \log(R)}$, while the semi-elasticity $s\eta_{r,VEL} = \frac{\partial(p+y-m)}{\partial(R)}$, therefore $\eta_{r,VEL} = s\eta_{r,VEL} \times R$, as $d\log(R) = \frac{dR}{R}$. Therefore, by specifying the money demand with the logarithm of real money as a function of the level of the nominal interest rate has the important implication of making the elasticity of the money demand with respect to the opportunity cost of holding money a function of the level of interest rates. This is crucial,

[3]Thus assuming $a_{31} = 1$

since it is undesirable to impose that the elasticity of money demand to interest rate is constant.

The third relation we estimate is an aggregate demand curve as shown in Table 4.3:

TABLE 4.3. LY= C(1)+ LYST +C(2)*(TBILL3-INFL(-1))

| Coefficient | Estimate | Std. Error | t-Statistic | Prob. |
|---|---|---|---|---|
| C(1) | 1.470880 | 0.274338 | 5.361572 | 0.0000 |
| C(2) | -0.383906 | 0.102396 | -3.749208 | 0.0002 |

| | |
|---|---|
| $R^2$ 0.970221 | Mean dependent var 820.4813 |
| Adjusted $R^2$ 0.970123 | S.D. dependent var 24.21989 |
| S.E. of regression 4.186429 | Akaike info criterion 2.870232 |
| Sum squared resid 5310.435 | Schwarz criterion 2.894627 |
| Log likelihood -868.4866 | $F$-statistic 9871.903 |
| Durbin–Watson stat 0.021376 | Prob(F-statistic) 0.000000 |

Note that LYST is included in the fitted relation with a coefficient constrained to unity. As a consequence, we can easily compute the level of long-run equilibrium real interest (as the real interest rate obtained by setting $y = y^*$); such a level is $3.82 = (1.47/0.38)$.

The fourth estimated relation is the aggregate supply function, as shown in Table 4.4.

TABLE 4.4. INFL=C(1)*INFL(-1)+C(2)*(LY-LYST)

| Coefficient | Estimate | Std. Error | t-Statistic | Prob. |
|---|---|---|---|---|
| C(1) | 0.9996 | 0.0032 | 319.10 | 0.0000 |
| C(2) | 0.027 | 0.0047 | 5.89 | 0.0000 |

| | |
|---|---|
| $R^2$ 0.99 | Mean dependent var 5.100013 |
| Adjusted $R^2$ 0.99 | S.D. dependent var 3.296546 |
| S.E. of regression 0.32 | Akaike info criterion 0.60 |
| Sum squared resid 32.14056 | Schwarz criterion 0.63 |
| Log likelihood -89.62183 | Durbin-Watson stat 1.54 |

Note that the estimated values for the parameters are extremely close to the case of maximum price stickiness and the adjustment of inflation with respect to the gap between output and potential output is significant but extremely slow.

### 4.5.3 *Simulating the effect of monetary policy*

Having estimated the model, we proceed to simulating it by considering the estimated equations as a system of differential equations, which can be solved after the specification of a money supply function. This procedure allows the construction of a baseline, which is used to evaluate the effect of monetary policy by specifying an alternative rule for monetary policy and by computing multipliers. The E-Views program solved1.prg allows the computation of the dynamic multipliers generated by a 1% increase in money supply. The program contains the following statements:

```
' This a program to compute dynamic multipliers
'first block
if @isobject(''m_temp'')=1 then
delete m_temp
endif
if @isobject(''dfbase'')=1 then
delete dfbase
endif
if @isobject(''dfshock'')=1 then
delete dfshock
endif
'second block
'baseline simulation
smpl 1986:01 2001:12
'define growth rate of money
genr x=6
model dfbase
'define exogenous variables
dfbase.append lm2=lm2(-12) +x
dfbase.append lyst=773.27+0.275*@TREND(1959:01)
'load endogenous variables
dfbase.merge df
copy dfbase m_temp
m_temp.append assign @all _bl
m_temp.solve
delete m_temp
group exog_bl d12lm2_bl d12lyst_bl
group endog_bl tbill3_bl infl_bl d12ly_bl
'third block
'disturbed simulation
smpl 1986:01 2001:12
'define shock to the growth rate of money
genr y=1
model dfshock
'exogenous variables
dfshock.append lm2=lm2(-12) +(x+y)
dfshock.append lyst=773.27+0.275*@TREND(1959:01)
'loading endogenous variables
```

```
dfshock.merge df
copy dfshock m_temp
m_temp.append assign @all _ds
m_temp.solve
delete m_temp
group exog_ds d12lm2_ds d12lyst_ds
group endog_ds tbill3_ds infl_ds d12ly_ds
plot tbill3_bl tbill3_ds
plot infl_bl infl_ds
plot d12ly_bl d12ly_ds
'fourth block
'computing dynamic multipliers
genr dm_tbill3=(tbill3_ds-tbill3_bl)/(x+y)
genr dm_infl=(infl_ds-infl_bl)/(x+y)
genr dm_d12ly=(d12ly_ds-d12ly_bl)/(x+y)
group dm dm_tbill3 dm_infl dm_d12ly
plot dm
```

The first block of the program defines objects that will contain the baseline model (`dfbase`) and the disturbed model (`dfshock`); it also defines a temporary object (`m_temp`) which will contain the model to simulate in each round. A baseline simulation is then created in the second block. The simulation sample is first chosen; as the model has been estimated over the sample 1959:07–1985:12 we proceed to simulate it from 1986:1 onwards. In fact, the sample for the simulation is purely artificial, since all series are model-generated when computing dynamic multipliers. Choosing a specific sample makes sense only when historical values are considered for some of the variables. Having chosen the sample we set the rate of growth of money $x$ at 6%, the exogenous policy controlled variable. Then all the estimated equations in the previous section are included in the model. The exogenous variables are included using an append statement, while the endogenous variables by importing directly into the model `dfbase` the model `df`, containing all the estimated equations. Then the model is solved dynamically by using the Gauss–Seidel procedure and the extension `_bl` is appended to all the generated variables. The variables are then grouped according to their status into exogenous and endogenous. In the third block a disturbed simulation is then created following the same steps, at the end of the block, simulated values for the endogenous variables are plotted. Finally, dynamic multiplier are computed, grouped into `dm`, and plotted in the fourth block.

We report the computed dynamic multipliers in Figure 4.2.

The 1% increase in the money supply has a one-to-one impact on inflation in the long-run and a zero impact on deviation of the GDP growth. Money is neutral in the long run, but it has a short-run impact on the output cycle as prices are sticky. As a consequence of price stickiness, we also observe a short-run liquidity effect on interest rates, while in the long run the Fisher relationship applies and monetary policy does not have any impact on real interest rates. Note that

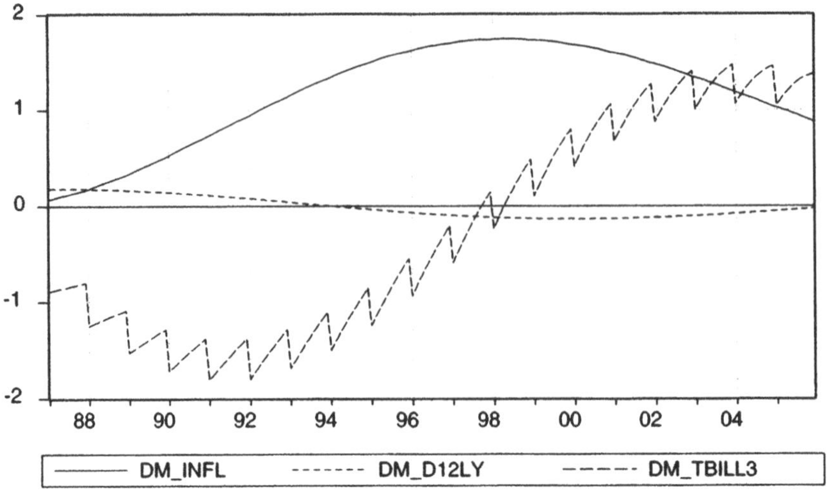


FIG. 4.2. Dynamic multipliers

there is some cyclicality in the interest rate multiplier, which is due to the cycle in nominal interest rates generated by the model. The cycle of output is not matched by any cycle in the money supply, which has only a trend. As a consequence, nominal interest rates reflect, to some extent, fluctuations in output. Setting the money supply as completely exogenous generates an artificial series incapable of replicating some features of the observed data. We shall re-address this point later.

At this stage it is more important to concentrate on the reliability of the description of the response of the economy to the monetary policy derived from the dynamic multipliers.

## 4.6 Assessing econometric evaluation of monetary policy

To have a first assessment of the reliability of our simulations, we use the following approach: we assume that the monetary authority has followed the rule which delivered the observed data on the money stock and, using such a variable as exogenous, we endogenously generate the relevant macroeconomic time-series for a sample covering both the estimation (up to 1985:12) and the simulation (from 1986:1 to 1996:3) periods. Such a result is obtained by solving the following version of the baseline model:

```
assign @all _fal
lyst=773.27+0.275*@TREND(1959:01)
'lm2=lm2(-12)+10
tbill3=(-1/1.758218)*(lm2-lp-ly) -(527.8596/1.758218)
ly=lyst+1.47-0.383*(tbill3-infl(-1))
```

```
(lp-lp(-12))=0.1 +0.975*(lp(-1)-lp(-13))+0.029*(ly-lyst)
INFL=(lp-lp(-12))
d12lm2=lm2-lm2(-12)
d12lyst=lyst-lyst(-12)
d12ly=ly-ly(-12)
cycle=ly-lyst
```

Note that now the equation for `lm2` is commented out: the model will be solved by taking `lm2` as exogenous and using the historical values for this variable.

We report in Figures 4.3 and 4.4 the simulated (defined with the suffix `_fal`) and observed relevant macroeconomic variables: cycle (defined as the deviation of output from trend output) and inflation.

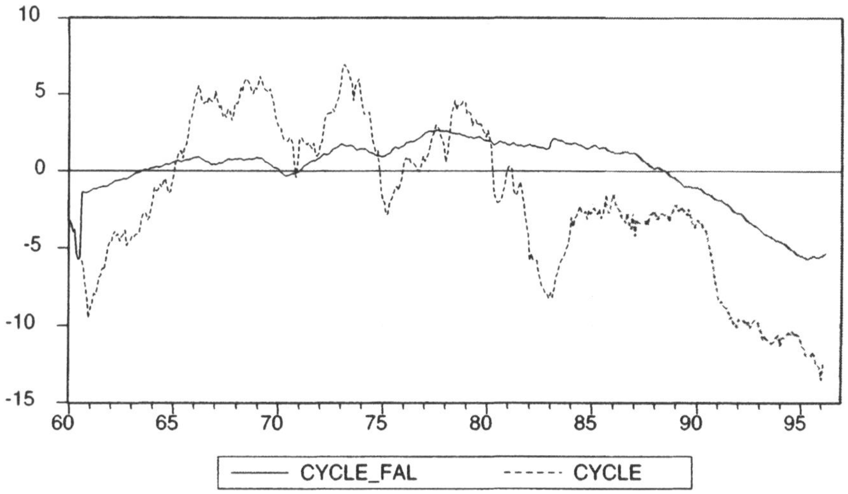


FIG. 4.3. Observed and simulated cycles

Shaded areas distinguish the simulation sample from the estimation sample. The analysis of Figures 4.3 and 4.4 reveals two problems. Over the estimation period the simulated series do not have a sufficiently rich dynamic to match with the observed time-series. However, there is no tendency for a systematic deviation of the simulated series from the observed ones: the difference between the model generated and the observed time-series has a long memory but there is a pattern for a reversion toward the zero mean. When we revert to the simulation period the first problem persists and, in addition, we start observing a systematic pattern in the divergence between the simulated and observed time-series. Such evidence probably justifies some scepticism towards econometric evaluation of monetary policy. To further elaborate on this point, we consider some diagnosis of the causes behind the problem to discuss the solutions proposed

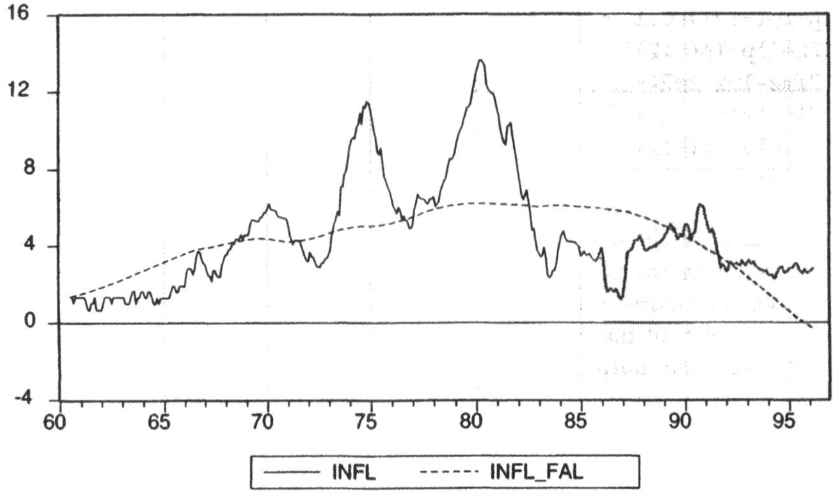


FIG. 4.4. Observed and simulated inflation

by recent developments in econometric modelling of the monetary transmission mechanism.

## 4.7 What is wrong with econometric policy evaluation?

The two problems with our application of the Cowles Commission approach are serious enough to warrant some discussion. We organize our discussion by dividing the explanation in two parts: those concentrating on modifications in the estimation technique and those suggesting modifications in the modelling strategy.

The small structural model we have considered is estimated using the single-equation OLS method. This method is clearly inappropriate, even by taking the a priori exogeneity assumptions on money supply and trend output as valid. Consider the money demand equation, along with the aggregate demand and supply schedules. These relations establish a simultaneous feedback between output, prices and the interest rate which make the OLS inappropriate as the estimation method. In the velocity equation, for example, the nominal interest rate, the only stochastic regressor, should correlate with the residuals, and therefore, the OLS estimate of the semi-elasticity of money demand with respect to interest rate should be biased. Biased estimates of the parameters of interest can obviously explain the disappointing performance of the model under simulation. However, this potential explanation does not seem to be the relevant one. We report in the following table the results of the estimation of the velocity equation by GIVE using valid instruments.

TABLE 4.5. VEL =C(1)+C(2)*TBILL3

| Coefficient | Estimate | Std. Error | $t$-Statistic | Prob. |
|---|---|---|---|---|
| C(1) | 527.41 | 0.439 | 1212 | 0.0000 |
| C(2) | 1.85 | 0.06 | 29.46 | 0.0000 |

| | |
|---|---|
| $R^2$ 0.72 | Mean dependent var 539.0975 |
| Adjusted $R^2$ 0.72 | S.D. dependent var 6.392876 |
| S.E. of regression 3.34 | Akaike info criterion 2.42 |
| Sum squared resid 3567.040 | Schwarz criterion 2.44 |
| Log likelihood -835.5954 | $F$-statistic 868 |
| Durbin–Watson stat 0.125 | Prob($F$-statistic) 0.000000 |

Instruments: C TBILL3(-1) LY(-1) LP(-1) LP(-2) LM2(-1)

Note that the GIVE estimates are not very different from the OLS. This result is robust to the consideration of full information estimation methods (a useful exercise). The observed problems in simulations do not seem to be explained by the chosen estimation method but rather by problems in identification and specification. These are the two issues closely addressed by modern approaches to econometric modelling. The first problem, i.e. the incapability of the estimated model to capture the observed dynamics of the variables of interest, can be explained by the following considerations:

1. The statistical model implicit in the estimated structure is too restrictive. There are two interpretations of the excessive simplicity in the specification: omission of relevant variables, and omission of the relevant dynamics for the included variables (note, for example, that the estimated money demand relation is a simple static equation).
2. The identifying restrictions, although necessary to make the estimation meaningful, deliver a structure which cannot adequately describe reality. Think of the money supply in the estimated model: if the monetary authority uses the money supply as an instrument to achieve given targets for the macroeconomic variables, then the money supply naturally reacts not only to the output and inflation but also to leading indicators for these variables. Assuming money supply as exogenous, the estimated model completely omits a relevant feedback and loses an important feature of the data. Moreover, by incorrectly assuming exogeneity, the model might induce a spurious statistic efficacy of monetary policy in the determination of macroeconomic variables. The endogeneity of money does generate correlations between macroeconomic and monetary variables, which, by invalidly assuming money as exogenous, can be interpreted as a causal relation running from money to the macroeconomic variables (the Sims critique).

The worsening of the model's performance under simulation can instead be explained by the following considerations:

1. Incorrect specification. Omitted variables have an effect which, if not detected when the model is estimated (possibly because the omitted variables were 'silent'), becomes relevant in explaining the parameters' instability of the estimated equations in the simulation period. Incorrectly specified dynamic models feature the parameters' instability in out-of-sample simulations.
2. Model simulation implies considering alternative monetary policy regimes. A change in regime might imply a structural shift in the parameters of the estimated equations, and, therefore, the model estimated under the 'baseline' regime cannot be used to evaluate the effect of the 'control' policy. In other words the Lucas critique applies.

In the next chapters we consider in turn all these explanations by discussing all the alternative modern approaches to applied macroeconometrics.

## 4.8 References

Bollerslev, T. (1986). 'Generalized Autoregressive Conditional Heteroscedasticity'. *Journal of Econometrics*, 31: 307-327.

Chow, G. C. and Lin, A. (1971).'Best Linear Unbiased Interpolation, Distribution and Extrapolation of a Time Series by Related Series'. *Review of Economics and Statistics*, 53:372-375

Doornik, J., and Hendry, D. F. (1996). *PcFIML: Interactive econometric modelling of dynamic system.* London: International Thompson Publishing.

Engle, R. F. (1982). Autoregressive conditional heteroscedasticity with estimates of the variance of United Kingdom inflation.

Goldberger, A. S. (1991). *A course in econometrics.* Cambridge, Massachusetts: Harvard University Press.

Hendry, D. F. (1976). 'The structure of simultaneous equation estimators'. *Journal of Econometrics*, 4: 51-88.

Hendry, D. F. (1996). *Dynamic Econometrics.* Oxford: Oxford University Press.

Klein, L. (1983). *Lectures in Econometrics.* Amsterdam: North-Holland.

Johnston, (1972). *Econometric Methods.* 2$^{nd}$ edition, New-York: McGraw-Hill.

Leeper, E. M., Sims, C. A., and Zha, T. (1996). 'What does monetary policy do?'. Mimeo. Available at ftp://ftp.econ.yale.edu/pub/sims/mpolicy.

Lucas, R. E. Jr. (1976). 'Econometric Policy Evaluation: A Critique'. In K. Brunner and A. Meltzer (eds.) *The Phillips curve and labor markets.* Amsterdam, North-Holland.

Pindyck, R. S. and Rubinfeld, D. L. (1981). *Econometric Models and Economic Forecast.* New York: McGraw Hill

Sargan, D. (1988). *Lectures on advanced econometric theory.* Oxford: Basil Blackwell.

Sims, C. A. (1980). 'Macroeconomics and Reality'. *Econometrica*, 48: 1-48.

Sims, C. A. (1992). 'Interpreting the Macroeconomic Time-Series Facts: the Effects of Monetary Policy'. *European Economic Review*, 36: 975-1011.

Spanos, A. (1990). 'The simultaneous-equations model revisited. Statistical adequacy and identification'. *Journal of Econometrics*, 44: 87-105.

White, A. (1980). 'A heteroscedastic consistent covariance matrix estimator and a direct test for heteroscedasticity'. *Econometrica*, 48: 817-838.

# 5

# LSE APPROACH

## 5.1 Introduction

The LSE approach explains the failure of the Cowles Commission methodology by attributing it to the lack of attention for the statistical model underlying the particular econometric structure adopted to analyse the effect of alternative monetary policies. The LSE methodology considers econometric policy evaluation an interesting and feasible exercise. However the way in which the Cowles Commission approach deals with a legitimate question is seen as incorrect. The lack of sufficient interest for the statistical model is at the root of the failure of the Cowles Commission approach to provide an acceptable answer to an interesting question. As seen from the application discussed in the previous chapter, the econometric analysis within the Cowles Commission tradition begins from the idea that the structural form of the process generating the data is known qualitatively, and the reduced form is then derived from such a structure. Within such a framework the validity of the reduced form is not tested. The LSE approach views this lack of validation of the reduced form as undermining the credibility of the structural parameter estimates. This approach recognizes that economic theory suggests the general specification of the relevant form, but the precise representation of the data generating process is almost never known in advance. Thus modelling procedures are required to determine the credibility of the estimated models. The reduced form takes a central role within this approach in that it represents the crucial probabilistic structure of the data (see Spanos 1990, Hendry, Neale and Srba 1988). The traditional logic of the Cowles Commission, according to which the reduced form is derived given the structural model, is reversed within the LSE approach. The reduced form is specified first, by defining a system via the set of variables considered, their classification into modelled and non-modelled variables (endogenous and exogenous in the traditional terminology) and the specification of the lag polynomials. The system is then validated by applying the three basic principles of econometrics: 'test, test and test'. The null hypothesis of interest is the absence of symptoms of mis-specification, such as residual non-normality, autocorrelation, heteroscedasticity, parameter non-constancy. If the null is not rejected and the system is considered as a congruent representation of the unknown data generating process, then non-stationarity can be dealt with and the long-run properties of the system can be identified by implementing cointegration analysis. Note again that such analysis is fully implemented on the reduced form and the identification of the structural long-run relationships is a totally separate problem from the identification of the structural short-run simultaneous relationships. In the last step a structural model is identified and estimated. No further validation is possible for just-identified models as they impose no restrictions on the system, while the validity of over-identified models is testable by testing the validity of the over-identifying restrictions implicitly imposed on the reduced form. Finally, policy simulation can be performed after testing that the necessary requirement for the model to be robust to the Lucas critique, i.e. superexogeneity of the relevant variables for the estimation of the parameters of interest, is satisfied.

## 5.2 The LSE diagnosis

The LSE diagnosis of the problems displayed by Cowles Commission models is simple:

> ... the statistical properties attributed to the structural estimators and related tests are in general invalid unless the probabilistic structure imposed on the data via the reduced form is invalid. A glance at the empirical literature confirms that not only are the statistical assumptions underlying the reduced form not tested, but the reduced form is rarely estimated explicitly. Indeed, the most popular estimation methods for the structural parameters are limited-information instrumental-variable methods such as two-stage least squares which do not even specify the implied reduced form... (Spanos 1990: 90).

Consider the structural model used to illustrate the Cowles Commission approach in the previous chapter,

$$\mathbf{A}\begin{bmatrix} y_t \\ p_t \\ R_t \\ m_t \\ y_t^* \end{bmatrix} = \mathbf{C}_0\begin{bmatrix} 1 \\ t \end{bmatrix} + \mathbf{C}_1\begin{bmatrix} y_{t-1} \\ p_{t-1} \\ R_{t-1} \\ m_{t-1} \\ y_{t-1}^* \end{bmatrix} + \mathbf{C}_2\begin{bmatrix} y_{t-2} \\ p_{t-2} \\ R_{t-2} \\ m_{t-2} \\ y_{t-2}^* \end{bmatrix} + \begin{bmatrix} \epsilon_{1t} \\ \epsilon_{2t} \\ \epsilon_{3t} \\ \epsilon_{4t} \\ \epsilon_{5t} \end{bmatrix} \tag{5.1}$$

$$\mathbf{A} = \begin{bmatrix} 1 & 0 & a_{13} & 0 & -1 \\ -a_{21} & 1 & 0 & 0 & a_{21} \\ -\frac{a_{31}}{a_{33}} & -\frac{1}{a_{33}} & 1 & \frac{1}{a_{33}} & 0 \\ 0 & 0 & 0 & 1 & 0 \\ 0 & 0 & 0 & 0 & 1 \end{bmatrix}$$

$$\mathbf{C}_0 = \begin{bmatrix} c_{0,11} & 0 \\ c_{0,21} & 0 \\ \frac{c_{0,31}}{a_{33}} & 0 \\ c_{0,41} & 0 \\ c_{0,51} & c_{0,52} \end{bmatrix}, \quad \mathbf{C}_1 = \begin{bmatrix} 0 & a_{13} & 0 \\ 0 & 2 & 0 \\ 0 & 0 & 0 \\ 0 & 0 & 1 \\ 0 & 0 & 0 \end{bmatrix}, \quad \mathbf{C}_2 = \begin{bmatrix} 0 & -a_{13} \\ 0 & -1 \\ 0 & 0 \\ 0 & 0 \\ 0 & 0 \end{bmatrix}.$$

Only parameters different from zero or one are to be considered 'free' and are then estimated to describe the economic properties of the adopted structure.

From this representation we immediately note the exogeneity assumptions imply a remarkable number of the restrictions on the set of the parameters of interest. Another substantial set of restrictions derives from the very limited dynamics adopted in the specification of the model. The implied reduced form features numerous restrictions, as easily checked by pre-multiplying the model by $\mathbf{A}^{-1}$ :

$$\begin{bmatrix} y_t \\ p_t \\ R_t \\ m_t \\ y_t^* \end{bmatrix} = \begin{bmatrix} d_{0,11} & d_{0,12} \\ d_{0,21} & d_{0,22} \\ d_{0,31} & d_{0,32} \\ d_{0,41} & 0 \\ d_{0,51} & d_{0,52} \end{bmatrix} \begin{bmatrix} 1 \\ t \end{bmatrix} + \begin{bmatrix} 0 & d_{1,112} & 0 & d_{1,13} & 0 \\ 0 & d_{1,22} & 0 & d_{1,23} & 0 \\ 0 & d_{1,32} & 0 & d_{1,33} & 0 \\ 0 & 0 & 0 & 1 & 0 \\ 0 & 0 & 0 & 0 & 0 \end{bmatrix} \begin{bmatrix} y_{t-1} \\ p_{t-1} \\ R_{t-1} \\ m_{t-1} \\ y_{t-1}^* \end{bmatrix}$$
$$\begin{bmatrix} 0 & d_{2,12} & 0 & 0 & 0 \\ 0 & d_{2,212} & 0 & 0 & 0 \\ 0 & d_{2,32} & 0 & 0 & 0 \\ 0 & 0 & 0 & 0 & 0 \\ 0 & 0 & 0 & 0 & 0 \end{bmatrix} \begin{bmatrix} y_{t-2} \\ p_{t-2} \\ R_{t-2} \\ m_{t-2} \\ y_{t-2}^* \end{bmatrix} + \mathbf{A}^{-1} \begin{bmatrix} \epsilon_{1t} \\ \epsilon_{2t} \\ \epsilon_{3t} \\ \epsilon_{4t} \\ \epsilon_{5t} \end{bmatrix}.$$

According to the LSE criticism, the validity of such a reduced form is not properly addressed by the Cowles Commission approach. Structural inference based on an improper statistical model is the LSE diagnosis for the failure of the Cowles Commission models, a verdict delivered from evaluating the properties of the residuals.

## 5.3 Reduction process

Econometric modelling is formalized within the LSE camp as the result of a reduction process. The starting point of the reduction process is a long way up: think of a vector $\mathbf{x}_t$ containing observations on all economic variables at time $t$. A sample of $T$ time-series observations on all the variables can be represented as follows:

$$\mathbf{X}_T^1 = \begin{bmatrix} \mathbf{x}_1 \\ . \\ . \\ . \\ \mathbf{x}_T \end{bmatrix}.$$

The starting point in reduction is a model for the data generating process (DGP). The DGP is described by the joint density function $D\left(\mathbf{X}_T^1, \boldsymbol{\theta}\right)$, we define $\mathbf{X}_{t-1}$ as the matrix including observations on all variables in $\mathbf{x}$ from time 1 to time $t-1$ and $\boldsymbol{\theta}$ as the set of parameters.

Model specification amounts to choosing a particular functional form for the density. Having chosen the model, a structure for this model is pinned down by identifying parameters and estimating them. In general, estimation is performed by considering the joint sample density function, known also as the likelihood function, which we can express as $D\left(\mathbf{X}_T^1 \mid \mathbf{X}_0, \boldsymbol{\theta}\right)$. The likelihood function is defined on the parameters space $\Theta$, given the observation of the observed sample $\mathbf{X}_T^1$ and of a set of initial conditions $\mathbf{X}_0$. Such initial conditions can be interpreted as the pre-sample observations on the relevant variables (which are usually not available). In case of independent observations, the likelihood function can be written as the product of the density functions for each observation. However, this is not the relevant case for time-series, as time-series observations are in general sequentially correlated. In this case, the sample density is then constructed using the concept of sequential conditioning. The likelihood function, conditioned with respect to initial conditions, can always be written as the product of a marginal density and a conditional density as follows:

$$D\left(\mathbf{X}_T^1 \mid \mathbf{X}_0, \boldsymbol{\theta}\right) = D\left(\mathbf{x}_1 \mid \mathbf{X}_0, \boldsymbol{\theta}\right) D\left(\mathbf{X}_T^2 \mid \mathbf{X}_1, \boldsymbol{\theta}\right).$$

Obviously, we also have

$$D\left(\mathbf{X}_T^2 \mid \mathbf{X}_0, \boldsymbol{\theta}\right) = D\left(\mathbf{x}_2 \mid \mathbf{X}_1, \boldsymbol{\theta}\right) D\left(\mathbf{X}_T^3 \mid \mathbf{X}_2, \boldsymbol{\theta}\right),$$

and, by recursive substitution, we eventually obtain:

$$D\left(\mathbf{X}_T^1 \mid \mathbf{X}_0, \boldsymbol{\theta}\right) = \prod_{t=1}^{T} D\left(\mathbf{x}_t \mid \mathbf{X}_{t-1}, \boldsymbol{\theta}\right).$$

Having obtained $D\left(\mathbf{X}_T^1 \mid \mathbf{X}_0, \boldsymbol{\theta}\right)$, we can in theory derive $D\left(\mathbf{X}_T^1, \boldsymbol{\theta}\right)$ by integrating with respect to $X_0$, the density conditional on pre-sample observations. In practice this could be intractable analytically as $D\left(X_0\right)$ is unknown. The hypothesis of stationarity becomes crucial at this stage, as stationarity restricts the memory of time-series and limits the effects of pre-sample observations to the first observations in the sample. This is why, in the case of stationary processes, initial conditions can be simply ignored. Clearly, the larger the sample, the better, as the weight of the information lost becomes smaller. Moreover, note also that, even by omitting initial conditions, we have:

$$D\left(\mathbf{X}_T^1 \mid \mathbf{X}_0, \boldsymbol{\theta}\right) = D\left(\mathbf{x}_1 \mid \mathbf{X}_0, \boldsymbol{\theta}\right) \prod_{t=2}^{T} D\left(\mathbf{x}_t \mid \mathbf{X}_{t-1}, \boldsymbol{\theta}\right).$$

Therefore the likelihood function is separated in the product on $T-1$ conditional distributions and one unconditional distribution. In the case of non-stationarity the unconditional distribution is not defined. On the other hand, in the case of stationarity, the DGP is completely described by the conditional density function $D\left(\mathbf{x}_t \mid \mathbf{X}_{t-1}, \boldsymbol{\theta}\right)$.

The baseline of the reduction process, the DGP or the Haavelmo distribution, is then completely described by $D\left(\mathbf{x}_t \mid \mathbf{X}_{t-1}, \boldsymbol{\theta}\right)$. The first step of the reduction process can be understood by partitioning $\mathbf{x}$ into three types of variables:

$$\mathbf{x}_t = \left(\mathbf{w}_t, \mathbf{y}_t, \mathbf{z}_t\right),$$

where $\mathbf{w}_t$ identifies variables which are unobservable or irrelevant to the problem investigated by the econometrician. In practice these variables are ignored, in theory such a result is obtained by factorizing the joint density and integrating it with respect to $\mathbf{w}_t$:

$$D(\mathbf{y}_t, \mathbf{z}_t \mid \mathbf{Y}_{t-1}, \mathbf{Z}_{t-1}, \boldsymbol{\beta}) = \iint D(\mathbf{y}_t, \mathbf{z}_t, \mathbf{w}_t \mid \mathbf{Y}_{t-1}, \mathbf{Z}_{t-1}, \mathbf{W}_{t-1}, \boldsymbol{\theta}) \\ D(\mathbf{W}_{t-1} \mid \mathbf{Y}_{t-1}, \mathbf{Z}_{t-1}, \boldsymbol{\theta})\, d\mathbf{W}_{t-1} d\mathbf{w}_t.$$

In this case we have a potential information loss which becomes real when the variables, judged irrelevant for the problem at hand, are relevant. In formal terms, we have no information loss only if

$$D(\mathbf{y}_t, \mathbf{z}_t \mid \mathbf{Y}_{t-1}, \mathbf{Z}_{t-1}, \boldsymbol{\beta}) = D(\mathbf{y}_t, \mathbf{z}_t, \mathbf{w}_t \mid \mathbf{Y}_{t-1}, \mathbf{Z}_{t-1}, \mathbf{W}_{t-1}, \boldsymbol{\theta}).$$

This is the statistical description of the model considered by the econometrician, i.e. the reduced form of the structure of interest. In general, at the empirical level, this is the earliest stage of the reduction process, in fact a reduced form for all the variables of interest (a VAR) is the most general model we fit to the data. However, such a general model viable for empirical estimation does not certainly coincide with the Haavelmo distribution for all economic variables.

How can we be sure that no loss of relevant information occurred in moving from the Haavelmo distribution to the estimated empirical model? By applying to our reduced form the three fundamental rules of LSE econometrics 'test, test and test'. $D(\mathbf{y}_t, \mathbf{z}_t \mid \mathbf{Y}_{t-1}, \mathbf{Z}_{t-1}, \boldsymbol{\beta})$ is empirically constructed by parameterizing $E(\mathbf{y}_t, \mathbf{z}_t \mid \mathbf{Y}_{t-1}, \mathbf{Z}_{t-1}, \boldsymbol{\beta})$ as

$$E(\mathbf{y}_t, \mathbf{z}_t \mid \mathbf{Y}_{t-1}, \mathbf{Z}_{t-1}, \boldsymbol{\beta}) = \begin{pmatrix} \boldsymbol{\beta}_{11}(L) & \boldsymbol{\beta}_{12}(L) \\ \boldsymbol{\beta}_{21}(L) & \boldsymbol{\beta}_{22}(L) \end{pmatrix} \begin{pmatrix} \mathbf{y}_{t-1} \\ \mathbf{z}_{t-1} \end{pmatrix}.$$

The vector of innovations $\mathbf{u}_t$ is derived from the specification of conditional means:

$$\mathbf{u}_t = \begin{pmatrix} \mathbf{y}_t \\ \mathbf{z}_t \end{pmatrix} - \begin{pmatrix} \boldsymbol{\beta}_{11}(L) & \boldsymbol{\beta}_{12}(L) \\ \boldsymbol{\beta}_{21}(L) & \boldsymbol{\beta}_{22}(L) \end{pmatrix} \begin{pmatrix} \mathbf{y}_{t-1} \\ \mathbf{z}_{t-1} \end{pmatrix}.$$

Going back to our application to the monetary transmission mechanism, the baseline of the investigation is a reduced form of the type

$$\begin{pmatrix} \mathbf{Y}_t \\ \mathbf{M}_t \end{pmatrix} = D_1(L) \begin{pmatrix} \mathbf{Y}_{t-1} \\ \mathbf{M}_{t-1} \end{pmatrix} + D_2 a_1 + \begin{pmatrix} \mathbf{u}_t^Y \\ \mathbf{u}_t^M \end{pmatrix}. \tag{5.2}$$

Any empirical model is in itself the product of some step in the reduction process. Thus, the starting point of the empirical analysis is the implementation of a battery of diagnostic tests, where the null hypothesis of interest is the validity of the baseline model as a simplified representation of the unknown DGP.

## 5.4 Test, test and test

Given that the GDP is unknown, the validity of reduction can be checked by ensuring that the vector of innovations $\mathbf{u}_t$ possesses all the features of true statistical innovations: absence of correlation, heteroscedasticity, non-normality. Any pattern of this type or any instability in the $\boldsymbol{\beta}$ parameters can then be interpreted as a signal of a loss of information that occurred in the hidden reduction from the DGP to the particular specification adopted. The three fundamental principles of the LSE methodology are 'test, test, and test' because only by implementing diagnostic checks we can discard invalid structural models. Testing usually concentrates on residuals because any non-randomness in residual behaviour can be interpreted as a signal of incorrect specification of the underlying model. The residuals of a statistical model are generated by the specification adopted by the econometrician and are a by-product of omitted variables (both in the sense of omitted important variables and of omitted lags of included variables), and errors-in-included-variables of several types (measurement or expectational errors). We illustrate how the relevant tests can be constructed with reference to the statistical model (5.2).

### 5.4.1 *Testing autocorrelated residuals*

Residual autocorrelation is usually tested via a Lagrange Multiplier test, which uses the following formulation:

$$\begin{pmatrix} \widehat{\mathbf{u}}_t^Y \\ \widehat{\mathbf{u}}_t^M \end{pmatrix} = \sum_{i=1}^{n} \boldsymbol{\delta}_i' \begin{pmatrix} \widehat{\mathbf{u}}_{t-i}^Y \\ \widehat{\mathbf{u}}_{t-i}^M \end{pmatrix} + D_1(L) \begin{pmatrix} \mathbf{Y}_{t-1} \\ \mathbf{M}_{t-1} \end{pmatrix} + D_2 a_1 + \begin{pmatrix} \mathbf{e}_t^Y \\ \mathbf{e}_t^M \end{pmatrix}. \tag{5.3}$$

Residual autocorrelation of the $n$-th order is checked by testing if the components of lagged fitted residuals, not explained by the regressors in the original model, are significant in explaining contemporaneous fitted residuals. A test against the null of absence of serial correlation of order n is implemented by considering lags up to the $n$-th of fitted residuals. The null hypothesis of interest is:

$$H_0 : \boldsymbol{\delta}_i = 0.$$

The test, based on the $R^2$ of the auxiliary system, is asymptotically distributed as a $\chi^2$ with $nm^2$ degrees of freedom, where $m$ is the number of the variables entering the reduced form, see Godfrey (1988). An $F$-approximation with small sample corrections is also available, see Kiviet (1986). The intuition of this procedure of model evaluation by variable addition is understood by considering that, under the null hypothesis, the component of lagged residuals not explained by the regressors in the model is not significant in explaining current residuals, see Pagan (1984).

### 5.4.2 *Testing heteroscedastic residuals*

To illustrate tests for the null of homoscedasticity, consider the simple case where we have a system including two variables, one monetary and one macroeconomic.

After estimation of (5.2), a test can be performed by running the following auxiliary model:

$$\begin{pmatrix} (\widehat{u}_t^Y)^2 \\ (\widehat{u}_t^M)^2 \\ (\widehat{u}_t^Y \widehat{u}_t^M) \end{pmatrix} = \boldsymbol{\delta}_0 + D^*(L) \begin{pmatrix} Y_{t-1}^2 \\ M_{t-1}^2 \\ Y_{t-1}M_{t-1} \end{pmatrix} + \begin{pmatrix} e_{1t} \\ e_{2t} \\ e_{3t} \end{pmatrix}. \tag{5.4}$$

Under the null hypothesis the variance-covariance of the system residuals is constant. Hence, we have

$$H_0 : D^*(L) = 0.$$

The test is easily generalized to systems of $m$ variables, with the proviso that, as $m$ gets large, it becomes unfeasible because of the limitation in degrees of freedom. The procedure is best interpreted as an extension of the heteroscedasticity tests proposed by White (1980) in the context of single-equation models. Of course, whenever the degrees of freedom problem is binding, a White test can be run on all the equations separately. Not rejecting the null in this case would satisfy a necessary condition for homoscedasticity of the system residuals. The condition is not sufficient because it does not provide a test for constancy of covariances. At the single equation level, the ARCH type of tests can also be run, see Engle (1982), by specifying the following models:

$$\begin{pmatrix} (\widehat{u}_t^Y)^2 \\ (\widehat{u}_t^M)^2 \end{pmatrix} = \boldsymbol{\delta}_0 + \sum_{i=1}^{n} \boldsymbol{\delta}_i' \begin{pmatrix} (\widehat{u}_{t-i}^Y)^2 \\ (\widehat{u}_{t-i}^M)^2 \end{pmatrix} + \begin{pmatrix} e_{1t} \\ e_{2t} \end{pmatrix}. \tag{5.5}$$

The null of interest is

$$H_0 : \boldsymbol{\delta}_i = 0.$$

Note that all the tests for heteroscedasticity presented here take some estimate of the variance-covariance matrix of the system residuals and check its constancy over time. The difference between different tests lies in the specification of the alternative, i.e. of the variables used to capture the fluctuations over time of the moments under the alternative distribution.

### 5.4.3 *Testing residuals normality*

Normality of residuals is a crucial property in that all the statistical framework used to 'test, test and test' is based on this assumption. A vector normality test has been proposed by Doornik and Hansen (1994).

The test is constructed by first standardizing the residuals $\left(\widehat{\mathbf{u}}_t^Y \ \widehat{\mathbf{u}}_t^M\right)$. Define the vector of standardized residuals $(\mathbf{r}_{1,\dots,}\mathbf{r}_T)$ as $\mathbf{R}$. Then $\mathbf{C} = T^{-1}\mathbf{R}'\mathbf{R}$ is the correlation matrix. The standardized residuals, normally distributed under the null with zero mean and variance-covariance matrix $\mathbf{C}$, can be transformed into an independent standard normal:

$$\mathbf{e}_t = \mathbf{E}\Lambda^{-\frac{1}{2}}\mathbf{E}'\mathbf{r}_t,$$

where $\Lambda$ is a diagonal matrix with the eigenvalues of $\mathbf{C}$ on the principal diagonal and the columns of $\mathbf{E}$ are the correspondent eigenvectors, such that $\mathbf{E}'\mathbf{E} = \mathbf{I}$, and $\Lambda = \mathbf{E}'\mathbf{C}\mathbf{E}$.

The test is performed by computing univariate skewness and kurtosis of each transformed residuals and comparing them with those of the normal distribution. Define $\mathbf{b}_1' = (b_{11}, ..., b_{1m})$, $\mathbf{b}_2' = (b_{21}, ..., b_{2m})$, as the vectors containing the sample estimates of the skewness and kurtosis of the transformed residuals of the $m$ equations included in the model we have that the test statistic:

$$\frac{T\mathbf{b}_1'\mathbf{b}_1}{6} + \frac{T(\mathbf{b}_2 - 3\mathbf{i})'(\mathbf{b}_2 - 3\mathbf{i})}{24} \overset{asy}{\sim} \chi^2(2m)$$

where $\mathbf{i}$ is the unit vector. As the above requires large samples, corrected versions are proposed and implemented in the Pc-FIML package.

### 5.4.4 *Testing parameter stability*

Within the LSE methodology, variable parameters is an oxymoron. In fact, Hendry (1995) makes clear that ' ... Models which have no set of constancies will be useless for forecasting the future, analysing economic policy, or test economic theories, since they lack entities on which to base those activities... '. Testing parameter constancy is therefore an important aspect of the diagnostic checking procedure. This is usually done within the LSE tradition by estimating models recursively and applying Chow (1960) tests for parameter stability.

Single equation Chow tests include one-step $F$-tests, break-point $F$-tests and forecast $F$-tests.

One-step forecasts tests are $F(1, t-k-1)$ under the null of constant parameters, for $t = N, ..., T$ and $k$ included regressors. A typical statistic is calculated as

$$\frac{(RSS_t - RSS_{t-1})(t-k-1)}{RSS_{t-1}}.$$

Where $RSS_t$ is the residual sum of squares computed from the estimation on $t$ observations. And they are computed by Pc-GIVE and Pc-FIML for all possible break points after initialization of the estimation.

Break-point $F$-tests are $F(T-t+1, t-k-1)$ for $t = N, ..., T$. The null of interest is the stability of parameters when the model is estimated on the sample 1 to $t$ against an alternative which allows any form of change over $t+1$ to $T$. A typical statistic is calculated as

$$\frac{(RSS_T - RSS_{t-1})(t-k-1)}{RSS_{t-1}(T-k-1)}.$$

Forecast $F$-tests are $F(T-N+1, M-k-1)$ for $t = N, ..., T$, they test stability of the model estimated on the sample 1 to $(N-1)$ against an alternative which allows any form of change over $N$ to $T$. A typical statistic is calculated as

$$\frac{(RSS_T - RSS_{N-1})(N-k-1)}{RSS_{N-1}(T-N-1)}.$$

All these tests can be extended to systems by defining $F$-approximations to likelihood ratio statistics.

Chow tests are tests for instability generated by a single-break point, occurring at a known date within the sample. Refinements of the testing procedure have been proposed to deal with breaks occurring at uncertain dates and with multiple breaks. Andrews (1993) proposes to deal with uncertainty by using trimming points to define a subsample in which the break is likely to have occurred, by then computing all possible Chow tests (in $\chi^2$ form) for every breakpoint. The largest statistic so obtained provides a stability test ('maximum Chow' test) for an unknown break point. The article provides the underlying distributional theory and critical values, which are functions of degrees of freedom and trimming points.

## 5.5 Testing a Cowles Commission model

We consider as a baseline model the following generalization of the statistical model underlying the simple Cowles Commission specification:

$$\begin{bmatrix} \pi_t \\ y_t \\ R_t \\ (m-p)_t \end{bmatrix} = \begin{bmatrix} d_{0,11} & d_{0,12} \\ d_{0,21} & d_{0,22} \\ d_{0,31} & d_{0,32} \\ d_{0,41} & d_{0,42} \end{bmatrix} \begin{bmatrix} 1 \\ t \end{bmatrix} + \sum_{i=1}^{6} D_i \begin{bmatrix} \pi_{t-i} \\ y_{t-i} \\ R_{t-i} \\ (m-p)_{t-i} \end{bmatrix} + \begin{bmatrix} u_{1t} \\ u_{2t} \\ u_{3t} \\ u_{4t} \end{bmatrix}. \tag{5.6}$$

We estimate the above specification by OLS, using Pc-FIML, over the sample 1959:7–1985:12. The residuals for the four equations in the system are reported in Figure 5.1, while diagnostic tests are reported in Table 5.1.

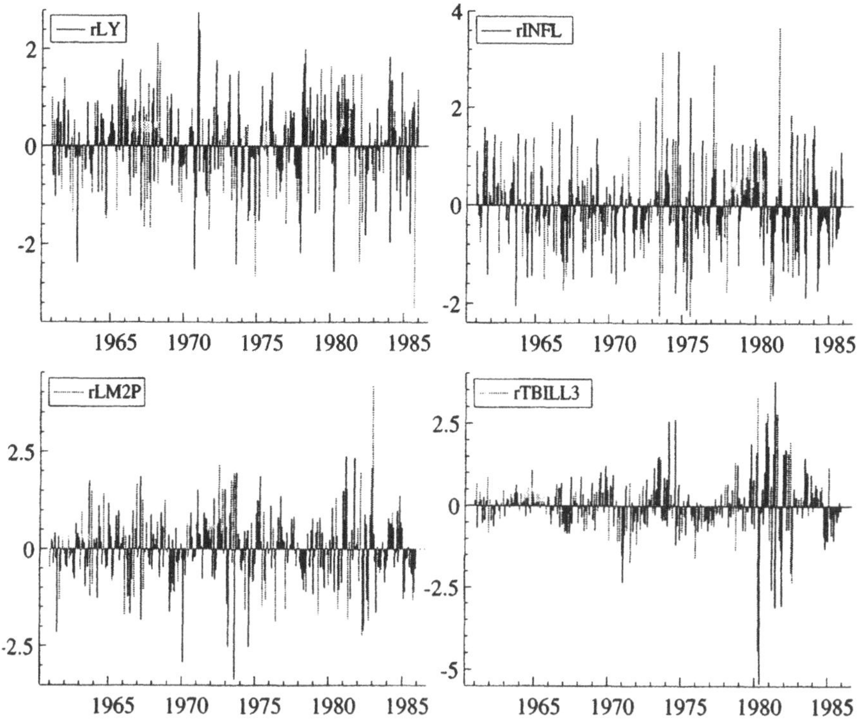


FIG. 5.1. Residuals from the estimation of model (5.6)

TABLE 5.1. Diagnostic tests

| | AR1–7 $F(7,267)$ | Norm. $\chi^2(2)$ | ARCH7 $F(7,260)$ | $X_i^2$ $F(50,223)$ |
|---|---|---|---|---|
| LY | 0.7691 [0.6137] | 4.9172 [0.0856] | 0.72095 [0.6543] | 0.60953 [0.9807] |
| INFL | 2.671 [0.0109] | 9.9844 [0.0068] | 0.922 [0.4898] | 1.5344 [0.0196] |
| LM2P | 1.9475 [0.0625] | 21.096 [0.0000] | 2.4126 [0.0208] | 1.1241 [0.2807] |
| TBILL3 | 2.1913 [0.0353] | 162.11 [0.0000] | 20.494 [0.0000] | 4.7914 [0.0000] |
| Vector | 2.4529 [0.0000] | 214.5 [0.0000] | - | 1.3827 [0.0000] |

The plot of the residuals and the results of the diagnostic tests reported in Table 5.1 prove that the adopted specification does not deliver an acceptable statistical model. Given that this model is more general than the simple specification used to illustrate the Cowles Commission approach, the results are valid *a fortiori* for such a model.

## 5.6 Searching for a congruent specification

In the previous section we have illustrated the diagnosis of the problems of the Cowles Commission models proposed by the LSE tradition. We consider now the prognosis, to begin the search of the final specification starting from an appropriate statistical model for the data. Looking at the behaviour of the residuals from the previous estimated model, we note that the equation for the interest rate shows a substantial degree of instability over the period 1979–82. In fact in this period a different monetary regime was adopted by the Fed who abandoned a strategy aimed at controlling interest rates to embrace a non-borrowed reserves targeting regime. As a consequence, the volatility of short-term interest rates changes dramatically over the period 1979–82. Such volatility goes back to pre-1979 levels only when non-borrowed reserves targeting is abandoned at the end of 1982 (see Walsh 1998). Mixing two different policy regimes is a recipe for parameter instability, therefore we concentrate on a single regime and shorten the sample to end the estimation in 1979:10. A second problem is detected by the diagnostics in the equation for inflation. Here, several outliers are generated by the oil price shocks of 1973 and 1979. To fix this problem we include among the variables in the system, an index of commodity prices. Such a variable can also be important in modelling the monetary policy-maker behaviour, if it plays a role as a leading indicator for inflation. Lastly, to model properly money demand it is necessary to consider explicitly the own return on money in the construction of the opportunity cost of holding this asset. A time-series for this variable is made available by the Fed at the internet site *http://www.bog.frb.fed.us/* We extend our baseline system and re-estimate it over the shortened sample with the new endogenous and exogenous variables. As the residuals show some persistent sign of non-normality we include a set of dummies to remove outliers (observations generating observed residuals of a magnitude exceeding, in absolute value, three times the standard deviation of fitted residuals). We then choose the following baseline model:

$$\begin{bmatrix} y_t \\ \pi_t \\ R_t^m \\ R_t^b \\ (m-p)_t \end{bmatrix} = \begin{bmatrix} d_{0,11} & d_{0,12} \\ d_{0,21} & d_{0,22} \\ d_{0,31} & d_{0,32} \\ d_{0,41} & d_{0,42} \\ d_{0,51} & d_{0,52} \end{bmatrix} \begin{bmatrix} 1 \\ t \end{bmatrix} + \sum_{i=1}^{6} D_i \begin{bmatrix} y_{t-i} \\ \pi_{t-i} \\ R_{t-i}^m \\ R_{t-i}^b \\ (m-p)_{t-i} \end{bmatrix} \tag{5.7}$$

$$+\sum_{i=0}^{6} F_i \Delta_{12} LPCM_{t-i} + \mathbf{g}'\mathbf{DUM}_t + \begin{bmatrix} u_{1t} \\ u_{2t} \\ u_{3t} \\ u_{4t} \end{bmatrix}.$$

$\mathbf{DUM}_t$ is a vector of dummy variables containing: dum7306,dum7307, dum7308, dum7310, dum7311, dum7312, dum7402, dum7403, dum7407, dum7408,dum7409, dum7501, dum7505, dum7806, dum7808, dum7811, dum7904. In general, dumMMYY is a variable taking value 1 in the MM month of the year YY and zero anywhere else.

We plot the residuals in Figure 5.2 and report the diagnostic tests in Table 5.2.

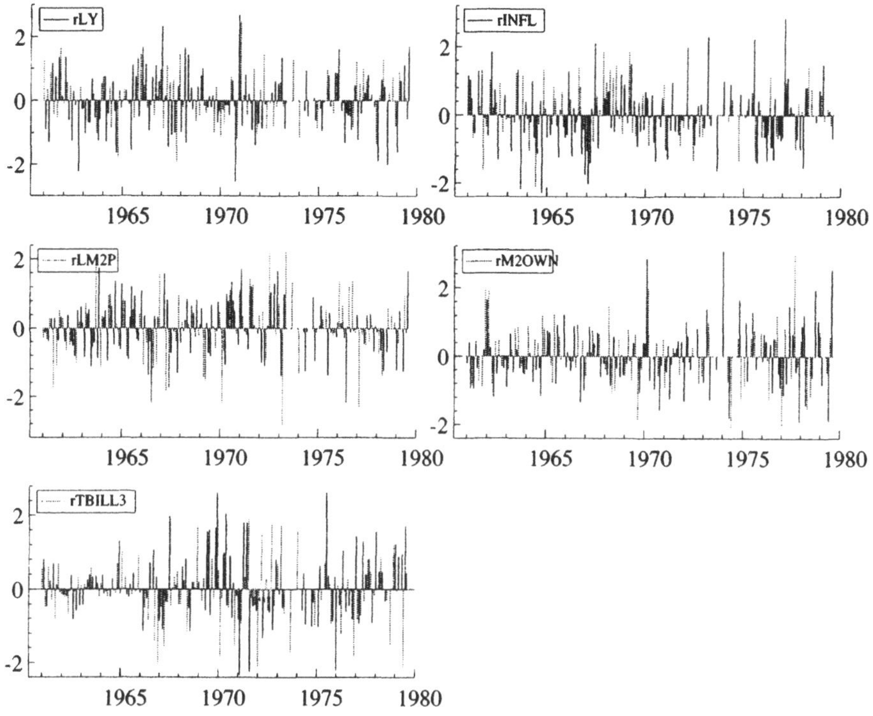


FIG. 5.2. Residuals from the estimation of model (5.7)

TABLE 5.2. Diagnostic tests

| | $AR$1-7 $F(7,267)$ | $Norm.\ \chi^2(2)$ | $ARCH7\ F(7,260)$ | $X_i^2\ F(50,223)$ |
|---|---|---|---|---|
| LY | 0.92159 [0.4913] | 1.577 [0.4545] | 1.0196 [0.4196] | 0.82561 [0.7929] |
| INFL | 1.4775 [0.1787] | 3.1857 [0.2033] | 0.38832 [0.9081] | 0.59005 [0.9874] |
| LM2P | 2.0011 [0.0580] | 3.04 [0.2187] | 0.49178 [0.8395] | 0.69226 [0.9418] |
| M2OWN | 5.2877 [0.0000] | 12.04 [0.0024] | 0.70325 [0.6693] | 1.0182 [0.4606] |
| TBILL3 | 1.0123 [0.4246] | 6.6683 [0.0356] | 2.8439 [0.0081] | 0.89271 [0.6835] |
| Vector | 1.4779 [0.0004] | 24.745 [0.0058] | - | 0.66171 [1.0000] |

The situation looks much improved now, although the equation for the own rate on money still shows some problems of autocorrelation and non-normality, signalled both by the single-equation and the system diagnostics. We attribute these problems to the peculiar time-series behaviour of this series and decide to proceed further in our analysis by considering (5.7) as a congruent representation for the unknown data generating process.

## 5.7 Cointegration analysis

The next step in the specification strategy is the identification of the long-run equilibria in our model. The number of cointegrating vectors can be detected by applying the Johansen procedure to identify the rank of the matrix $\Pi$ in the following reparameterization of our model:

$$\begin{bmatrix} \Delta y_t \\ \Delta \pi_t \\ \Delta R_t^m \\ \Delta R_t^b \\ \Delta (m-p)_t \end{bmatrix} = \begin{bmatrix} d_{0,11} \\ d_{0,21} \\ d_{0,31} \\ d_{0,41} \\ d_{0,51} \end{bmatrix} + \sum_{i=0}^{6} F_i \Delta_{12} LPCM_{t-i} + \mathbf{g}'\mathbf{DUM}_t$$

$$+ \sum_{i=1}^{5} D_i \begin{bmatrix} \Delta y_{t-i} \\ \Delta \pi_{t-i} \\ \Delta R_{t-i}^m \\ \Delta R_{t-i}^b \\ \Delta (m-p)_{t-i} \end{bmatrix} + \Pi \begin{bmatrix} y_{t-6} \\ \pi_{t-6} \\ R_{t-6}^m \\ R_{t-6}^b \\ (m-p)_{t-6} \end{bmatrix} + \begin{bmatrix} u_{1t} \\ u_{2t} \\ u_{3t} \\ u_{4t} \\ u_{5t} \end{bmatrix}.$$

We have already seen in Chapter 2 that two identification schemes deliver alternative representations of the long-run equilibria based on over-identifying restrictions not rejected by the data. The first scheme is centred upon a money demand relation, while the second upon an interest rate reaction function. We have also shown that the analysis of the adjustment parameters makes the second scheme preferable. On the basis of these results, we opt for the second identification scheme and proceed to specify a structural model for the policy rates, output and inflation. Within such a scheme, real money is completely determined by the demand side and loses any interest for the analysis of monetary policy. When the researcher loses interest in real money the return on money also becomes uninteresting. Our economic interpretation of the results of the cointegration analysis makes our baseline reduced form unnecessarily complicated. The natural question at this point regards the legitimacy of a simplification of the model in moving from the reduced form to the structural model of interest.

## 5.8 Specifying a structural model

Having validated the reduced form, the econometrician is left with the problem of identifying the appropriate structure. Moreover, we have seen that the reduced form might constitute, in itself, a model unnecessarily complicated for the problem at hand. Then we should identify the cases in which further simplification, obtained by reducing the dimension of the estimated system, is viable with no loss of relevant information for the purposes of analysis.

### 5.8.1 *Exogeneity*

Suppose that the relevant problem is inference on subset $\boldsymbol{\beta}_1$ of the parameters determining the joint density of $\mathbf{y}_t$, and $\mathbf{z}_t$. In general it is always possible to re-write $D(\mathbf{y}_t, \mathbf{z}_t \mid \mathbf{Y}_{t-1}, \mathbf{Z}_{t-1}, \boldsymbol{\beta})$ as follows:

$$\begin{aligned} & D(\mathbf{y}_t, \mathbf{z}_t \mid \mathbf{Y}_{t-1}, \mathbf{Z}_{t-1}, \boldsymbol{\beta}) \\ & = D(\mathbf{y}_t \mid \mathbf{z}_t, \mathbf{Y}_{t-1}, \mathbf{Z}_{t-1}, \boldsymbol{\beta}_1, \boldsymbol{\beta}_2) \, D(\mathbf{z}_t \mid \mathbf{Y}_{t-1}, \mathbf{Z}_{t-1}, \boldsymbol{\beta}_1, \boldsymbol{\beta}_2). \end{aligned} \tag{5.8}$$

The general case admits as a specific case the existence of a 'sequential cut', which we represent as follows:

$$\begin{aligned} & D(\mathbf{y}_t, \mathbf{z}_t \mid \mathbf{Y}_{t-1}, \mathbf{Z}_{t-1}, \boldsymbol{\beta}) \\ & = D(\mathbf{y}_t \mid \mathbf{z}_t, \mathbf{Y}_{t-1}, \mathbf{Z}_{t-1}, \boldsymbol{\beta}_1) \, D(\mathbf{z}_t \mid \mathbf{Y}_{t-1}, \mathbf{Z}_{t-1}, \boldsymbol{\beta}_2). \end{aligned} \tag{5.9}$$

If so and if the set on which the parameters $\boldsymbol{\beta}_1$are defined is totally independent from the set on which the parameters $\boldsymbol{\beta}_2$ are defined ($\boldsymbol{\beta}_1$ and $\boldsymbol{\beta}_2$ are *variation free*) then inference on $\boldsymbol{\beta}_1$can be performed by concentrating only on the conditional density for $\mathbf{y}_t$, without explicitly treating the marginal density for $\mathbf{z}_t$. To have an intuition for this argument, think of the problem of deriving an estimator of $\boldsymbol{\beta}_1$ by using (5.9) as the likelihood function. Taking logarithms of (5.9) we have:

$$\begin{aligned} \ln D(\mathbf{y}_t, \mathbf{z}_t \mid \mathbf{Y}_{t-1}, \mathbf{Z}_{t-1}, \boldsymbol{\beta}) = & \ln D(\mathbf{y}_t \mid \mathbf{z}_t, \mathbf{Y}_{t-1}, \mathbf{Z}_{t-1}, \boldsymbol{\beta}_1) \\ & + \ln D(\mathbf{z}_t \mid \mathbf{Y}_{t-1}, \mathbf{Z}_{t-1}, \boldsymbol{\beta}_2) \end{aligned} \tag{5.10}$$

from which it is clear that the logarithm of the joint process equals the sum of two factors. The second factor is a constant with respect to $\boldsymbol{\beta}_1$, thus it does not affect the maximum likelihood estimator of $\boldsymbol{\beta}_1$ and can be ignored when the main interest of research is inference on $\boldsymbol{\beta}_1$. When the sequential cut can be operated and $\boldsymbol{\beta}_1$ and $\boldsymbol{\beta}_2$ are 'variation free', $\mathbf{z}_t$ is said to be weakly exogenous for the estimation of $\boldsymbol{\beta}_1$. Weak exogeneity can be confronted with Granger non-causality (see Granger 1987). $\mathbf{y}_t$ Granger-causes $\mathbf{z}_t$ if the knowledge of $\mathbf{y}_t$ helps the prediction of $\mathbf{z}_{t+j}$, $j > 0$. Granger-causality is independent from the choice of the parameters of interest, while weak exogeneity is obviously dependent. As a consequence, it is perfectly admissible that $\mathbf{z}_t$ is not Granger-caused by $\mathbf{y}_t$ but these variables are not weakly exogenous for the estimation of the parameters of interest. Think of the following case:

$$\begin{aligned} & D(\mathbf{y}_t, \mathbf{z}_t \mid \mathbf{Y}_{t-1}, \mathbf{Z}_{t-1}, \boldsymbol{\beta}) \\ & = D(\mathbf{y}_t \mid \mathbf{z}_t, \mathbf{Y}_{t-1}, \mathbf{Z}_{t-1}, \boldsymbol{\beta}_1, \boldsymbol{\beta}_2) \, D(\mathbf{z}_t \mid \mathbf{Z}_{t-1}, \boldsymbol{\beta}_1, \boldsymbol{\beta}_2). \end{aligned} \tag{5.11}$$

The link between Granger-causality and weak exogeneity is established by the concept of strong exogeneity, which is defined as the intersection of the two concepts, therefore we have strong exogeneity when the joint density can be factorized as follows:

$$\begin{aligned} & D(\mathbf{y}_t, \mathbf{z}_t \mid \mathbf{Y}_{t-1}, \mathbf{Z}_{t-1}, \boldsymbol{\beta}) \\ &= D(\mathbf{y}_t \mid \mathbf{z}_t, \mathbf{Y}_{t-1}, \mathbf{Z}_{t-1}, \boldsymbol{\beta}_1)\, D(\mathbf{z}_t \mid \mathbf{Z}_{t-1}, \boldsymbol{\beta}_2). \end{aligned} \tag{5.12}$$

Weak exogeneity constitutes the basis for the definition of a third concept of exogeneity: superexogeneity. Superexogeneity requires weak exogeneity and that the conditional model $D(\mathbf{y}_t \mid \mathbf{z}_t, \mathbf{Y}_{t-1}, \mathbf{Z}_{t-1}, \boldsymbol{\beta}_1)$ is structurally invariant, i.e. changes in the distribution of the marginal model for $\mathbf{z}_t$ do not affect the $\boldsymbol{\beta}_1$ parameters.

These three concepts are useful in defining the validity of the reduction from the data congruent reduced form and the adopted structural model:

1. if the objective of the analysis is inference on the $\boldsymbol{\beta}_1$ parameters, then the joint density can be reduced to a conditional model if $\mathbf{z}_t$ is weakly exogenous for the estimation of the parameters of interest;
2. if the objective of the analysis is dynamic simulation, then the joint density can be reduced to a conditional model if $\mathbf{z}_t$ satisfies the conditions for strong exogeneity;
3. finally, if the objective of the analysis is econometric policy evaluation, then the joint density can be reduced to a conditional model if $\mathbf{z}_t$ satisfies the conditions for superexogeneity.

Tests for the validity of all these three concepts have been developed to sustain the validity of the last stage of the reduction processes.

### 5.8.2 *Exogeneity in ECM representations*

To illustrate how the concepts of exogeneity are applied to linear dynamic models, consider the following DGP:

$$\begin{aligned} y_t &= a0_{12} z_t + \varepsilon_{1t} \\ \varepsilon_{1t} &= \rho \varepsilon_{1t-1} + u_{1t}, \quad 0 < \rho < 1 \\ a0_{21} y_t + a0_{22} z_t &= a1_{21} y_{t-1} + a1_{22} z_{t-1} + \varepsilon_{2t} \\ \varepsilon_{2t} &= \varepsilon_{2t-1} + u_{2t} \end{aligned} \tag{5.13}$$

$$\begin{pmatrix} u_{1t} \\ u_{2t} \end{pmatrix} n.i.d. \left[ \begin{pmatrix} 0 \\ 0 \end{pmatrix}, \begin{pmatrix} \sigma_{11} & 0 \\ 0 & \sigma_{22} \end{pmatrix} \right].$$

This is a non-stationary process, integrated of the first order, admitting one cointegrating vector. The non-stationarity of the process stems from the presence of a unit root in $\varepsilon_{2t}$, while the cointegrating vector is defined by $y_t - a_{12} z_t$, as $\varepsilon_{1t}$ is stationary. The system (5.13) can be reparameterized as follows:

$$\mathbf{A}_0 \begin{pmatrix} \Delta y_t \\ \Delta z_t \end{pmatrix} = \mathbf{A}_1 \begin{pmatrix} \Delta y_{t-1} \\ \Delta z_{t-1} \end{pmatrix} + \mathbf{C} \begin{pmatrix} y_{t-1} \\ z_{t-1} \end{pmatrix} + \begin{pmatrix} u_{1t} \\ u_{2t} \end{pmatrix} \tag{5.14}$$

$$\mathbf{A}_0 = \begin{pmatrix} 1 & -a0_{12} \\ a0_{21} & a0_{22} \end{pmatrix}, \mathbf{A}_1 = \begin{pmatrix} 0 & 0 \\ a1_{21} & a1_{22} \end{pmatrix},$$
$$\mathbf{C} = \begin{pmatrix} -(1-\rho) & a0_{12}(1-\rho) \\ 0 & 0 \end{pmatrix}$$
$$\mathbf{C} = \mathbf{A}_0 \boldsymbol{\alpha}\boldsymbol{\beta}'.$$

Note that (5.14) can be considered a congruent representation of the DGP, as it features well-behaved residuals. This is not true of (5.13), whose residuals are autocorrelated. Autocorrelation is generated by the omitted first-order dynamics in the static equation. The omitted dynamics admit specific restrictions known as COMFAC (common factor restriction).[1]

To analyse the different concepts of exogeneity, consider the probabilistic structure of the data underlying model (5.14). In other words, let us derive the reduced form associated with (5.14):

$$\begin{pmatrix} \Delta y_t \\ \Delta z_t \end{pmatrix} = \begin{pmatrix} \frac{a0_{12}a1_{21}}{k} & \frac{a0_{12}a1_{22}}{k} \\ \frac{a1_{21}}{k} & \frac{a1_{22}}{k} \end{pmatrix} \begin{pmatrix} \Delta y_{t-1} \\ \Delta z_{t-1} \end{pmatrix} \tag{5.15}$$
$$+ \begin{pmatrix} -\frac{a0_{22}(1-\rho)}{k} \\ \frac{a0_{21}(1-\rho)}{k} \end{pmatrix} \begin{pmatrix} 1 & -a0_{12} \end{pmatrix} \begin{pmatrix} y_{t-1} \\ z_{t-1} \end{pmatrix} \tag{5.16}$$
$$+ \begin{pmatrix} \frac{a0_{22}}{k} & \frac{a0_{12}}{k} \\ \frac{-a0_{21}}{k} & \frac{1}{k} \end{pmatrix} \begin{pmatrix} u_{1t} \\ u_{2t} \end{pmatrix}, \tag{5.17}$$
$$k = \frac{1}{a0_{22} - a0_{21}a0_{12}}. \tag{5.18}$$

From the reduced form we find that the conditional joint density of $y_t$ and $z_t$ can be written as:

$$\begin{pmatrix} \Delta y_t \\ \Delta z_t \end{pmatrix} \mid I_{t-1} \Big) \; n.i.d. \left[ \begin{pmatrix} \mu_y \\ \mu_z \end{pmatrix}, \begin{pmatrix} \sigma_{yy} & \sigma_{yz} \\ \sigma_{yz} & \sigma_{zz} \end{pmatrix} \right], \tag{5.19}$$

where

$$\mu_y = \frac{a0_{12}a1_{21}}{k}\Delta y_{t-1} + \frac{a0_{12}a1_{22}}{k}\Delta z_{t-1} - \frac{a0_{22}(1-\rho)}{k}(y_{t-1} - a0_{12}z_{t-1}),$$
$$\mu_z = \frac{a1_{21}}{k}\Delta y_{t-1} + \frac{a1_{22}}{k}\Delta z_{t-1} + \frac{a0_{21}(1-\rho)}{k}(y_{t-1} - a0_{12}z_{t-1}),$$
$$\sigma_{yy} = \left(\frac{a0_{22}}{k}\right)^2 \sigma_{11} + \left(\frac{a0_{12}}{k}\right)^2 \sigma_{22},$$
$$\sigma_{zz} = \left(\frac{a0_{21}}{k}\right)^2 \sigma_{11} + \left(\frac{1}{k}\right)^2 \sigma_{22},$$
$$\sigma_{yz} = -\left(\frac{a0_{22}}{k}\right)\left(\frac{a0_{21}}{k}\right)\sigma_{11} + \left(\frac{a0_{12}}{k}\right)\left(\frac{1}{k}\right)\sigma_{22}.$$

[1]The common factor restriction is singular in that the effects of the omitted dynamic can be cured by a Cochrane-Orcutt estimator (static model + autocorrelated error terms).

By applying the known properties of the multivariate normal, we derive from the statistical representation of the data the conditional mean of $\Delta y_t$ with respect to $\Delta z_t$ and $I_{t-1}$ as follows:

$$E\left(\Delta y_t \mid \Delta z_t, I_{t-1}\right) = \mu_y + \frac{\sigma_{yz}}{\sigma_{zz}}\left(z - \mu_z\right). \tag{5.20}$$

$z_t$ is weakly exogenous for the estimation of the parameters of interest if the conditional mean for $\Delta y_t$ derived from (5.20) coincides with the conditional mean for $\Delta y_t$ derived from the first equation of model (5.14). As the conditional mean from the first equation of (5.14) is:

$$E\left(\Delta y_t \mid \Delta z_t, I_{t-1}\right) = a0_{12}\Delta z_t - (1-\rho)\left(y_{t-1} - a0_{12}z_{t-1}\right), \tag{5.21}$$

the weak exogeneity of $\Delta z_t$ for the estimation of the parameter $a0_{12}$ is obtained when $a0_{21} = 0$. Strong exogeneity requires Granger non-causality in addition to weak exogeneity, thus it is satisfied when $a0_{21} = 0$, $a1_{21} = 0$.

Superexogeneity requires weak exogeneity and independence of the parameters of interest from the distribution of $\Delta z_t$. In our example, whenever the conditions for weak exogeneity are satisfied, superexogeneity also holds. To show a case in which this does not happen, consider the following modification of our DGP:

$$\begin{aligned} y_t &= a0_{12}E\left(z_{t+1} \mid I_t\right) + \varepsilon_{1t} \\ z_t &= a1_{22}z_{t-1} + \varepsilon_{2t} \end{aligned} \tag{5.22}$$

$$\begin{pmatrix} \varepsilon_{1t} \\ \varepsilon_{2t} \end{pmatrix} n.i.d. \left[\begin{pmatrix} 0 \\ 0 \end{pmatrix}, \begin{pmatrix} \sigma_{11} & 0 \\ 0 & \sigma_{22} \end{pmatrix}\right].$$

Here the conditional mean $E\left(y_t \mid z_t, I_{t-1}\right)$ is given by the following expression:

$$E\left(y_t \mid z_t, I_{t-1}\right) = a0_{12}a1_{22}z_t \tag{5.23}$$

and it depends on $a1_{22}$, the parameter determining the conditional mean of $z_t$.

We conclude with the following remarks.

1. Exogeneity is defined independently from the parameters defining the cointegrating vectors, but it is related to the weights. Weak exogeneity has a precise relation with the direction of adjustment in presence of disequilibria.
2. Our example above is a special case, as we take a diagonal variance-covariance matrix. In general, weak exogeneity requires a lower triangular structure and absence of correlation in the variance covariance-matrix.
3. Note the impossibility of reverse regression. The conditions of weak exogeneity of $\Delta z_t$ for the estimation of $a0_{12}$ are mutually exclusive with the condition of weak exogeneity of $\Delta y_t$ for the estimation of $\frac{1}{a0_{12}}$.

### 5.8.3 *Testing exogeneity*

The preceding example shows how weak exogeneity can be tested for within the framework of cointegration. To provide a more general introduction to the issue of testing exogeneity, consider a bivariate process for two generic variables $y_t$ and $z_t$ conditioned with respect to the information available $I_{t-1}$, which includes all past history for the process

$$\begin{pmatrix} y_t \\ z_t \end{pmatrix} \mid I_{t-1} \Big) \, n.i.d. \left[ \begin{pmatrix} \mu_t^y \\ \mu_t^z \end{pmatrix}, \begin{pmatrix} \sigma_t^{yy} & \sigma_t^{yz} \\ \sigma_t^{yz} & \sigma_t^{zz} \end{pmatrix} \right]. \tag{5.24}$$

The conditional model for $y_t$ can be written as

$$(y_t \mid z_t, I_{t-1}) \, n.i.d. \left[ \frac{\sigma_t^{yz}}{\sigma_t^{zz}} (z_t - \mu_t^z) + \mu_t^y, \sigma_t^{yy} - \left( \frac{\sigma_t^{yz}}{\sigma_t^{zz}} \right) \right], \tag{5.25}$$

and the marginal model for $z_t$ is instead

$$(z_t \mid I_{t-1}) \, n.i.d. \, (\mu_t^z, \sigma_t^{zz}). \tag{5.26}$$

The parameters of interest feature the following relationship:

$$\mu_t^y = \beta \mu_t^z + \mathbf{w}_t' \boldsymbol{\delta}, \tag{5.27}$$

of which, for the sake of exposition, we consider the special case

$$y_t = \beta z_t + \mathbf{w}_{t-1}' \boldsymbol{\delta}_t + u_t, \tag{5.28}$$

where $\mathbf{w}_{t-1}$ is included in $I_{t-1}$.

Weak exogeneity of $z_t$ for the estimation of $\beta$ implies that this parameter can be estimated directly from (5.28) without any loss of relevant information. For this we need a sequential cut and need that the conditional model does not depend on $\mu_t^z, \sigma_t^{yz}, \sigma_t^{zz}$. To formally pin down the conditions for weak exogeneity substitute (5.27) in (5.25) obtaining:

$$(y_t \mid z_t, I_{t-1}) \sim n.i.d. \left[ E(y_t \mid z_t, I_{t-1}), \sigma_t^{yy} - \left( \frac{\sigma_t^{yz}}{\sigma_t^{zz}} \right) \right] \tag{5.29}$$

$$E(y_t \mid z_t, I_{t-1}) = \beta z_t + \mathbf{w}_{t-1}' \boldsymbol{\delta} + \left( \frac{\sigma_t^{yz}}{\sigma_t^{zz}} - \beta \right) (z_t - \mu_t^z).$$

Therefore we have weak exogeneity of $z$ for the estimation of $\beta$, if the following condition is satisfied:

$$\frac{\sigma_t^{yz}}{\sigma_t^{zz}} = \beta.$$

From this condition we can easily understand the tests for exogeneity available in the literature (see Hausman 1978, Wu 1973), which are based on two-stage procedures.

In the first stage, $\mu_t^z$ is parameterized by fitting a conditional model for $z_t$ of the following type:

$$z_t = \mathbf{s}_t'\boldsymbol{\pi} + u_t, \tag{5.30}$$

where the vector $\mathbf{s}$ includes all the variables necessary to obtain a satisfactory specification for $z_t$. In the second stage, the significance of residuals from (5.30) in equation (5.28) and the null of weak exogeneity coincide with the null of non-significance of such a constructed variable. This argument can be extended to test the null of superexogeneity (see Engle and Hendry 1993, Favero and Hendry 1992, Ericsson and Irons 1994). The alternative hypothesis is now complicated as follows:

$$\beta\left(\mu_t^z, \sigma_t^{zz}\right) = \beta_0 + \beta_1 \mu_t^z + \beta_2 \sigma_t^{zz} + \beta_3 \frac{\sigma_t^{zz}}{\mu_t^z}, \tag{5.31}$$

and the null of interest is weak exogeneity augmented by $\beta_1 = \beta_2 = \beta_3 = 0$.

To see how the test is derived, substitute from (5.31) and (5.27) in (5.25), obtaining:

$$\left(y_t \mid z_t, I_{t-1}\right) \sim n.i.d.\ \left(\mu_t, \Omega_t\right) \tag{5.32}$$

$$\mu_t = \beta_0 z_t + \mathbf{w}_{t-1}'\boldsymbol{\delta} + \left(\frac{\sigma_t^{yz}}{\sigma_t^{zz}} - \beta_0\right)\left(z_t - \mu_t^z\right) + \beta_1\left(\mu_t^z\right)^2 + \beta_2 \sigma_t^{zz}\mu_t^z + \beta_3 \sigma_t^{zz}$$

$$\Omega_t = \sigma_t^{yy} - \left(\frac{\sigma_t^{yz}}{\sigma_t^{zz}}\right).$$

By using the first-order expansion:

$$\frac{\sigma_t^{yz}}{\sigma_t^{zz}} = \delta_0 + \delta_1 \sigma_t^{zz},$$

we reach the following estimable relation:

$$\begin{aligned} y_t = {} & \beta_0 z_t + \mathbf{w}_{t-1}'\boldsymbol{\delta} + \left(\delta_0 - \beta_0\right)\left(z_t - \mu_t^z\right) \\ & + \delta_1 \sigma_t^{zz}\left(z_t - \mu_t^z\right) + \beta_1\left(\mu_t^z\right)^2 + \beta_2 \sigma_t^{zz}\mu_t^z + \beta_3 \sigma_t^{zz}, \end{aligned}$$

where the null hypothesis of interest can now be empirically tested by parameterizing the first two moments of the conditional model for $z_t$.

Hendry (1988) provides an alternative assessment of superexogeneity by analysing the encompassing implications of feedback versus feedforward models.

This procedure is based on the explicit consideration of two alternative specifications for the DGP.

The feedback model, denoted by $H_b$, is:

$$\begin{aligned} y_t &= \boldsymbol{\beta}'\mathbf{z}_t + v_t, \qquad (5.33)\\ E_b\left(\mathbf{z}_t v_t\right) &= 0. \end{aligned}$$

The feedforward model, denoted by $H_f$, is:

$$\begin{aligned} y_t &= \boldsymbol{\delta}' E\left(\mathbf{z}_{t+1} \mid I_t\right) + \epsilon_t, \qquad (5.34)\\ \mathbf{z}_t &= \boldsymbol{\gamma}_t \mathbf{z}_{t-1} + \mathbf{u}_t, \qquad (5.35)\\ E_f\left(\mathbf{z}_t \epsilon_t\right) &= 0,\\ \mathbf{u}_t &\sim i.d.\left(0, \Omega_t\right). \end{aligned}$$

Note that in $H_f$ the parameters of the marginal model for $\mathbf{z}_t$ are a function of time through $\boldsymbol{\gamma}_t$ and $\Omega_t$. Moreover, we restrict ourselves to the case in which the only relevant information in $I_t$ to predict $\mathbf{z}_{t+1}$ are the realizations at time $t$ of $\mathbf{z}$.

We can now explore the encompassing predictions of each model for the other. We do so by evaluating the performance of each model when the congruent representation of the DGP is the alternative model.

When (5.33) and (5.30) are a congruent representation of the DGP, the following implications hold:

1. when $\boldsymbol{\gamma}_t$ and $\Omega_t$ are non-constant, also the projection of $y_t$ on $\mathbf{z}_{t-1}$ is non-constant, then
$$E_b\left(y_t \mid \mathbf{z}_{t-1}\right) = \boldsymbol{\beta}'\boldsymbol{\gamma}_t \mathbf{z}_{t-1};$$
2. the error-variance is also non-constant:
$$\begin{aligned} y_t - E_b\left(y_t \mid \mathbf{z}_{t-1}\right) &= \boldsymbol{\beta}'\mathbf{u}_t + v_t = \varphi_t,\\ E_b\left(\varphi_t^2\right) &= \sigma_v^2 + \boldsymbol{\beta}'\Omega_t\boldsymbol{\beta}; \end{aligned}$$
3. the projection of $y_t$ on $\mathbf{z}_{t-1}$ should fit worse than the behavioural model (5.33):
$$E_b\left(\varphi_t^2\right) = \sigma_v^2 + \boldsymbol{\beta}'\Omega_t\boldsymbol{\beta} > \sigma_v^2;$$
4. the behavioural model (5.33) should feature constant parameters.

When instead (5.34) and (5.30) are a congruent representation of the DGP, the following implications hold:

1. the conditional model cannot be constant when the marginal model for $\mathbf{z}_t$ is sufficiently variable since
$$E_f\left(y_t \mid \mathbf{z}_t\right) = \boldsymbol{\delta}'\boldsymbol{\gamma}_t \mathbf{z}_{t-1};$$

2. the projection of $y_t$ on $\mathbf{z}_{t-1}$ is non-constant but with the parameter vector $\boldsymbol{\delta}'\gamma_t\gamma_{t+1}$;
3. no variance ranking is possible as

$$y_t - E_f(y_t \mid \mathbf{z}_t) = \epsilon_t,$$

as in (5.34).

The analysis of the encompassing implications of the two cases reveals that when the feedback model is stable and the marginal process is not, the feed-forward specification cannot be a congruent representation of the DGP. As a consequence, the relevance of the Lucas critique could be analysed by assessing simultaneously the stability of the feedback structural model and of the marginal models for the regressors in the feedback model. This procedure deserves some discussion.

A first observation is related to the power of tests for structural stability. For the procedure to work, it is essential that the marginal model is sufficiently variable and that such variability is detectable through tests for parameters' stability. As we have already seen, the issue is not trivial, since multiple breaks at unknown points are not easily detected.

Setting aside the power of the tests, there is a logical issue related to the reduction procedure. If parameter stability is taken as one of the criteria for congruency, then congruent reduced forms should never feature parameter instability. In practice, as we have seen in our application, congruent specifications often need the inclusion of dummies. Therefore, the significance of the same dummies in different equations of the adopted model could be exploited to apply the procedure for the evaluation of the relevance of the Lucas critique.

A related question refers to the power of the procedure in the case of limited information, i.e. when parameter instability is generated by omitted variables in the marginal models. Hendry (1988) explicitly considers such a case, by adopting the following alternative specification for the marginal model:

$$\mathbf{z}_t = \gamma_1\mathbf{z}_{t-1} + \gamma_2\mathbf{s}_{t-1} + \mathbf{u}_{2t}, \tag{5.36}$$

$$\mathbf{u}_{2t} \sim i.d.\,(0, \Omega_2)\,. \tag{5.37}$$

When (5.36) is a congruent representation of the DGP, (5.30) features instability because of a limited-information problem: the omission of $\mathbf{s}_{t-1}$ from the relevant information set. However, if (5.30) is observed, then the relation between $\mathbf{z}_t$ and $\mathbf{s}_t$ cannot be constant. It must be the case that:

$$\mathbf{x}_t = \boldsymbol{\mu}_t\mathbf{z}_t + \boldsymbol{\xi}_t,$$

$$\boldsymbol{\xi}_t \sim i.d.\,(0, \Xi_t)\,,$$

and then

$$\gamma_t = \gamma_1 + \gamma_2\boldsymbol{\mu}_t,$$

$$\Omega_t = \Omega_2 + \gamma_2\Xi_t\gamma_2'.$$

The result of the stability of the feedback model paired with the instability of the (mis-specified) marginal model can still rule out the congruency of the feedforward model.

## 5.9 A model of the monetary transmission mechanism

To illustrate the specification of a structural model for the monetary transmission mechanism, we consider as a baseline the cointegrated reduced form discussed in one of the previous sections:

$$\begin{bmatrix} \Delta y_t \\ \Delta \pi_t \\ \Delta R_t^b \end{bmatrix} = \begin{bmatrix} d_{0,11} \\ d_{0,21} \\ d_{0,31} \end{bmatrix} + \sum_{i=0}^{6} F_i \Delta_{12} LPCM_{t-i} + \mathbf{g}'\mathbf{DUM}_t \tag{5.38}$$

$$+\sum_{i=1}^{5} D_i \begin{bmatrix} \Delta y_{t-i} \\ \Delta \pi_{t-i} \\ \Delta R_{t-i}^b \end{bmatrix} + \begin{bmatrix} \alpha_{11} \\ \alpha_{21} \\ \alpha_{31} \end{bmatrix} \left(R_{t-1}^b - R_{t-1}^{b*}\right) + \begin{bmatrix} u_{1t} \\ u_{2t} \\ u_{3t} \end{bmatrix},$$

$$R_{t-1}^{b*} = \pi_{t-1} + 0.22 y_{t-1} - 0.08t.$$

Note that (5.38) is the result of the reduction of the baseline model, which contains five equations. The original model delivered two cointegrating relationships. We have identified the first one as an interest rate reaction function and the second one as a rule for determining the interest rate on bank deposits. To describe the monetary transmission mechanism under interest rate targeting, we need to supplement the interest rate reaction function with equations for the target variables, inflation and output. Real money, being demand determined, loses interest and so does the opportunity cost of holding money. Therefore, we have omitted from the original model the two equations determining real money and the interest rate on bank deposits together with the equilibrium relationships for the latter. The validity of this step in the reduction process is testable. Congruency of our selected specification requires that the weights on the second cointegrating vector can be constrained to zero in our three maintained equations, that the weights on the first cointegrating vector can be constrained to zero in the equations for real money and the interest rate on bank deposits, and, finally, that the lagged value of real money and the interest rate on bank deposits do not significantly enter system (5.38). Having asserted the validity of this further step in reduction, we proceed to the specification of the following structural model:

$$\Delta y_t = \underset{(0.03)}{0.23} + \underset{(0.06)}{0.33}\,\Delta y_{t-1} - \underset{(0.09)}{0.21}\,\Delta R_{t-3}^b - \underset{(0.46)}{1.19}\,DUM7312 \tag{5.39}$$

$$-\underset{(0.46)}{1.11}\,DUM7308$$

$$\Delta\pi_t = \underset{(0.02)}{-0.05} + \underset{(0.03)}{0.08}\,\Delta y_{t-1} + \underset{(0.03)}{0.06}\,\Delta y_{t-5} + \underset{(0.05)}{0.2}\,\Delta\pi_{t-5} \tag{5.40}$$
$$+\underset{(0.05)}{0.14}\,\Delta\pi_{t-6} + \underset{(0.005)}{0.03}\,\Delta_{12}LPCM_{t-1} - \underset{(0.006)}{0.02}\,\Delta_{12}LPCM_{t-2}$$
$$-\underset{(0.27)}{0.92}\,DUM7307 + \underset{(0.26)}{0.87}\,DUM7308 + \underset{(0.26)}{0.69}\,DUM7407$$
$$-\underset{(0.25)}{0.56}\,DUM7408 + \underset{(0.25)}{1.04}\,DUM7409 - \underset{(0.25)}{0.75}\,DUM7505,$$

$$\Delta R_t^b = -\underset{(3.08)}{8.34} + \underset{(0.13)}{0.31}\,\Delta\pi_t + \underset{(0.03)}{0.08}\,\Delta y_{t-3} + \underset{(0.06)}{0.36}\,\Delta R_{t-1}^b \tag{5.41}$$
$$+\underset{(0.006)}{0.01}\,\Delta_{12}LPCM_t - \underset{(0.005)}{0.013}\Delta_{12}LPCM_{t-1}$$
$$-\underset{(0.018)}{0.04}\left(R_{t-1}^b - R_{t-1}^{b*}\right) + \underset{(0.24)}{0.60}\,DUM7306$$
$$+\underset{(0.28)}{0.71}\,DUM7307 - \underset{(0.24)}{0.90}\,DUM7310 + \underset{(0.25)}{1.06}\,DUM7311$$
$$-\underset{(0.24)}{0.76}\,DUM7312 - \underset{(0.24)}{0.86}\,DUM7402 + \underset{(0.24)}{1.13}\,DUM7403$$
$$+\underset{(0.25)}{1.64}\,DUM7408 - \underset{(0.28)}{1.72}\,DUM7409 - \underset{(0.24)}{0.72}\,DUM7501$$
$$+\underset{(0.23)}{0.49}\,DUM7808 + \underset{(0.28)}{0.57}\,DUM7811.$$

LR test of over-identifying restrictions: $\chi^2(89) = 95.3354\ [0.3037]$.

The model is estimated over the sample 1961:2–1979:8 by FIML. The 89 over-identifying restrictions imposed by the reduced form implicit in our structure on the unconstrained reduced form are not rejected. The first equation can be interpreted as an aggregate demand equation along which the output gap (deviation of output from a stochastic trend) depends on lagged change in nominal interest rates. The second equation is the stylized aggregate supply which determines inflation as a function of past inflation, the commodity price inflation and the output gaps. Finally, the third equation is an interest rate reaction function which describes short-run dynamics around a long-run solution determined by response of interest rates to inflation and output. Note that, because of the dynamic specification, the response of the monetary instruments to fluctuations in the target variables is different in the short-run and in the long-run. To illustrate the within sample performance of the model we report actual and fitted values in Figure 5.3.

## 5.10 Simulating monetary policy

We are now in the position of simulating the effects of monetary policy. We simulate the impact of a hundred basis point exogenous monetary policy shock by computing dynamic multipliers. The baseline model is obtained by simulating dynamically, for given values of the exogenous variables, the three endogenous variables. In practice these variables are generated by equations (5.40),

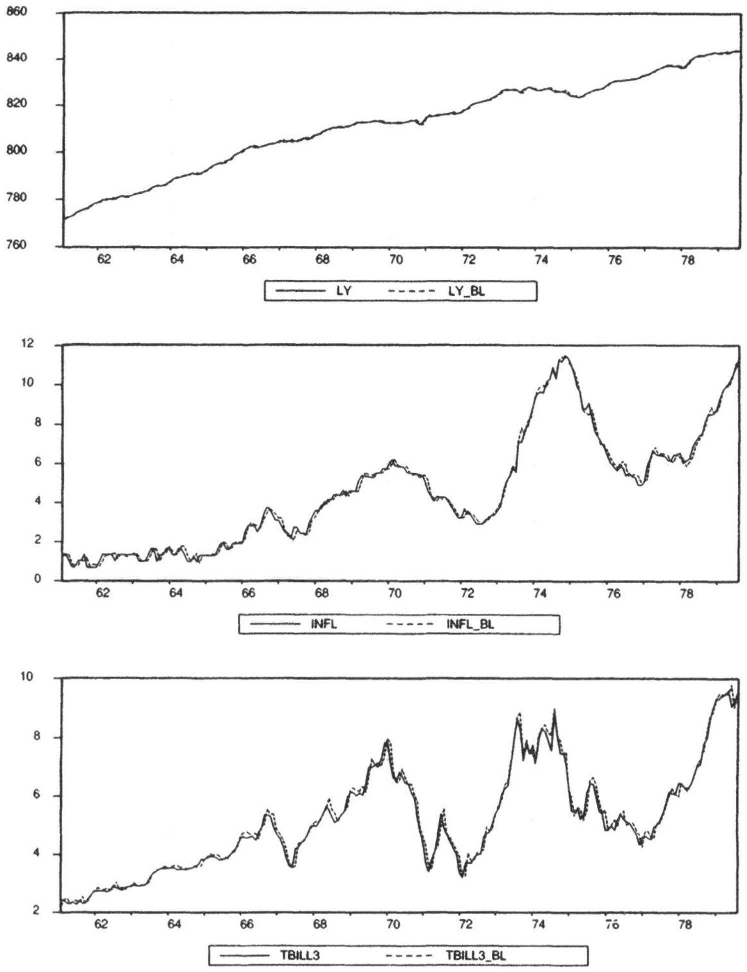


FIG. 5.3. Actual and fitted values from the structural model

(5.39), (5.41) over the sample considered for estimation. The perturbed solution is obtained by adding an exogenous one-off 100 basis point shock to equation (5.41) in the first period of the simulation. Obviously a one-off hundred basis point shock to the first difference of the policy rates is a permanent one hundred basis points shock to the level of policy rates. Dynamic multipliers are then computed by adapting the E-Views procedures already discussed in Chapter 4. All computations are available in the file lse.wf1. We report dynamic multipliers in Figure 5.4.

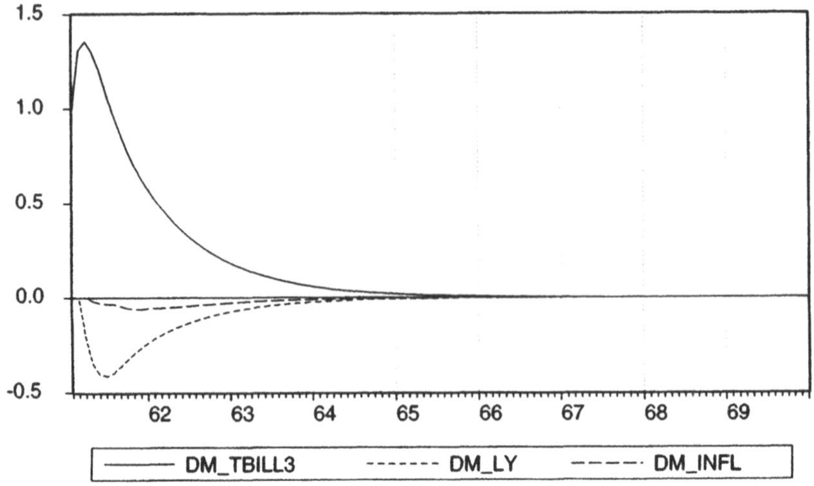


FIG. 5.4. Dynamic multipliers

Dynamic multipliers confirm the stability of the model and reveal a much stronger impact of monetary policy on output fluctuations than on inflation. Note also that the pattern of multipliers is much smoother than the corresponding pattern for the model used to illustrate the Cowles Commission strategy. Such smoothness is a consequence of the better dynamic specification of the LSE model.

### 5.10.1 *Model evaluation*

To complete our comparative evaluation of the LSE and the Cowles Commission specifications we have still to consider out-of-sample evaluation, where the performance of the Cowles Commission specification was at its worst. We simulate the LSE model dynamically over the period 1985:01–1996:03. In doing so we deliberately skip the period of non-borrowed reserves targeting where our specification is clearly not appropriate. The dynamically simulated series are reported with the actual series in Figure 5.5.

Figure 5.5 shows an improved performance with respect to the Cowles Commission specification but clearly there are problems in the out-of-sample simulation. The implementation of diagnostic tests guarantees the quality of the within sample results but cannot insure against structural shifts in parameters: congruent models within sample might perform very poorly in out-of-sample simulations.

### 5.10.2 *Testing the Lucas critique*

Our simple model of the monetary transmission mechanism offers an opportunity to implement empirically tests for superexogeneity.

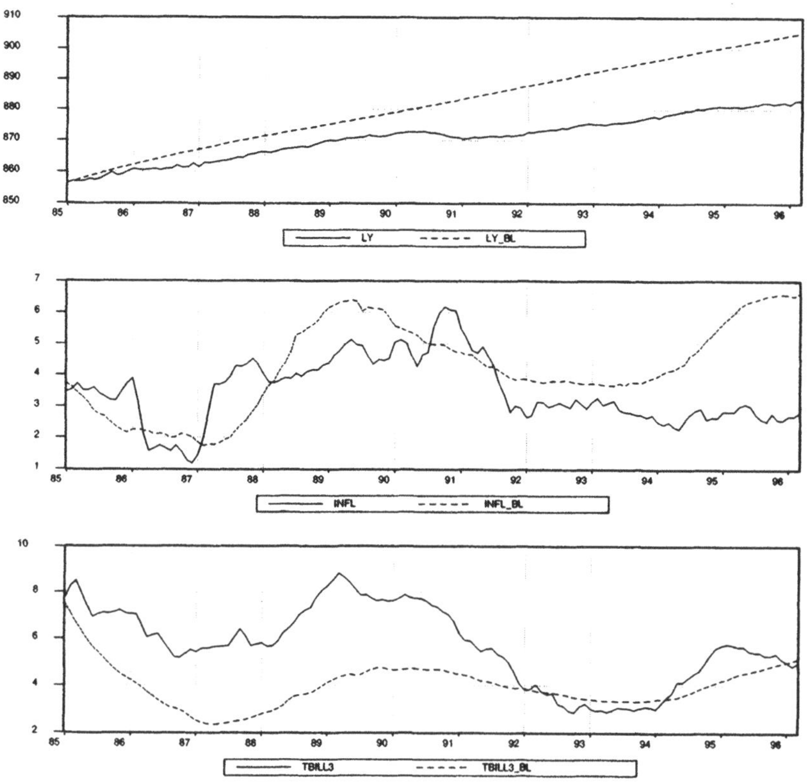


FIG. 5.5. Out-of-sample dynamic simulation: actual and simulated (_bl) series

In our discussion of identification in Chapter 3 we have shown that when a central bank faces the following intertemporal optimization problem:

$$\min \quad E_t \sum_{i=0}^{\infty} \delta^i L_{t+i}, \tag{5.42}$$

where:

$$L = \frac{1}{2}\left[(\pi_t - \pi^*)^2 + \lambda x_t^2\right] \tag{5.43}$$

under the constraints of the following specification for aggregate supply and demand in a closed economy:

$$x_{t+1} = \beta_x x_t - \beta_r \left(i_t - E_t \pi_{t+1} - \bar{r}\right) + u_{t+1}^d, \tag{5.44}$$

$$\pi_{t+1} = \pi_t + \alpha_x x_t + u_{t+1}^s. \tag{5.45}$$

As shown by Svensson (1997), the optimal interest rate rule can be written as:

$$i_t = \bar{r} + \pi^* + \left(\frac{1+\alpha_x\beta_r}{\alpha_x\beta_r}\right)(E_t\pi_{t+1} - \pi^*) \tag{5.46}$$
$$+\frac{\beta_x}{\beta_r}x_t + \frac{\lambda}{\delta\alpha_x k}\frac{1}{\alpha_x\beta_r}E_t x_{t+1}.$$

where $k$ is a combination of parameters describing the structure of the economy and the preferences of the central banker. We then have an intertemporal optimization framework which offers a feedforward monetary rule, in which output gap and inflation are not superexogenous for the estimation of the parameters of interest. Contrast this specification with equation (5.41) in our model. Our estimated equation is a feedback specification, which does not include explicitly expectations and whose parameters are estimated independently from those in the aggregate demand and supply schedules. Therefore, we have a natural candidate to test the validity of the Lucas critique. Tests of feedforward versus feedback model are difficult to apply in that we have designed our model to pass diagnostic tests. However, note that the reaction function and the aggregate supply and demand equation contain a common set of dummies. This is a clear indication of common outliers in the three equations which does not refute the hypothesis of validity of the feedforward interpretation. The presence of dummies shall also impact on the Engle–Hendry superexogeneity tests. This test is applicable by exploiting the specification of supply and demand equations to derive proxies for the first two moments in the conditional model for these two variables and then by adding them to the interest rate reaction function. The impact of the dummies on the test is determined by the fact that they capture some portion of the variability in the additional regressors on which joint significance is tested.

## 5.11 What have we learned?

In our opinion, the major strengths of the LSE methodology are related to a careful diagnosis of the problems of the Cowles Commission approach and to the attempt of giving 'scientific dignity' to the specification of dynamic econometric models. The concept of cointegration fits naturally in the context of dynamic specification of ECM models. Such research strategy is based on a multi-step framework: specification of the VAR and its deterministic component, identification of the number of cointegrating vectors, identification of the parameters in cointegrating vectors, tests on the speed of adjustment with respect to disequilibria. The results of the final test depend on the outcome of the previous stages in the empirical analysis, but the outcome of each step is not so easily and uniquely established empirically. The reduction process has been criticized by macroeconomists for its tendency to deliver preferred specification 'a bit over-cooked' and to loosen considerably the link between econometric models and economic theory. Consider the following money demand specification, taken from Baba, Hendry, and Starr (1992), as a typical LSE model:

$$\begin{aligned}\Delta (m-p)_t = & \underset{[0.097]}{-0.334}\Delta_4 (m-p)_{t-1} - \underset{[0.039]}{0.156}\Delta^2 (m-p)_{t-4} \qquad (5.47)\\ & \underset{[0.015]}{-0.249}\left(m-p-\frac{1}{2}y\right)_{t-2} - \underset{[0.046]}{0.33}\,\Delta\hat{p} - \underset{[0.132]}{1.097}\Delta_4 p_{t-1}\\ & \underset{[0.079]}{+0.859}V_t + \underset{[1.49]}{11.68}\Delta SV_{t-1} - \underset{[0.104]}{1.409}AS_t - \underset{[0.063]}{0.973}AR_{1t}\\ & \underset{[0.049]}{-0.255}\Delta R_{ma,t} + \underset{[0.055]}{0.435}R_{nsa,t} + \underset{[0.07]}{0.395}\Delta Ay_t + \underset{[0.003]}{0.013}D_t\\ & \underset{[0.02]}{+0.352} + \hat{u}_t,\end{aligned}$$

where heteroscedasticity consistent estimators are reported in brackets. The Baba–Hendry–Starr specification for US money demand is estimated on quarterly data covering the period 1960–1988. $m$ is the logarithm of M1; $y$ is the logarithm of real GNP using 1982 as base year; $p$ is the logarithm of the deflator; $\Delta^2$ is the square of the difference operator, $\Delta$; $\Delta\widehat{p}_t = \Delta(1+\Delta)\, p_t$; $\Delta_4 (m-p)_{t-1} = 0.25\left((m-p)_{t-1} - (m-p)_{t-5}\right)$; $V_t$ is a nine-quarter moving average of quarterly averages of twelve-month moving standard deviations of 20-year bond yields; $SV_t = \max(0, S_t) * V_t$ where S is the spread between the 20-year Treasury bond yield and the coupon equivalent yield on a one-month T-bill; $AS_t = 0.5\,(S_t + S_{t-1})$; $AR_{1t}$ is a two-quarter moving average of the one-month T-bill yield; $R_{ma,t}$ is the maximum of a passbook savings rate, a weighted certificate of deposit rate and a weighted money market mutual fund rate; $R_{nsa,t}$ is the average of weighted NOW and SuperNow rates; $Ay_t = 0.5\,(y_t + y_{t-1})$and $D_t$ is a credit control dummy which is –1 in 1980(2), 1 in 1980(3), and zero everywhere else. Baba–Hendry–Starr report 11 diagnostics; all passed.

The achievement of data congruency implies some evident cost in terms of the parsimony of the specification and economic interpretability of the results. Equation (5.47) also illustrates why the LSE methodology is not easily applied to systems of equations, even of very limited dimensions. General-to-specific methodology is usually applied in single-equation specification (money demand and consumption of non-durables functions are the preferred application of the LSE approach), applications to systems with few variables are reported in the literature but it becomes very hard and very rare to apply such methodology when the dimension of the system exceeds a small dimension (say five equations). Moreover, we have seen that the applicability of the concept of cointegration is very rapidly complicated as $n$ increases in $n$-variate systems.

Faust and Whiteman (1997) note that (5.47) is a much richer specification than the one implicitly contained in the standard VAR approach, including moving averages and moving standard deviations of interest rates. I am somewhat sceptical that such a specification could be produced by a VAR approach to cointegration, or by any VAR analysis. Criticisms of the use of variables generated by this are mainly based on the argument that, by construction, they capture within-sample fluctuations in the data and their performance out-of-sample worsens considerably. Moreover such transformations, being data-instigated, are usually related to theory with some difficulties. Many applied macroeconometricians feel not at ease in using variables which perform well empirically but whose links with theory are not so clear. Of course, for the LSE methodology, this is a problem with the profession rather than with the econometric methodology. In fact, this is probably the centre of the debate.

## 5.12 References


Andrews, D. W. (1993). 'Tests for parameter instability and structural change with unknown change point'. *Econometrica*, 61: 821–853.

Baba, Y., Hendry, D. F., and Starr, R. M. (1992). 'The demand for M1 in the USA, 1960–1988'. *Review of Economic Studies*, 59: 25–61.

Chow, G. C. (1960). 'Tests of equality between sets of coefficients in two linear regressions'. *Econometrica*, 28: 591–605.

Doornik, J., and Hendry, D. F. (1997). *PcFIML 9.0. Interactive econometric modelling of dynamic systems.* Oxford: Thomson Publishing.

Doornik, J., and Hansen, H. (1994). *A practical test of multivariate normality.* Oxford: Nuffield College.

Engle, R. F. (1982). 'Autoregressive conditional heteroscedasticity, with estimates of the variance of United Kingdom inflations'. *Econometrica*, 50: 987–1007.

Engle, R. F. and Hendry, D. F. (1993). 'Testing superexogeneity and invariance in regression models'. *Journal of Econometrics*, 56: 119–139.

Ericsson, N. R., and Irons, J. S. (1994). *Testing Exogeneity.* Oxford: Oxford University Press.

Faust, J. and Whiteman, C. H. (1997). 'General-to-specific procedures for fitting a data-admissible, theory-inspired, congruent, parsimonious, encompassing, weakly-exogenous, identified, structural model to the DGP: a translation and a critique'. Board of Governors of the Federal Reserve System, International Finance Discussion Papers, 576.

Favero, C. A., and Hendry, D. F. (1992). 'Testing the Lucas critique: a Review'. *Econometric Reviews*, 11: 265-306.

Godfrey, L. G. (1988). *Misspecification tests in Econometrics.* Cambridge: Cambridge University Press.

Granger, C. W. J. (1987). 'Equilibrium, causality and error correction models'. *Economic Notes*, 1: 6-21.

Hausman, J. A. (1978). 'Specification tests in econometrics'. *Econometrica*, 46: 1251-1271.

Hendry, D. F. (1988). 'The encompassing implications of feedback versus feedforward mechanisms in econometrics'. *Oxford Economic Papers*, 4:133-147.

Hendry, D. F. (1995). *Dynamic Econometrics.* Oxford: Oxford University Press.

Hendry, D. F., Neale, A., and Srba, F. (1988). 'Econometric analysis of small linear systems using PC-FIML'. *Journal of Econometrics*, 38: 203-226.

Johansen, S., and Nielsen, B.G. (1993). 'Asymptotics for the cointegration rank test tests in the presence of intervantion dummies'. *Manual for the simulation program DisCo.* Manual and program are available at the URL http://www.nuff.ox.ac.uk/users/nielsen/disco.html.

Kiviet, J. F. (1986). 'On the rigour of some mis-specification tests for modelling dynamic relationships'. *Review of Economic Studies*, 53: 241-261.

Osterwald-Lenum, M. (1992). 'A note with quantiles of the asymptotic distribution of the maximum likelihood cointegration rank test statistics'. *Oxford Bulletin of Economics and Statistics*, 54: 461-472.

Pagan, A.(1984). 'Model evaluation by variable addition'. In Hendry, D.F. and Wallis, K. F., (eds.), *Econometrics and Quantitative Economics*, Oxford: Basil Blackwell.

Spanos, A.(1990) 'The simultaneous-equations model revisited. Statistical adequacy and identification'. *Journal of Econometrics*, 44: 87-105.

Svensson, L.E.O. (1997) 'Inflation Forecast Targeting: Implementing and Monitoring Inflation Targets', *European Economic Review*, 41: 1111-1146.

Walsh, C. (1998). *Monetary theory and policy.* Cambridge, Massachusetts: MIT Press.

White, H. (1980). 'A heteroscedasticity-consistent covariance matrix estimator and a direct test for heteroscedasticity'. *Econometrica*, 48: 817-838.

Wu, D. (1973). 'Alternative tests of independence between stochastic regressors and disturbances'. *Econometrica*, 41: 733-750.

# 6

# VAR APPROACH

## 6.1 Introduction: why VAR models?

The LSE methodology has interpreted the failure of the traditional Cowles Commission approach, heralded by the critiques of Lucas (1976) and Sims (1980*a*), as the result of using mis-specified and ill-identified models. The LSE methodology, however, does not question the potential of macroeconometric modelling for simulation and econometric policy evaluation. In fact, at the stage of simulation and policy evaluation, there is no difference between the traditional Cowles Commission approach and the LSE approach. The LSE solution to the problems of traditional macroeconometric modelling concentrates on the stages of identification and specification. The importance of estimation is de-emphasized, in that congruency of the specification is considered as a much higher priority than the choice of the most appropriate estimator. No innovation is proposed at the stage of simulation and policy evaluation: the traditional methods are applied, after having tested, tested, and tested.

The VAR approach shares with the LSE methodology the diagnosis of the problem of Cowles Commission models but also questions the potential of traditional macroeconometric modelling for policy simulation and econometric policy evaluation. VAR models of the monetary transmission mechanism differ from structural LSE models as to the purpose of their specification and estimation. In the traditional approach the typical question asked within a macroeconometric framework is 'What is the optimal response by the monetary authority to movement in macroeconomic variables to achieve given targets for the same variables?' The VAR approach fully recognizes the potential of the Lucas critique and acknowledges that questions like 'How should a central bank respond to shocks in macroeconomic variables?' are to be answered within the framework of quantitative monetary general equilibrium models of the business cycle. So the answer should rely on a theoretical model rather than on an empirical *ad hoc* macroeconometric model. Within this framework, there emerges a new role for empirical analysis, which is to provide evidence on the stylized facts to include in the theoretical model adopted for policy analysis and to decide between competing general equilibrium monetary models. The operationalization of this research program is very well described in a recent paper by Christiano, Eichenbaum and Evans (1998). There are three relevant steps:

1. monetary policy shocks are identified in actual economies;

2. the response of relevant economic variables to monetary shocks is then described;
3. finally, the same experiment is performed in the model economies to compare actual and model-based responses as an evaluation tool and a selection criterion for theoretical models.

LSE-type structural models and VAR models of the monetary transmission mechanism have a common structure which, using the notation of Chapter 3, is represented as follows:

$$\mathbf{A}\begin{pmatrix}\mathbf{Y}_t\\ \mathbf{M}_t\end{pmatrix} = \mathbf{C}(L)\begin{pmatrix}\mathbf{Y}_{t-1}\\ \mathbf{M}_{t-1}\end{pmatrix} + \mathbf{B}\begin{pmatrix}\nu_t^Y\\ \nu_t^M\end{pmatrix} \tag{6.1}$$

where $\mathbf{Y}$ and $\mathbf{M}$ are vectors of macroeconomic (non-policy) variables (e.g. output and prices) and variables controlled by the monetary policy-maker (e.g. interest rates and monetary aggregates containing information on monetary policy actions) respectively. Matrix $\mathbf{A}$ describes the contemporaneous relations among the variables and $\mathbf{C}(L)$ is a matrix finite-order lag polynomial. $\nu \equiv \begin{pmatrix}\nu^Y\\ \nu^M\end{pmatrix}$ is a vector of structural disturbances to the non-policy and policy variables; non-zero off-diagonal elements of $\mathbf{B}$ allow some shocks to affect directly more than one endogenous variable in the system. The main difference between the two approaches lies in the aim for which models are estimated.

Traditional Cowles Commission structural models are designed to identify the impact of policy variables on macroeconomic quantities to determine the value to be assigned to the monetary instruments ($\mathbf{M}$) to achieve a given target for the macroeconomic variables ($\mathbf{Y}$). The policy variables in $\mathbf{M}$ are considered as exogenous on the grounds that these are the instruments controlled by the policy-maker. Identification in traditional structural models is obtained without assuming the orthogonality of structural disturbances. Dynamic multipliers are used to describe the impact of monetary policy variables on macroeconomic quantities. In the computation of dynamic multipliers the responses of macroeconomic variables to monetary policy can be, and usually is, obtained without decomposing monetary policy into its endogenous and exogenous components.

The assumed exogeneity of the monetary variables in the traditional approach makes the model invalid for policy analysis if monetary policy reacts endogenously to macroeconomic variables. The LSE methodology would recognize the problem of the invalid exogeneity assumption for $\mathbf{M}$, it would then proceed to the identification of an alternative enlarged model.[1] However, the new model would still be used for simulation and econometric policy evaluation, whenever the appropriate concept of exogeneity (respectively strong and super) where satisfied by the adopted specification.

[1]Presumably, such identification would be obtained through the imposition of a priori restrictions on the dynamics of the lagged variables.

VAR modelling would reject the Cowles Commission identifying restrictions as 'incredible' for reasons not very different from the ones pinned down by the LSE approach, however, VAR models of the transmission mechanism are not estimated to yield advice on the best monetary policy. They are rather estimated to provide empirical evidence on the response of macroeconomic variables to monetary policy impulses in order to discriminate between alternative theoretical models of the economy. It then becomes crucial to identify monetary policy actions using restrictions independent from the competing models of the transmission mechanism under empirical investigation, taking into account the potential endogeneity of policy instruments.

In a series of recent papers, Christiano, Eichenbaum and Evans (1996*a*)–(1996*b*) apply the VAR approach to derive 'stylized facts' on the effect of a contractionary policy shock, and conclude that plausible models of the monetary transmission mechanism should be consistent at least with the following evidence on price, output and interest rates: *(i)* the aggregate price level initially responds very little; *(ii)* interest rates initially rise, and *(iii)* aggregate output initially falls, with a $j$-shaped response, with a zero long-run effect of the monetary impulse. Such evidence leads to the dismissal of traditional real business cycle models, which are not compatible with the liquidity effect of monetary policy on interest rates, and of the Lucas (1972) model of money, in which the effect of monetary policy on output depends on price misperceptions. The evidence seems to be more in line with alternative interpretations of the monetary transmission mechanism based on sticky prices models (Goodfriend and King 1997), limited participation models (Christiano and Eichenbaum 1992) or models with indeterminacy–sunspot equilibria (Farmer 1997).

Having stated the objective of VAR models we are now in the position to assess how identification, estimation and simulation are implemented to analyse the monetary transmission mechanism.

VAR models concentrate on shocks. First the relevant shocks are identified, and the response of the system to shocks is described by analysing impulse responses (the propagation mechanism of the shocks), forecasting error variance decomposition, and historical decomposition.

## 6.2 Identification and estimation

We introduced the identification problem for VAR in Chapter 3.

The structural model (6.1) is not directly observable; however a VAR can be estimated as the reduced form of the underlying structural model:

$$\begin{pmatrix} \mathbf{Y}_t \\ \mathbf{M}_t \end{pmatrix} = \mathbf{A}^{-1}\mathbf{C}(L) \begin{pmatrix} \mathbf{Y}_{t-1} \\ \mathbf{M}_{t-1} \end{pmatrix} + \begin{pmatrix} \mathbf{u}_t^Y \\ \mathbf{u}_t^M \end{pmatrix}, \tag{6.2}$$

where $\mathbf{u}$ denotes the VAR residual vector, normally independently distributed with full variance-covariance matrix $\Sigma$. The relation between the residuals in $\mathbf{u}$ and the structural disturbances in $\boldsymbol{\nu}$ is therefore:

$$\mathbf{A}\begin{pmatrix}\mathbf{u}_t^Y\\ \mathbf{u}_t^M\end{pmatrix}=\mathbf{B}\begin{pmatrix}\boldsymbol{\nu}_t^Y\\ \boldsymbol{\nu}_t^M\end{pmatrix}. \tag{6.3}$$

Undoing the partitioning we have

$$\mathbf{u}_t=\mathbf{A}^{-1}\mathbf{B}\boldsymbol{v}_t,$$

from which we can derive the relation between the variance-covariance matrices of $\mathbf{u}_t$ (observed) and $\boldsymbol{\nu}_t$ (unobserved) as follows:

$$E\left(\mathbf{u}_t\mathbf{u}_t'\right)=\mathbf{A}^{-1}\mathbf{B}E\left(\boldsymbol{v}_t\boldsymbol{v}_t'\right)\mathbf{B}'\mathbf{A}^{-1}.$$

Substituting population moments with sample moments we have:

$$\widehat{\sum}=\widehat{\mathbf{A}}^{-1}\mathbf{B}\mathbf{I}\widehat{\mathbf{B}}'\widehat{\mathbf{A}}^{-1}, \tag{6.4}$$

$\widehat{\sum}$ contains $n(n+1)/2$ different elements, which is the maximum number of identifiable parameters in matrices **A** and **B**. Therefore, a necessary condition for identification is that the maximum number of parameters contained in the two matrices equals $n(n+1)/2$, such a condition makes the number of equations equal to the number of unknowns in system (6.4). As usual, for such a condition also to be sufficient for identification no equation in (6.4) should be a linear combination of the other equations in the system (see Amisano and Giannini 1996, Hamilton 1994). As for traditional models, we have the three possible cases of under-identification, just-identification and over-identification. The validity of over-identifying restrictions can be tested via a statistic distributed as a $\chi^2$ with a number of degrees of freedom equal to the number of over-identifying restrictions. Once identification has been achieved, the estimation problem is solved by applying generalized method of moments estimation. We describe this class of estimators in the next chapter.

In practice, identification requires the imposition of some restrictions on the parameters of **A** and **B**. This step has been historically implemented in a number of different ways. We concentrate on the most widely used strategies in the next subsections.

### 6.2.1 *Choleski decomposition*

In the famous article which introduced VAR methodology to the profession, Sims (1980*a*) proposed the following identification strategy, based on the Choleski decomposition of matrices:

$$\mathbf{A}=\begin{pmatrix}1 & 0\,0 & & 0\\ a_{21} & 1\,0 & & 0\\ . & .\;1 & & .\\ a_{n1} & . & a_{nn-1} & 1\end{pmatrix},\qquad \mathbf{B}\begin{pmatrix}b_{11} & 0 & 0 & 0\\ 0 & b_{22} & 0 & 0\\ . & . & b_{ii}. & .\\ 0 & 0 & 0 & b_{nn}\end{pmatrix}. \tag{6.5}$$

This is obviously a just-identification scheme, where the identification of structural shocks depends on the ordering of variables. It corresponds to a recursive economic structure, with the most endogenous variable ordered last.

### 6.2.2 *Structural models with contemporaneous restrictions*

In this identification scheme some a priori information is used to impose restrictions on the elements of matrices **A** and **B**, different from the Choleski ordering. If the objective of VAR is to provide evidence to choose between competing models, the identifying restrictions should be independent from the theoretical predictions of those models. The recent literature on the monetary transmission mechanism (see Strongin 1995, Bernanke and Mihov 1995, Christiano, Eichenbaum and Evans 1996, Leeper, Sims and Zha 1996), offers good examples on how these kind of restrictions can be derived. VARs of the monetary transmission mechanism are specified on six variables, with the vector of macroeconomic non-policy variables including gross domestic product (GDP), the consumer price index (P) and the commodity price level (Pcm), the vector of policy variables includes the federal funds rate (FF), the quantity of total bank reserves (TR) and the amount of non-borrowed reserves (NBR). Given the estimation of the reduced form VAR for the six macro and monetary variables, a structural model is identified by: (*i*) assuming orthogonality of the structural disturbances; (*ii*) imposing that macroeconomic variables do not simultaneously react to monetary variables, while the simultaneous feedback in the other direction is allowed, and (*iii*) imposing restrictions on the monetary block of the model reflecting the operational procedures implemented by the monetary policy-maker. All identifying restrictions satisfy the criterion of independence from specific theoretical models. In fact, within the class of models estimated on monthly data, restrictions (*ii*) are consistent with a wide spectrum of alternative theoretical structures and imply a minimal assumption on the lag of the impact of monetary policy actions on macroeconomic variables, whereas restrictions (*iii*) are based on institutional analysis. Restrictions (*ii*) are made operational by setting to zero an appropriate block of elements of the **A** matrix.

The contemporaneous relations among the Fed funds rate and the reserve aggregates are derived, as in Bernanke and Mihov (1995), from a specific model of the reserve market:

$$u^{TR} = -\alpha u^{FF} + \nu^{D} \tag{6.6}$$
$$u^{BR} = \beta u^{FF} + \nu^{B} \tag{6.7}$$
$$u^{NBR} = \phi^{D}\nu^{D} + \phi^{B}\nu^{B} + \nu^{S}. \tag{6.8}$$

Equations (6.6) and (6.7) describe banks' demand equations (expressed in innovation, i.e. VAR residual–form) for total, TR, and borrowed, BR, reserves (time subscripts are omitted): the federal funds rate affects negatively the demand for total reserves (6.6) and positively the demand for borrowed reserves.[2] $\nu^D$ and $\nu^B$ are disturbances to total and borrowed reserves respectively. The supply of non-borrowed reserves in (6.8) reflects the behaviour of the Federal Reserve. In

[2]We assume from the start that movements in the discount rate, which would enter (6.7) with a negative sign, are completely anticipated, so that the innovation in the Fed funds-discount rate differential is entirely attributable to the former rate.

particular, by means of open-market operations, the Fed can change the amount of NBR supplied to the banking system in response to (readily observed) disturbances to total and borrowed reserves demand. Moreover, variations in non-borrowed reserves may be due to monetary policy shocks unrelated to reserves demand behaviour. In (6.8) the coefficients $\phi^D$ and $\phi^B$ measure the reaction of the Fed to total and borrowed reserve demand movements respectively, and $\nu^S$ represents the monetary policy shock to be empirically identified. The market for reserves featuring the assumed simultaneous relations is described by Figure 6.1.

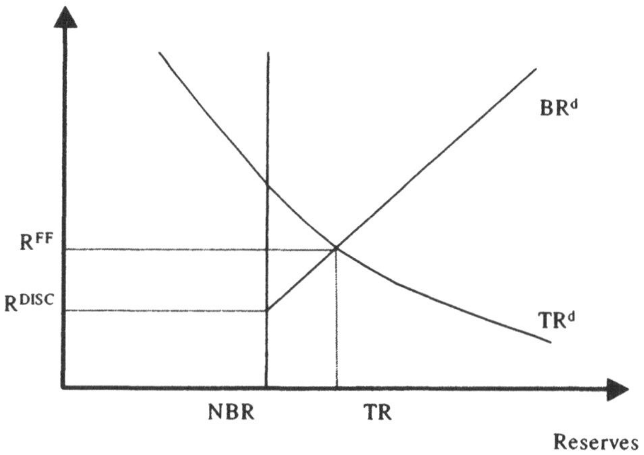


FIG. 6.1. The US market for bank reserves

Combining the market for reserves with the macroeconomic variables, we can explicitly rewrite (6.3) as follows:

$$\begin{pmatrix} 1 & 0 & 0 & 0 & 0 & 0 \\ a_{21} & 1 & 0 & 0 & 0 & 0 \\ a_{31} & a_{32} & 1 & 0 & 0 & 0 \\ a_{41} & a_{42} & a_{43} & 1 & -\frac{1}{\beta} & \frac{1}{\beta} \\ a_{51} & a_{52} & a_{53} & \alpha & 1 & 0 \\ a_{61} & a_{62} & a_{63} & 0 & 0 & 1 \end{pmatrix} \begin{pmatrix} u_t^{GDP} \\ u_t^{P} \\ u_t^{Pcm} \\ u_t^{FF} \\ u_t^{TR} \\ u_t^{NBR} \end{pmatrix} = \begin{pmatrix} 1 & 0 & 0 & 0 & 0 & 0 \\ 0 & 1 & 0 & 0 & 0 & 0 \\ 0 & 0 & 1 & 0 & 0 & 0 \\ 0 & 0 & 0 & -\frac{1}{\beta} & 0 & 0 \\ 0 & 0 & 0 & 0 & 1 & 0 \\ 0 & 0 & 0 & \phi^B & \phi^D & 1 \end{pmatrix} \begin{pmatrix} \nu_{1t}^{NP} \\ \nu_{2t}^{NP} \\ \nu_{3t}^{NP} \\ \nu_t^{B} \\ \nu_t^{D} \\ \nu_t^{S} \end{pmatrix}. \qquad (6.9)$$

Several features of (6.9) must be noted. First, VAR residuals from the first three equations, describing the non-policy part of the system, are orthogonalized simply by assuming a recursive (Choleski) structure for the corresponding block of the **A** matrix. This procedure yields orthogonal disturbances to which we do not attach a specific 'structural' interpretation, labelling them simply as $\nu_i^{NP}$ $(i = 1, 2, 3)$, where NP denotes a non-policy shock.

Second, as shown by Bernanke and Mihov (1995), the general formulation in (6.9) is still not identified, but identification can be completed by a careful analysis of the operational procedures followed by the central bank.

- Case 1: Federal funds targeting.

In this case we have $\varphi^d = 1, \varphi^b = -1$. Central bank uses NBR to neutralize shocks coming from banks' and households' behaviour. We then have for the monetary block identification:

$$\begin{bmatrix} u_t^{TR} \\ u_t^{NBR} \\ u_t^{FF} \end{bmatrix} = \begin{bmatrix} 1 & \frac{\alpha}{\beta+\alpha} & 0 \\ 1 & 1 & -1 \\ 0 & -\frac{1}{\beta+\alpha} & 0 \end{bmatrix} \begin{bmatrix} \nu_t^D \\ \nu_t^S \\ \nu_t^B \end{bmatrix}.$$

The model is now over-identified. Note that this identification scheme is equivalent to a Choleski identification with the ordering Federal funds rate, total reserves and non-borrowed reserves Choleski plus some additional within equation and cross equations restrictions.

- Case II: targeting NBR.

$\varphi^d = 0, \varphi^b = 0$.

$$\begin{bmatrix} u_t^{TR} \\ u_t^{NBR} \\ u_t^{FF} \end{bmatrix} = \begin{bmatrix} \frac{\beta}{\beta+\alpha} & \frac{\alpha}{\beta+\alpha} & \frac{\alpha}{\beta+\alpha} \\ 0 & 1 & 0 \\ \frac{1}{\beta+\alpha} & -\frac{1}{\beta+\alpha} & -\frac{1}{\beta+\alpha} \end{bmatrix} \begin{bmatrix} \nu_t^D \\ \nu_t^S \\ \nu_t^B \end{bmatrix}$$

Monetary policy shocks now coincide with the VAR innovations for non-borrowed reserves, NBR, while the Federal funds rate reflects all type of shocks.

- Case III: Strongin identification (1994).

Shocks to reserves are demand shocks which the central bank has to accommodate. Therefore monetary policy shocks are the shocks to NBR orthogonal to shocks to TR. Moreover, the central bank does not react to borrowed reserves. $\alpha = 0, \varphi^b = 0$,

$$\begin{bmatrix} u_t^{TR} \\ u_t^{NBR} \\ u_t^{FF} \end{bmatrix} = \begin{bmatrix} 1 & 0 & 0 \\ \varphi^d & 1 & 0 \\ -\frac{\varphi^d-1}{\beta} & -\frac{1}{\beta} & -\frac{1}{\beta} \end{bmatrix} \begin{bmatrix} \nu_t^D \\ \nu_t^S \\ \nu_t^B \end{bmatrix}$$

NBR is now the variable from which monetary policy shocks are extracted.

- Case IV: controlling borrowed reserves.

In this case TR – NBR is only a function of shocks $\nu^s$. $\varphi^d = 1, \varphi^b = \frac{\alpha}{\beta}$. We have:

$$\begin{bmatrix} u_t^{TR} \\ u_t^{NBR} \\ u_t^{FF} \end{bmatrix} = \begin{bmatrix} 1 & \frac{\alpha}{\beta+\alpha} & \frac{\alpha}{\beta} \\ 1 & 1 & \frac{\alpha}{\beta} \\ 0 & -\frac{1}{\beta+\alpha} & -\frac{1}{\beta} \end{bmatrix} \begin{bmatrix} \nu_t^D \\ \nu_t^S \\ \nu_t^B \end{bmatrix}.$$

It is easily seen that an alternative regime would imply identification which is technically not far from Choleski's triangularization, with different ordering of the monetary variables. In a Fed funds targeting regime Federal funds rate does not react contemporaneously to the other monetary variables while in a non-borrowed reserves targeting regime it is NBR that does not react contemporaneously to the other two monetary shocks. Moreover, information on the operating procedure by the Fed are important in determining the appropriate identification scheme and, more importantly, VAR models of the monetary transmission mechanism should be estimated within a single policy regime. Bagliano and Favero (1998) provide evidence on the structural instability of VAR of the MTM estimated across different monetary policy regimes.

### 6.2.3 *Structural VARs with long-run restrictions*

Often long-run behaviour of shocks provide restrictions acceptable within a wide range of theoretical models. A typical restriction compatible with virtually all macroeconomic models is that in the long-run demand shocks have zero impact on output. Blanchard and Quah (1989) show how these restrictions can be used to identify VARs.

The structural model of interest is specified by posing $\mathbf{A}$ equal to the identity matrix and by imposing no restriction on the $\mathbf{B}$ matrix. We then have the following specification for a generic vector of variables $\mathbf{y}_t$:

$$\mathbf{y}_t = \sum_{i=1}^{p} \mathbf{A}_i \mathbf{y}_{t-i} + \mathbf{B}\mathbf{v}_t$$

from which one can derive the matrix which describes the long-run effect of the structural shocks on the variables of interest as follows:

$$\left(\mathbf{I} - \sum_{i=1}^{p} \mathbf{A}_i\right)^{-1} \mathbf{B}\mathbf{v}_t = -\Pi^{-1}\mathbf{B}\mathbf{v}_t.$$

Coefficients in $\Pi$ are obtained from the reduced form, therefore, we are able to impose long-run restrictions given the estimation of the reduced form.

Two points are worth noting:

1. $(I - A_1)$ is -$\Pi$, for this matrix to be invertible the VAR must be specified on stationary variables;
2. the long-run restrictions are restrictions on the cumulative impulse response function.

Let us now consider the Blanchard and Quah (1989) dataset. The authors aim at separating demand shocks from supply shocks, they consider a VAR on two variables, the unemployment rate, $UN$, and the quarterly rate of growth of GDP, $\Delta LY$. The original sample contains quarterly data from 1951:2 to 1987:4, we have retrieved the two series from Datastream and they are available only for the sample 1951:2–1987:4. The series are available in the file bq.wks. The VAR is specified with 8 lags, a constant, and a deterministic trend (in the original paper a break in the constant for ΔLY is also allowed but we do not allow it here) as follows:

$$\begin{pmatrix} \Delta LY_t \\ UN_t \end{pmatrix} = A_1 \begin{pmatrix} \Delta LY_{t-1} \\ UN_{t-1} \end{pmatrix} + \ldots + A_8 \begin{pmatrix} \Delta LY_{t-8} \\ UN_{t-8} \end{pmatrix} + A_9 \begin{pmatrix} 1 \\ t \end{pmatrix} + \begin{pmatrix} u_{1t} \\ u_{2t} \end{pmatrix}.$$

The structure of interest is the following:

$$\begin{pmatrix} \Delta LY_t \\ UN_t \end{pmatrix} = A_1 \begin{pmatrix} \Delta LY_{t-1} \\ UN_{t-1} \end{pmatrix} + \ldots A_8 \begin{pmatrix} \Delta LY_{t-8} \\ UN_{t-8} \end{pmatrix} + A_9 \begin{pmatrix} 1 \\ t \end{pmatrix}$$
$$+ \begin{pmatrix} b_{11} & b_{12} \\ b_{21} & b_{22} \end{pmatrix} \begin{pmatrix} v_{1t} \\ v_{2t} \end{pmatrix}.$$

To obtain the identifying restrictions consider that

$$\begin{pmatrix} \Delta LY_t \\ UN_t \end{pmatrix} = \left( \mathbf{I} - \sum_{i=1}^{p} \mathbf{A}_i \right)^{-1} \begin{pmatrix} b_{11} & b_{12} \\ b_{21} & b_{22} \end{pmatrix} \begin{pmatrix} v_{1t} \\ v_{2t} \end{pmatrix}$$
$$= \begin{pmatrix} k_{11} & k_{12} \\ k_{21} & k_{22} \end{pmatrix} \begin{pmatrix} b_{11} & b_{12} \\ b_{21} & b_{22} \end{pmatrix} \begin{pmatrix} v_{1t} \\ v_{2t} \end{pmatrix}.$$

Demand shocks are identified by imposing that their long-run impact on the level of output is zero:

$$k_{11}b_{11} + k_{12}b_{21} = 0.$$

Note that by imposing the restriction that the cumulative impulse response of the rate of output growth to a demand shock is zero we impose the restriction that the impulse response of the level of output to a demand shock is zero in the long run. As the variables are stationary the long-run response of $\Delta LY$ and $UN$ to all shocks is zero by definition.

We implement the procedure on the data by using Malcolm (1998), a package written by Rocco Mosconi for RATS.

We start from the estimation of the VAR, we then implement the Johansen procedure on this VAR, we make sure that the null of stationarity is not rejected. We then retrieve the Π matrix. $\Pi = \begin{bmatrix} 0.1451 & 0.2168 \\ -0.5741 & -0.0693 \end{bmatrix}$, then:

$$(-\Pi)^{-1} = \begin{bmatrix} -0.1451 & -0.2168 \\ 0.5741 & 0.0693 \end{bmatrix}^{-1} = \begin{bmatrix} 0.60572 & 1.8949 \\ -5.0179 & -1.2683 \end{bmatrix},$$

and our long-run identifying restriction is

$$0.60572b_{11} + 1.8949b_{21} = 0.$$

Note the difference between this methodology and the Choleski decomposition, which would simply restrict $b_{21}$ to zero.

### 6.2.4 *Identification in cointegrated VARs*

Let us consider now how the identification problem changes when we have a cointegrated VAR. Considering, for simplicity, only first-order dynamics, the cointegrated reduced form is:

$$\Delta \mathbf{y}_t = \Pi \mathbf{y}_{t-1} + \mathbf{v}_t,$$

where $\Pi = \boldsymbol{\alpha}\boldsymbol{\beta}'$. As we know, identification of the cointegrating vectors is a problem totally separated from identification of the structural shocks of interest. Therefore, having solved the identification of the cointegrating relationships, we still have to deal with the problem of posing appropriate restrictions on the parameters of the **B** matrix in order to pin down the shocks $\mathbf{u}_t$

$$\Delta \mathbf{y}_t = \Pi \mathbf{y}_{t-1} + \mathbf{B}\mathbf{u}_t.$$

In the context of cointegration, the identification problem can be solved in a very natural way. Consider, for simplicity, the case of a bivariate model $\mathbf{y}_t = (y_t, x_t)$, in which variables are non-stationary $I(1)$ but cointegrated with a cointegrating vector $(1, -1)$, so the rank of the $\Pi$ matrix is 1 and we use the following representation of the stationary reduced form:

$$\begin{pmatrix} \Delta y_t \\ \Delta x_t \end{pmatrix} = \begin{pmatrix} \alpha_{11} \\ \alpha_{21} \end{pmatrix} \begin{pmatrix} 1 & -1 \end{pmatrix} \begin{pmatrix} y_{t-1} \\ x_{t-1} \end{pmatrix} + \begin{pmatrix} b_{11} & b_{12} \\ b_{21} & b_{22} \end{pmatrix} \begin{pmatrix} v_{1t} \\ v_{2t} \end{pmatrix}. \tag{6.10}$$

Model (6.10) can be re-written as follows Mellander, Vredin and Warne (1993):

$$\begin{aligned} \begin{pmatrix} -1 & 1 \\ 0 & 1 \end{pmatrix} \begin{pmatrix} (1-L) & 0 \\ 0 & 1 \end{pmatrix} \begin{pmatrix} (y_t - x_t) \\ \Delta x_t \end{pmatrix} &= \begin{pmatrix} \alpha_{11} & 0 \\ \alpha_{21} & 0 \end{pmatrix} \begin{pmatrix} (y_{t-1} - x_{t-1}) \\ \Delta x_{t-1} \end{pmatrix} \\ &\quad + \begin{pmatrix} b_{11} & b_{12} \\ b_{21} & b_{22} \end{pmatrix} \begin{pmatrix} v_{1t} \\ v_{2t} \end{pmatrix}. \end{aligned} \tag{6.11}$$

The two representations are completely identical (they feature the same residuals). The second representation has been widely used in research based on present value models. The cointegrating properties of the system suggest the presence of two types of shocks: a permanent one (related to the single common trend shared by the two variables) and a transitory one (related to the cointegrating relation). It seems therefore natural to identify one shock as permanent and the other as transitory. Given that we have a stationary system, the identification of shocks is obtained by deriving long-run responses of the variables of interest to relevant shocks. From (6.11) we have:

$$\left( \begin{pmatrix} -1 & 1 \\ 0 & 1 \end{pmatrix} \begin{pmatrix} (1-L) & 0 \\ 0 & 1 \end{pmatrix} - \begin{pmatrix} \alpha_{11}L & 0 \\ \alpha_{21}L & 0 \end{pmatrix} \right) \begin{pmatrix} (y_t - x_t) \\ \Delta x_t \end{pmatrix} = \begin{pmatrix} b_{11} & b_{12} \\ b_{21} & b_{22} \end{pmatrix} \begin{pmatrix} v_{1t} \\ v_{2t} \end{pmatrix},$$

from which long-run responses are obtained by setting $L = 1$ and by inverting the matrix pre-multiplying variables in the stationary representation of VAR

$$\begin{pmatrix} (y_t - x_t) \\ \Delta x_t \end{pmatrix} = \begin{pmatrix} -\alpha_{11} & 1 \\ -\alpha_{21} & 1 \end{pmatrix}^{-1} \begin{pmatrix} b_{11} & b_{12} \\ b_{21} & b_{22} \end{pmatrix} \begin{pmatrix} v_{1t} \\ v_{2t} \end{pmatrix} \tag{6.12}$$

$$\begin{pmatrix} (y_t - x_t) \\ \Delta x_t \end{pmatrix} = \begin{pmatrix} \frac{-b_{11}+b_{21}}{\alpha_{11}-\alpha_{21}} & -\frac{b_{12}-b_{22}}{\alpha_{11}-\alpha_{21}} \\ \frac{-\alpha_{21}b_{11}+\alpha_{11}b_{21}}{\alpha_{11}-\alpha_{21}} & \frac{-\alpha_{21}b_{12}+\alpha_{11}b_{22}}{\alpha_{11}-\alpha_{21}} \end{pmatrix} \begin{pmatrix} v_{1t} \\ v_{2t} \end{pmatrix}. \tag{6.13}$$

Thus $v_{2t}$ can be identified as the transitory shock by imposing the following restriction:

$$-\alpha_{21}b_{12} + \alpha_{11}b_{22} = 0$$

which, given knowledge of the $\boldsymbol{\alpha}$ parameters from the cointegration analysis, provides the just-identifying restriction for the parameters in **B**. Note that, there is one case in which this identification is equivalent to the Choleski ordering, the case in which $\alpha_{11} = 0$. Note that this is the case in which $\Delta y_t$ is weakly exogenous for the estimation of $b_{21}$. An application of this identifying scheme is provided in Favero, Giavazzi and Spaventa (1997) where the procedure is implemented to separate international from local factors in the determination of interest rates fluctuations.

## 6.3 Why shocks?

Having identified the 'monetary rule' by proposing an explicit solution to the problem of the endogeneity of money, the VAR approach concentrates on deviations from the rule. Deviations from the rule are obtained either by changing the systematic component of monetary policy or by considering exogenous shocks, which leave systematic monetary policy unaltered. In the former case the deviation from the rule is obtained by changing some parameters in the **A** matrix describing the simultaneous relations among variables, while in the latter case the parameters in the matrices **A** and **B** are left unaltered. Consider for example the case of Federal funds targeting. The first type of deviations is obtained by modifying the response of the Federal funds rates to macroeconomic conditions, i.e. fluctuations in output, commodity prices and the consumer price index, while the second type of deviations is obtained by considering an exogenous shock which does not alter the response of the monetary policy-maker to macroeconomic conditions. VAR modelers have exclusively concentrated on simulating shocks, leaving the systematic component of monetary policy unaltered.

The VAR approach to the monetary transmission mechanism has been criticized on the basis that it views central banks as 'random number generators'. This is incorrect, since monetary policy rules are explicitly estimated in structural VAR models. However, the focus is not on rules but on deviations from rules, since only when central banks deviate from their rules it becomes possible to collect interesting information on the response of macroeconomic variables to monetary policy impulses, to compare with the predictions of the alternative theoretical models. In fact, deviations from monetary policy rules provide researchers with the best opportunity to detect the response of macroeconomic variables to monetary impulses unexpected by the market. The first chain of most models of the monetary transmission mechanism links the policy rates to the term structure of the interest rates and the most popular model of the term structure, the expectational model, predicts that the term structure does not generally react to expected monetary impulses. The monetary impulses relevant to the transmission analysis are therefore structural shocks in (6.1).

Recently, McCallum (1999) has criticized the choice of VAR modelers of concentrating on shocks which leave the systematic component of monetary policy unaltered. It is argued that the emphasis on the shock component is misplaced because the unsystematic portion of policy-instrument variability is small in relation to the variability of the systematic component.

> ...Indeed, it is conceivable that the policy behaviour could be virtually devoid of any unsystematic component. In the limit, that is, the variance of the shock component could approach zero. But this would not imply that monetary policy is unimportant for price level behaviour, central bank's main responsibility... (McCallum 1999:5).

The simulation of systematic monetary policy requires, for robustness to the Lucas critique, the specification of a forward-looking model in which 'deep parameters' are identified independently from nuisance parameters describing expectations formation and dependent on the policy regime. This is what McCallum (1999) effectively does in a series of papers where the impact of modifications in the monetary policy-maker reaction function is dynamically simulated.

However, it is important to note that McCallum's work aims not at model selection but rather at model simulation. The question of using the empirical evidence to judge between different theoretical models is not addressed in McCallum's work, based on a specific model.

If VAR models are, instead, used to describe the empirical evidence relevant to the choice between alternative theoretical models, then there is a possible defence of the choice of concentrating on shocks rather than on the systematic components of monetary policy. Such a defence is related to the Lucas critique.

Consider the following data generating process:

$$\begin{aligned} y_t &= a_1 m_{t+1}^e + a_2 y_{t-1} + u_{1t} \\ m_t &= b_0 + b_1 y_{t-1} + b_2 m_{t-1} + u_{2t}, \end{aligned}$$

where $y$ is the macroeconomic variable and $m$ is the monetary policy variable.

The DGP is the relevant theoretical model, which is unknown to the empirical researcher. The empirical researcher tries instead to describe the empirical relation between the monetary instruments and the macroeconomic variables by specifying the following structural VAR:

$$\begin{aligned} y_t &= c_o + c_1 m_t + c_2 y_{t-1} + v_{1t} \\ m_t &= b_0 + b_1 y_{t-1} + b_2 m_{t-1} + v_{2t}, \end{aligned} \tag{6.14}$$

in which the restrictions $c_o = a_1 b_0$, $c_1 = a_1 b_2, c_2 = a_2 + a_1 b_1$ hold.

Equation (6.14) is not viable for econometric evaluation of systematic monetary policy, in that the parameters in the equation for $y$ cannot be kept constant when the systematic component of the monetary policy rule is altered. However, the simulation of the dynamic impact of a monetary policy shock identified *à la* Choleski ordering $m$ first is still viable in that it is performed while keeping all parameters constant.

Note that this small example reiterates the importance of estimating parameters in structural VAR models by concentrating on a single policy regime, in fact regime shifts require different parameterization. This reflects the fact, noted by Keating(1990), that a forward-looking DGP imposes cross-equation restrictions on parameters in a VAR.

Last, but certainly not least, a crucial assumption in structural VAR modelling is that structural shocks are linear combinations of the residuals in reduced form VAR models. Lippi and Reichlin (1993) argue that modern macroeconomic models which are linearized into dynamic systems tend to include non-invertible moving average components and structural shocks are therefore not identifiable. In fact, the linearized modern macroeconomic models of the monetary transmission mechanism, which we shall describe in the next chapters, deliver short VARs. In such models structural shocks are combinations of the residuals in the reduced form VARs (the Wold innovations) and the Lippi–Reichlin critique does not seem to be applicable (for a further discussion of this point see Amisano and Giannini 1996).

## 6.4 Description of VAR models

After the identification of structural shocks of interest, the properties of VAR models are described using impulse response analysis, variance decomposition and historical decomposition. Consider a structural VAR model for a generic vector $\mathbf{y}_t$, containing $m$ variables:

$$\mathbf{A}_0 \mathbf{y}_t = \sum_{i=1}^{p} \mathbf{A}_i \mathbf{y}_{t-i} + \mathbf{B}\mathbf{v}_t,$$

which we can rewrite as:

$$\begin{aligned} \left[\mathbf{A}_0 - \mathbf{A}\left(L\right)\right] \mathbf{y}_t &= \mathbf{B}\mathbf{v}_t \\ \mathbf{A}\left(L\right) &= \sum_{i=1}^{p} \mathbf{A}_i L^i. \end{aligned}$$

By inverting $[\mathbf{A}_0 - \mathbf{A}(L)]$ (under the assumption of invertibility of this polynomial) we obtain the moving average representation for our VAR process:

$$\begin{aligned} \mathbf{y}_t &= \mathbf{C}(L)\,\mathbf{v}_t, \qquad (6.15)\\ \mathbf{y}_t &= \mathbf{C}_0\mathbf{v}_t + \mathbf{C}_1\mathbf{v}_{t-1} + ... + \mathbf{C}_s\mathbf{v}_{t-s},\\ \mathbf{C}(L) &= [\mathbf{A}_0 - \mathbf{A}(L)]^{-1},\\ \mathbf{C}_0 &= \mathbf{A}_0^{-1}\mathbf{B}. \end{aligned}$$

To illustrate the concept of an *impulse response function,* we interpret the generic matrix $\mathbf{C}_s$ within the moving average representation as follows:

$$\mathbf{C}_s = \frac{\partial \mathbf{y}_{t+s}}{\partial \mathbf{v}_t}.$$

The generic element $\{i, j\}$ of matrix $\mathbf{C}_s$ represents the impact of a shock hitting the $j$-th variable of the system at time $t$ on the $i$-th variable of the system at time $t+s$. As $s$ varies we have a function describing the response of variable $i$ to an impulse in variable $j$. For this function of partial derivative to be meaningful we must allow that a shock to variable $j$ occurs while all other shocks are kept to zero. Of course this is allowed for structural shocks, as they are identified by imposing they are orthogonal to each other. Note, however that the concept of an impulse response function is not applicable to reduced form VAR innovations, which, in general, are correlated to each other.

*Historical decomposition* is obtained by using the structural MA representation to separate series in the components (orthogonal to each other) attributable to the different structural shocks.

Finally *forecasting error variance decomposition* (FEVD) is obtained from (6.15) by deriving the error in forecasting $\mathbf{y}_s$ period in the future as:

$$(\mathbf{y}_{t+s} - E_t\mathbf{y}_{t+s}) = \mathbf{C}_0\mathbf{v}_t + \mathbf{C}_1\mathbf{v}_{t-1} + ... + \mathbf{C}_s\mathbf{v}_{t-s}$$

from which we can construct the variance of such forecasting error as:

$$Var\,(\mathbf{y}_{t+s} - E_t\mathbf{y}_{t+s}) = \mathbf{C}_0 I\mathbf{C}_0' + \mathbf{C}_1 I\mathbf{C}_1' + ... + \mathbf{C}_s I\mathbf{C}_s'$$

from which we can compute the share of the total variance attributable to the variance of each structural shock. Note again that such composition makes sense only if shocks are orthogonal to each other. Only in this case we can write the variance of the total forecasting error as a sum of variances of the single shocks (as the covariance terms are zero following the orthogonality property of structural shocks).

To illustrate the three concepts consider the following bivariate VAR, in which structural parameters have been identified and estimated via a Choleski decomposition:

$$\begin{pmatrix} y_{1t} \\ y_{2t} \end{pmatrix} = \begin{pmatrix} a_{11} & a_{12} \\ a_{21} & a_{22} \end{pmatrix} \begin{pmatrix} y_{1t-1} \\ y_{2t-1} \end{pmatrix} + \begin{pmatrix} b_{11} & 0 \\ b_{21} & b_{22} \end{pmatrix} \begin{pmatrix} v_{1t} \\ v_{2t} \end{pmatrix}.$$

The MA representation is

$$\begin{pmatrix} y_{1t} \\ y_{2t} \end{pmatrix} = \begin{pmatrix} b_{11} & 0 \\ b_{21} & b_{22} \end{pmatrix} \begin{pmatrix} v_{1t} \\ v_{2t} \end{pmatrix} + \begin{pmatrix} a_{11} & a_{12} \\ a_{21} & a_{22} \end{pmatrix} \begin{pmatrix} b_{11} & 0 \\ b_{21} & b_{22} \end{pmatrix} \begin{pmatrix} v_{1t-1} \\ v_{2t-1} \end{pmatrix}$$
$$+ \ldots + \begin{pmatrix} a_{11} & a_{12} \\ a_{21} & a_{22} \end{pmatrix}^s \begin{pmatrix} b_{11} & 0 \\ b_{21} & b_{22} \end{pmatrix} \begin{pmatrix} v_{1t-s} \\ v_{2t-s} \end{pmatrix},$$

from which impulse response functions, historical decomposition and forecasting error variance decomposition are immediately obtained.

## 6.5 Monetary policy in closed economies

Cumulative work on the analysis of the monetary transmission mechanism in the US led to the specification of a VAR system which has by now become the standard reference model. We have already seen and discussed this benchmark specification which contains six variables: gross domestic product (GDP), the consumer price index (P) and the commodity price level (Pcm) together with the federal funds rate (FF), the quantity of total bank reserves (TR) and the amount of non-borrowed reserves (NBR).

It is interesting to see how the specification of the benchmark model has developed over time. Initially models were estimated on a rather limited set of variables, i.e. prices, money and output, and identified imposing a diagonal form on the matrix **B** and a lower triangular form on the matrix **A** with money coming last in the ordering of the variables included in the VAR (Choleski identification). This first type of models is discussed in Leeper, Sims and Zha (1996), we replicate their results on the dataset lszusa.wf1. The underlying structural model is specified as follows:

$$\mathbf{A}_0 \mathbf{y}_t = \sum_{i=1}^{k} \mathbf{A}_i \mathbf{y}_{t-i} + \mathbf{B} \boldsymbol{v}_t \tag{6.16}$$

$$\mathbf{y}_t = \begin{bmatrix} p_t \\ y_t \\ m_t \end{bmatrix}, \qquad \mathbf{A}_0 = \begin{bmatrix} 1 & 0 & 0 \\ a_{21} & 1 & 0 \\ a_{31} & a_{32} & 1 \end{bmatrix}$$

$$\mathbf{B} = \begin{bmatrix} b_{11} & 0 & 0 \\ 0 & b_{22} & 0 \\ 0 & 0 & b_{33} \end{bmatrix}, \qquad \boldsymbol{\nu}_t \sim n.i.d.\,(0, I)\,.$$

All variables are expressed in logarithms. Identification is Choleski-type with money ordered last. This is a model geared to deliver monetary policy shocks, so the identification of shocks to LP and LY does not matter. As Leeper, Sims and Zha did, we have estimated the model on the sample 1960:1–1996:3, including six lags of each variable. The impulse responses obtained are reported in Figure 6.2.

Prices slowly react to monetary policy, output responds in the short run, in the long run (from two years after the shock onwards) prices start adjusting

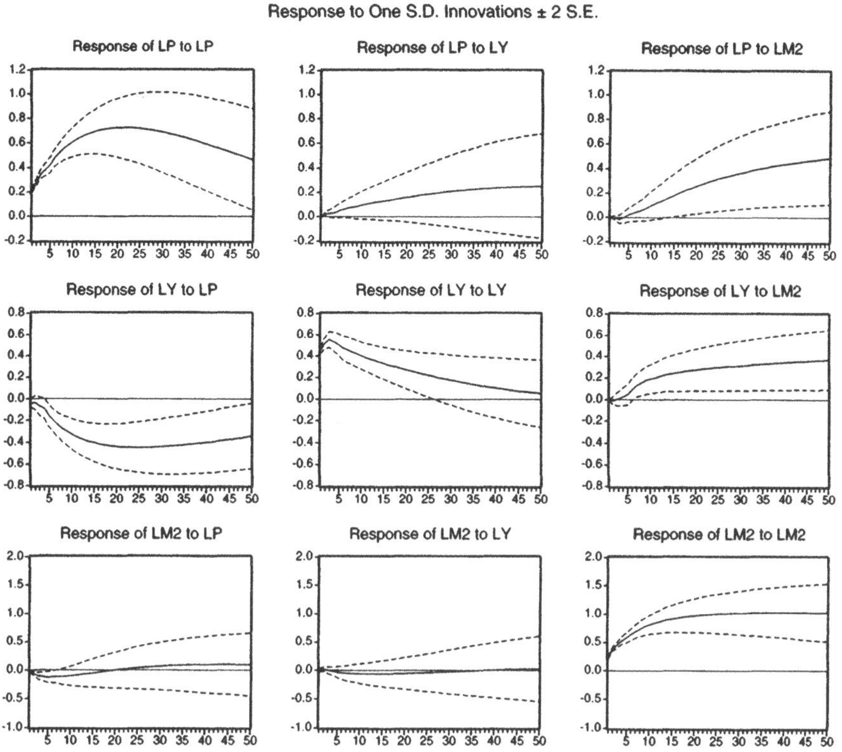


FIG. 6.2. Impulse response functions in a three-variables VAR of the MTM

and the significant effect on output vanishes. There is no strong evidence for the endogeneity of money. This is easily checked by looking at the estimated parameters in $\mathbf{A}_0$ and by analysing FEVD in Figure 6.3.

Macroeconomic variables play a very limited role in explaining the variance of the forecasting error of money, while money instead plays an important role in explaining fluctuations of both the macroeconomic variables.

Sims (1980) extended the VAR to include the interest rate on Federal funds ordered just before money as a penultimate variable in the Choleski identification. The idea is to see the robustness of the above results after identifying the part of money which is endogenous to the interest rate. Impulse response functions are modified as in Figure 6.4, while FEVD is modified as in Figure 6.5.

Impulse response functions and FEVD raise a number of issues.

1. Though little of the variation in money is predictable from past output and prices, a considerable amount becomes predictable when past short-term interest rates are included in the information set.

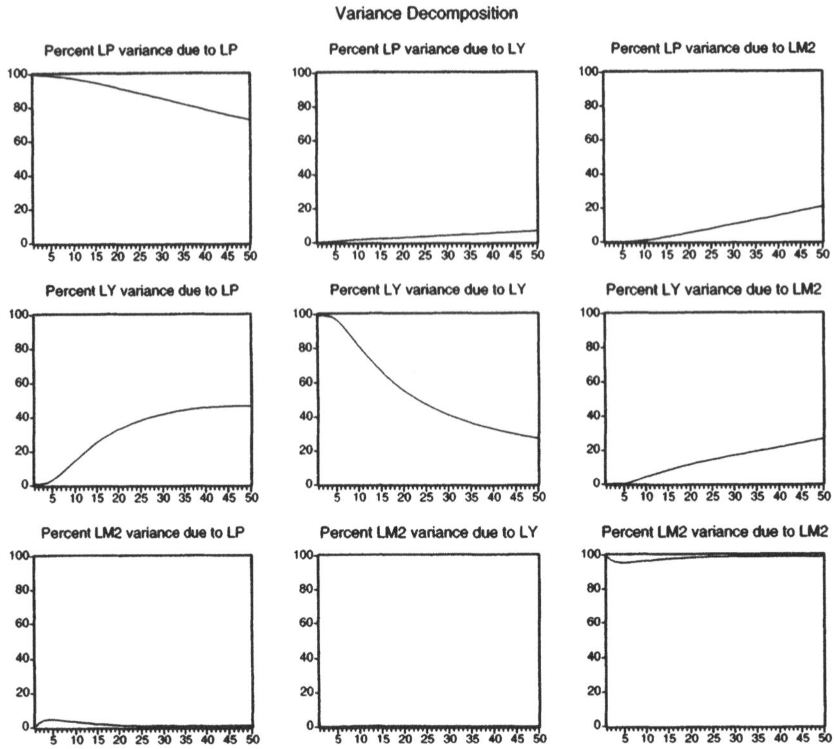


FIG. 6.3. FEVD in a three-variables VAR of the MTM

2. It is difficult to interpret the behaviour of money as driven by money supply shocks. The response to money innovations gives rise to the 'liquidity puzzle': the interest rate declines very slightly contemporaneously in response to a money shock to start increasing afterwards.

3. There are also difficulties with interpreting shocks to interest rates as monetary policy shocks. The response of prices to an innovation in interest rates gives rise to the 'price puzzle': prices increase significantly after an interest rate hike. An accepted interpretation of the liquidity puzzle relies on the argument that the money stock is dominated by demand rather than supply shocks. Moreover, the interpretation of money as demand shocks driven is consistent with the impulse response of money to interest rates. Note also that, even if the money stock were to be dominated by supply shocks, it would reflect both the behaviour of central banks and the banking system. For both these reasons the broad monetary aggregate has been substituted by narrower aggregates, bank reserves, on which it is easier to identify shocks mainly driven by the behaviour of the monetary policy

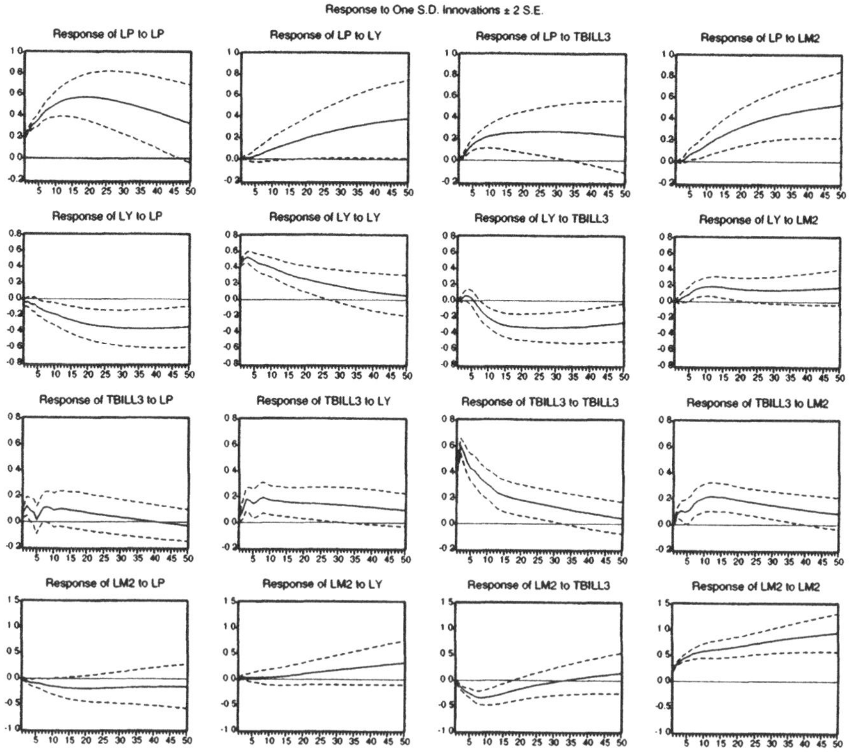


FIG. 6.4. Impulse responses in a four-variables VAR of the MTM

maker. The 'price puzzle' has been attributed to mis-specification of the four-variables VAR used by Sims. Suppose that there exists a leading indicator for inflation to which the Fed reacts. If such a leading indicator is omitted from the VAR, then we have an omitted variable positively correlated with inflation and interest rates. Such omission makes the VAR mis-specified and explains the positive relation between prices and interest rates observed in the impulse response functions. It has been observed (see Christiano, Eichenbaum and Evans 1996, Sims 1996) that the inclusion of a Commodity Price Index in the VAR solves the 'price puzzle'.

Our brief historical record of the empirical analysis of closed economy VAR of the MTM has brought us to the justification of the six variables included in what is by now known as the benchmark VAR model. We have already discussed its identification, let us now examine impulse response functions derived by using the Federal fund targeting identifying restrictions and reported in Figure 6.6.

The evidence reported in the impulse response functions represents the relevant stylized facts to include in theoretical models of the MTM. This kind

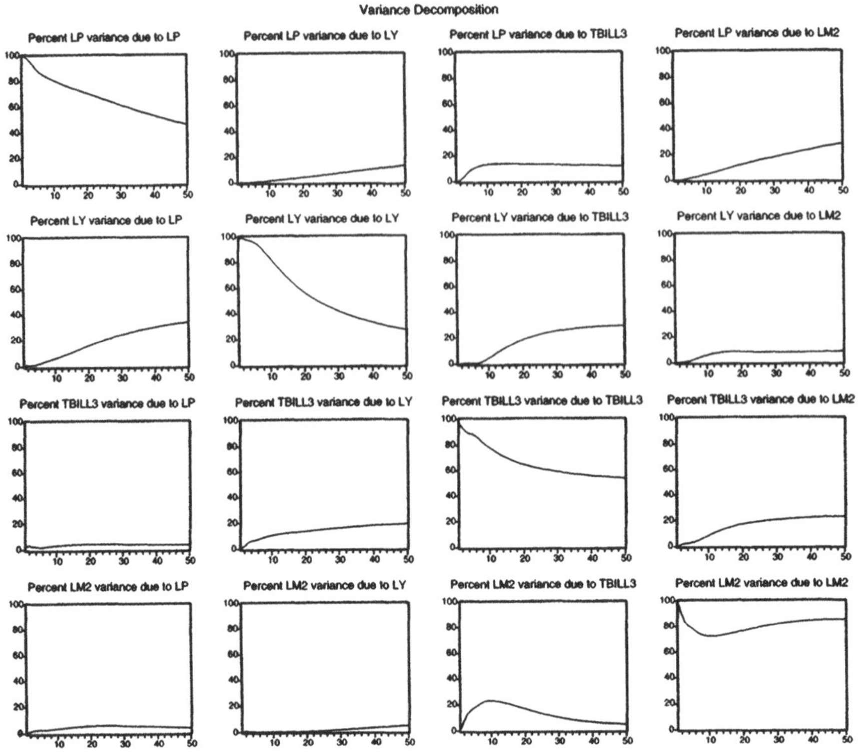


FIG. 6.5. FEVD in a four-variable VAR of the MTM

of evidence has established that plausible models of the monetary transmission mechanism should be consistent at least with the following evidence on price, output and interest rates: *(i)* the aggregate price level initially responds little; *(ii)* interest rates initially rise, and *(iii)* aggregate output initially falls, with a $j$-shaped response, and a zero long-run effect of the monetary impulse.

## 6.6 Monetary policy in open economies

Various papers have examined the effects of monetary shocks in open economies, but this strand of literature has been distinctly less successful in providing accepted empirical evidence than the VAR approach in closed economies.

The first results have been provided by Eichenbaum and Evans (1995), using an open-economy VAR with the following structure:

$$\mathbf{A}_0 \mathbf{y}_t = \sum_{i=1}^{k} \mathbf{A}_i \mathbf{y}_{t-i} + \mathbf{B}\boldsymbol{v}_t, \tag{6.17}$$

where $\mathbf{y}_t = \left\{ \mathrm{Y}_t^{US}, \mathrm{P}_t^{US}, \mathrm{NBRX}_t^{US} \text{ (or } \mathrm{FF}_t), \mathrm{Y}_t^{FOR}, \mathrm{P}_t^{FOR}, \mathrm{R}_t^{FOR}, \mathrm{e}_t \text{ (or } \mathrm{q}_t) \right\}$.

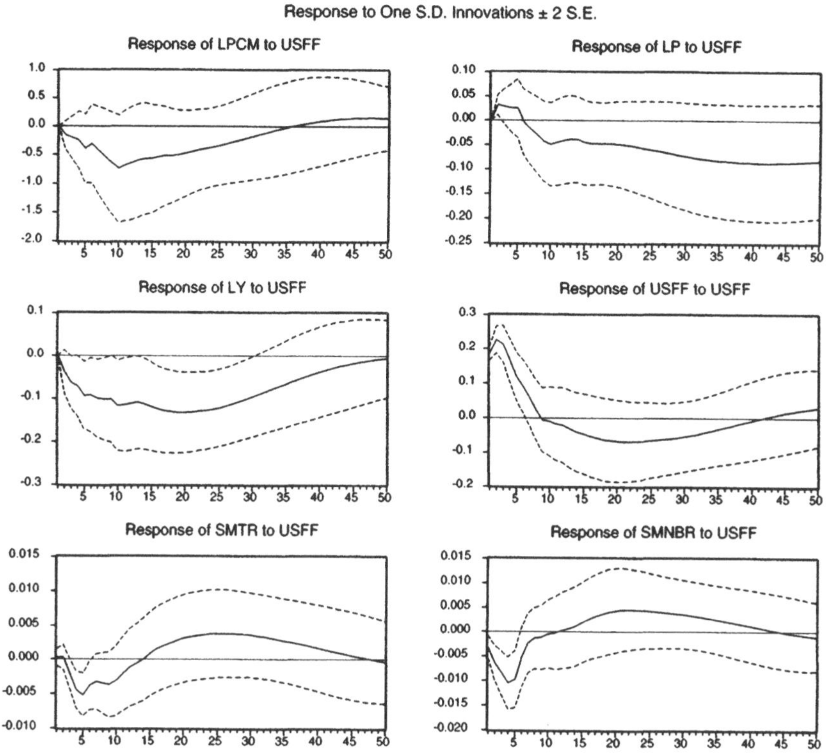


FIG. 6.6. Impulse response functions in a six-variables VAR of the MTM

$Y^{US}, P^{US}$ are logarithms of US output and price, $NBRX^{US}$ is the ratio of non-borrowed to total reserves (the appropriate variable from which one can extract monetary policy shocks under a regime of non-borrowed reserves targeting). FF is the Federal Funds rate, which is considered as an alternative to $NBRX^{US}$, and it is an informative variable for the extraction of monetary policy shocks under the regime of interest rate targeting; $Y^{FOR}, P^{FOR}$, and $R^{FOR}$ are respectively the logarithms of output, prices, and the level of short-term interest rate in the foreign country; $e$ is the nominal bilateral exchange rate, while $q$ is the real bilateral exchange rate. The matrix **B** is diagonal and **A** is lower-triangular. The empirical analysis is implemented by considering in turn, as a foreign country, each of the G7 countries on a sample of monthly data from 1974:1 to 1990:5. The following evidence emerges: ($i$) a restrictive US monetary policy shock generates a significant and persistent appreciation of the US dollar; ($ii$) a restrictive US monetary policy shock generates a significant and persistently larger effect on the domestic interest rate with respect to the foreign rate; ($i$) and ($ii$) imply a sharp deviation from the uncovered interest parity condition in favour of

US dollar-denominated investments (the 'forward-discount puzzle'); (*iii*) identified US monetary policy shocks are not different from the shocks derived within closed-economy VARs (*iv*) the closed-economy response of US prices and output to monetary policy shocks is robust to the extension of the VAR to the open economy; (*v*) a restrictive foreign monetary policy shock generates an appreciation of the US dollar (the 'exchange-rate puzzle'); and (*vi*) the response of the real exchange rate to the US and foreign monetary policy shocks does not differ significantly from the response of the nominal exchange rate. Such evidence is substantially confirmed by the work of Schlagenhauf and Wrase (1995), who consider a very similar specification for the G5 countries over the sample 1972:2–1990:2, using quarterly data. Some considerations should help to interpret the above results.

First, the empirical models are estimated over samples including shifts in the US and foreign monetary policy regimes, therefore, parameter instability is a potential problem.

Second, the extension to the open economy features the omission from the VAR of the commodity price index and of the monetary variables irrelevant to the extraction of the policy shocks. While the simplification of the monetary block is sustainable in the light of the absence of contemporaneous feedback between the informative variables and the other monetary variables under the chosen identification schemes, the omission of the commodity price index is unjustifiable as it leads to the same mis-specification as in the closed economy model for US monetary policy shocks. Moreover, such an omission might well also bias the identification of the foreign monetary policy shocks if the commodity price index is regarded as a leading indicator of inflation by the foreign policy-maker.

In conclusion, it is passible to argue that the observed puzzles might depend on the incorrect specification of the VAR.

Third, on the identification scheme, while some rationale can be provided for a quasi-recursive scheme in closed economies, a similar justification is much harder to provide in open economies. In fact, the recursive identification scheme with the exchange rate ordered last implies that neither the US nor the foreign monetary authority react contemporaneously to exchange rate fluctuations. This assumption seems sustainable for the US (the Fed benign neglect for the dollar) but it is certainly heavily questionable when the foreign countries are considered, as they are much more open economies than the US.

The failure of the recursive identification scheme could also be responsible for the observation of the puzzles.

In fact, most of the recent empirical work aims at breaking such a recursive structure.

Kim and Roubini (1997) have attempted this by introducing a structural identification by the explicit consideration of a money demand and supply functions. Their specification for the generic non-US country is:

$$\mathbf{A}_0\mathbf{y}_t = \sum_{i=1}^{k}\mathbf{A}_i\mathbf{y}_{t-i} + \mathbf{B}\boldsymbol{v}_t \tag{6.18}$$

$$\mathbf{y}_t = \begin{bmatrix} \mathrm{OPW}_t \\ \mathrm{FF}_t \\ \mathrm{Y}_t^{FOR} \\ \mathrm{P}_t^{FOR} \\ \mathrm{M}_t^{FOR} \\ \mathrm{R}_t^{FOR} \\ \mathrm{e}_t \end{bmatrix}, \quad \mathbf{A}_0 = \begin{bmatrix} 1 & 0 & 0 & 0 & 0 & 0 & 0 \\ a_{21} & 1 & 0 & 0 & 0 & 0 & 0 \\ a_{31} & 0 & 1 & 0 & 0 & 0 & 0 \\ a_{41} & 0 & a_{43} & 1 & 0 & 0 & 0 \\ 0 & 0 & a_{53} & a_{54} & 1 & a_{56} & 0 \\ a_{61} & 0 & 0 & 0 & a_{65} & 1 & a_{67} \\ a_{71} & a_{72} & a_{73} & a_{74} & a_{75} & a_{76} & 1 \end{bmatrix} \tag{6.19}$$

$$\nu_t \sim n.i.d.\,(0, I) \tag{6.20}$$

with $\mathrm{R}^{FOR}$ denoting the short-term non-US policy rate, $\mathrm{M}^{FOR}$ a monetary aggregate (M0 or M1), $\mathrm{P}^{FOR}$ the log of consumer price index, $\mathrm{Y}^{FOR}$ the log of industrial production, OPW the world index of oil price in dollars, FF the Federal funds rate, and e the nominal exchange rate against the dollar. **B** is a diagonal matrix. The model is estimated over the sample 1974:7–1992:5, on monthly data. The main differences between the proposed structural identification and the recursive identification schemes can be understood by analysing the $\mathbf{A}_0$ matrix. Some elements under the principal diagonal are set to zero to allow the introduction of simultaneous feedbacks between demand and supply for money and central bank behaviour and exchange rates. The estimated model is over-identified with 23 parameters estimated in the $\mathbf{A}_0$ and **B** matrix, out of a possible maximum of 28. The over-identifying restrictions are tested and not rejected. The identifying restrictions are rather standard. The US economy is taken as exogenous and the exchange rate does not enter in the Fed reaction function, US output and prices are not included in the VAR, while a simultaneous feedback is allowed between money demand and supply (the central bank rule). According to this rule, contemporaneous US interest rate movements are relevant to the foreign central bank only if they affect the exchange rate. Only the exchange rate is allowed to contemporaneously react to news in all the other variables.

Unfortunately the coefficients in the $\mathbf{A}_0$ matrix are estimated rather imprecisely. If we consider the case of the US versus Germany, the only significant parameters in the matrix are $a_{53}$ and $a_{72}$. The first parameter is difficult to interpret, given that the identification scheme does not explicitly address aggregate demand and supply shocks, while the point estimate of the second parameter implies an appreciation of the dollar against the Deutschmark in response to a US restrictive monetary policy. The potential simultaneous feedback between foreign monetary policy and the exchange rate does not seem to be empirically relevant. However, all the puzzles disappear and the empirical results for the impulse response functions are broadly in line with results from the US closed economy model. Given that this VAR included some proxy for the commodity price index the evidence cannot be decisive on the source of the 'puzzles', although the fact that the simultaneous feedback between foreign interest rates and the exchange rate is not significant is consistent with attributing a substantial role to commodity prices.

Also in this case the sample considered spans different regimes, moreover, this methodology brings broad monetary aggregates back into the specification. Interestingly, money is now used to extract demand rather than supply shocks, however, the specification of money demand implicit in the VAR might not be rich enough to capture the dynamic in the data. As pointed out by Faust and Whiteman (1997), single equation work by Hendry and colleagues on money demand has clearly shown the importance of including in the model the opportunity cost of holding money, which is often a spread between the interest rates. Interest spreads capturing the opportunity cost of holding money are never included in VAR models of the MTM. An identification similar to the one adopted by Kim and Roubini (1997) is the one proposed for the Canadian case by Cushman and Zha (1997), who aid the structural identification by explicitly introducing the trade sector into the model.

An interesting alternative approach to the identification of the simultaneous feedback between non-US interest rates and exchange rates is proposed by Smets (1996)–(1997). Smets considers the following structural model for non-US countries:

$$\mathbf{A}_0\mathbf{y}_t = \sum_{i=1}^{k}\mathbf{A}_i\mathbf{y}_{t-i} + \mathbf{B}\boldsymbol{v}_t \tag{6.21}$$

$$\mathbf{y}_t = \begin{bmatrix} \Delta y_t \\ \Delta p_t \\ R_t \\ \Delta e_t \end{bmatrix}, \quad \mathbf{B} = \begin{bmatrix} b_{11} & b_{12} & 0 & 0 \\ \frac{-(k_{11}b_{11}+k_{13}b_{31}+k_{14}b_{41})}{k_{12}} & b_{22} & 0 & 0 \\ b_{31} & b_{32} & 1 & 0 \\ b_{41} & b_{42} & b_{43} & b_{44} \end{bmatrix}$$

$$\mathbf{A}_0 = \begin{bmatrix} 1 & 0 & 0 & 0 \\ 0 & 1 & 0 & 0 \\ 0 & 0 & 1-\omega & \omega \\ 0 & 0 & 0 & 1 \end{bmatrix}$$

where $\Delta y_t$ is output growth, $\Delta p_t$ is inflation, $R$ is a short-term interest rate and $\Delta e_t$ is the exchange rate appreciation. No US variables are introduced, and the commodity price index is also excluded. However, Smets is more ambitious and aims at identifying both macroeconomics and monetary shocks. Three type of restrictions are imposed. First the semi-structural restrictions, macro variables do not react contemporaneously to monetary variables. Second, macroeconomic supply shocks are identified for macroeconomic demand shocks by assuming that the long-run effect of demand shocks on output is zero. Third, monetary policy shocks are identified from exchange rate shocks by assuming that the central bank reacts proportionally to interest rate and exchange rate developments (short-term Monetary Condition Indexes). Macroeconomic shocks are separated into demand and supply shocks by noting that the long-run response of output to a demand shock is given by element $(1,1)$ of the matrix $\left(A_0 - \sum_{i=1}^{k} A_i\right)^{-1} B$. Given the block-recursiveness assumption on $A_0$, the elements of $\left(A_0 - \sum_{i=1}^{k} A_i\right)^{-1}$ relevant to determine the element (1,1) of $\left(A_0 - \sum_{i=1}^{k} A_i\right)^{-1} B$ are not functions of the $A_0$ matrix and therefore from the estimation of the reduced-form VAR one can retrieve all the elements in the $A_i$ matrix and generate an identifying restriction for the structural parameters in the $B$ matrix by setting the element (1,1) $\left(A_0 - \sum_{i=1}^{k} A_i\right)^{-1} B$ to zero. In practice, given that

$$\left(A_0 - \sum_{i=1}^{k} A_i\right)^{-1} = \begin{bmatrix} k_{11} & k_{12} & k_{13} & k_{14} \\ k_{21} & k_{22} & k_{23} & k_{24} \\ k_{31} & k_{32} & k_{33} & k_{34} \\ k_{41} & k_{42} & k_{43} & k_{44} \end{bmatrix},$$

one can show that $k_{11}, k_{12}, k_{13}, k_{14}$ are determined independently from the parameters in $A_0$, therefore restricting to zero the long-run effect of demand shock on output, we have $b_{21} = -\left(k_{11}b_{11} + k_{13}b_{31} + k_{14}b_{41}\right)/k_{12}$.

Lastly in the monetary block, monetary policy shocks are identified from exchange rate shocks by assuming that the appropriate indicator of exogenous monetary stance is a short-term MCI where the exchange rate and interest rate are appropriately weighted. The weights can be estimated or imposed given the knowledge of the relative weights in several central banks MCIs. This approach encompasses as a special case, the pure interest-rate targeting and the pure exchange-rate targeting. The main empirical problems with this procedure are the instability of the estimated $\omega$ and the potentially disruptive implications of mis-specification for the identification of aggregate demand and supply shocks (see Faust and Leeper 1997).

### 6.6.1 *Replicating the empirical evidence*

The dataset berlin.wf1 contains the relevant variables to replicate the open-economy VAR models discussed so far.

We first estimate a benchmark open-economy model for the US and the German economy without including the Commodity Price Index. The model is estimated on monthly data over the sample 1983:1–1997:12. The VAR is specified by including six lags of US industrial production, the US consumer price index, Federal funds rate, German industrial production, German consumer price index, German call money rate, and the US-dollar/Deutschmark nominal exchange rate (unit of DM for one US dollar). The choice of the sample is motivated by the need of having a single monetary policy regime for the US, featuring Fed funds targeting; see Bagliano and Favero (1998). Impulse responses for all variables to US and German monetary policy shocks are reported in Figures 6.7 and 6.8.

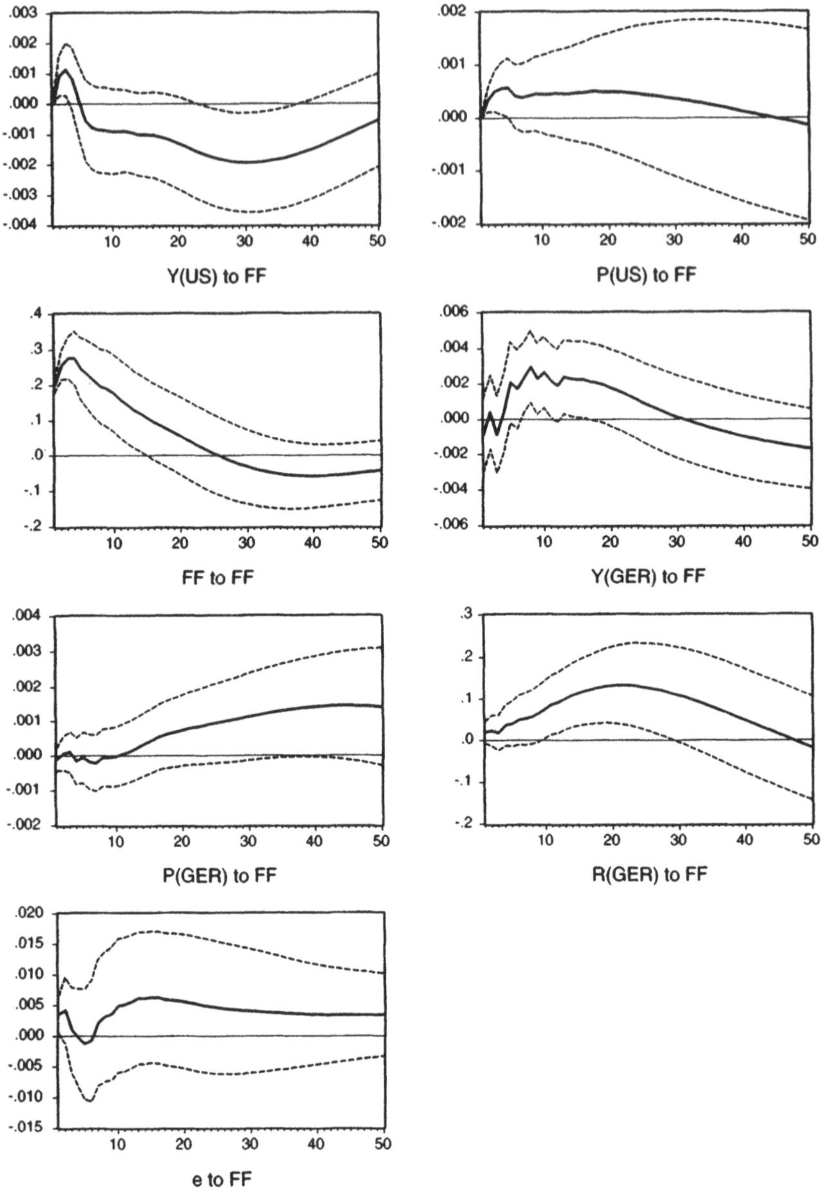


FIG. 6.7. Impulse responses to US monetary policy shock in the benchmark VAR open-economy model (dashed lines: 2 standard error bands)

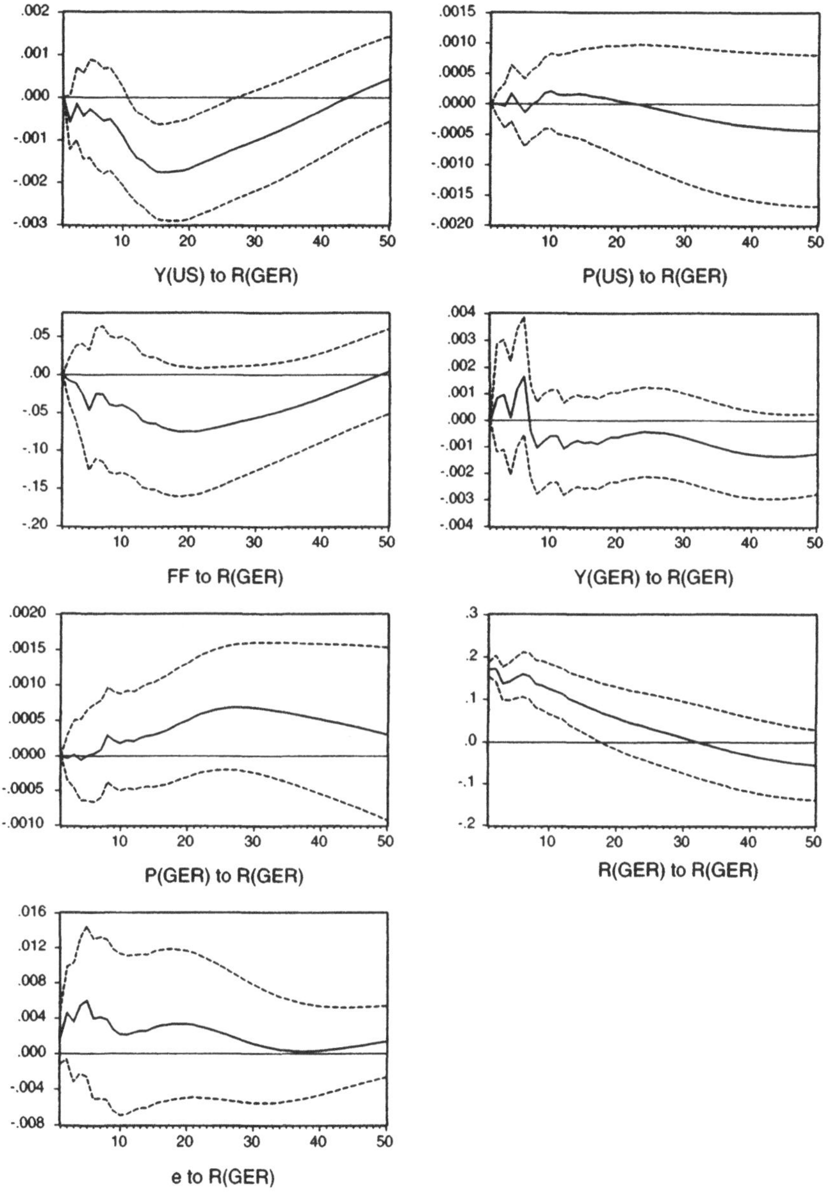


FIG. 6.8. Impulse responses to German monetary policy shock in the benchmark VAR open-economy model (dashed lines: 2 standard error bands)

We have confirmation of all the facts and puzzles observed in the literature. The analysis of the contemporaneous feedback between variables within the recursive specification provides evidence on the endogeneity of US monetary policy, which reacts significantly to internal conditions, and of the German monetary policy which reacts to both internal conditions and, less significantly to US monetary policy. The exchange rate reacts contemporaneously significantly to US monetary policy (positive interest rate shock in the US induces appreciation of the US dollar *vis-à-vis* the DM) and to macroeconomic conditions in the US and Germany (a positive shock in US industrial production and in German price lead contemporaneously to an appreciation of the US dollar) both are not contemporaneously significantly affected by German monetary policy.

The analysis of the responses to monetary impulses in the US and Germany confirms all the main findings of the literature namely:

- a significant U-shaped response of US output to US monetary policy;
- the existence of a price puzzle both for the US and Germany;
- the existence of a forward-discount puzzle generated by US monetary policy restriction;
- exchange-rate puzzle for German monetary policy shock.

### 6.6.2 *Omitted variables*

Our analysis of VAR models of the monetary transmission mechanism has shown the crucial importance of the Commodity Price Index in the derivation of monetary policy shocks. The arguments made for the inclusion of this variable in closed-economy VAR of the monetary transmission mechanism are also compelling for open-economy VAR. Possibly puzzles observed in open economies are related to mis-specification, via the omission of a commodity price index in the benchmark open-economy VAR. We consider this potential explanation, by concentrating on an open-economy VAR model linking the US and the German economy.

We include a commodity price index by keeping the Choleski identification and considering Pcm as a macroeconomic variables influencing both US and German monetary policy. The new impulse responses are reported in Figures 6.9 and 6.10. The results in the two figures show that the inclusion of commodity prices solves the price puzzle for both countries, moreover also the forward-discount bias puzzle and the exchange-rate puzzle tend to disappear. Finally, although we do not observe a symmetric contemporaneous effect of the US and German monetary policy on the exchange rate, the impulse response functions of the exchange rate to the two monetary shocks over a horizon of four year show a remarkable degree of symmetry.

Although the inclusion of commodity prices seems clearly relevant, we have opened the issue of potential simultaneity between the exchange rate and the policy rate in a small open economy and not yet addressed it. We shall consider this issue by looking at the more general problem of assessing the reliability of the measurement of monetary policy with VAR models.

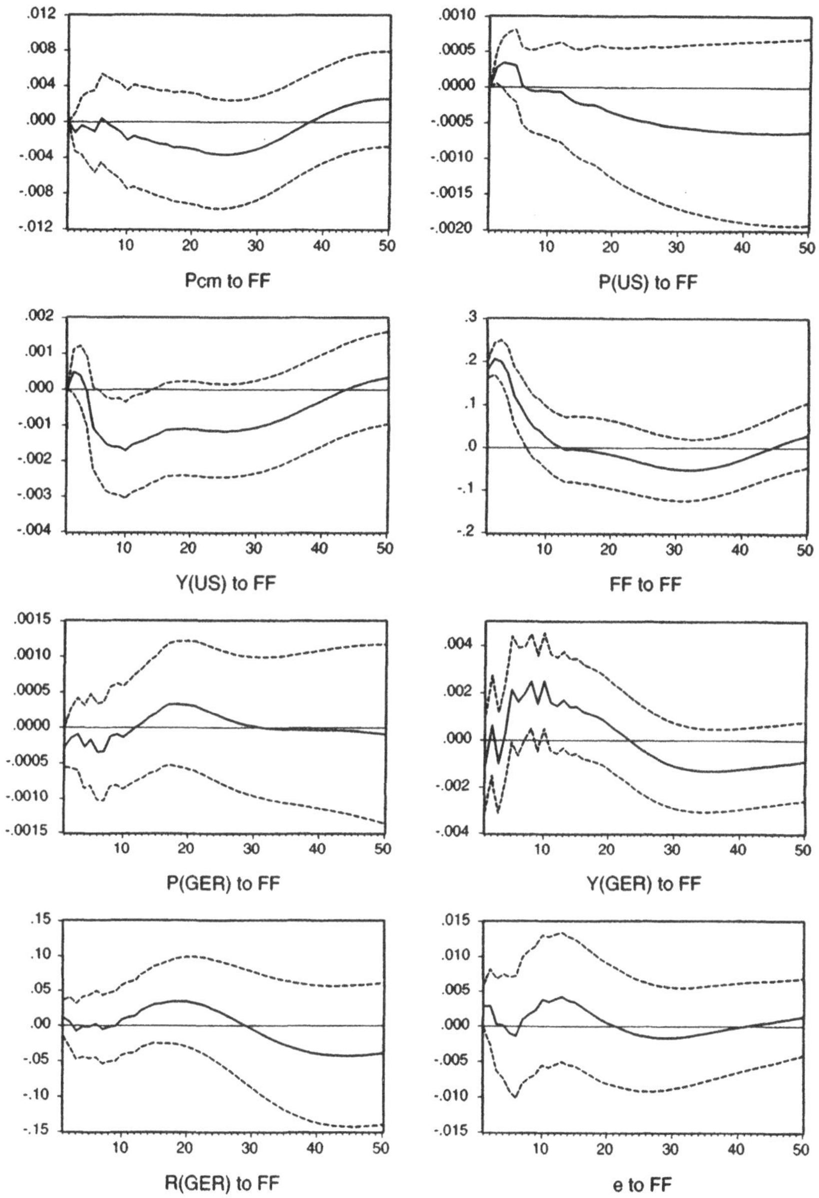


FIG. 6.9. Impulse responses to the US monetary policy shock in the benchmark VAR with commodity price index (dashed lines: 2 standard error bands)

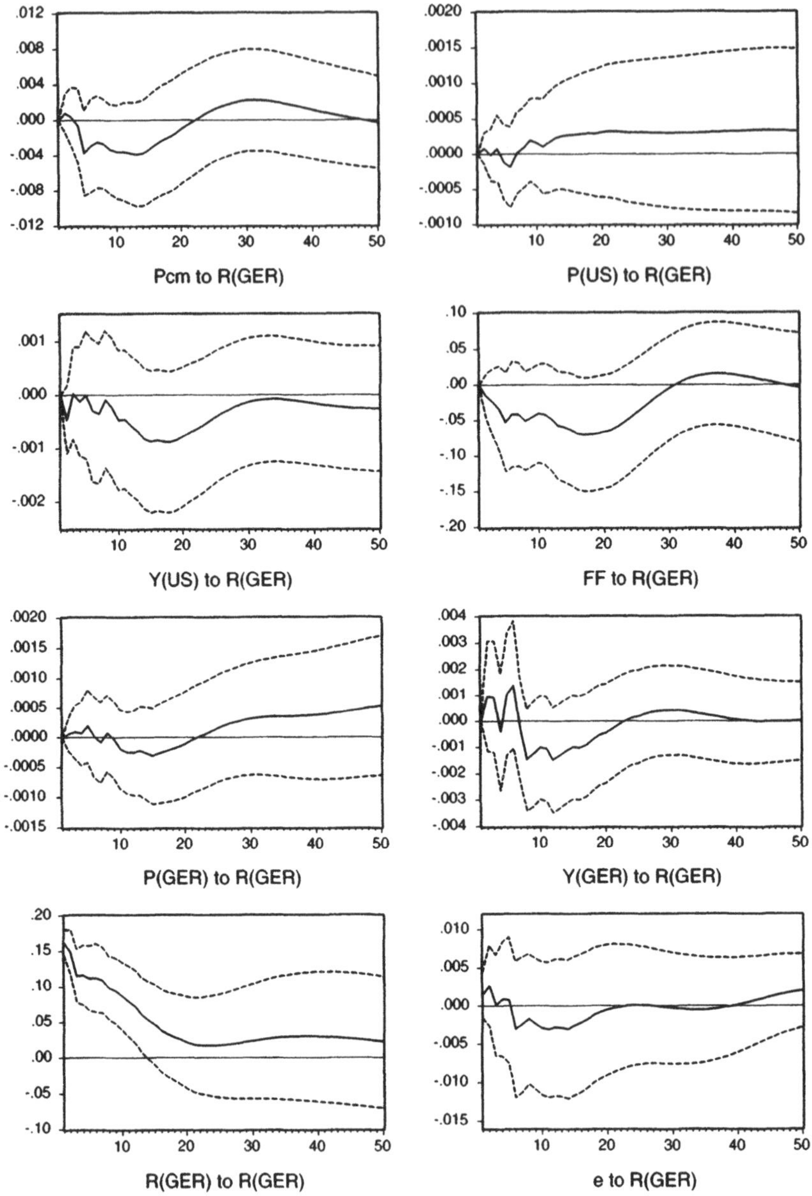


FIG. 6.10. Impulse responses to German monetary policy shock in the benchmark VAR with commodity price index (dashed lines: 2 standard error bands)

## 6.7 VAR and non-VAR measures of monetary policy

Econometric measurement of monetary policy has always been a debated issue. VAR models are linear, constant-parameter autoregressive distributed lag models, bound to include a very limited number of variables with a parsimonious lag parameterization. The crucial step to deriving evidence from the data using VARs, is the possibility of posing identifying restrictions independently from theoretical models. We have illustrated how a consensus has been reached in the case of closed economies and how the same result has not yet been achieved for open economies. We have provided an interpretation of this difference in the light of the difficulties in identifying monetary policy shocks in open economies. Recently, VAR based monetary policy shocks have been compared with monetary policy shocks measured by alternative approaches. We think that these developments can be useful not only to evaluate VAR methodologies, but also to help identification when, as in the case of the open economy models, the traditional VAR methods have difficulties in delivering the necessary number of identifying restrictions.

### 6.7.1 *Non-VAR measures of monetary policy shocks*

Historically, alternatives to econometric measurement of monetary policy have always been considered, think for example of qualitative indicators of monetary policy derived adopting the 'narrative approach' of Romer and Romer (1989; 1994). In a recent paper, Leeper (1996) shows that even the dummy variable generated by the 'narrative approach' (identifying episodes of deliberate monetary contractions) is predictable from past macroeconomic variables, thus reflecting the endogenous response of policy to the economy, and the estimated coefficients cannot provide an unbiased estimate for the response of the macroeconomic variables to a monetary impulse.

Recently the attention of monetary economists has turned to financial markets, which are a potential source of powerful information and measurement of monetary policy. We consider a variety of measures of monetary policy derived from financial markets and assess their role in the evaluation of VAR-based monetary policy shocks in open and closed economies.

A first alternative was proposed by Rudebusch (1998) and further analysed by Brunner (1996). Monetary policy shocks are derived from the thirty-day Federal funds future contracts, which have been quoted on the Chicago Board of Trade since October 1988, and are bets on the average overnight Federal funds rate for the delivery month, the variable included in benchmark VARs. Shocks are constructed as the difference between the Federal funds rate at month $t$ and the thirty-day federal funds future at month $t-1$. Such a choice is based on the evidence that the regression of the Federal funds rate (FF) at $t$ on the thirty-day Federal funds future (FFF) at $t-1$ produces an intercept not significantly different from zero, a slope coefficient not significantly different from one, and serially uncorrelated residuals:

$$\mathrm{FF}_t = -\underset{(0.0436)}{0.037} + \underset{(0.007)}{0.999}\mathrm{FFF}_{t-1} + \widehat{u}_t$$
$$R^2 = 0.99, \qquad \sigma = 0.145, \qquad \mathrm{DW} = 1.86.$$

Note that this procedure produces shocks, labelled FFF, comparable to the reduced form innovations from the VAR and not to the structural monetary policy shocks, because surprises relative to the information available at the end of month $t-1$ may reflect endogenous policy responses to news about the economy that become available in the course of month $t$. However, if an identification scheme is available, then innovations derived from the future contracts can be transformed in the relevant shocks by applying to them the standard VAR identification procedure. A non-trivial problem with this procedure comes from the fact that Federal funds future are available from 1988 onwards. Future contracts on the one-month Eurodollar are available on a more extended sample. Given that the properties of the series generated by the one-month Eurodollar are very close to the properties of Federal funds future, the direct measurement based on one-month Eurodollar could be used on an extended sample.

A second non-VAR measure of policy shocks is based on the work of Skinner and Zettelmeyer (1996). They derive a measure of unanticipated monetary policy shocks by following a two-step methodology: first, using information from central bank reports and newspapers they make a list of days on which monetary policy announcements occurred; second, monetary policy shocks are identified with the changes in the three-month interest rate on the days of policy announcements. The validity of such a procedure requires that:

1. short rates (e.g. the overnight rate) are affected by policy;
2. arbitrage is effective between the overnight and the three-month interest rates;
3. the impact of other news affecting the three-month rate on the day of the policy decision is negligible;
4. policy actions are not endogenous responses to information that becomes available on the day when the decision is made.

To ensure that conditions 3 and 4 are applicable, Skinner and Zettelmeyer go through reports of the policy actions and exclude from their sample those which do not conform to requirements 3 and 4. The main problem with the index obtained this way is that it can only pin down shocks associated to monetary policy decisions reflected in some action on controlled variables, whereas shocks associated with *no* action (while some action was expected by the markets) are neglected.

An alternative approach which might overcome this problem has been proposed by Bagliano and Favero (1998), applying the methodology set out in Svensson (1994) and Soderlind and Svensson (1997). The methodology is based on the use of instantaneous forward rates as monetary policy indicators. Forward rates are interest rates on investments made at a future date, the settlement date, and expiring at a date further into the future, the maturity date. Instantaneous forward interest rates are the limit as the maturity date and the settlement date approach one another.

To illustrate our derivation of the spot rate let us start by the consideration of a *zero-coupon* bond issued at time $t$ with a face value of 1, maturity of $m$ years and price $P_{mt}^{ZC}$. The simple yield $Y_{mt}$ is related to the price as follows:

$$P_{mt}^{ZC} = \frac{1}{(1+Y_{mt})^m}. \tag{6.22}$$

Defining the spot rate $r_{mt}$ as $\log(1+Y_{mt})$, which is the continuously compounded yield, and the discount function $D_{mt}$ as the price at time $t$ of a zero coupon that pays one unit at time $t+m$, we then have:

$$P_{mt}^{ZC} = \exp(-mr_{mt}) = D_{mt}. \tag{6.23}$$

Consider now a *coupon* bond that pays a coupon rate of $c$ per cent annually and pays a face value of 1 at maturity. The price of the bond at trade date is given by the following formula:

$$P_{mt} = \sum_{k=1}^{m} cD_{kt} + D_{mt}. \tag{6.24}$$

Given the observation of prices of coupon bonds, spot rates on the zero coupon equivalent are derived by fitting a discount function based on the following specification for the spot rates:

$$\begin{aligned} r_{kt} = \beta_0 + \beta_1 \frac{1-\exp\left(-\frac{k}{\tau_1}\right)}{\frac{k}{\tau_1}} + \beta_2 \left(\frac{1-\exp\left(-\frac{k}{\tau_1}\right)}{\frac{k}{\tau_1}} - \exp\left(-\frac{k}{\tau_1}\right)\right) \\ +\beta_3 \left(\frac{1-\exp\left(-\frac{k}{\tau_2}\right)}{\frac{k}{\tau_2}} - \exp\left(-\frac{k}{\tau_2}\right)\right). \end{aligned} \tag{6.25}$$

Such a specification was originally introduced by Svensson (1994) and it is an extension of the parameterization proposed by Nelson and Siegel (1987). Implied forward rates can be calculated from spot rates. A forward rate at time $t$ with trade date $t+t'$ and settlement date $t+T$ is calculated as the return on an investment strategy based on buying zero-coupon bonds at time $t$ maturing at time $t+T$ and selling at time $t$, zero-coupon bonds maturing at time $t+t'$. The forward rate is related to the spot rate by the following formula:

$$f_{t+T,t+t',t} = \frac{Tr_{T,t} - t'r_{t',t}}{T-t'} \tag{6.26}$$

so the forward rate for a one-year investment with settlement in two years and maturity in three years is equal to three times the three-year spot rate minus twice the two-year spot rate. The instantaneous forward rate is the rate on a forward contract with an infinitesimal investment after the settlement date:

$$f_{mt} = \lim_{T \to m} f_{t+T,t+m,t}. \tag{6.27}$$

In practice, we identify the instantaneous forward rate with an overnight forward rate, a forward rate with maturity one day after the settlement. The relation between instantaneous forward rate and spot rate is then:

$$r_{mt} = \frac{\int_{\tau=t}^{t+m} f_{\tau t} d\tau}{m}$$

or, equivalently

$$f_{mt} = r_{mt} + m\frac{\partial r_{m,t}}{\partial m}. \tag{6.28}$$

Given specification (6.25) for the spot rate, the resulting forward function is:

$$f_{kt} = \beta_0 + \beta_1 \exp\left(-\frac{k}{\tau_1}\right) + \beta_2 \frac{k}{\tau_1} \exp\left(-\frac{k}{\tau_1}\right) + \beta_3 \frac{k}{\tau_2} \exp\left(-\frac{k}{\tau_2}\right). \tag{6.29}$$

Therefore, as $k$ goes to zero, the spot and the forward rates coincide at $\beta_0 + \beta_1$ and as $k$ goes to infinity, the spot and the forward rates coincide at $\beta_0$. The forward rate function features a constant, an exponential term decreasing when $\beta_1$ is positive, and two 'hump-shaped' terms. In principle $\beta_0+\beta_1$ can be restricted to match the observed overnight rate, but we do not follow this strategy. In fact, by definition a monetary policy shock implies a jump in, at least, the short end of the term structure. Forcing the smooth instantaneous forward rate curve to fit exactly the observed overnight rate would not allow us to seize an eventual expected monetary policy action. For this reason, we exclude the overnight rate from the information used for estimation. Then, exploiting the continuity of the functional form, we reconstruct the very short end of the term structure allowing for a gap between the estimated overnight and the observed overnight rates. Such a gap represents the jump in the very short end of the term structure associated with expectations of intervention by the central bank. An example can clarify matters. On the occasion of the meeting held on the 2nd of December 1993 the Bundesbank reduced the repurchase rate by 25 basis points. On the close of the markets before the meeting we observed the structure of spot rates relevant to the estimation of our yield curves reported in Table 6.1.

TABLE 6.1. German interest rates

| Date | 30/11/93 | 2/12/93 |
|---|---|---|
| o/n | 6.70 | 6.35 |
| seven-days | 6.44 | 6.31 |
| one-month | 6.44 | 6.31 |
| three-month | 6.19 | 6.06 |
| six-month | 5.81 | 5.75 |
| one-year | 5.37 | 5.25 |
| two-year | 5.08 | 5.03 |
| three-year | 5.05 | 5.02 |
| four-year | 5.16 | 5.15 |
| five-year | 5.3 | 5.29 |
| seven-year | 5.69 | 5.68 |
| ten-year | 6.16 | 6.17 |

In Figure 6.11 we report Nelson–Siegel interpolants. More precisely we report the two instantaneous forward curves associated, respectively, to the spot curve estimated excluding the overnight rate (IFW) and to the spot curve estimated including the overnight rate (IFOY).

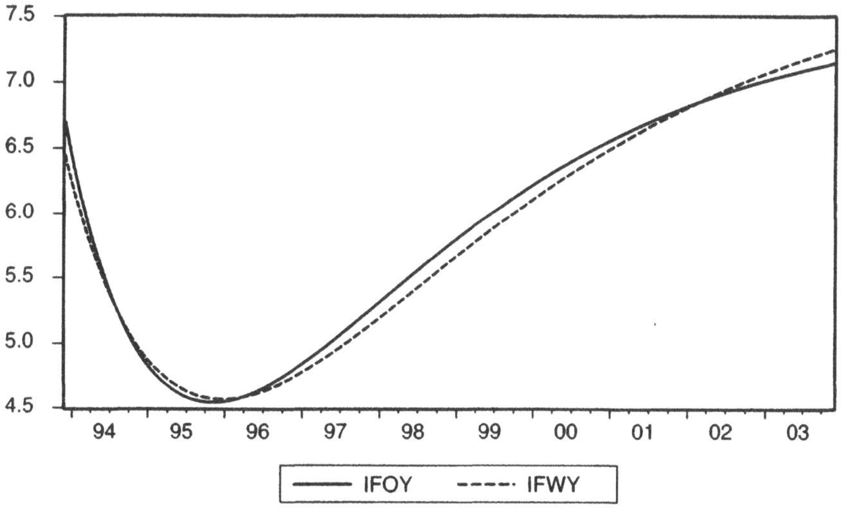


FIG. 6.11. Estimated forward-rate curves on the 30 Novermber 1993 with and without the overnight rate

Fitting the curve on the data including the overnight without allowing for a jump in the term structure from the date of the Bundesbank Council meeting afterwards would have spuriously generated an interest rate shock.

If the pure expectational model is valid and there is no term premium, then instantaneous forward rates at future dates can be interpreted as the expected spot interest rates for those future rates. The observable equivalent of the instantaneous forward rate is the overnight rate.

The following strategy for identification of monetary policy shocks directly exploits the relation between spot rates and instantaneous forward rates:

1. exploiting the fact that intervention on policy rates for Germany and the US takes place on the occasions of regular meetings of the Bundesbank Council and of the Federal Open Market Committee (FOMC) (since 1994), collect data on the term structure of interest rates the day before the monetary policy meetings. Observations on one-day, seven-day rate, one-month euro, three-month euro, six-month euro, twelve-month euro, three-, five-, seven-, and ten-year fixed interest rate swap are available on Datastream and other databases;

2. estimate a term structure for spot rates and the associated curve of instantaneous rates;

3. interpret the instantaneous rate as the overnight rate, and from the curve derive the expected implicit overnight rate for the day after the monetary policy meeting;

4. derive monetary policy shocks, subtracting from the observed overnight rate the day after the policy meeting the overnight rate implicit in the curve the day before the policy meeting;

5. aggregate the above daily measures (concentrated in a few special days) to construct monthly measures of shocks.

There are several difficulties that one should overcome in constructing this measure of monetary policy shocks. Following Bagliano and Favero (1999), we illustrate examples of monetary shocks generated by unanticipated action or by unanticipated inaction by the Bundesbank, and examples of markets' anticipation of Bundesbank behaviour when expectations on monetary policy turned out to be correct and no shocks were observed. We consider the sample 1984–1997.

Consider first July 1988. In this month the Bundesbank Council met twice, on the 14th and on the 28th. During the first Council the Bundesbank didn't take any action, during the second Council it was decided to raise the Lombard Rate by 50bp. In Figure 6.12 we report the weekly and the overnight rate, along with the monetary policy action (PMA).

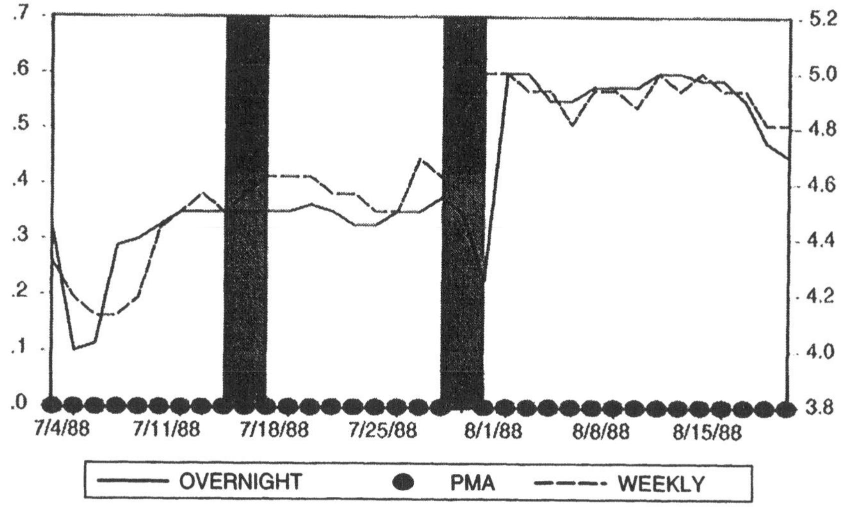


FIG. 6.12. Monetary policy interventions and short-term interest rates in Germany, July 1988

We shade areas of the three days centred around the meetings. Note that no monetary policy action was expected during the first meeting, while some action was expected before the second one. Six days before the meeting the weekly rate contains the first six days of maturity which doesn't include the action and the seventh one which, instead, does include it, so the weekly rate should start to 'reflect' the monetary policy action six days before the meeting. The weight of the seventh day is one-seventh, so the information doesn't appear clearly six days before, but as we approach the date of the council the weight of the action becomes greater and the expectation discloses itself. In fact, the weekly rate starts reacting three days before the meeting. It is also possible that the market realizes that the Bundesbank will act only a few days before the Council (say less than six days before), in this case the weekly rate starts reacting later than six days before the Council. The weekly rate should be the best observed interest rate to identify expectations on monetary policy actions. In fact, Council meetings take place fortnightly and the one-month rate immediately before any meeting reflects expectations on the outcome of the following two meetings.

The second episode we consider is the tightening of monetary policy that occurred after German reunification in January–February 1991. Two meetings were held in this period, on the 17th of January and the 2nd of February. As Figure 6.13 clearly shows, the weekly rate increased sharply just before the first Council revealing an expected increase in interest rates.

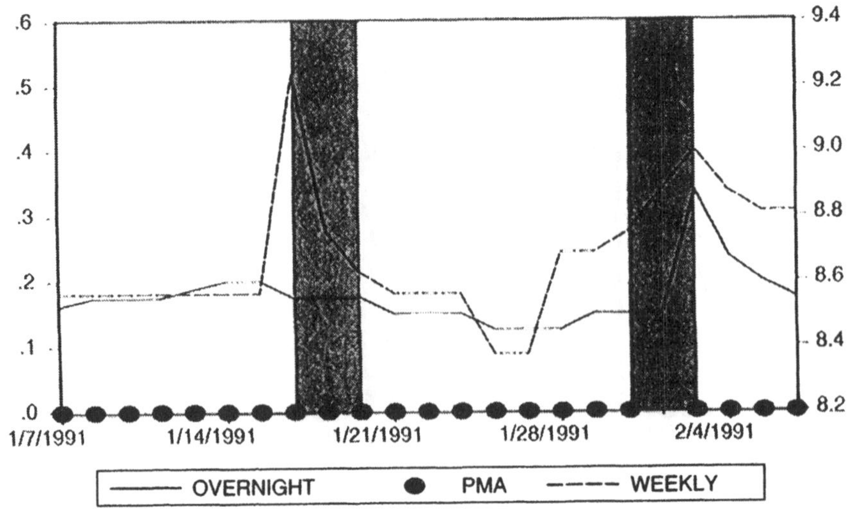


FIG. 6.13. Monetary policy interventions and short-term interest rates in Germany, January 1991

The Bundesbank didn't act on that meeting. We immediately observe that the expected tightening happened during the following Council meeting, when the Bundesbank raised the discount rate and the Lombard rate by 50 bp. To summarize, on the 14th of January we observed a monetary policy shock arising from an anticipated action that didn't occur, meanwhile on the 2nd of February there is no shock as the policy move has been correctly anticipated.

The third episode we single out occurred in December 1991 (see Figure 6.14) when the Bundesbank tightened the monetary policy, once again raising the discount rate and the Lombard rate by 50 bp. The dates of the Bundesbank Councils are the 5th and the 19th of December. During the latter meeting the Bundesbank surprised the market, and we observe a shock arising from an unexpected policy action.

The main strength of the methodology based on forward interest rate curves is its flexibility and capability to capture shocks independently from the specification and parameterization of a linear autoregressive model. The main limitation of this approach is caused by the volatility of very short-term rates not related to expectations on monetary policy. Figures 6.15 and 6.16 report daily observations on the overnight and the weekly rates for the estimation sample period used in the VAR.

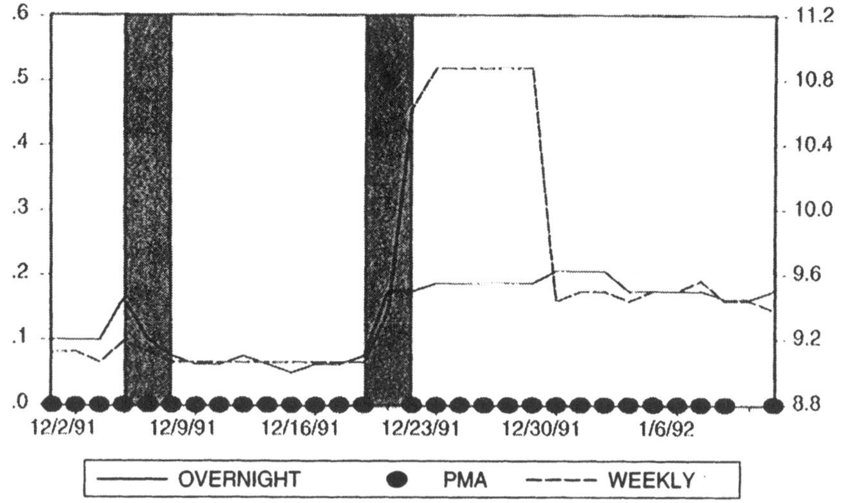


FIG. 6.14. Monetary policy interventions and short-term interest rates in Germany, December 1991

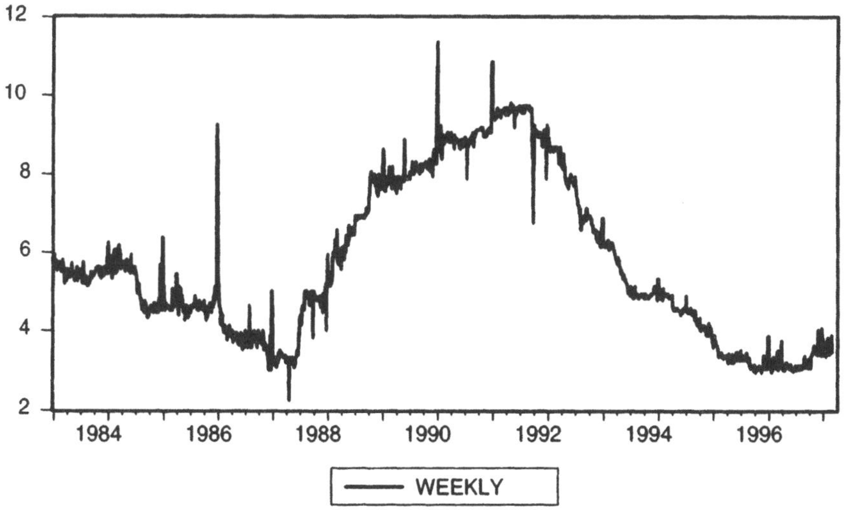


FIG. 6.15. The German seven-day rate

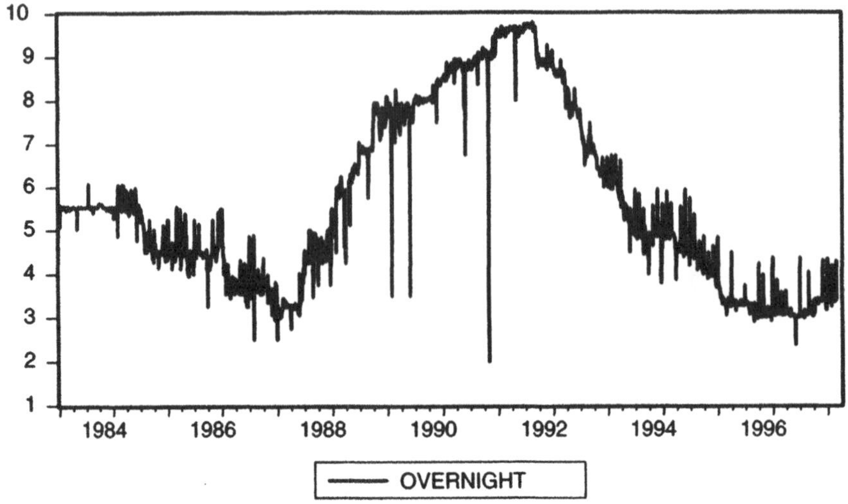


FIG. 6.16. The German overnight rate

We immediately note a number of blips in the series. They can be damaging to our methodology whenever they happen on occasion of a Bundesbank Council meeting.

Most of those blips are generated by banks' reserves' management which run into a non-perfectly liquid market, such as on the occasion of the last day of the average reserves maintenance period. We make an effort to render our inference robust to blips.

In fact, we have estimated our curves starting from the seven-day rather than the overnight rate, and our methodology of estimation considers the information contained in the whole term structure. However, we have run a further check and avoid labelling as policy shocks all unexpected movements in policy rates which have disappeared within a week after the Council meeting. Such correction led us to single out two outliers in 1988:9 and 1991:12. The 1988:9 outlier, whose determination is described in Figure 6.13, is the only one of a relevant magnitude.

In Figure 6.17 we report the behaviour of the seven-day and the one-month rate in the course of September 1988.

No policy intervention was decided in September 1988, however, just before the meeting of mid-September we observe a hike in the seven-day rate. Such a hike is not reflected in the term structure for longer maturities (we report one-month for reference). This hike would have been labelled as a shock by the methodology; however, as it is reversed within the week after the meeting this episode should be considered as a monetary policy shock.

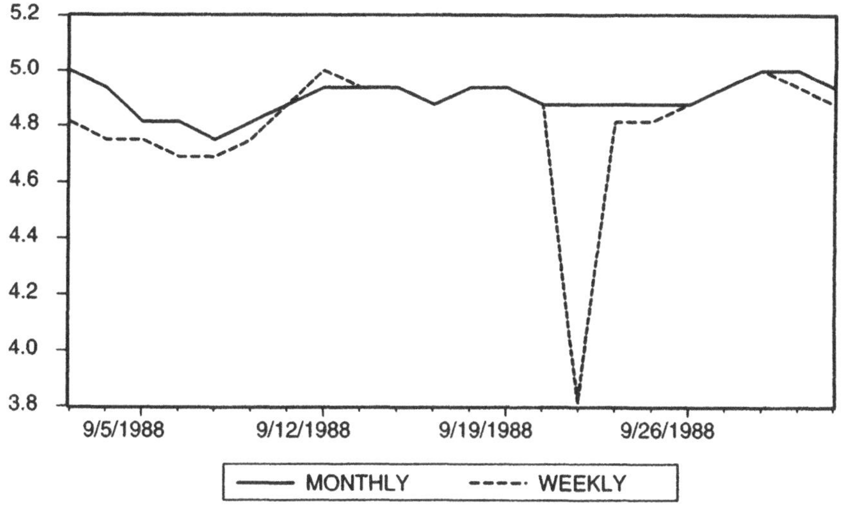


FIG. 6.17. The German seven-day and one-month rate in September 1988

## 6.8 Empirical results

Non-VAR measures of monetary policy can be directly compared with VAR measures; they can also be used to assess the robustness of the VAR-based descriptions of the monetary transmission mechanism, finally, they can be exploited, within a VAR, to aid identification of other structural shocks. To illustrate these possibilities we consider in turn the closed economy (US) case and the open economy (US–Germany) case.

### 6.8.1 *Closed economy (US)*

To evaluate the role of non-VAR based measures of monetary policy shock, we first estimate the closed-economy four-variable version of the VAR model for the US and compute impulse response functions of all variables to a shock in the Federal funds rate. Our model is specified as follows:

$$\mathbf{A}\begin{pmatrix} Y_t^{US} \\ Pcm_t \\ P_t^{US} \\ FF_t \end{pmatrix} = \mathbf{C}(L)\begin{pmatrix} Y_{t-1}^{US} \\ Pcm_{t-1} \\ P_{t-1}^{US} \\ FF_{t-1} \end{pmatrix} + \mathbf{B}\begin{pmatrix} \nu_t^1 \\ \nu_t^2 \\ \nu_t^3 \\ \nu_t^{FF} \end{pmatrix} \tag{6.30}$$

where **A** is lower-triangular and **B** is diagonal.

The ordering chosen allows for a contemporaneous response of the policy rate to innovations in output, consumer prices and the commodity price level. The orthogonalized residual of the Federal funds rate equation, $\nu^{FF}$, is identified as a monetary policy shock. No structural interpretation is given to the (orthogonalized) residuals from the other equations in the system. We consider two non-VAR measures of monetary policy, derived respectively from one-month

Eurodollar forward rate (EUR$) and from the estimation of the instantaneous forward rate curve on the occasions of FOMC meetings ($IFS^{US}$). These alternative shocks are plotted with the VAR-based shocks in Figures 6.18 and 6.19.

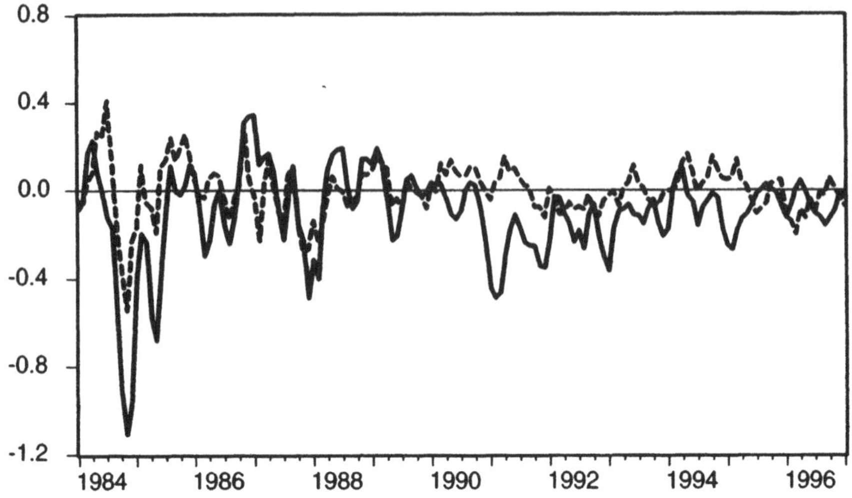


FIG. 6.18. Three-month centred moving averages of EUR$ shocks (solid line) and closed-economy VAR monetary policy shocks (dotted line)

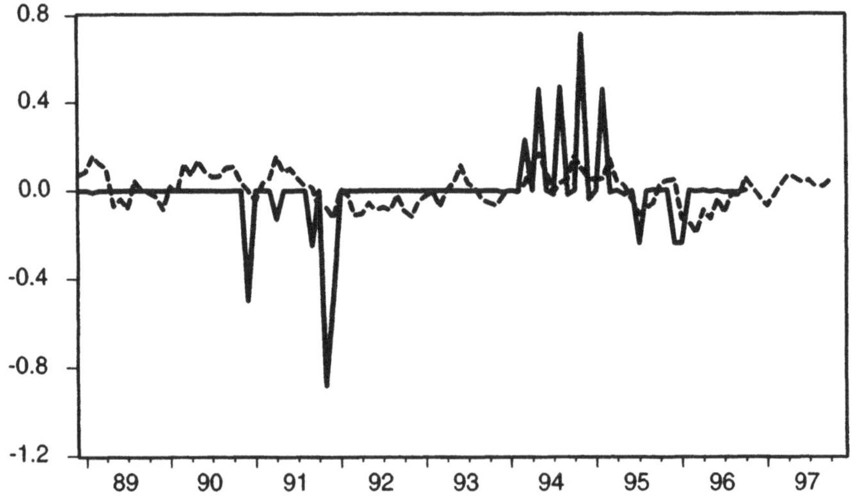


FIG. 6.19. $IFS^{US}$ shocks (solid line) and closed-economy VAR monetary policy shocks (dotted line)

Note that the EUR\$ measure is available on a larger sample than the $\text{IFS}^{US}$ measure as the practice of modifying monetary policy rates on the occasions of given and announced dates started only in the 1990s. We report in Table 6.2 the correlations of VAR and non-VAR measures of monetary policy.

TABLE 6.2. VAR and non-VAR monetary policy shocks

Sample: 1988:11–1996:10

Correlation coefficients (standard errors on the diagonal)

| | $EUR\$$ | $IFS^{US}$ | $\nu^{FF}$ |
|---|---|---|---|
| $EUR\$$ | 0.185 | - | - |
| $IFS^{US}$ | 0.203 | 0.169 | - |
| $\nu^{FF}$ | 0.352 | 0.319 | 0.123 |

Sample: 1988:11–1996:10

| | $EUR\$$ | $\nu^{FF}$ |
|---|---|---|
| $EUR\$$ | 0.277 | - |
| $\nu^{FF}$ | 0.500 | 0.211 |

Rudebusch (1996), using the Federal funds future contracts, obtains similar results to those obtained in our shorter sample and concludes that VAR-based measures of monetary policy do not make sense. We note that much better results are obtained in the enlarged sample. To provide further evidence we specify a VAR augmented by the non-VAR measures of monetary policy shocks, considered as an exogenous variable. Following Amisano and Giannini (1996), we represent the estimated system as follows:

$$\mathbf{A}\begin{pmatrix} \mathrm{Y}_t^{US} \\ \mathrm{Pcm}_t \\ \mathrm{P}_t^{US} \\ \mathrm{FF}_t \end{pmatrix} = \mathbf{C}(L)\begin{pmatrix} \mathrm{Y}_{t-1}^{US} \\ \mathrm{Pcm}_{t-1} \\ \mathrm{P}_{t-1}^{US} \\ \mathrm{FF}_{t-1} \end{pmatrix} + \begin{pmatrix} g_1 \\ g_2 \\ g_3 \\ g_4 \end{pmatrix} x_t + \mathbf{B}\begin{pmatrix} \nu_t^1 \\ \nu_t^2 \\ \nu_t^3 \\ \nu_t^{FF} \end{pmatrix} \tag{6.31}$$

$$x = \mathrm{EUR\$}, \mathrm{IFS}^{US}$$

where $\mathbf{A}$ is lower-triangular and $\mathbf{B}$ is diagonal. The estimated values of the coefficients $g_i$ are reported in Table 6.3.

TABLE 6.3. Coefficients on $EUR\$$ and $IFS^{US}$ in the benchmark VAR

| Sample 1988:11–1997:11 | | | | |
|---|---|---|---|---|
| | $Y^{US}$ | $Pcm$ | $P^{US}$ | $FF$ |
| $EUR\$$ | 0.0061<br>(0.0032) | 0.0055<br>(0.0121) | 0.0013<br>(1.0633) | 0.468<br>(0.097) |
| $IFS^{US}$ | 0.0025<br>(0.0031) | 0.0082<br>(0.0116) | 0.0009<br>(0.0013) | 0.356<br>(0.099) |
| Sample: 1984:1–1997:11 | | | | |
| | $Y^{US}$ | $Pcm$ | $P^{US}$ | $FF$ |
| $EUR\$$ | 0.0026<br>(0.0016) | 0.0007<br>(0.0006) | 0.0058<br>(0.0063) | 0.552<br>(0.062) |

We note that none of the macroeconomic variables responds to the non-VAR monetary policy shocks, while the Federal fund rate does. As suggested by the correlations between shocks, results are stronger on the larger sample. We then concentrate on this sample and compare impulse responses to monetary policy shocks in the traditional benchmark VAR specification with impulse responses to non-VAR monetary policy shocks in our augmented specification.

The results, shown in Figure 6.20, illustrate that a contractionary monetary policy shock produces the expected negative effect on output and a persistent effect on the Federal funds rate.

The inclusion of the commodity price index is successful in solving the price puzzle: the consumer price level does not show a 'perverse' response to restrictive policy.

The pairs of impulse response functions, based on the VAR and the non-VAR shocks, describe a very similar transmission mechanism, supporting the evidence already provided by Brunner (1996) and Bagliano and Favero (1998) with different exogenous measures.

Despite a correlation of 0.5 between EUR$ and the measure of policy shock obtained from the benchmark VAR, the dynamic effects of monetary policy show very close features.

The different measures capture unexpected variations in the policy rate related to monetary policy and the existence of other non-policy disturbances does not change the basic features of the response to a policy shock.

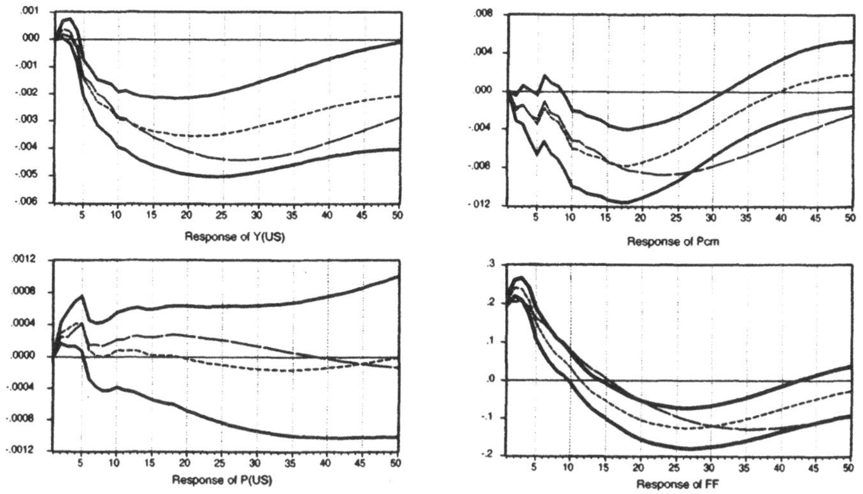


FIG. 6.20. Responses to EUR$ shocks (solid line) and to VAR-based structural shocks $\nu^{FF}$ (dotted line) with one standard deviation confidence intervals from the benchmark VAR

### 6.8.2 *Open economy (US–Germany)*

Let us now consider the open-economy version of the VAR system. We begin by a baseline specification which includes the commodity price index:

$$\mathbf{A}\begin{pmatrix} \mathrm{Y}_t^{US} \\ \mathrm{Pcm}_t \\ \mathrm{P}_t^{US} \\ \mathrm{FF}_t \\ \mathrm{Y}_t^{GER} \\ \mathrm{P}_t^{GER} \\ e_t \\ \mathrm{R}_t^{GER} \end{pmatrix} = \mathbf{C}(L)\begin{pmatrix} \mathrm{Y}_{t-1}^{US} \\ \mathrm{Pcm}_{t-1} \\ \mathrm{P}_{t-1}^{US} \\ \mathrm{FF}_{t-1} \\ \mathrm{Y}_{t-1}^{GER} \\ \mathrm{P}_{t-1}^{GER} \\ e_{t-1} \\ \mathrm{R}_{t-1}^{GER} \end{pmatrix} + \mathbf{B}\begin{pmatrix} \nu_t^1 \\ \nu_t^2 \\ \nu_t^3 \\ \nu_t^{FF} \\ \nu_t^5 \\ \nu_t^6 \\ \nu_t^e \\ \nu_t^{RGER} \end{pmatrix} \tag{6.32}$$

where $\mathbf{A}$ is lower-triangular and $\mathbf{B}$ is diagonal. As we have done for the closed economy case, we compare the orthogonalized residual of the German call money rate equation ($\nu^{RGER}$) with the non-VAR measure of German monetary policy shocks $IFS^{GER}$, derived from instantaneous forward rates. Figure 6.21 and Table 6.4 confirm the results for correlations obtained in the closed-economy case.

TABLE 6.4. VAR and non-VAR monetary policy shocks

Sample: 1984:1–1997:11

| | $IFS^{GER}$ | $\nu^{RGER}$ |
|---|---|---|
| $IFS^{GER}$ | 0.194 | - |
| $\nu^{RGER}$ | 0.163 | 0.169 |

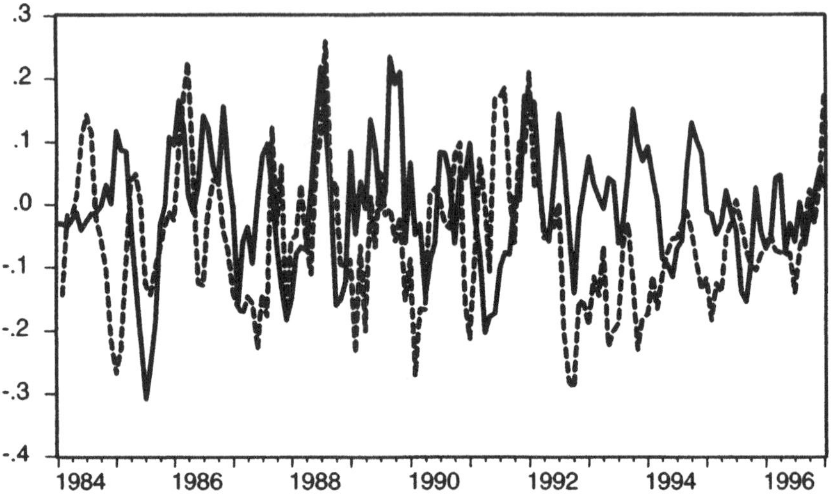


FIG. 6.21. Three-month centred moving averages of $IFS^{GER}$ shocks (solid line) and open-economy VAR German monetary policy shocks (dotted line)

As in the closed-economy case, we augment the previously estimated system by including the exogenous measure of German monetary policy shocks $IFS^{GER}$ described in the previous section.

The open-economy VAR is now the following:

$$\mathbf{A}\begin{pmatrix} \mathrm{Y}_t^{US} \\ \mathrm{Pcm}_t \\ \mathrm{P}_t^{US} \\ \mathrm{FF}_t \\ \mathrm{Y}_t^{GER} \\ \mathrm{P}_t^{GER} \\ e_t \\ \mathrm{R}_t^{GER} \end{pmatrix} = \mathbf{C}(L)\begin{pmatrix} \mathrm{Y}_{t-1}^{US} \\ \mathrm{Pcm}_{t-1} \\ \mathrm{P}_{t-1}^{US} \\ \mathrm{FF}_{t-1} \\ \mathrm{Y}_{t-1}^{GER} \\ \mathrm{P}_{t-1}^{GER} \\ e_{t-1} \\ \mathrm{R}_{t-1}^{GER} \end{pmatrix} + \begin{pmatrix} g_1 \\ g_2 \\ g_3 \\ g_4 \\ g_5 \\ g_6 \\ g_7 \\ g_8 \end{pmatrix} IFS_t^{GER} + \mathbf{B}\begin{pmatrix} \nu_t^1 \\ \nu_t^2 \\ \nu_t^3 \\ \nu_t^{FF} \\ \nu_t^5 \\ \nu_t^6 \\ \nu_t^e \\ \nu_t^{RGER} \end{pmatrix}. \quad (6.33)$$

Using our exogenous measure of monetary policy shocks in combination with a Choleski ordering with the German policy rate coming last, we are able to directly address the issue of simultaneity between German monetary policy and the exchange rate. The contemporaneous effect of a monetary policy shock on the exchange rate is given by the coefficient on $IFS^{GER}$ in the exchange rate equation ($g_7$), while the response of the German interest rate to innovations in the exchange rate is endogenized by the ordering chosen. As shown in Table 6.5, we do not observe a significant contemporaneous feedback between the German interest rate and the exchange rate in any direction. In our framework, this is a testable proposition rather than an assumed identified restriction. We note that our measure of monetary policy shocks significantly enters in the German policy rate equation and that the contemporaneous response of the US output to German monetary policy shocks is small but marginally significant.[3]

TABLE 6.5. Coefficients on $IFS^{GER}$ and simultaneous responses of $e$

| | $Y^{US}$ | $Pcm$ | $P^{US}$ | $FF$ | $Y^{GER}$ | $P^{GER}$ | $e$ | $R^{GER}$ |
|---|---|---|---|---|---|---|---|---|
| $IFS^{GER}$ | −0.007 | −0.01 | −0.0013 | −0.0892 | 0.00002 | 0.0029 | 0.0084 | 0.230 |
| | (0.002) | (0.008) | (0.0008) | (0.1146) | (0.0011) | (0.007) | (0.0127) | (0.097) |
| $e$ | 1.36 | −0.15 | −0.15 | 0.022 | 0.045 | 2.44 | −0.007 | −0.008 |
| | (0.037) | (0.11) | (1.09) | (0.0083) | (0.126) | (0.79) | (0.002) | (0.01) |

The pair of impulse response functions shown in Figure 6.22, along with one standard deviation bands, confirm qualitatively the results obtained for the closed US economy: measuring monetary policy shocks using financial market data does not alter the main features of the monetary transmission mechanism for Germany.

## 6.9 Conclusions

The VAR approach to the monetary transmission mechanism aims at the derivation of stylized facts to help the selection of the theoretical model to use for simulating the effects of monetary policy. The identification of parameters in this type of model does not allow us to separate deep parameters describing taste and technology from expectational parameters dependent on policy regimes. However, by estimating this model on a single policy regime and by describing the responses of variables to structural shocks of interest, it is hoped to derive some stylized facts on the monetary transmission mechanism.

Unfortunately, structural shocks are not directly observable and the imposition of a set of identifying restrictions is a necessary prerequisite for the analysis. Given the aim of the analysis, it is essential that identifying restrictions are posed

[3] We report impulse responses based on restricting such a coefficient to zero; relaxing this restriction does not affect the shape and magnitude of the impulse responses.

independently from specific theories. All the developments of the Choleski ordering that we have discussed in the chapter provide the researcher with tools for achieving this aim. In particular, we have shown how information from financial markets can be used both to assess robustness of results derived within traditional VAR models of the monetary transmission mechanism and to aid identification in cases when traditional analysis does not deliver a sufficient number of restrictions. Within this framework it is also natural that the number of identifying restrictions is kept at a minimum.

VAR models of the monetary transmission mechanism are very rarely cointegrated VARs. We have seen that multivariate cointegration analysis requires the solution of a long-run identification problem, and that imposing cointegrating restrictions on a VAR in levels increases efficiency in the estimator at the cost of potential inconsistency, when the incorrect identifying restrictions are imposed. The monetary transmission mechanism is a short-run phenomenon and this explains why researchers prefer to employ unrestricted VARs to evaluate impulse response analysis over a short to medium horizon. Cointegrated VARs are however an almost inevitable choice when the relevant, theory-neutral restrictions, are long-run ones.

As VAR models are the natural empirical counterparts of dynamic general equilibrium models, their statistical adequacy is not as closely scrutinized as the adequacy of reduced-form specifications within the LSE approach. In particular, in numerous applications outliers are not removed and non-normality of residuals is a common feature. Parameter stability is also an issue in the debate.

Our analysis of VAR-based empirical evidence of the monetary transmission mechanism has shown that the main problem with the empirical evidence provided by these models is uncertainty. Large standard errors are associated with the point estimates of impulse response functions. The more so in the case of VAR in open economies, where practitioners have developed the habit of reporting one standard deviation bands rather than two standard deviation bands. The main consequence of such uncertainty is that the aim of the exercise, once again model selection, is difficult to achieve in practice.

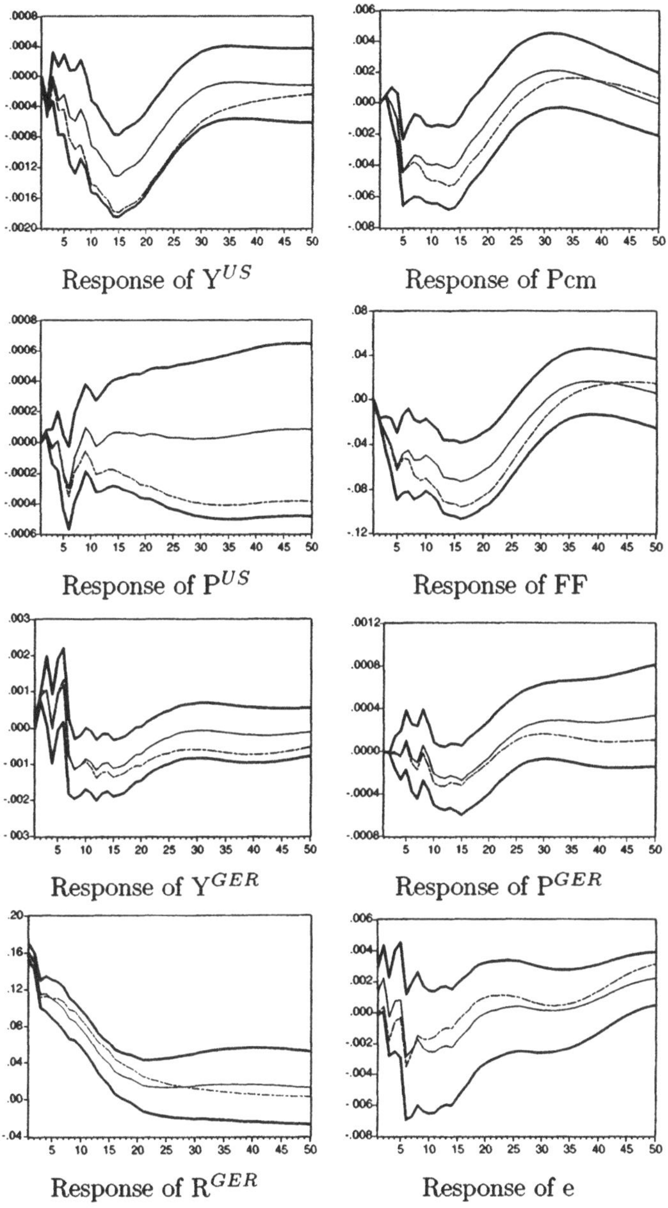


FIG. 6.22. Responses to IFS$^{GER}$ shocks (solid line) and to VAR-based structural shocks $\nu^{RGER}$ (dotted line) with one standard deviation confidence intervals from the benchmark VAR

## 6.10 References


Amisano, G., and Giannini, C. (1996). *Topics in Structural VAR Econometrics.* Springer–Verlag.

Bagliano, F. C., and Favero, C. A. (1998). 'Measuring Monetary Policy with VAR models: an evaluation'. *European Economic Review,* 42, 6: 1069-1112.

Bagliano, F. C., and Favero, C. A. (1999). 'Information from financial markets and VAR measures of monetary policy'. *European Economic Review,* 43, 6: 825-838.

Bernanke, B. S. and Blinder, A. (1992). 'The Federal Funds Rate and the channels of monetary transmission'. *American Economic Review,* 82: 901-921.

Bernanke, B. S. and Mihov, I. (1998). 'Measuring monetary policy'. *Quarterly Journal of Economics,* 113, 3: 869-902.

Bernanke, B. S. and Mihov, I. (1996). 'What Does the Bundesbank Target?'. NBER working paper No. 5764.

Bernanke, B. S. and Mihov, I. (1998). 'The liquidity effect and long-run neutrality'. NBER working paper No. 6608.

Blanchard, O. J., and Quah, D. T. (1989). 'The dynamic effects of aggregate demand and supply disturbances'. *American Economic Review,* 79: 655-73.

Brunner, A. (1996). 'Using measures of expectations to identify the effects of a monetary policy shock'. Board of Governors of the Federal Reserve System, International Finance Discussion Paper No. 537.

Campbell, J. (1995). 'Some Lessons from the Yield Curve'. *Journal of Economic Perspectives,* 9, 3: 129-152.

Christiano, L. J., and Eichenbaum, M. (1992). 'Liquidity Effects and the Monetary Transmission Mechanism'. *American Economic Review,* 82, 2: 346-353.

Christiano, L. J., Eichenbaum, M., and Evans, C. L. (1996a). 'The Effects of Monetary Policy Shocks: Evidence from the Flow of Funds'. *Review of Economics and Statistics,* 78: 16-34.

Christiano, L. J., Eichenbaum, M., and Evans, C. L. (1996b). 'Monetary Policy Shocks and their Consequences: Theory and Evidence'. Paper presented at ISOM.

Christiano, L. J., Eichenbaum, M., and Evans, C. L. (1998). 'Monetary Policy shocks: what have we learned and to what end?'. NBER working paper No. 6400.

Clarida, R., and Gali, J. (1994). 'Sources of real exchange rate fluctuations: how important are nominal shocks?'. Carnegie-Rochester Conference Series on Public Policy 41: 1-56.

Clarida. R., and Gertler, M. (1996). 'How the Bundesbank conducts monetary policy'. NBER working paper No. 5581.

Cochrane, J. (1994). 'Permanent and Transitory Components of GNP and Stock Prices'. *Quarterly Journal of Economics,* 241-267.

Cushman, D. O., and Zha, T. (1997). 'Identifying monetary policy in a small open economy under flexible exchange rates'. *Journal of Monetary Economics*, 39: 433-448.

Doornik, J., and Hendry, D. F. (1996). *PcFIML: Interactive econometric modelling of dynamic system.* London: International Thompson Publishing.

Eichenbaum, M., and Evans, C. (1995). 'Some Empirical Evidence on the effects of monetary policy on real exchange rates'. *Quarterly Journal of Economics*, 110: 975-1009.

Farmer, R. E. A. (1997). 'Money in a Real Business Cycle Model'. Mimeo, Dept. of Economics, UCLA.

Faust, J., and Leeper, E. M. (1997). 'When do long run identifying restrictions give reliable results?'. *Journal of Business and Economic Statistics*, 15, 3: 345-353.

Faust, J., and Whiteman, C. H. (1997). 'General-to-Specific procedures for fitting a data-admissible, theory inspired, congruent, parsimonious, encompassing, weakly exogenous, identified, structural model to the DGP: A translation and critique'. Board of Governors of the Federal System, International Finance Discussion Paper 576.

Favero, C. A., Giavazzi, F., and Spaventa, L. (1996). 'High-yields. The spread on German interest rates'. *The Economic Journal*, 107: 956-985.

Favero, C. A., Pifferi, M., and Iacone, F. (1996). 'Monetary Policy, Forward Rates and Long Rates: Does Germany Differ from the United States?'. CEPR Discussion Paper No. 1456.

Goodfriend, M., and King, R. (1997). 'The Newclassical Synthesis and the Role of Monetary Policy'. Paper presented at the 12th NBER Annual Macroeconomic Conference.

Gordon, D., and Leeper, E. M. (1994).'The Dynamic Impacts of Monetary Policy: an Exercise in Tentative Identification'. *Journal of Political Economy*, 102: 1228-1247.

Grilli, V., and Roubini, N. (1996). 'Liquidity and Exchange Rates: Puzzling Evidence from the G-7 Countries'. Mimeo, Yale University.

Grilli, V., and Roubini, N. (1996). 'Liquidity Models in Open Economies: Theory and Empirical Evidence'. *European Economic Review*, 4: 847-859.

Hamilton, J. (1994). *Time-Series Analysis.* Princeton: Princeton University Press.

Hendry, D. F. (1996). *Dynamic Econometrics.* Oxford: Oxford University Press.

Keating, J. W. (1990) 'Identifying VAR Models under Rational Expectations'. *Journal of Monetary Economics*, 25: 453-476.

Kim, S., and Roubini, N. (1997). 'Liquidity and Exchange Rates in the G-7 Countries: Evidence from identified VARs'. Mimeo.

Leeper, E. M., Sims, C. A., and Zha, T. (1996). 'What does monetary policy do?'. Available at http://eco-072399b.princeton.edu/yftp/bpea/bpeaf.pdf

Leeper, E. M. (1997). 'Narrative and VAR approaches to monetary policy: common identification problems'. *Journal of Monetary Economics.*

Lippi, M., and Reichlin, L. (1993). 'The dynamic effects of aggregate demand and supply disturbances: comment'. *American Economic Review*, 83, 3: 644-652.

Lucas, R. E. Jr. (1972). 'Expectations and the Neutrality of Money'. *Journal of Economic Theory*, 4, April: 103-124.

Lucas, R. E. Jr. (1976). 'Econometric Policy Evaluation: A Critique'. In K. Brunner and A. Meltzer (eds.) *The Phillips curve and labor markets.* Amsterdam: North-Holland.

McCallum, B. (1994). 'A reconsideration of the uncovered interest parity relationship'. *Journal of Monetary Economics,* 33: 105-132.

McCallum, B. (1999). 'Analysis of the monetary transmission mechanism: methodological issues'. Paper presented at the Deutsche Bundesbank conference 'The monetary transmission process: recent developments and lessons for Europe', Frankfurt.

McCallum, B., and Nelson, E. (1999). 'An optimizing IS-LM specification for monetary and business cycle analysis'. *Journal of Money Credit and Banking*, 31.

Mellander, E., Vredin, A., and Warne, A. (1993). Stochastic trends and economic fluctuations in a small open economy. *Journal of Applied Econometrics.*

Mosconi, R. (1998). *Malcolm. The theory and practice of cointegration analysis in RATS.* Venice: Cafoscarina.

Nelson, C. R., and Siegel, A. F. (1987). 'Parsimonious modelling of yield curves'. *Journal of Business,* 60: 473-489.

Obstfeld, M., and Rogoff, K. (1996). *Foundations of International Economics.* Cambridge, Massachusetts: MIT Press.

Romer, C. D., and Romer, D. H. (1989). 'Does Monetary Policy Matter? A New Test in the Spirit of Friedman and Schwartz'. In O.J. Blanchard and S. Fischer (eds.), *NBER Macroeconomics Annual.* MIT Press, 121-170.

Romer, C. D., and Romer, D. H. (1994). 'Monetary Policy Matters'. *Journal of Monetary Economics,* 34: 75-88.

Rudebusch, G. D. (1998). 'Do Measures of Monetary Policy in a VAR Make Sense?'. *International Economic Review*, 39: 907-931.

Schlagenhauf, D. E., and Wrase, J. M. (1995). 'Liquidity and Real Activity in a simple open economy model'. *Journal of Monetary Economics,* 35: 431-461.

Sims, C. A. (1980a). 'Macroeconomics and Reality'. *Econometrica*, 48: 1-48.

Sims, C. A. (1980b). 'Comparison of interwar and postwar business cycles: monetarism reconsidered'. *American Economic Review*, May: 250-257.

Sims, C. A. (1992). 'Interpreting the Macroeconomic Time-Series Facts: the Effects of Monetary Policy'. *European Economic Review*, 36: 975-1011.

Sims, C. A., Stock, J. H., and Watson, M. (1990). 'Inference in linear time-series models with some unit roots'. *Econometrica*, 58: 113-144.

Sims, C. A., and Zha, T. (1996). 'Does Monetary Policy Generate Recessions?'. Mimeo. Available at ftp://ftp.econ.yale.edu/pub/sims/mpolicy

Skinner, T., and Zettelmeyer, J. (1996). 'Identification and effects of monetary policy shocks: an alternative approach'. Mimeo, MIT, September.

Smets, F. (1996). 'Measuring Monetary Policy in the G7 countries: interest rates versus exchange rates'. Presented at CEPR-Banca d'Italia workshop on Model Specification, Identification and Estimation in Empirical Macroeconomics.

Smets, F. (1997). 'Measuring Monetary Policy Shocks in France, Germany and Italy: the role of the exchange rate'. BIS Working Paper No.42.

Soderlind, P., and Svensson, L. E. O. (1997). 'New techniques to extract market expectations from financial instruments'. *Journal of Monetary Economics*, 40: 383-42.

Strongin, S. (1995). 'The identification of monetary policy disturbances. Explaining the liquidity puzzle'. *Journal of Monetary Economics*, 35: 463-497.

Svensson, L. E. O. (1994). 'Estimating and interpreting forward interest rates: Sweden 1992-1994'. CEPR Discussion Paper No.105.

Uhlig, H. (1997). 'What are the effects of monetary policy ? Results from an agnostic identification procedure'. Mimeo.
Available at http://cwis.kub.nl/~few5/center/staff/uhlig/home.htm.

# 7

# INTERTEMPORAL OPTIMIZATION AND GMM METHOD

## 7.1 Introduction

The intertemporal optimization approach to macroeconomic theory takes the Lucas critique seriously and relies on the belief that questions like 'How should a central bank respond to shocks in macroeconomic variables?' are to be answered within the framework of quantitative monetary general equilibrium models of the business cycle.

The evaluation of the effects of monetary policy is a question for theoretical models rather than for empirical *ad hoc* macroeconometric models. We have seen that VAR-based empirical evidence helps the selection of the relevant theoretical model. However, once the model selection problem has been solved, there are two relevant issues: parameterization and simulation. In this chapter we mainly concentrate on parameterization while we devote the next chapter to simulation and policy evaluation. The intertemporal optimization approach takes no interest in the parameters estimated by traditional macroeconometric modelling, since it delivers parameters which are convolutions of 'deep' and expectational parameters. Deep parameters describe tastes and technology and are invariant to policy regimes, expectational parameters are instead dependent on the specific policy regime.

Interestingly, the intertemporal optimization–rational expectations paradigm generates an alternative econometric approach to estimate deep parameters of interest in a very natural way: the generalized methods of moments (GMM).

This chapter is devoted to the illustration of the empirically relevant aspect of the GMM methodology. We consider applications to consumers' behaviour and the estimation of monetary policy rules. We start by illustrating the close relationship between the econometric methodology and the intertemporal optimization achieved by the implementation of the GMM method in the estimation of Euler equations. We then consider the technical aspects of the definition of the estimator, the problems related to the estimation of the covariance matrix and the inference within GMM models.

Having considered the technical aspects of the estimator, we evaluate its success in the neo-classical camp and its extremely rare utilization by Keynesian macroeconomists by giving an econometric interpretation to a statement by Mankiw, Rotemberg and Summers (1985) who assert that:

> ... *The major difference between modern neoclassical and traditional Keynesian macroeconomic theories is that the former regard observed levels of employment, consumption and output as realizations from dynamic*

*optimizing decisions by both households and firms, while the latter regard them as reflecting constraints on households and firms ...*

We conclude by showing applications of the GMM approach to the estimation of deep parameters describing (representative) consumer behaviour and to the estimation of deep parameters describing central banks' preferences in monetary policy rules.

## 7.2 Euler equations and closed form solutions

Consider the standard optimization problem for the representative consumer:

$$\max_{c_{t+i},A_{t+i}} E_t \sum_{i=0}^{\infty} (1+\delta)^{-i} U(c_{t+i}), \tag{7.1}$$

subject to the following constraints

$$A_{t+i} = (1+r) A_{t+i-1} + y_{t+i} - c_{t+i},$$

$$\lim_{i\to\infty} E_t A_{t+i} (1+r)^{-i} = 0,$$

where $y$ is disposable labour income, $c$ is consumption of non-durable goods and services, $A$ is wealth (a single financial asset) giving a return of $r$, $U$ is a utility function featuring both intertemporal and intra-temporal separability. All variables are expressed in real terms. The $\delta$ parameter describes the rate of the intertemporal preferences of the representative consumer, who has an infinite horizon and does not face liquidity constraints of any form. Therefore, she can run negative balances of $A$ in any period with the only constraint that the present discounted value of wealth in time $t$ approaches zero as $t$ approaches infinity (transversality condition). Lastly, we denote the expectation formed conditionally upon the information set available at time $t$ by $E_t$.

We solve the intertemporal optimization problem by finding the maximum of the following Lagrangian function:

$$\max_{c_{t+i},A_{t+i}} E_t \sum_{i=0}^{\infty} (1+\delta)^{-i} G_{t+i}, \tag{7.2}$$

$$G_{t+i} = U(c_{t+i}) + \lambda_{t+i} \left(A_{t+i} - (1+r) A_{t+i-1} - y_{t+i} + c_{t+i}\right).$$

We assume that the real return is non-stochastic and that utility function features constant relative risk aversion (CRRA):

$$U(c_{t+i}) = \frac{c_{t+i}^{1-\gamma}}{1-\gamma}, \tag{7.3}$$

where the $\gamma$ parameter describes the consumer's risk aversion. This specification completes the set-up of our problem. We note that there are two parameters which describe tastes and could be defined as deep in Lucas's terminology: $\gamma$ and $\delta$.

First-order conditions for optimality could be stated as follows:

$$E_t\left(c_{t+i}^{-\gamma}\right) + E_t\lambda_{t+i} = 0 \qquad \forall\, i, \tag{7.4}$$

$$E_t\lambda_{t+i} - E_t\left(\frac{1+r}{1+\delta}\lambda_{t+i+1}\right) = 0 \qquad \forall\, i.$$

By eliminating the Lagrange multipliers and considering the specific case of $i = 0$, we obtain:

$$E_t\left(\frac{1+r}{1+\delta}c_{t+1}^{-\gamma} - c_t^{-\gamma}\right) = 0. \tag{7.5}$$

Some considerations of equation (7.5), known as the Euler equation, are in order. First, this relation clearly confutes the idea that economic theory mainly gives predictions on the long-run behaviour of economic variables: in fact, the Euler equation imposes restrictions on the short-run dynamics of economic variables. Second, the only parameters entering equation (7.5) are $\gamma$ and $\delta$, the 'deep' parameters describing consumers' preferences. Third, as equation (7.5) represents not the closed form solution of the intertemporal optimization problem but only the first-order condition for optimality, it cannot be interpreted as a consumption function. However, from (7.5) we derive the falsifiable proposition that, under the joint hypothesis of rational expectations, the only significant variable in predicting consumption at time $t+1$ given the information available at time $t$ is consumption at time $t$. Under our hypotheses, the logarithm of consumption behaves as a 'random walk' (Hall 1978). The conditional expectation for time $t+1$ taken at time $t$ of the expression between brackets in (7.5) is zero, and such an expression is orthogonal to any variable other than consumption included in the agent's information set at time $t$. Labelling the expression between brackets in (7.5) as $f_{t+1}$we have:

$$E_t f_{t+1} = 0, \quad E_t f_{t+1}\mathbf{z}_t = 0, \tag{7.6}$$

where $\mathbf{z}$ is a vector containing any economic variable observable at time $t$.

Note that the Euler equation does not have any implication for the relation between consumption and other economic variables: the significance of income in explaining contemporaneous fluctuations in consumption is perfectly compatible with our intertemporal optimization model, which only rules out the significance of income at time $t$ in explaining the difference between the marginal utility of savings at time $t$ for time $t+1$ (if the consumer does not consume one unit at time $t$, she will invest it in the financial asset and have $(1+r)$ units at time $t+1$, the discounted value of this quantity being $(1+r)/(1+\delta)$) and the marginal utility of consumption at time $t$. Finally, note that if the rate of intertemporal preference and the interest rate are equal, fluctuations in consumption are determined exclusively by stochastic shocks. To further illustrate the relationship between the Euler equation and consumption function and to provide a firmer background to our discussion of econometric methodology we take advantage of the simplicity of our specification to derive analytically a closed form solution to our intertemporal optimization problem. To simplify matters even further let us assume 'certainty equivalence'.

From the first-order conditions we derive the following relationship between consumption at time $t$ and consumption in any period following $t$:

$$c_{t+i} = c_t \left( \frac{1+r}{1+\delta} \right)^{i/\gamma}. \tag{7.7}$$

Now aggregate, over time, the period budget constraint and impose the transversality condition to obtain:

$$\sum_{i=0}^{\infty} \frac{c_{t+i}}{(1+r)^i} = \sum_{i=0}^{\infty} \frac{y_{t+i}}{(1+r)^i} + (1+r) A_{t-i}. \tag{7.8}$$

By using (7.7) in (7.8) to substitute consumption in all future periods with an expression in terms of current consumption, we obtain:

$$c_t = (\rho - 1) \left( \sum_{i=0}^{\infty} \frac{y_{t+i}}{(1+r)^i} + (1+r) A_{t-i} \right) \tag{7.9}$$

where $\rho = \frac{(1+\delta)^{\frac{1}{\gamma}}}{(1+r)^{\frac{1}{\gamma}-1}}$ is assumed to be greater than one. When $\delta = r$ the expression (7.9) simplifies to the following:

$$c_t = r \left( \sum_{i=0}^{\infty} \frac{y_{t+i}}{(1+r)^i} + (1+r) A_{t-i} \right). \tag{7.10}$$

Equation (7.10) represents the closed form solution to the intertemporal optimization problem and is the structural consumption function for our representative consumer under the hypothesis of certainty equivalence. Note that consumption is a function of permanent income, which includes current income, and that the reaction of consumption to modifications in the real interest rate depends on income and substitution effects. The sign of the income effect depends on the consumer's financial position: if the consumer is in debt ($A_{t-1} < 0$) the income effect is negative, while for a consumer in credit ($A_{t-1} > 0$) the income effect is positive. The substitution effect is always negative, as an increase in the interest rate lowers the discounted stream of future income.

The closed form solution is useful to understand the scepticism of neo-classical economists towards the use of empirical *ad hoc* structural macroeconometric models to simulate the effects of macroeconomic policy. To grasp the intuition[1] let us re-write relation (7.9) omitting the 'perfect foresight':

$$c_t = (\rho - 1)\left(\sum_{i=0}^{\infty} \frac{E_t y_{t+i}}{(1+r)^i} + (1+r)\, A_{t-1}\right) + \varepsilon_t, \tag{7.11}$$

$$\varepsilon_t = (\rho - 1) \sum_{i=0}^{\infty} \frac{(y_{t+i} - E_t y_{t+i})}{(1+r)^i}.$$

In order to interpret (7.11) in the light of traditional *ad hoc* macroeconometric models, which do not usually explicitly incorporate expectations, we need to solve for future income in terms of current income. We do so by assuming a simple autoregressive process for income:

$$y_t = a_1 y_{t-1} + u_t. \tag{7.12}$$

Using (7.12) repeatedly in (7.11) we have:

$$c_t = (\rho - 1)(1+r)\, A_{t-1} + (\rho - 1) \frac{1+r}{1+r-a_1} y_t + \varepsilon_t. \tag{7.13}$$

Parameters in (7.13) are convolutions of the deep parameters contained in $\rho$ and of the expectational parameter $a_1$, which changes every time the process generating income is modified. Moreover, given the estimation of (7.13), the structural parameters describing consumer's tastes, $\delta$ and $\gamma$, are even unidentifiable. Note also that the residual term in (7.13) is, by construction, autocorrelated. If we can represent autocorrelation in the following, simple, manner,

$$\varepsilon_t = \delta \varepsilon_{t-1} + v_t \tag{7.14}$$

then the best representation of the data generating process is:

$$\begin{aligned}\Delta c_t = {} & (\rho - 1)(1+r)\, \Delta A_{t-1} + (\rho - 1) \frac{1+r}{1+r-a_1} \Delta y_t \\ & - (1-\delta)\left(c_{t-1} - (\rho - 1)(1+r)\, A_{t-2} - (\rho - 1) \frac{1+r}{1+r-a_1} y_{t-1}\right) + v_t,\end{aligned} \tag{7.15}$$

which, obviously, is an error correction mechanism (ECM). Clearly when the income generating process is constant, a specification like (7.15) will perform extremely well in fitting the data. Note that such a specification can be obtained without any reference to the theoretical intertemporal optimization approach, being derived by the LSE-type econometric specification search within the class of ECM representations of cointegrating regressions. However, if the data generating process is the one postulated by the intertemporal optimization theory,

[1]This amounts to a little cheating, which simplifies matters greatly without having any substantial effect on our final conclusions.

then the estimated model cannot be used for policy simulation. No empirical questions involving simulating the impact on consumption of different policies determining the income process can be answered meaningfully on the basis of the estimation of a model like (7.15). The estimated parameters are a function of the parameters in the income process and become misleading if the interesting policy to simulate implies a change in the income generating process. Within the intertemporal optimization framework, the answer to the interesting policy question should rely on the theoretical model rather than on an empirical *ad hoc* macroeconometric model. Therefore, the impact of different policy on consumption is to be based on the direct simulation of alternative processes for income within the framework of the theoretical model (7.11). Obviously, to implement meaningfully this approach, some estimate of the parameter $\rho$ and hence of the parameters $\delta$ and $\gamma$, which describe appropriately the preferences of consumers are needed. Now, the Euler equation immediately qualifies as the best relation for empirical estimation for the identification of the parameters of interest. It allows identification of the parameters of interest and does not depend on expectational parameters. Moreover, it leads naturally to the implementation of the generalized method of moments estimator. We devote the next section to the econometric analysis of this estimator.

## 7.3 Estimating Euler equations: the GMM method

Generalizing the results illustrated in the previous section we can represent the first-order condition from a generic intertemporal optimization problem as:

$$E_t \left[ f \left( \mathbf{x}_{t+i}, \boldsymbol{\theta} \right) \mathbf{z}_t \right] = 0 \tag{7.16}$$

where $\theta$ is the $(p \times 1)$ vector containing the parameters of interest and $\mathbf{z}$ is the $(n \times 1)$ vector of variables that theory suggests is orthogonal to $f(\mathbf{x}_{t+i}, \boldsymbol{\theta})$. In our example $\theta = (\delta, \gamma)$, $f(\mathbf{x}_{t+i}, \boldsymbol{\theta}) = \left( \frac{1+r}{1+\delta} c_{t+1}^{-\gamma} - c_t^{-\gamma} \right)$ and $\mathbf{z}_t$ contains any variables observable at time $t$ other than consumption.

It is intuitively clear that a necessary condition for the identification of parameters of interest is $n \geq p$, with over-identification in the case of strict inequality and just-identification in the case of equality. If $n < p$, then the parameters of interest are not identified. Let us concentrate on the over-identification case, of which just-identification is a special case. This is the relevant case in numerous economic examples, as deriving Euler equations from intertemporal optimization and rational expectations usually selects a potentially infinite number of valid instruments. Think of our application to the consumer problem: any lagged variable is a valid instrument under the null that the rational expectations/intertemporal optimization model is a data generating process.

The estimator is 'naturally' derived from (7.16) by substituting population moments with sample moments:

$$\frac{1}{T}\sum_{t=1}^{T}\left[f\left(\mathbf{x}_{t+i},\boldsymbol{\theta}\right)\mathbf{z}_t\right]=0 \tag{7.17}$$

where $T$ is the size of the available sample. Obviously, in the case of over-identification (7.17) produces a system of $n$ equations with $p$ unknowns, which does not admit a unique solution. This problem is solved by considering $p$ linear combinations of the $n$ first-order conditions and therefore by minimizing the 'Euclidean distance' between $\frac{1}{T}\sum_{t=1}^{T}\left[f\left(\mathbf{x}_{t+i},\boldsymbol{\theta}\right)\mathbf{z}_t\right]$ and the null vector. This implies solving the following minimization problem:

$$\min_{\boldsymbol{\theta}}\left(\sum_{t=1}^{T}\left[f\left(\mathbf{x}_{t+i},\boldsymbol{\theta}\right)\mathbf{z}_t\right]\right)'\mathbf{A}\left(\sum_{t=1}^{T}\left[f\left(\mathbf{x}_{t+i},\boldsymbol{\theta}\right)\mathbf{z}_t\right]\right), \tag{7.18}$$

where $\mathbf{A}$ is a an appropriate $(n\times n)$ weighting matrix. By defining a $(T\times n)$ matrix $F\left(\mathbf{x}_{t+i},\mathbf{z}_t,\boldsymbol{\theta}\right)$, with typical element $f\left(\mathbf{x}_{t+i},\boldsymbol{\theta}\right)z_{jt}$, where $j=1,...,n$, $t=1,...,T$, the minimization problem can be re-written as:

$$\min_{\boldsymbol{\theta}}\ i'F\left(\mathbf{x}_{t+i},\mathbf{z}_t,\boldsymbol{\theta}\right)\mathbf{A}F\left(\mathbf{x}_{t+i},\mathbf{z}_t,\boldsymbol{\theta}\right)i,$$

where $i$ is a $(T\times 1)$ identity vector. One can show that any symmetric positive definite matrix $\mathbf{A}$ will yield a consistent estimate of the vector of parameters of interest. However, Hansen (1982) has shown that a necessary (but not sufficient) condition to obtain an asymptotically efficient estimate of $\theta$ is to set $\mathbf{A}$ equal to the inverse of the covariance matrix of the sample moments. The intuition behind this choice is simple: less weight is put on the more imprecise conditions. Therefore if $\Psi=Var\left(\sum_{t=1}^{T}\left[f\left(\mathbf{x}_{t+i},\boldsymbol{\theta}\right)\mathbf{z}_t\right]\right)$, GMM estimates are obtained by solving the following minimization problem:

$$\min_{\boldsymbol{\theta}}\left(\sum_{t=1}^{T}\left[f\left(\mathbf{x}_{t+i},\boldsymbol{\theta}\right)\mathbf{z}_t\right]\right)'\Psi^{-1}\left(\sum_{t=1}^{T}\left[f\left(\mathbf{x}_{t+i},\boldsymbol{\theta}\right)\mathbf{z}_t\right]\right). \tag{7.19}$$

Note that in general, as $\Psi$ is a function of $\boldsymbol{\theta}$, it is necessary to proceed in at least two steps. Exploiting the fact that any arbitrary weighting matrix will deliver consistent estimates of $\boldsymbol{\theta}$, this vector of parameters is estimated first, then a $\widehat{\Psi}$ is constructed and the minimization of (7.19) is then performed. Of course, the two-step procedure is easily extended to an iterative procedure.

Hansen (1982) has shown that the minimized criterion function can be also used to test the validity of instruments in the case of over-identification. In fact the quantity:

$$J=\left(\sum_{t=1}^{T}\left[f\left(\mathbf{x}_{t+i},\widehat{\theta}\right)\mathbf{z}_t\right]\right)'\widehat{\Psi}^{-1}\left(\sum_{t=1}^{T}\left[f\left(\mathbf{x}_{t+i},\widehat{\theta}\right)\mathbf{z}_t\right]\right), \tag{7.20}$$

is distributed as a $\chi^2$ with $n-p$ degrees of freedom. The quantity (7.20) is known in the literature as the $J$-statistic. GMM is a very general class of estimators and many of the known estimators can be set up as special cases of GMM. Consider, for example, the generalized instrumental variables estimator.

The relevant problem is to estimate the vector of unknown parameters $\boldsymbol{\beta}$ in the linear model:

$$\mathbf{y} = \mathbf{X}\boldsymbol{\beta} + \mathbf{u}, \tag{7.21}$$

where $y$ is a $(T \times 1)$ vector of observations on the dependent variable, $\mathbf{X}$ is a $(T \times p)$ matrix of observations on the explanatory variables, $\boldsymbol{\beta}$ is the $(p \times 1)$ vector of parameters of interest, and $\mathbf{u}$ is the $(T \times 1)$ vector of observations on the error term with zero mean and variance-covariance matrix equal to $\sigma^2 I$. Assume that $\mathbf{X}$ are not weakly exogenous for the estimation of the parameters of interest, we then have:

$$p \lim \frac{1}{T}\mathbf{X}'\mathbf{u} \neq \mathbf{0}. \tag{7.22}$$

However, there exists a $\mathbf{Z}$ matrix containing $T$ observations on $n$ valid instruments, for which we have:

$$p \lim \frac{1}{T}\mathbf{Z}'\mathbf{u} = \mathbf{0}. \tag{7.23}$$

Condition (7.23), which defines instruments as valid, also gives a set of orthogonality restrictions to construct a GMM estimate. Let us concentrate on the over-identification case, where $n > p$. Applying formula (7.19), the relevant estimate is derived by solving the following problem:

$$\min_{\boldsymbol{\beta}} \left(\mathbf{u}'\mathbf{Z}\Psi^{-1}\mathbf{Z}'\mathbf{u}\right) \tag{7.24}$$

where the appropriate choice for the matrix $\Psi$ is:

$$\Psi = E\left(\mathbf{Z}'\mathbf{u}\mathbf{u}'\mathbf{Z}\right) = \sigma^2\mathbf{Z}'\mathbf{Z}. \tag{7.25}$$

Therefore, the GMM estimate will minimize the following criterion:

$$\min_{\boldsymbol{\beta}} \left(\frac{1}{\sigma^2}\mathbf{u}'\mathbf{Z}\left(\mathbf{Z}'\mathbf{Z}\right)^{-1}\mathbf{Z}'\mathbf{u}\right) \tag{7.26}$$

which admits GIVE as the solution:

$$\widehat{\boldsymbol{\beta}} = \left(\mathbf{X}'\mathbf{Z}\left(\mathbf{Z}'\mathbf{Z}\right)^{-1}\mathbf{Z}'\mathbf{X}\right)^{-1}\mathbf{X}'\mathbf{Z}\left(\mathbf{Z}'\mathbf{Z}\right)^{-1}\mathbf{Z}'\mathbf{y}. \tag{7.27}$$

Similarly, the $J$-statistic takes the following form:

$$J = \frac{\widehat{\mathbf{u}}'\mathbf{Z}\left(\mathbf{Z}'\mathbf{Z}\right)^{-1}\mathbf{Z}'\widehat{\mathbf{u}}}{s^2} \tag{7.28}$$

where $\widehat{\mathbf{u}} = \mathbf{y} - \mathbf{X}\widehat{\boldsymbol{\beta}}$ and $s^2 = \widehat{\mathbf{u}}'\widehat{\mathbf{u}}/T$. Equation (7.28) is distributed as a $\chi^2$ with $n - p$ degrees of freedom and it is the well-known test for the validity of instruments originally proposed by Sargan (1988) within the context of the GIVE estimator.

### 7.3.1 *Covariance matrix estimation*

So far we have implicitly considered the case in which the empirical moments were serially independent. In general it is worthwhile to relax such an assumption, as in many macroeconometric applied cases some dependence in the empirical moments are generated. Think, for example, of the case of the estimation of central bank reaction functions (Taylor 1999). As we shall see later, a central bank's policy rule can be specified by assuming that central banks set their instrument, the interest rate, to react to the contemporaneous output gap, the difference between them implies current and potential output, and to deviation of future expected inflation from its target. Future inflation is the relevant variable because the existence of lags between monetary action and their effect on the economy makes reacting to contemporaneous targets useless. The literature takes the relevant horizon for future inflation to be about one year. So the following rule could be specified on monthly data:

$$r_t = a_0 + a_1 E_t \left(\pi_{t+12} - \pi_t^*\right) + a_2 E_t \left(y_t - y_t^*\right) + v_t, \tag{7.29}$$

where $v_t$ is an exogenous i.i.d. disturbance. To fit (7.29) to the data, the unobservable forecast variables are eliminated by rewriting the rule in terms of the realized variables as follows:

$$\begin{aligned} r_t &= a_0 + a_1 \left(\pi_{t+12} - \pi_t^*\right) + a_2 \left(y_t - y_t^*\right) + \varepsilon_t, & (7.30)\\ \varepsilon_t &= a_1 \left[E_t \left(\pi_{t+12} - \pi_t^*\right) - \left(\pi_{t+12} - \pi_t^*\right)\right] & (7.31)\\ &\quad + a_2 \left[E_t \left(y_t - y_t^*\right) - \left(y_t - y_t^*\right)\right] + v_t. \end{aligned}$$

Labelling as $\mathbf{z}_t$ the vector of variables within the central bank's information set at the time the interest rate is chosen, we can construct the GMM estimator using the following set of orthogonality conditions:

$$E_t \left(\varepsilon_t \mid \mathbf{z}_t\right) = 0. \tag{7.32}$$

However, by construction, the composite disturbance term $\varepsilon_t$ features an MA(11) structure and empirical moments cannot be considered as serially independent.

To deal with this case we rewrite $\Psi$, the covariance matrix of the empirical moments, as:

$$\Psi = \lim_{T\to\infty} \left[\frac{1}{T}\sum_{p=1}^{T}\sum_{q=1}^{T} E\left(F_p'\left(\mathbf{x}_{t+i}, \mathbf{z}_t, \boldsymbol{\theta}\right) F_q\left(\mathbf{x}_{t+i}, \mathbf{z}_t, \boldsymbol{\theta}\right)\right)\right], \tag{7.33}$$

where $F_q\left(\mathbf{x}_{t+i}, \mathbf{z}_t, \boldsymbol{\theta}\right)$ is the $q^{th}$ row of the $(T \times n)$ matrix $F\left(\mathbf{x}_{t+i}, \mathbf{z}_t, \boldsymbol{\theta}\right)$. The first step to find a consistent estimator of $\Psi$ is to define the autocovariances of the empirical moments as:

$$\Gamma(j) = \frac{1}{T}\sum_{p=j+1}^{T} E\left(F_p'\left(\mathbf{x}_{t+i}, \mathbf{z}_t, \boldsymbol{\theta}\right) F_{p-j}\left(\mathbf{x}_{t+i}, \mathbf{z}_t, \boldsymbol{\theta}\right)\right) \quad \text{for } j \geq 0 \qquad (7.34)$$

$$\Gamma(j) = \frac{1}{T}\sum_{p=-j+1}^{T} E\left(F_{p+j}'\left(\mathbf{x}_{t+i}, \mathbf{z}_t, \boldsymbol{\theta}\right) F_{p}\left(\mathbf{x}_{t+i}, \mathbf{z}_t, \boldsymbol{\theta}\right)\right) \quad \text{for } j \leq 0. \qquad (7.35)$$

In terms of the $(n \times n)$ matrices $\Gamma(j)$, the right-hand side of (7.33) without the limit becomes:

$$\Psi^n = \sum_{j=-n+1}^{n-1} \Gamma(j). \qquad (7.36)$$

If there were no serial correlations between observations, then only $\Gamma(0)$ would be non-zero and we would have

$$\Psi^n = \Gamma(0) = \frac{1}{T}\sum_{p=1}^{T} E\left(F_p'\left(\mathbf{x}_{t+i}, \mathbf{z}_t, \boldsymbol{\theta}\right) F_p\left(\mathbf{x}_{t+i}, \mathbf{z}_t, \boldsymbol{\theta}\right)\right), \qquad (7.37)$$

which could be useful to deal with heteroscedasticity in the empirical moments. To see this point empirically, let us consider again the case of GIVE with heteroscedastic disturbances.

The relevant problem is to estimate the vector of unknown parameters $\boldsymbol{\beta}$ in the linear model:

$$\mathbf{y} = \mathbf{X}\boldsymbol{\beta} + \mathbf{u}, \qquad (7.38)$$

where $y$ is a $(T \times 1)$ vector of observations on the dependent variable, $\mathbf{X}$ is a $(T \times p)$ matrix of observations on the explanatory variables, $\boldsymbol{\beta}$ is the $(p \times 1)$ vector of parameters of interest, and $\mathbf{u}$ is the $(T \times 1)$ vector of observations on the error term with zero mean and variance-covariance matrix equal to $\Omega$, where

$$\Omega = \begin{bmatrix} \sigma_1^2 & \cdot & 0 \\ \cdot & \cdot & \cdot \\ 0 & 0 & \sigma_T^2 \end{bmatrix}.$$

As before we assume that $\mathbf{X}$ are not weakly exogenous for the estimation of the parameters of interest, but there exists a $\mathbf{Z}$ matrix containing $T$ observations on $n$ valid instruments. Applying formula (7.19), the relevant estimate is derived by solving the following problem:

$$\min_{\beta}\left(\mathbf{u}'\mathbf{Z}\Psi^{-1}\mathbf{Z}'\mathbf{u}\right), \qquad (7.39)$$

where the appropriate choice for the matrix $\Psi$ is:

$$\Psi = \Gamma(\mathbf{0}) = \mathbf{Z}'\Omega\mathbf{Z} = \frac{\mathbf{1}}{\mathbf{T}}\sum_{\mathbf{p}=1}^{\mathbf{T}} \mathbf{E}\left(u_p^2\right)\mathbf{Z}_p'\mathbf{Z}_p, \qquad (7.40)$$

which can be consistently estimated by using any consistent estimator of the parameters of interest and substituting $E\left(u_p^2\right)$ with the square of the corresponding residual.

This estimator is interpretable as an extension of the heteroscedasticity consistent estimator proposed by White (1980) within the OLS framework to the GIVE case.

Having discussed this application, let us return to the general case of serial correlation of unknown form. As remarked by Davidson and MacKinnon (1993) it is tempting to estimate the autocovariances simply by omitting the expectations in expression (7.40), evaluating the $F_p$ at some consistent preliminary estimate of the vector of parameters of interest, and then by substituting the $\widehat{\Gamma}(j)$ obtained into (7.37) in order to obtain a suitable estimate of $\Psi$. This would generalize the procedure implemented in the case $\Psi = \Gamma(0)$. However, while the sample autocovariance matrix of order zero evaluated at a consistent estimate of $\boldsymbol{\theta}$ without the expectation is a consistent estimate of the true autocovariance matrix of order zero $\Gamma(\mathbf{0})$, the sample autocovariance of order $j$ evaluated in the same manner is inconsistent for the true autocovariance matrix of order $j$. To see this think of the case $j = T - 1$, when $\Gamma(j)$ has only one term. No law of large numbers can conceivably apply to a single term and therefore $\widehat{\Gamma}(j)$ will tend to zero as $T$ goes to infinity on the account of the factor $T^{-1}$ in the definition. An empirical solution is to limit our attention to models in which the autocovariance of order $j$ does not tend to zero as $T$ goes to infinity. Then, it seems reasonable to truncate the sum by eliminating terms for which $|j|$ is greater than some threshold $p$. We then have

$$\widehat{\Psi} = \widehat{\Gamma}(0) + \sum_{j=1}^{p} \left[ \widehat{\Gamma}(j) + \widehat{\Gamma}(-j) \right]. \tag{7.41}$$

The choice of $p$, the lag truncation parameter is not a difficult issue. In many cases the appropriate lag truncation parameter is suggested by the model which leads the specification of the orthogonality condition. In our above example of the policy rule, the obvious choice is $p = 11$. In case the choice of the lag truncation parameter is not suggested by the economic problem at hand, statistical criteria, related to the number of observations in the sample and to the length of the memory of the data (i.e. degree of autocorrelation in the sample moments) can be chosen.[2] There is however a more serious difficulty than the choice of the lag truncation parameter associated with (7.41), in fact it need not be positive definite. Newey and West (1987) have proposed a solution to this problem: multiply the sequence of the $\widehat{\Gamma}(j)$'s by a sequence of weights that decreases as $|j|$ increases. Specifically, they propose the following estimator:

$$\widehat{\Psi} = \widehat{\Gamma}(0) + \sum_{j=1}^{p} \left[ 1 - \frac{j}{p+1} \right] \left[ \widehat{\Gamma}(j) + \widehat{\Gamma}(-j) \right]. \tag{7.42}$$

For a complete discussion of the properties of this estimator and for some alternative solutions to the positive definiteness problem see Andrews (1991).

[2]See, for example, E-Views 3 User's Guide, Chapter 18: 488-492.

Consider once again the GIVE example in which the matrix $\Omega$ takes now a very general form: it is full and allows for heteroscedasticity and autocorrelation of an unknown form. The GMM estimator now becomes:

$$\widehat{\beta} = \left(\mathbf{X}'\mathbf{Z}\widehat{\Psi}^{-1}\mathbf{Z}'\mathbf{X}\right)^{-1}\mathbf{X}'\mathbf{Z}\widehat{\Psi}^{-1}\mathbf{Z}'\mathbf{y}, \tag{7.43}$$

which is also known as the two-step two-stage least squares. In fact, after a preliminary consistent estimate of the parameters of interest is derived by an ordinary IV procedure, $\widehat{\Psi}$ is constructed, having chosen the lag truncation parameter and applying the Newey–West correction. The estimation of $\widehat{\Psi}$ allows the construction of more efficient estimate of the vector of parameters of interest via formula (7.43). The estimator proposed by Cumby, Huizinga and Obstfeld (1983), derived in the framework of rational expectations models, can be considered as a special case of the above estimator. Lastly note that, as far as inference is concerned, the $J$-statistic can still be constructed as in the simple case of not autocorrelated and homoscedastic sample moments with the appropriate estimator of the variance-covariance matrix of the sample moments.

## 7.4 The limits to Euler equation–GMM approach

In this section we consider the limits to the Euler equation–GMM approach both from theoretical and applied points of view. The analysis of the theoretical problems aims to show the difficulties in implementing GMM when market imperfections are brought into the intertemporal optimization approach. The empirical problems are related to the nature of deep parameters estimated by GMM. Such parameters should describe taste and technology and, by their nature, should, therefore, be constant over different sample periods. However, they do not seem to be constant.

### 7.4.1 *Theoretical problems*

To show the difficulties in implementing the GMM estimation of the Euler equation derived outside the pure neo-classical paradigm take the Mankiw *et al.* (1985) quotation reported at the beginning of this chapter literally and introduce liquidity constraints in the intertemporal optimization problem for the representative consumer. We have:

$$\max_{c_{t+i},A_{t+i}} E_t \sum_{i=0}^{\infty} (1+\delta)^{-i} U\left(c_{t+i}\right), \tag{7.44}$$

subject to the following constraints:

$$\begin{aligned} A_{t+i} &= (1+r) A_{t+i-1} + y_{t+i} - c_{t+i}, \\ \lim_{i\to\infty} E_t A_{t+i} (1+r)^{-i} &= 0, \\ A_{t+i} &\geq b_{t+i}. \end{aligned}$$

The only difference with the problem originally considered is that we have introduced a finite, although not necessarily positive, limit $b$ to the stock of debt available to the consumer in each period.

The liquidity constraint can be re-written as follows:

$$H_{t+i} = (1+r)^{i+1} A_{t-1} + \sum_{i=0}^{\infty} (1+r)^{-i} (y_{t+i} - c_{t+i}) - b_{t+i} \geq 0, \tag{7.45}$$

and the intertemporal optimization problem becomes

$$\max_{c_{t+i}, A_{t+i}} E_t \sum_{i=0}^{\infty} (1+\delta)^{-i} G_{t+i}, \tag{7.46}$$

$$G_{t+i} = U(c_{t+i}) + \lambda_{t+i} (A_{t+i} - (1+r) A_{t+i-1} - y_{t+i} + c_{t+i}) + \mu_{t+i} H_{t+i},$$

where $\lambda$ is the Lagrange multiplier associated with the stock-flow relationship between wealth and savings and $\mu$ is the Lagrange multiplier associated with the existence of liquidity constraints. When the liquidity constraint does not bind and $\mu = 0$, we are back to the original intertemporal optimization problem. Maintaining the CRRA parameterization for the utility function, the first-order conditions for optimization are now:

$$E_t \left(c_{t+i}^{-\gamma}\right) - E_t \lambda_{t+i} = E_t \left(\frac{1+\delta}{1+r}\right)^{-i} \mu_{t+i}, \quad \forall\, i, \tag{7.47}$$

$$E_t \lambda_{t+i} - E_t \left(\frac{1+r}{1+\delta} \lambda_{t+i+1}\right) = 0, \quad \forall\, i.$$

Setting $i = 0$ and combining the first-order conditions, we derive the Euler equation as:

$$E_t \left(\frac{1+r}{1+\delta} c_{t+1}^{-\gamma} - c_t^{-\gamma} - \left(\frac{1+\delta}{1+r}\right) \mu_{t+i} + \mu_t\right) = 0. \tag{7.48}$$

Analysing equation (7.48) we note immediately that the specification of the utility function and the assumption of rational expectations are insufficient to eliminate all the non-observable variables from the Euler equation. Therefore, GMM becomes empirically unfeasible. This simple example shows rather clearly why when constraints are introduced in the intertemporal optimization problem, the GMM method becomes much less popular.

Several solutions have been proposed to the problem generated by the introduction of liquidity constraints, but none of them replicate the neat correspondence between the solution to the economic problem and implementation of the econometric methodology obtained in the case of intertemporal optimization without market imperfections.

Deaton (1991; 1992) observes the impossibility of finding an analytical solution to (7.48) and proposes to characterize the properties of the numerical solution obtained under the hypothesis of simple DGP for the income process. However, even for a very simple autoregressive process for income, the computational burden is rather heavy. Pesaran and Smith (1994) propose to approximate the unknown Lagrange multipliers by a general function of observable variables. Within this context, it is important to gather institutional information to help the identification of the appropriate functional form and the appropriate argument for such a function. Favero and Pesaran (1994) apply this methodology to the empirical modelling of oil investment using institutional and geological information to identify the appropriate function. Abandoning time-series there is the possibility of reverting to panel data to identify liquidity constrained agents, see Zeldes (1989). Brave attempts to identify the relevance of liquidity constraints using time-series data have been proposed by Campbell and Mankiw (1987), and Jappelli and Pagano (1989). Aggregate time-series consumption is thought of as the result of the aggregation of consumption by two types of agents: liquidity constrained and liquidity unconstrained. To allow aggregation, utility is assumed to be quadratic, and the behaviour of the unconstrained agents is described by the usual Euler equation while constrained agents are assumed to consume all their disposable income in each period. By assuming that a fixed proportion of income accrues to each type of agents, the Euler equation for the unconstrained agents and the consumption function for the constrained agents are aggregated into a macroeconomic consumption function, which takes the form of an ECM model. One of the estimated parameters in such a consumption function is the proportion of income accruing to the constrained agents. The importance of liquidity constraints in the economy can therefore be empirically evaluated on macro time-series data. It is unclear, however, why the proportion of income accruing to the liquidity constrained agents is thought of as a parameter rather than a variable.

### 7.4.2 *Empirical problems*

The main empirical problem with the GMM approach to estimate structural parameters has been noted by a series of authors (see, for example, Ghysels and Hall 1990*a*; 1990*b*, Garber and King 1983, Oliner, Rudebusch and Sichel 1992) for the US data. Some observed that in general the parameters estimated on aggregate time-series data by implementing GMM on Euler equations derived by different intertemporal optimization problems are unstable over time. Such instability is clearly incompatible with their nature as parameters describing taste and technology suggested by the theoretical models. There are several possible interpretations of instability: it could signal the incorrect specification of the estimated model or it could be generated by the fact that representative agent models are applied on aggregate data without taking proper care of aggregation. The second interpretation has generated a research program which refrains from estimating the 'deep' parameters from aggregate macroeconomic time-series. 'Deep' parameters are instead taken from microeconometric studies on disaggregated data. Using these parameters, theoretical models are then calibrated and simulated to compare properties of real and simulated macroeconomic time-series. We shall concentrate on the calibration methodology in the next chapter. We now conclude our analysis of the GMM method by looking at empirical applications of this methodology.

## 7.5 Application to the consumer's problem

The first illustrative example which we consider involves the estimation of the Euler equation (7.5):

$$E_t\left(\frac{1+r_{t+1}}{1+\delta}c_{t+1}^{-\gamma} - c_t^{-\gamma}\right) = 0,$$

using a dataset on monthly US data, which is the version of the Hansen and Singleton (1983) dataset made available as a tutorial dataset for Microfit version 4.0 (see Pesaran and Pesaran 1997). The dataset is available in Excel format as hs.xls. It contains monthly data for the sample 1959:3–1978:12 on the following variables:

X1: ratio of consumption in time period $t-1$ to consumption in time period $t$

X2: one plus the one-period real return on stocks.

Estimation of the Euler equation is implemented using the appropriate routine in E-Views, using the Bartlett weights and the Newey–West criterion to choose the lag truncation parameter. The results are reported in Table 7.1.

TABLE 7.1. C(1)*(X1^C(2))*X2-1

| Coefficient | Estimate | Std. Error | $t$-Statistic | Prob. |
|---|---|---|---|---|
| C(1) | 0.998082 | 0.004465 | 223.5548 | 0.0000 |
| C(2) | 0.891202 | 1.814987 | 0.491024 | 0.6239 |

| | |
|---|---|
| S.E. of regression 0.041502 | $J$-statistic 0.006453 |
| Sum squared resid 0.404766 | Durbin–Watson stat 1.828192 |

Instrument list: C X1(-1) X2(-1)

Note that the parameters are estimated by using the following three orthogonality conditions:

$$E_t\left(\frac{1+r_{t+1}}{1+\delta}\left(\frac{c_t}{c_{t+1}}\right)^{\gamma} - 1\right) = 0,$$

$$E_t\left(\frac{1+r_{t+1}}{1+\delta}\left(\frac{c_t}{c_{t+1}}\right)^{\gamma} - 1\right) r_t = 0,$$

$$E_t\left(\frac{1+r_{t+1}}{1+\delta}\left(\frac{c_t}{c_{t+1}}\right)^{\gamma} - 1\right)\left(\frac{c_{t-1}}{c_t}\right) = 0.$$

Therefore we have one over-identifying restriction whose validity can be tested by using the $J$-statistic. Such a statistic, distributed as a $\chi^2$ with one degree of freedom, is easily computed multiplying by the number of observations the $J$-statistic reported in the E-Views output. Given that the observed value is 1.5294 ($237 \times 0.006453$), we do not reject the null of validity of instruments. Note that the coefficient of risk aversion is estimated rather poorly, while the discount factor is instead estimated with high precision. To evaluate the relevance of the correction for heteroscedasticity and correlation of unknown form, we implement the GMM without such correction. This result is obtained by defining a variable $u_t$ taking a value of zero everywhere and estimating the following model:

$$u_{t+1} = \frac{1+r_{t+1}}{1+\delta}\left(\frac{c_t}{c_{t+1}}\right)^{\gamma} - 1 + \varepsilon_{t+1}. \tag{7.49}$$

The GMM estimates are obtained by estimating (7.49) by instrumental variables, using the constant, $r_t$, and $(c_{t-1})/(c_t)$ as instruments. The results of the TSLS estimation are reported in Table 7.2.

TABLE 7.2. U=C(1)*(X1^C(2))*X2-1

| Coefficient | Estimate | Std. Error | $t$-Statistic | Prob. |
|---|---|---|---|---|
| C(1) | 0.998945 | 0.004947 | 201.9470 | 0.0000 |
| C(2) | 0.864734 | 2.044035 | 0.423052 | 0.6726 |

| | |
|---|---|
| S.E. of regression 0.041545 | Durbin–Watson stat 1.829335 |
| Sum squared resid 0.405609 | |

Instrument list: X1(-1 )X2(-1 )C

The results are unaltered. A useful exercise left to the reader is the assessment of the stability over time of estimated parameters.

## 7.6 GMM and monetary policy rules

We have already introduced the discussion of the estimation of monetary rules by GMM to illustrate the issue of the possibility of correlation in the sample moments. We now investigate this topic at greater depth, referring to the empirical work by Clarida, Gali and Gertler (1997; 1998). Specification (7.29), although useful for some illustrative purposes, is unsuccessful in capturing the observed persistence in the interest rates. In the literature the following empirical model is usually specified:

$$r_t^* = \bar{r} + a_1 E_t\left(\pi_{t+12} - \pi^*\right) + a_2 E_t\left(y_t - y_t^*\right), \tag{7.50}$$

$$r_t = (1-\rho)\, r_t^* + \rho r_{t-1} + v_t, \tag{7.51}$$

where $r^*$ is the target interest rate and $a_0$ is the equilibrium value for $r^*$. The partial adjustment mechanism introduced by equation (7.51) is justified by the empirical observation of tendency of central banks to smooth interest rates (see Goodfriend 1991). Moreover, a constant target rate of inflation is assumed in the estimated version of the rule. The empirical model for the policy rates becomes:

$$\begin{aligned} r_t = &(1-\rho)\left[\bar{r} + a_1 E_t\left(\pi_{t+12} - \pi^*\right) + a_2 E_t\left(y_t - y_t^*\right)\right] \\ &+\rho r_{t-1} + v_t. \end{aligned} \tag{7.52}$$

From which, by eliminating the unobserved forecast variables, we obtain:

$$\begin{aligned} r_t = &(1-\rho)\,\bar{r} + a_1(1-\rho)\,\pi_{t+12} + a_2(1-\rho)\left(y_t - y_t^*\right) \\ &+\rho r_{t-1} + \epsilon_t, \end{aligned}$$

where

$$\epsilon_t = v_t - a_1(1-\rho)\left(\pi_{t+12} - E_t\pi_{t+12}\right) - a_2(1-\rho)\left(y_t - E_t y_t\right).$$

Then, since $E_t\left[\epsilon_t \mid \mathbf{u}_t\right] = 0$, where $\mathbf{u}_t$ includes all the variables in the central bank's information set at the time interest rates are chosen, we derive the following set of orthogonality conditions:

$$\begin{aligned} &E_t\left[f_t \mid \mathbf{u}_t\right] = 0 \\ &f_t = r_t - (1-\rho)\,\bar{r} - a_1(1-\rho)\,\pi_{t+12} - a_2(1-\rho)\left(y_t - y_t^*\right) - \rho r_{t-1} \end{aligned} \tag{7.53}$$

GMM can be used in this framework to estimate the parameters of interest $a_0, a_1, a_2$ and $\rho$. The $J$-test for the validity of over-identifying restrictions can then assess if the simple specification of the monetary policy rule in (7.53) omits important variables which enter the central bank rule. Obvious candidates for the role of omitted variables are monetary aggregates, foreign interest rates, long-term interest rates, exchange-rate fluctuations and possibly stock-markets overvaluation (do central banks care of 'irrational exuberance'?). Moreover the estimation of parameters of interest allows some relevant consideration on monetary policy. Given (7.50), one can write an equilibrium relation for the real interest rate as follows:

$$rr_t^* = \bar{rr} + (a_1 - 1)\,E_t\left(\pi_{t+12} - \pi^*\right) + a_2 E_t\left(y_t - y_t^*\right), \tag{7.54}$$

where $\bar{rr}$ is the equilibrium real interest rate, independent from monetary policy. Equation (7.54) illustrates the critical role of parameter $a_1$. If $a_1 > 1$ the target real rate is adjusted to stabilize inflation, while with $0 < a_1 < 1$ it instead moves to accommodate inflation: the central bank raises the nominal rate in response to an expected rise in inflation but it does not increase it sufficiently to keep the real rate from declining. Taylor (1998) and Clarida, Gali, Gertler (1998) have shown that $0 < a_1 < 1$ are consistent with the possibility of persistent, self-fulfilling fluctuations in inflation and output. Therefore the value of one for $a_1$ is a crucial discriminatory criterion to judge central bank behaviour. Clarida,

Gali and Gertler show that in the pre-October 1979 period the Fed rule features rules $a_1 < 1$, while the post-October 1979 period features $a_1 > 1$. Finally, it is possible to use the fitted values for the parameters $a_0$, and $a_1$ to recover an estimate of the central banks' constant target inflation rate $\pi^*$. The empirical model does not allow separate identification of the equilibrium inflation rate and of the equilibrium real interest rate but it does provide a relation between them conditional upon $a_0$, and $a_1$. Given that $a_0 = \bar{r} - a_1\pi^*$ and $\bar{rr} = \bar{r} - \pi^*$, we have then:

$$\pi^* = \frac{\bar{rr} - a_0}{a_1 - 1} \tag{7.55}$$

which establishes a relation between the target rate of inflation and the equilibrium real interest rate defined by the parameters $a_0$, and $a_1$ in the policy rule. Clarida, Gali and Gertler (1997) set the real interest rate to the average in the sample and use (7.55) to recover the implied value for $\pi^*$.

The database CGG contains monthly data for the US and German economy taken from Datastream and from the database on US monthly data used in Leeper, Sims and Zha (1996), which should enable replication of the reaction function estimated by the authors, as well as testing for a number of interesting over-identifying restrictions. The following variables for the sample 1979:1–1996:12 are available:

gercmr: German average (of the month) call money rate;
ger10y: redemption yield on German 10-year government bonds;
gercp: German consumer price index;
gerinfter: Bundesbank announced rate of medium term unavoidable inflation;
germ1: German M1;
germ3: German M3;
gerip: German Industrial Production;
pcm: IMF world commodity price index (in US dollars);
smnbr: US smoothed (by a 36-month moving average) non-borrowed reserves;
smtr: US smoothed (by a 36-month moving average) total reserves;
totmkus_dy_01: US stock market dividend-yield;
Totmkus_pe_01: US stock market price-earning ratio;
totmkus_pi_01: US stock market price index;
us10y: redemption yield on US 10-year government bonds;
uscp: US consumer price index;
usdm: US dollar/ DM exchange rate;
usfdtrg: US Federal Funds target;
usff: US average Federal Funds rate;
usip: US industrial production;
uslabcose: US unit labour cost;
usm2sa: US M2;
usmanhera: US manufacturing hourly earnings;
usoperate: US capacity utilisation rate.

### 7.6.1 *The estimation of a baseline policy rule for the Fed*

We concentrate first on the US case, trying to replicate the results in Clarida, Gali and Gertler (1997). A series of empirical problems must be solved in order to perform GMM estimation of the monetary policy rule. The first issue we take is the measurement of the output gap. Clarida, Gali and Gertler take as the measurement the deviation of the logarithm of industrial production from a quadratic trend. This is easily obtained by taking the residuals of an OLS regression of the logarithm of industrial production on a constant, a linear trend and a quadratic trend. Such measurement of the cycle would be correct only if the logarithm of industrial production features a deterministic quadratic trend. To check the robustness of the definition of the cycle to alternative de-trending methods we compare the original proposal (USGAP1) of the authors with the difference between industrial production and a Hodrick–Prescott filter with the penalty parameter set to 14400 (USGAP2) and with the demeaned capacity utilization rate (USGAP3). We construct USGAP1, USGAP2, and USGAP3, on the sample 1981:10–1997:12, as we want to start estimation of the policy rule from 1982:10 (the beginning of the interest rate targeting regime). We report the alternative measures of output gaps in Figure 7.1.

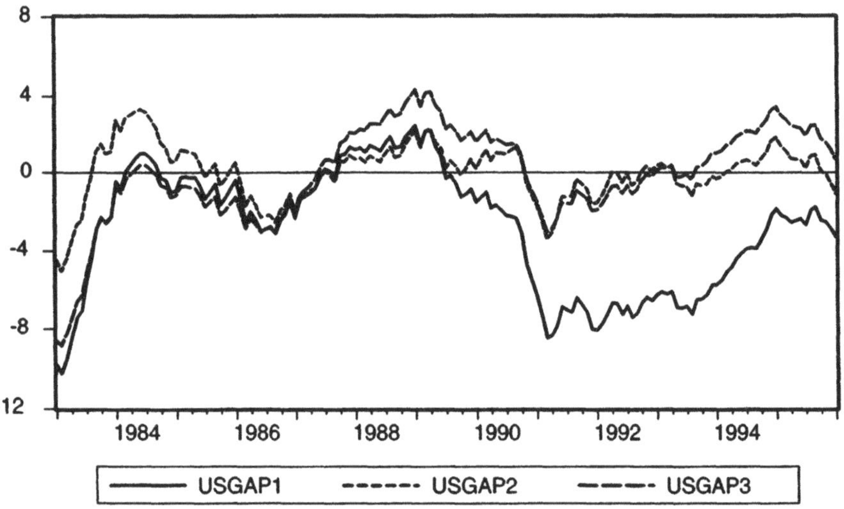


FIG. 7.1. Alternative measures of US output gap

We note that the three different measures do not show evident discrepancies as far as the location of the turning points in the cycle is concerned up to 1990, from 1990 onwards USGAP1 signals a persistent recession, not shared by the other two measures. Obviously, such a difference does show up in a corresponding difference in policy rates. Orphanides (1999) has extensively considered the problem of measuring the output gap to show that different behaviour by the Fed in the course of the 1970s and the 1980s can be explained by different measures of the output gaps rather than by different parameters in the reaction function. To keep our results comparable with those of Clarida, Gali and Gertler, we keep USGAP1 as the relevant measure for the gap. Checking robustness to different de-trending choices could be an interesting exercise.

The second empirical problem is the choice of the instruments. Here we follow Clarida, Gali and Gertler, by taking as instruments the constant, the first six lags, the ninth and the twelfth lag of output gap, the first six lags, the ninth and the twelfth lag of the federal fund rate, the first six lags, the ninth and the twelfth lag of inflation, the first six lags, the ninth and the twelfth lag of the logarithm IMF commodity price index.

We then implement estimation by GMM, using the correction for heteroscedasticity and autocorrelation of unknown form with a lag truncation parameter of 12 and choosing Bartlett weights to ensure positive definiteness of the estimated variance-covariance matrix. The results reported in Table 7.3 are obtained by implementing GMM in E-Views.

TABLE 7.3. GMM estimation of 7.52

| Coefficient | Estimate | Std. Error | $t$-Statistic | Prob. |
|---|---|---|---|---|
| C(1) | 2.87 | 0.99 | 2.90 | 0.0038 |
| C(2) | 0.92 | 0.012 | 73.82 | 0.0004 |
| C(3) | 1.73 | 0.25 | 6.87 | 0.0000 |
| C(4) | 0.66 | 0.10 | 6.60 | 0.0000 |

| | |
|---|---|
| $R^2$ 0.98 | Mean dependent var 6.713957 |
| Adjusted $R^2$ 0.98 | S.D. dependent var 2.191514 |
| S.E. of regression 0.28 | Sum squared resid 13.74 |
| Durbin–Watson stat 1.06 | $J$-statistic 0.0611 |

Thus we have estimated $a_0 = 2.87$, $a_1 = 1.73$, and $a_2 = 0.66$, while $\rho = 0.92$. The estimates are in line with those obtained by Clarida, Gali and Gertler, with $a_1 > 1$, with some slight differences. Such differences can be explained by their choice of a second-order lag in the adjustment, while we restrict ourselves to first-order dynamics.[3]

The statistic for the validity of instruments, distributed as a $\chi^2$ with 29 degrees of freedom (33 instruments for 4 parameters) takes the value of 10.45 ($0.0611 \times 171$ as the reported statistic in E-Views is divided by the number of observations) and does not reject the null of validity of instruments. If we follow the practice suggested by Clarida, Gali and Gertler to derive an estimate for the inflation target by using the estimated parameters and the average real interest

[3] Checking this empirically could be a useful exercise.

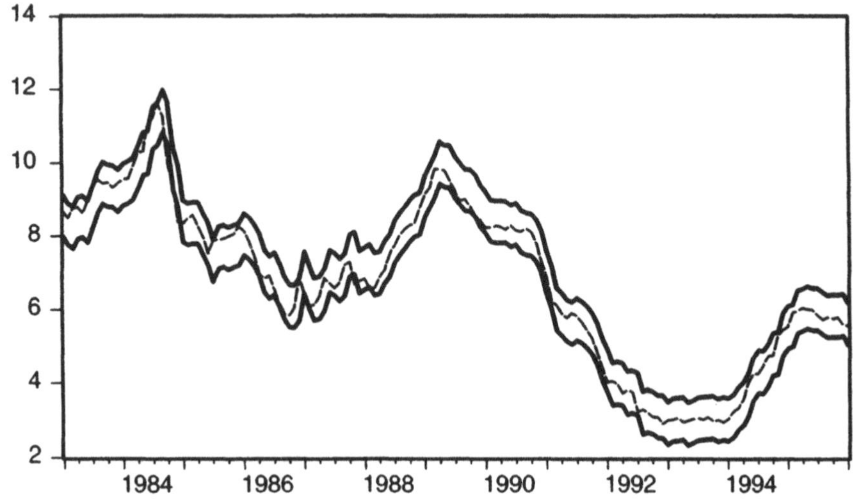


FIG. 7.2. Observed US policy rates and the 95 per cent confidence interval from the estimated policy rule

rate over the sample as a proxy for the real equilibrium interest rate, we get a point estimate of 0.5 with a rather wide confidence interval (as the 95 confidence interval for $a_0$ spans 0.89–4.85). Overall, the rule is rather successful in explaining the Fed behaviour as illustrated in Figure 7.2, where we report observed policy rates and the 95 per cent confidence interval from our estimated equation.

### 7.6.2 *Does the Fed care for long-term interest rates?*

Within the GMM framework it is easy to check the importance of omitted variables in the policy rule. In fact if there are such variables, then the orthogonality condition should be violated and the test for the validity of instruments should then reject the null hypothesis. There is a rather wide range of literature concentrating on the importance of long-term interest rates for the Fed explicitly related to their signalling role for 'inflation scares'. As pointed out by Goodfriend (1991), the behaviour of long-term interest rates could be informative on agents' expectations for inflation and on the effects of monetary policy on such expectations. Campbell (1995) concentrates on the collapse of bond prices in 1994, relating it to movements in the term premium generated by a rise in expected inflation, unmatched by any movement in the same direction in actual inflation. Looking at the 1994 data we see clearly that the Fed reacted lately to the increase in long-term interest rates and it took several tightening steps in the target federal funds rate to convince markets of the central bank determination in fighting inflation. In fact only after several tightening movements in the policy rate the long-term interest rate started reverting its upward trend. All this discussion shows that there are serious theoretical and policy reasons for the central bank to monitor long-term interest rates, and the omission of long-term interest rates from the rule seems an obvious candidate for putting our testing procedure at work. We then re-estimate the baseline model by including the level of contemporaneous long-term interest rates in the set of instruments and we obtain the results shown in Table 7.4.

TABLE 7.4. GMM estimation of 7.52

| Coefficient | Estimate | Std. Error | $t$-Statistic | Prob. |
|---|---|---|---|---|
| C(1) | 4.23 | 1.10 | 3.84 | 0.0002 |
| C(2) | 0.95 | 0.007 | 120.63 | 0.0000 |
| C(3) | 1.48 | 0.27 | 5.37 | 0.0000 |
| C(4) | 0.86 | 0.11 | 7.47 | 0.0000 |

| | |
|---|---|
| $R^2$ 0.98 | Mean dependent var 6.713957 |
| Adjusted $R^2$ 0.98 | S.D. dependent var 2.191514 |
| S.E. of regression 0.27 | Sum squared resid 12.69 |
| Durbin–Watson stat 1.17 | $J$-statistic 0.067 |

The point estimates of the parameters are slightly modified but the tests for validity of instruments do not reject the null ($0.067 \times 171 = 11.45$). In the light of this evidence we can conclude that the long-term interest rate affects the Fed behaviour as a leading indicator for future inflation but not as an independent argument of the monetary policy rule.

## 7.7 Interest rate rules and central banks' preferences

Monetary policy rules like those we have considered so far are empirically successful and useful to show how the GMM methodology is applied. However, they are not in line with our introduction to the GMM methodology since they are not derived explicitly from an intertemporal optimization problem and therefore no deep parameters describing central banks' preferences are identifiable. In fact it is perhaps surprising that the GMM methodology has been used to estimate reaction functions, while the optimization problem of the central banks provides first-order conditions which are instead a more natural object of GMM estimation. Following Svensson (1998), we consider the simplest possible version of the inflation targeting problem. The central bank faces the following intertemporal optimization problem:

$$\min \quad E_t \sum_{i=0}^{\infty} \delta^i L_{t+i}, \tag{7.56}$$

where:

$$L = \frac{1}{2}\left[ (\pi_t - \pi^*)^2 + \lambda x_t^2 \right], \tag{7.57}$$

where $E_t$ denotes expectations conditional upon the information set available at time $t$, $\delta$ is the relevant discount factor, $\pi_t$ is inflation at time $t$, $\pi^*$ is the target level of inflation, $x$ represents deviations of output from its natural level, $\lambda$ is a parameter which determines the degree of flexibility in inflation targeting. When $\lambda = 0$ the central bank is a strict inflation targeter. As the monetary instrument is the policy rate, $i_t$, the structure of the economy must be described to obtain an explicit form for the policy rule. We consider the following specification for aggregate supply and demand in a closed economy:

$$x_{t+1} = \beta_x x_t - \beta_r \left(i_t - E_t\pi_{t+1} - \bar{r}\right) + u_{t+1}^d, \tag{7.58}$$

$$\pi_{t+1} = \pi_t + \alpha_x x_t + u_{t+1}^s. \tag{7.59}$$

As shown in Svensson (1997), the first-order conditions for optimality can be written as:

$$\frac{dL}{di_t} = (E_t\pi_{t+2} - \pi^*) = -\frac{\lambda}{\delta\alpha_x k} E_t x_{t+1} \tag{7.60}$$

$$k = 1 + \frac{\delta\lambda k}{\lambda + \delta\alpha_x^2 k}.$$

Note that (7.60) delivers the set of orthogonality conditions, which constitute the natural object for GMM estimation. Joint estimation of (7.59) , (7.58) and (7.60) allows identification and estimation of the parameters describing the structure of the economy and the ones describing the central banks' preferences. Alternatively (7.59) , (7.58) and (7.60) can be used to derive an interest rate rule. By substituting from (7.59) in (7.58), we obtain:

$$E_t\pi_{t+2} = E_t\pi_{t+1} + \alpha_x[\beta_x x_t - \beta_r(i_t - E_t\pi_{t+1} - \bar{r})], \tag{7.61}$$

and by substituting (7.61) in (7.4) we derive a standard interest rate rule:

$$i_t = \bar{r} + \pi^* + \left(\frac{1 + \alpha_x\beta_r}{\alpha_x\beta_r}\right)(E_t\pi_{t+1} - \pi^*) + \frac{\beta_x}{\beta_r} x_t + \frac{\lambda}{\delta\alpha_x k}\frac{1}{\alpha_x\beta_r} E_t x_{t+1}. \tag{7.62}$$

A number of comments on this rule are in order:

1. If the rule is estimated as a single equation, then the fitted parameters are convolutions of the parameters describing the central banks' preferences $(\pi^*, \lambda, \delta)$ and of those describing the structure of the economy $\left(\alpha_x, \beta_r, \beta_x, \bar{r}\right)$. Thus the estimated parameters in the interest rate rules are not 'deep' in the sense of Lucas (1976).
2. As the structure of the economy cannot be identified from the estimation of the rule only, it is impossible to assess if the responses of central banks to output and inflation are consistent with the parameters describing the impact of the policy instrument on these variables. Note, for example, that the estimation of an interest rate rule relating the policy rate to the output

gap and to the deviation of expected inflation from the target does not help to distinguish a strict inflation targeter ($\lambda = 0$), in the terminology of Svensson, from a flexible inflation targeter ($\lambda > 0$).

3. Econometric identification of the rule requires the timing assumption that the central bank can set policy rates in response to contemporaneous macro variables in the economy, but policy rates do not have a contemporaneous impact on those variables. This assumption is commonly used to identify VAR models of the monetary transmission mechanism.
4. In order to make (7.62) consistent with the data, the rule has been interpreted as delivering 'target' interest rates, and a sluggish adjustment of actual to target rates has been imposed (Clarida, Gali and Gertler, 1997). Direct estimation of the policy rule does not allow us to identify a structure of central banks' preferences which is consistent with interest rate smoothing.
5. There is only one empirical implication of the rule which can be confronted with the data independently from the identification of the parameters of interest, namely whether the parameter describing the reaction of policy rates to a gap between expected and target inflation is larger than one. In fact a monetary policy which accommodates changes in inflation, $\partial i_t / \partial E_t \pi_{t+1} \leq 1$, will not, in general, converge to the target rate $\pi^*$. This empirical prediction is the one which has attracted most of the discussion on estimated monetary policy rules (see Clarida, Gali and Gertler, 1997).

To provide a better mapping from central banks' behaviour to their preferences, a strategy closer to the spirit of intertemporal optimization seems more appropriate. First, estimate the structure of the economy to identify the parameters of the aggregate supply and demand functions. Second, estimate the Euler equation for the solution of the intertemporal optimization problem to identify central banks' preferences. In this step (and in reference to the simple example analysed above), given the knowledge of $\alpha_x$and $\beta_r$, we can identify directly, from the estimation of the first-order conditions (7.4), the $\lambda$ and $\pi^*$ associated with each assumed value of the discount rate, $\delta$. Third, test if the monetary policy rule consistent with the structure of the economy and the preferences of the central bank matches the actual behaviour of policy rates. This strategy has been followed by Favero and Rovelli (1999), whose empirical investigation leads to the selection of a strict inflation targeting with real interest rate smoothing (with estimated relative weights of about four to one) as the best model to describe the Fed behaviour in the 1980s.

## 7.8 References

Andrews, D. W. K. (1991). 'Heteroscedasticity and autocorrelation consistent covariance matrix estimation'. *Econometrica*, 59: 249–254.

Campbell, J. (1995). 'Some Lessons From the Yield Curve'. *Journal of Economic Perspectives*, 9: 129-152.

Campbell, J., and Mankiw, G. (1987). 'Permanent Income, Current Income and Consumption'. NBER Working Paper No. 2436.

Clarida, R., and Gertler, M. (1996). 'How the Bundesbank conducts monetary policy'. NBER working paper No. 5581.

Clarida, R., Gali, J., and Gertler, M. (1997). 'Monetary policy rules in practice: some international evidence'. CEPR discussion paper series No. 1750.

Clarida, R., Gali, J., and Gertler, M. (1998). 'Monetary policy rules and macroeconomic stability: evidence and some theory'. CEPR discussion paper series No. 1908.

Cumby, R. E., Huizinga, J., and Obstfeld, M. (1983). 'Two-step two-stage least squares estimation in models with rational expectations'. *Journal of Econometrics*, 21: 333-355.

Davidson, R., and MacKinnon, J. G. (1993). *Estimation and inference in econometrics.* Oxford: Oxford University Press.

Deaton, A. (1991). 'Savings and Liquidity Constraints'. *Econometrica*, 59, 5: 1221-1248.

Deaton, A. (1992). *Understanding Consumption.* Oxford: Oxford University Press.

Eviews 3 (1997). *User's Guide.* Quantitative Micro Software.

Favero, C. A., and Pesaran, M. H., (1994). 'Oil Investment in the North Sea'. *Economic Modelling*, 11: 308-329.

Favero, C. A., and Rovelli, R. (1999). 'Modelling and identifying central banks' preferences'. CEPR discussion paper No. 2178.

Garber, P., and King, R. K. (1983). 'Deep Structural Escavation? A Critique of the Euler Equation Methods'. NBER technical Working Paper No. 31.

Ghysels, E., and Hall, A. (1990a). 'A Test for Structural Stability of Euler Conditions Parameters Estimated via the generalized method of moments Estimator'. *International Economic Review*, 2, 31: 355-364.

Ghysels, E., and Hall, A. (1990b). 'Are Consumption-Based Intertemporal Capital Asset Pricing Models Structural'. *Journal of Econometrics* 45, 1-2: 121-139.

Goodfriend, M. (1991). 'Interest rate smoothing and the conduct of monetary policy'. *Carnegie-Rochester Conference on Public Policy*, 7-30.

Hall, R. E. (1978). 'Stochastic implications of the Life-Cycle Permanent Income hypothesis: theory and evidence'. *Journal of Political Economy*, 86: 972-987.

Hansen, L. (1982). 'Large Sample Properties of The Generalized Method of Moments Estimators'. *Econometrica*, 50: 1029-1053.

Hansen, L., and Singleton, K. (1982). 'Generalized Instrumental Variables Estimation of Nonlinear Rational Expectations Models'. *Econometrica*, 50: 1269-1291.

Hansen, L., and Singleton, K. (1983). 'Stochastic consumption, risk aversion, and the temporal behavoiur of asset returns'. *Journal of Political Economy*, 91: 249-265, 1983.

Jappelli, T., and Pagano, M. (1989). 'Consumption and Capital Market Imperfections: An International Comparison'. *American Economic Review*, 79, 5: 1089-1105.

Leeper, E. M., Sims, C. A., and Zha, T. (1996). 'What does monetary policy do?'. Available at ftp://ftp.econ.yale.edu/pub/sims/mpolicy

Lucas, R. E. Jr. (1976). 'Econometric Policy Evaluation: A Critique'. In K. Brunner and A. Meltzer (eds.) *The Phillips curve and labor markets*. Amsterdam: North-Holland.

Mankiw, G., Rotemberg, L., and Summers, L. (1985). 'Intertemporal Substitution in Economics'. *Quarterly Journal of Economics*, 85: 225-251.

Newey, W. K., and West, K. D. (1987). 'A simple, positive semi-definite, heteroscedasticity and autocorrelation consistent covariance matrix'. *Econometrica*, 55: 703-708.

Oliner, S., Rudebusch, G., and Sichel, D. (1992). 'The Lucas Critique Revisited: Assessing the Stability of Empirical Euler Equations'. Board of Governors of the Federal Reserve System, D.P. 130.

Orphanides, A. (1999). 'The quest for prosperity without inflation'. Paper presented at the conference on 'Monetary Policy-making under uncertainty', Frankfurt, December 3-4.

Pesaran, M. H., and Smith, R. (1994). 'Theory and Evidence in Economics'. *Journal of Econometrics*.

Pesaran, M. H., and Pesaran, B. (1997). *Working with Microfit 4.0. Interactive econometric analysis*. Oxford: Oxford University Press.

Sargan, D. (1988). *Lectures on advanced econometric theory*, M.Desai (ed.). Oxford: Basil Blackwell.

Svensson, L. E. O. (1997). 'Inflation Forecast Targeting: Implementing and Monitoring Inflation Targets'. *European Economic Review*, 41: 1111-1146.

Svensson, L. E. O. (1998). 'Monetary Issues for the ESCB'. Presented at the Carnegie-Rochester Conference. Available at http://www.iies.su.se/leosven/

Taylor, J. B. (1993). 'Discretion versus policy rules in practice'. *Carnegie-Rochester Conference series on Public Policy*, 39: 195-214.

Taylor, J. B. (1998). 'The robustness and efficiency of monetary policy rules as guidelines for interest rate setting by the European central bank'. Paper presented at the Conference on Monetary Policy Rules, Stockholm, 12-13 June.

Taylor, J. B. (1999). *Monetary Policy Rules*. Chicago: University of Chicago Press.

White, A. (1980). 'A heteroscedastic consistent covariance matrix estimator and a direct test for heteroscedasticity'. *Econometrica*, 48: 817-838.

Zeldes, S. P. (1989). 'Consumption and Liquidity Constraints: An Empirical Investigation'. *Journal of Political Economy*, 97, 2: 305-346.

# 8

# CALIBRATION

## 8.1 Introduction

The calibration approach takes the intertemporally optimized model to the data to answer specific economic questions[1]. The essence of this methodology can be described in six steps; see Canova and Ortega (1997) and Cooley (1997):

1. formulation of an economic question;
2. selection of a model design which bears some relevance to the question asked;
3. choice of functional forms for the primitives of the model to find a solution for the endogenous variables in terms of the exogenous variables and the parameters;
4. choice of parameters and stochastic processes for the exogenous variables and simulation of paths for the endogenous variables of the model;
5. selection of a metric to compare the outcomes of the model relative to a set of 'stylized facts';
6. policy analyses, if required.

We illustrate the methodology by considering the question of the relative relevance of supply-side technological shocks and monetary policy in determining fluctuations in macroeconomic variables. We do so by introducing money in the utility function and by then modifying the traditional artificial economies considered in the calibration camp in which money is typically a 'veil'. Obviously, there are no logical objections against the use of intertemporally optimized models in which monetary policy is not ineffective as a consequence of some market imperfections or some 'cash in advance' constraints. In fact, the diffusion of calibrated models featuring short-run effectiveness of monetary policy has recently increased in the literature. We consider a model, proposed by McCallum and Nelson (1997), which is directly comparable with models used in previous sections of the book since it can be reparameterized as a forward-looking IS–LM framework. Equipped with this model design, we illustrate the main steps of the calibration approach. In describing step 5 we show how the impulse response derived from the artificial economy differ from the impulse responses described in Chapter 6 and representing the benchmark stylized facts on the effect of monetary policy on macroeconomic variables. Lastly, we discuss policy analyses.

[1]This chapter has been jointly written with Marco Maffezzoli.

## 8.2 Model design

Our model design is taken from McCallum and Nelson (1999*a*). The economy is inhabited by a large number of infinitely-living identical price-taking households. They can be aggregated into a single representative household, whose preferences are summarized by the following intertemporal utility function

$$U_t = E_t \left[ \sum_{s=t}^{\infty} \frac{\beta^{s-t}}{1-\mu} \left[ \widetilde{C}_s^{1-\mu} + \theta \left( \frac{\widetilde{M}_s}{P_s} \right)^{1-\mu} \right] \right], \tag{8.1}$$

where $\mu \in (0, \infty)$ is the reciprocal of the intertemporal elasticity of substitution, $\beta \in (0,1)$ is the intertemporal discount factor, $\widetilde{C}_t \in R^+$ is the real consumption level at date $t$. Tilded variables refer to individual quantities. Non-tilded variables, instead refer to aggregate per household quantities. $\widetilde{M_t/P_t} \in R^+$ is the stock of real money balances held at the start of period $t$, and $\theta \in (0, \infty)$ is the relative weight of real money balances in the utility function.

> *... the rationale for the inclusion of $\frac{\widetilde{M}_t}{P_t}$ is of course that holdings of the economy's medium of exchange provide transaction services that reduce ... (the) resources needed in 'shopping' for the numerous distinct consumption goods whose aggregate is represented by $\widetilde{C}_t$...* (McCallum and Nelson 1999*a*: 15)

Each household produces a single good using the following constant-returns-to-scale Cobb–Douglas production function:

$$\widetilde{Y}_t = a_t \widetilde{K}_t^{1-\alpha} \left( Z_t \widetilde{n}_t \right)^{\alpha} \tag{8.2}$$

with $\alpha \in (0,1)$, where $\widetilde{K}_t \in R^+$ is the stock of capital held by the household at date $t$, $Z_t = \gamma^t \in R^{++}$ is labour-augmenting exogenous technical progress, $n_t \in [0,1]$ is the labour input, and $a_t \in R$ is a stochastic measure of total factor productivity (TFP). We assume that the natural logarithm of $a_t$ follows a first-order univariate AR process:

$$\ln(a_{t+1}) = (1-\rho)\ln(a) + \rho \ln(a_t) + \epsilon_t^a \tag{8.3}$$

where $a$ is the unconditional mean, $\rho \in (0,1)$ the persistence parameter, and $\epsilon_t \sim N(0, \sigma_a^2)$, the i.i.d. innovation. By adequately choosing units, we impose $a = 1$.

Each household inelastically supplies one unit of labour to a competitive labour market, from which the same household as a producer purchases the labour input at the real wage rate $W_t$. Furthermore, a market for one-period government bonds exists. These bonds pay between date $t$ and $t+1$ a real interest rate equal to $r_t$.

The representative household's budget constraint has the following specification:

$$\widetilde{K}_{t+1}+(1+\pi_{t+1})\frac{\widetilde{M}_{t+1}}{P_{t+1}}+\widetilde{B}_{t+1}=(1-\delta)\widetilde{K}_t+\frac{\widetilde{M}_t}{P_t}+(1+r_t)\widetilde{B}_t \quad (8.4)$$
$$+a_t\widetilde{K}_t^{1-\alpha}(Z_t\widetilde{n}_t)^{\alpha}-\widetilde{C}_t-(\widetilde{n}_t-1)W_t-V_t,$$

where $\widetilde{B}_t \in R^+$ is the number of real government bonds held at the beginning of period $t$, $P_t$ is the money price of goods, $\pi_{t+1}=(P_{t+1}-P_t)/P_t$ is the inflation rate, $V_t$ is a lump-sum tax levied on the household, and $\delta$ is the depreciation rate.

The presence of exogenous technical progress introduces a non-stationary component in the system. This implies that the model does not converge to a steady-state in the long-run. The original non-stationary model can be transformed into a stationary one simply by normalizing all equations with respect to $Z_t$.[2] Normalization of equation (8.1) delivers:

$$U_t=E_t\left[\sum_{i=0}^{\infty}\frac{\widetilde{\beta}^i}{1-\mu}\left(\widetilde{c}_{t+i}^{1-\mu}+\theta(\widetilde{m}_{t+i})^{1-\mu}\right)\right], \quad (8.5)$$

where $\widetilde{\beta}=\beta\gamma^{1-\mu}$, $\widetilde{c}_t=\widetilde{C}_t/Z_t$, and $\widetilde{m}_t=\widetilde{M}_t/(P_tZ_t)$. To ensure finiteness of our objective function, we impose that $\widetilde{\beta}<1$. Similarly, normalizing (8.4) we obtain:

$$\gamma\widetilde{k}_{t+1}+(1+\pi_{t+1})\gamma\widetilde{m}_{t+1}+\gamma\widetilde{b}_{t+1}=(1-\delta)\widetilde{k}_t+\widetilde{m}_t+(1+r_{t+1})\widetilde{b}_t \quad (8.6)$$
$$+a_t\widetilde{k}_t^{1-\alpha}\widetilde{n}_t^{\alpha}-\widetilde{c}_t-(\widetilde{n}_t-1)w_t-v_t,$$

where lower case letters identify normalized variables.

### 8.2.1 *Households*

The representative household solves a stochastic optimal control problem, with consumption and labour as control variables, and capital, money, and bonds as endogenous state variables. Formally, (8.5), evaluated at date 0, is maximized subject to (8.6) and the initial conditions for all endogenous state variables.

In order to obtain the first-order conditions, we form a Lagrangian in expectations:

$$L=E_t\sum_{i=0}^{\infty}\widetilde{\beta}^i\left[\left(\frac{\widetilde{c}_{t+i}^{1-\mu}+\theta\widetilde{m}_{t+i}^{1-\mu}}{1-\mu}\right)+\widetilde{\lambda}_{t+i}\Psi_{t+i}\right]$$
$$\Psi_{t+i}=(1-\delta)\widetilde{k}_{t+i}+\widetilde{m}_{t+i}+(1+r_{t+i})\widetilde{b}_{t+i}+a_{t+i}\widetilde{k}_{t+i}^{1-\alpha}\widetilde{n}_{t+i}^{\alpha}-\widetilde{c}_{t+i}$$
$$-(\widetilde{n}_{t+i}-1)w_{t+i}-v_{t+i}-\gamma\widetilde{k}_{t+i+1}-(1+\pi_{t+i+1})\gamma\widetilde{m}_{t+i+1}-\gamma\widetilde{b}_{t+i+1}$$

[2]Since $\gamma$ is exogenous, the normalization can be easily reversed: the original and the transformed models are isomorphic. Any qualitative conclusion we may reach studying the normalized model can be immediately extended to the original one.

where $\widetilde{\lambda}_{t+i}$ is a vector of present-value costate variables, and derive it with respect to $\widetilde{c}_{t+i}$, $\widetilde{n}_{t+i}$, $\widetilde{k}_{t+i}$, $\widetilde{m}_{t+i}$, $\widetilde{b}_{t+i}$ and $\widetilde{\lambda}_{t+i}$. The first-order conditions for optimality are:

$$E_t\left(\widetilde{c}_{t+i}^{-\mu}\right) = E_t\left(\widetilde{\lambda}_{t+i}\right) \tag{8.7}$$

$$E_t\left(\alpha a_{t+i}\widetilde{k}_{t+i}^{1-\alpha}\widetilde{n}_{t+i}^{\alpha-1}\right) = E_t\left(w_{t+i}\right) \tag{8.8}$$

$$\widetilde{\beta}E_t\left[\widetilde{\lambda}_{t+i}\left(1-\alpha\right)a_{t+i}\widetilde{k}_{t+i}^{-\alpha}\widetilde{n}_{t+i}^{\alpha} + \widetilde{\lambda}_{t+i}\left(1-\delta\right)\right] = \gamma E_t\widetilde{\lambda}_{t+i-1} \tag{8.9}$$

$$\widetilde{\beta}E_t\left(\theta\widetilde{m}_{t+i}^{-\mu} + \widetilde{\lambda}_{t+i}\right) = E_t\left[1+\pi_{t+i}\right]\gamma\widetilde{\lambda}_{t+i-1} \tag{8.10}$$

$$\widetilde{\beta}E_t\left(\widetilde{\lambda}_{t+i}\left(1+r_{t+i}\right)\right) = \gamma E_t\widetilde{\lambda}_{t+i-1} \tag{8.11}$$

$$\begin{aligned}\gamma\widetilde{k}_{t+i+1} + \left(1+\pi_{t+i+1}\right)\gamma\widetilde{m}_{t+i+1} + \gamma\widetilde{b}_{t+i+1} &= \left(1-\delta\right)\widetilde{k}_{t+i} + \widetilde{m}_{t+i} \\ &\quad + \left(1+r_{t+i}\right)\widetilde{b}_{t+i} + a_{t+i}\widetilde{k}_{t+i}^{1-\alpha}\widetilde{n}_{t+i}^{\alpha} \\ &\quad - \widetilde{c}_{t+i} - \left(\widetilde{n}_{t+i}-1\right)w_{t+i} - v_{t+i}.\end{aligned} \tag{8.12}$$

Conditions (8.7)–(8.12), together with the following transversality condition:

$$\lim_{i\to\infty} E_0\left[\widetilde{\beta}^i\widetilde{\lambda}_{t+i}\left(\widetilde{k}_{t+i+1} + \widetilde{m}_{t+i+1} + \widetilde{b}_{t+i+1}\right)\right] = 0, \tag{8.13}$$

are necessary and sufficient for the household's problem, i.e. they completely characterize the sequence of probability measures that solve the household's stochastic optimal control problem. Given that the state variables are always positive, we may rewrite (8.13) as three separated transversality conditions:

$$\lim_{i\to\infty} E_0\widetilde{\beta}^i\widetilde{\lambda}_{t+i}\widetilde{k}_{t+i+1} = 0,\ \lim_{i\to\infty} E_0\left[\widetilde{\beta}^i\widetilde{\lambda}_{t+i}\widetilde{m}_{t+i+1}\right] = 0, \tag{8.14}$$
$$\lim_{i\to\infty} E_0\left[\widetilde{\beta}^i\widetilde{\lambda}_{t+i}\widetilde{b}_{t+i+1}\right] = 0.$$

### 8.2.2 *Government*

The government's budget constraint, written in per household terms, is:

$$-v_t = \left(1+\pi_{t+1}\right)\gamma m_{t+1} - m_t + \gamma b_{t+1} - \left(1+r_t\right)b_t, \tag{8.15}$$

where $m_t$ is the per household real money supply and $b_t$ is the per household supply of government bonds.

The dynamics of government bonds has to satisfy also the so-called no-Ponzi game (NPG) condition:

$$\lim_{s\to\infty} E_t\left[\prod_{j=t}^{s}\left(1+r_j\right)^{-1}b_{t+s+1}\right] \geq 0. \tag{8.16}$$

The NPG condition states that the present value of government bonds cannot be strictly negative in the long run. In other words, it rules out the possibility for the government to repay existing debt contracting always issuing new debt. The (intratemporal) budget constraint (8.15) together with the NPG condition (8.16) forms an intertemporal budget constraint.

For the sake of simplicity, we impose that normalized lump-sum taxes are constant over time, i.e. that $v_t = v$ for each $t$. Furthermore, we assume that the nominal money stock grows at an exogenously given rate $\eta_t$:

$$M_t = \prod_{i=0}^{t} \eta_i M_0. \tag{8.17}$$

Finally, we assume that the logarithm of $\eta_t$ follows a stationary AR process:

$$\ln\left(\eta_{t+1}\right) = (1-\zeta)\ln(\eta) + \zeta \ln(\eta_t) + \epsilon_t^m \tag{8.18}$$

where $\eta$ is the unconditional mean, $\zeta \in (0,1)$ the persistence parameter, and $\epsilon_t \sim N\left(0, \sigma_m^2\right)$ the i.i.d. innovation.

Equation (8.17) can be interpreted as a 'degenerated' version of the central banker reaction function, since monetary policy, i.e. the growth rate of nominal money balances, does not depend on any endogenous variable.[3] In this framework, then, monetary policy shocks can be modelled as unexpected shocks to the exogenous growth rate of nominal money balances. In other words, they coincide with the i.i.d. innovations in (8.18).

## 8.3 Dynamic equilibrium

To characterize a dynamic equilibrium we note that all households are identical, therefore, in equilibrium, individual and aggregate per household quantities have to coincide; which implies that all tildes can be dropped. Furthermore, we impose the following conditions:

$$\widetilde{n}_t = n_t = 1, \quad \widetilde{m}_t = m_t = \frac{M_t}{\gamma^t P_t}, \quad \widetilde{b}_t = b_t, \tag{8.19}$$

where $M_t$ is the per household nominal money supply. Equation (8.19) equates demand and supply for the labour input, the stock of nominal money balances, and the stock of government bonds.

Combining (8.17) and (8.19) with the definition of inflation rate we obtain:

$$1 + \pi_{t+1} = \frac{\eta_t}{\gamma}\frac{m_t}{m_{t+1}}. \tag{8.20}$$

Two comments are in order here:

[3]Christiano, Eichenbaum and Evans (1998) bridge the gap between the VAR-based empirics on the monetary transmission mechanism and the simple rules like this considered in theoretical models by showing that any equilibrium allocation generated under an endogenous policy rule can be replicated by an adequately parameterized recursive exogenous policy rule. In other words simplified rules like the one considered here share impulse response functions and stochastic properties with endogenous policy rules estimated in VAR models of the monetary transmission mechanism.

1. The variable $m_t$, a state variable from the household point of view, becomes a forward-looking aggregate decision variable when considered from the aggregate point of view. This is because the nominal money supply is exogenous, while the demand for real money balances is endogenous. The price level, $P_t$, has to equate supply and demand, i.e. under rational expectations, it has to satisfy the first-order condition governing the accumulation of real money balances, equation (8.10). The price level, then, substitutes $M_t$ as an aggregate endogenous variable, with the difference that $P_t$ is not a state variable, but a forward-looking variable that can be treated as a costate variable. The variable $m_t$, then, is the ratio between $M_t\gamma^{-t}$, an exogenous process, and $P_t$. To stress this point, we may rewrite $m_t$ as $1/p_t$, where $p_t = \gamma^t P_t/M_t$ is a normalized stationary variable.
2. Since both the nominal money supply and the lump-sum transfers are exogenous, bonds have to counterbalance seigniorage in order to keep the government budget balanced. The supply of government bonds is then, in some sense, exogenous too; more precisely, it is beyond government control. The demand for government bonds is, however, still endogenous. The real interest rate, $r_t$, has to equate supply and demand for bonds, i.e. under rational expectations, has to satisfy condition (8.11). It also becomes an aggregate forward-looking decision variable.

By substituting the government budget constraints and (8.20) in the household first-order conditions, we obtain a system of stochastic difference equations that fully describe a dynamic competitive equilibrium in our economy. We write the system by setting $i = 1$ in our first-order conditions and by dropping, for the sake of simplicity, the optimality condition for labour supply

$$c_t^{-\mu} = \lambda_t \tag{8.21}$$

$$E_t\left[\lambda_{t+1}\left[(1-\alpha)\,a_{t+1}k_{t+1}^{-\alpha} + 1 - \delta\right]\right] = \frac{\gamma}{\widetilde{\beta}}\lambda_t \tag{8.22}$$

$$\widetilde{\beta}E_t\left(\theta p_{t+1}^{\mu} + \lambda_{t+1}\right) = E_t\left(\frac{p_{t+1}}{p_t}\right)\eta_t\lambda_t \tag{8.23}$$

$$E_t\left[\lambda_{t+1}\left(1 + r_{t+1}\right)\right] = \frac{\gamma}{\widetilde{\beta}}\lambda_t \tag{8.24}$$

$$\gamma k_{t+1} = (1-\delta)\,k_t + a_t k_t^{1-\alpha} - c_t \tag{8.25}$$

$$\gamma b_{t+1} = \frac{1-\eta_t}{p_t} + (1+r_t)\,b_t - v_t. \tag{8.26}$$

Furthermore, the transversality conditions (8.14) can be restated as:

$$\lim_{t\to\infty} E_0\widetilde{\beta}^t\lambda_t k_{t+1} = 0,\ \lim_{t\to\infty} E_0\left[\widetilde{\beta}^t\frac{\lambda_t}{p_{t+1}}\right] = 0, \tag{8.27}$$

$$\lim_{t\to\infty} E_0\left[\widetilde{\beta}^t\lambda_t b_{t+1}\right] = 0.$$

Note that the last transversality condition in (8.27) implies the NPG condition (8.16). Note furthermore that, as in Bénassy (1995), the dynamics of consumption and investment are driven by real shocks only (consider equations (8.21), (8.22), and (8.25): they represent a stand-alone Brock–Mirman model). The 'real' world is in some sense completely separated from the 'monetary' world. The dynamics of government debt, on the other side, is driven by both monetary and real shocks. This 'separation' result is of course not robust, depending on our restrictive assumptions for the structure of preferences and the money creation process.

In summary, equations (8.21)–(8.26), together with the initial conditions and (8.27), form a system of stochastic difference equations that completely describe the competitive equilibrium allocations for our economy. The solution to such a system is an infinite sequence of conditional probability measures that converge in the long run to an invariant, or unconditional, distribution; in other words, it is a sequence $\{P_t(c_t, p_t, r_t, \lambda_t, b_t, a_t, \eta_t, k_0, b_0, a_0, \eta_0)\}_0^\infty$, where each $P_t(\cdot)$ represents a probability measure on $R_+^\infty$, converging to $P(c, p, r, \lambda, k, b, 1, \eta)$ as $t \to \infty$. Given the recursive structure of our system, a solution can also be seen as a set of aggregate decision rules for $c_t, p_t, r_t, \lambda_t, k_{t+1}$ and $b_{t+1}$, expressed as functions of $k_t, b_t, a_t$ and $\eta_t$.

## 8.4 An IS–LM interpretation

McCallum and Nelson (1999*a*) show that a version of the intertemporally optimized model we have considered so far can be reparameterized in terms of a traditional IS–LM framework. In fact, the addition of an expectational term is sufficient to make the standard IS function match a fully optimizing model, whereas no changes are needed for the LM function.

To show this point, combine (8.23) with (8.21) and (8.24), obtaining:

$$E_t\left(\theta m_{t+1}^{-\mu} + c_{t+1}^{-\mu}\right) = \left[1 + E_t\left(\pi_{t+1}\right)\right] E_t\left[c_{t+1}^{-\mu}\left(1 + r_{t+1}\right)\right]. \qquad (8.28)$$

Following Sargent (1987), we can approximate[4] (8.28) with:

$$E_t\left(\theta m_{t+1}^{-\mu}\right) = E_t\left(c_{t+1}^{-\mu}\right)\left\{\left[1 + E_t\left(\pi_{t+1}\right)\right]\left[1 + E_t\left(r_{t+1}\right)\right] - 1\right\}. \qquad (8.29)$$

Equation (8.29) is equivalent to:

$$E_t\left(\theta m_{t+1}^{-\mu}\right) = E_t\left(c_{t+1}^{-\mu}\right) E_t\left(i_{t+1}\right), \qquad (8.30)$$

where $i_{t+1} = (1 + \pi_{t+1})(1 + r_{t+1}) - 1$ is the nominal interest rate between date $t$ and $t + 1$. Furthermore, we can combine (8.21) and (8.22) to get:

$$\widetilde{\beta} E_t\left[c_{t+1}^{-\mu}\left(1 + r_{t+1}\right)\right] = \gamma c_t^{-\mu}. \qquad (8.31)$$

Now consider equations (8.30) and (8.31). The first one differs only by a random term from a standard LM function $m_t = \mathrm{LM}(c_t, i_t)$, where the real money balances depend on a transaction variable and an opportunity cost variable. The

[4]Given two random variables, $x$ and $y$, we have that $E(xy) = E(x)E(y) + Cov(x, y)$. Sargent (1987: 94-95) approximates the conditional covariance term by zero.

second one, instead, can be interpreted as an extended IS function by imposing a further assumption. If, as stated in McCallum and Nelson (1999*a*: 7–10), we are able to approximate fluctuations in income with fluctuations in consumption (at least for business cycle purposes), then we may substitute it in (8.31), and get an extended IS function of the form $y_t = \text{IS}\left[E_t\left(y_{t+1}\right), E_t\left(r_{t+1}\right)\right]$. The previous IS function is non-standard since it incorporates expectational terms for both the income level and the real interest rate. This forward-looking aspect is usually absent in standard IS–LM analysis.

## 8.5 Choice of parameters

The theoretical framework developed in the previous sections is of limited use, at least from an empirical point of view, without the specification of a value for all deep parameters in the model. The choice of a particular parameterization, however, cannot be arbitrary, but needs some kind of empirical foundation. The literature on intertemporally optimized models has shown a clear preference for calibrating rather than estimating parameters of interest. To discuss this choice a brief comparative revision of the two approaches might be helpful.

We summarize the estimation approach in Figure 8.1.

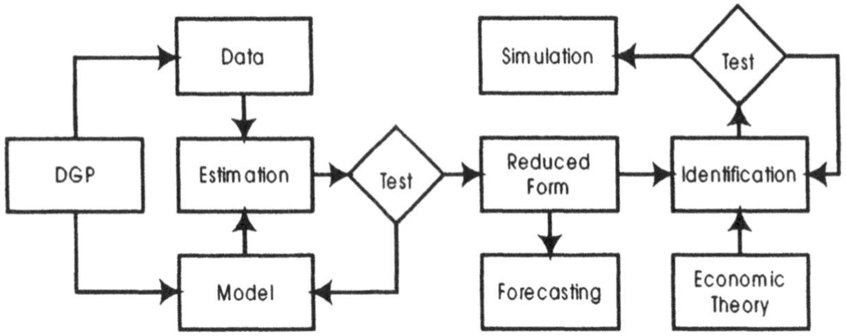


FIG. 8.1. The estimation approach

The estimation approach would start from the assumption of the existence of a data generating process (DGP) summarizing the true multivariate stochastic process that governs the observed macroeconomic variables. The unknown DGP would then be approximated by a statistical model, the reduced form, whose congruency is to be assessed on the basis of diagnostic tests. If the null hypothesis of congruency is not rejected, then the reduced form is directly available for forecasting.

The estimation of deep parameters requires the specification of a structural model. Such a model is usually identified by imposing further, testable, restrictions on the reduced form. If such over-identifying restrictions are not rejected, then a set of structural parameters is identifiable and, after estimation, the model can be used for simulation exercises.

The LSE approach to estimation works rather nicely when applied to data-driven dynamic specifications loosely related to theory, but it is much less likely to succeed when applied to an intertemporally optimized model of the kind we have considered in this chapter. Microeconomic foundations are usually obtained at the inevitable cost of simplification. Clearly, in numerous cases, theoretical models are far too simple representations of reality (the partial super-neutrality of money that characterizes our framework is in clear contrast with many stylized monetary facts discussed in the literature). Most likely, any formal test would conclude that the model is statistically false, if enough observed data were available. Such a result would take us to reject the whole analysis, preventing us from doing any kind of numerical exercise. As clearly stated by Eichenbaum (1995: 1609),

> *Since all models are wrong along some dimension of the data the classic Haavelmo (1944) program is not going to be useful in this context. We do not need high powered econometrics to tell us that models are false. We know that.*

A critical question arises at this point. Is the incapability to completely explain the observed data a sufficient argument for rejection of an economic model? A researcher might after all be interested in establishing how far a simple model like ours can go. A model can be statistically refuted because it simply does not catch any feature of the data; however, it can be refuted also because it performs poorly in only a few dimensions, while performing well in others. The researcher may then be interested in actually identifying the dimensions in which the model is more at odds with the data. The hope is, of course, that such pieces of information may improve our understanding, and help us in building a better model, one that may actually be a congruent representation of the DGP. As suggested again by Eichenbaum (1995),

> *What we do need are interesting diagnostic tools to help us understand the dimensions along which mis-specified models do well and the dimensions along which they do poorly.*

The standard econometric approach is of little use from this point of view, since the formal tests often do not suggest any explicit alternative to the model under examination, providing no help in the theoretical respecification of the model.

To summarize, then, the strong prior against the statistical truth of our model, together with the interest in studying its numerical properties anyway, suggests following a different approach than the formal econometric one previously described. The approach described here is known as calibration, and was introduced in macroeconomics[5] by Kydland and Prescott (1982). It is extensively described in Cooley (1997), among others; he states (p. 56) that

[5] Calibration was initially used in computable general equilibrium models of public finance and international trade, as noted by Cooley (1997). The use of calibration methods is widespread among natural sciences as well, as remarked by Gallant (1995).

> *calibration is a strategy for finding numerical values for the parameters of artificial economic worlds...[it] uses economic theory extensively as the basis for restricting a general framework and mapping that framework into the measured data.*

In other words, the aim of calibration is not to provide a congruent representation of the data, but simply to find values for the deep parameters of the model that are jointly compatible with the theory and the data in particular well-specified dimensions. Figure 8.2 crudely summarizes the calibration approach.

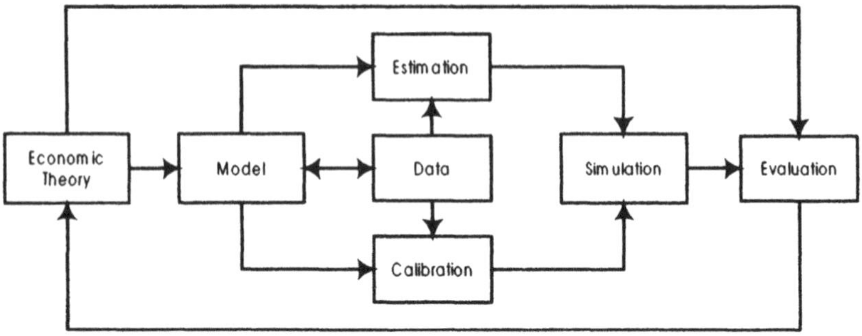


FIG. 8.2. Calibration approach

The main difference between calibration and standard econometrics lies in the bi-directional relationship among theory and measurement that characterize the former. In econometrics, this relationship goes in one direction only, from data to theory; the econometrician conditions the information set on available data, and searches for the most likely theoretical structure to have generated them. As stated in Cooley (1995, p. 60),

> *the calibration approach ... views the appropriate data or measurements as something to be determined in part by the features of the theory...*

First of all, a preliminary, non-theoretical, inspection of the data identifies some general stylized facts that any economic model should internalize. A classical example here is offered by Kaldor's stylized facts on growth but, as we have shown in Chapter 6, structural VAR models identified via restrictions independent from predictions of specific theoretical models can be also used to this end. The theoretical framework at hand, then, integrated by these observed stylized facts, provides the parametric class of models whose performance we want to evaluate (the neo-classical theoretical framework, together with Kaldor's stylized facts, generates the standard neo-classical growth model characterized by long-run balanced growth).

Once a particular model has been developed, it precisely defines the quantities of interest to be measured, and suggests how available measurements have to be reorganized if they are inconsistent with the theory. For instance, the concept of investment in our model is a fairly broad one; since no government or foreign sectors are explicitly modelled, to obtain a measure of investment that matches our theoretical concept we need to reorganize the data, and sum up private fixed investment, private consumption of durable goods, government investment, and net exports. Furthermore, by assuming a 'Cobb–Douglas' production function, we clearly identify total factor productivity, one of the model's two stochastic components, with the standard Solow residuals. Such a series can be reconstructed from the series on output, labour and capital.

Then, measurements are used to give empirical content to the theory, and in particular to provide empirically based values for the unknown parameters. They are chosen, according to Cooley (1997: 58),

> *so that the behavior of the model economy matches features of the measured data in as many dimensions as there are unknown parameters...*

In other words, we need first to specify some features of the data for the model to reproduce; of course, these features have to be different from the ones under examination. In our case, the features we want to match are long-run features of the real and monetary variables, our main interest being the short-run cyclical properties of the model. Then, we need to find some one-to-one relationship between these features and the deep parameters of the model. Finally, we invert this relationship, and find the parameters' values that make the model replicate the observed features.

From this point of view, calibration can be interpreted as a method of moments estimation procedure that focuses on a limited parameters' subset, setting only the discrepancy between some simulated and observed moments to zero. Christiano and Eichenbaum (1992) generalize this idea and propose a variant of Hansen's (1982) GMM procedure to estimate and assess stochastic general equilibrium models using specific moments of the actual data. Other possibilities are described in Diebold *et al.* (1994), who minimize the discrepancy between the spectrum of the observed and simulated series at particular frequencies. These procedures are formal developments of the basic methodological approach, and share with standard calibration the focus on a limited set of previously selected moments, while standard econometric methods use, in principle, the whole available information set, weighting different moments exclusively according to how much information on them is contained in the actual data, as for example in the maximum likelihood methods.

Generally, not all parameters can be calibrated, simply because there are more unknown parameters than invertible relationships. A subset of them has to be left to more standard econometric techniques. This implies that formal statistical estimation and calibration are not perfect substitutes, but partial complements. For instance, by assuming a constant long-run growth rate we identify the exogenous growth component with a linear trend in logarithms, that can be easily estimated by regressing a time trend on the natural logarithm of output, using ordinary least squares. Note, however, that in the traditional approach to calibration, these estimates are used quite differently than in econometrics. In the former, the focus is limited to the parameters' point estimates, the stochastic nature of these estimates is generally ignored, and the estimation procedure is seen more as a purely mechanical device. Some more recent studies, such as Eichenbaum (1991), stress the importance of taking into account the parameters' variability, and provide different ways to map the parameters' uncertainty onto the predicted moments' uncertainty. For instance, Canova (1994) and DeJong *et al.* (1994) simulate and evaluate the basic real business cycle model by drawing both the shocks and the parameters from a priori densities.

There is a diffused practice in the calibration literature to borrow parameter values from previous studies, often just for comparison purposes. The abuse of this practice is unfortunately widespread. Note that it is admissible only if the measurements used in these studies refer to the same theoretical concepts, and if the way they were reorganized is completely compatible with our needs. We will follow this practice too, and borrow many parameter values from Cooley and Prescott (1995), Cooley and Hansen (1995), and Gavin and Kydland (1999). Cooley and Prescott carefully calibrate a standard real business cycle model to the US economy which is perfectly compatible with the real side of our economy; Cooley and Hansen estimate the stochastic properties of money growth; Gavin and Kydland study the long-run properties of money's income velocity. Both studies focus on the monetary aggregate defined as M1.

Once a parameterization is available, we can simulate the model and perform many different kinds of numerical exercises. The results are then evaluated, and answers to the main questions are provided. For instance, the ability of the model to reproduce some particular features (of course, the ones that are different from those used to calibrate it) of the data can be judged. The conclusions drawn may then stimulate further theoretical developments.

The metric chosen to compare the observed properties and the simulated ones is a critical issue. In the traditional calibration procedure, an informal, 'aesthetic', metric is used. In the words of Kydland and Prescott (1996: 75),

> *the sampling distribution of this set of statistics can be determined to any degree of accuracy for the model and compared with the values of the set of statistics for the actual economy.*

No formal measure of the distance between simulated and observed properties is provided, and certainly not a statistical one. This informal evaluation procedure, however, is perfectly in line with the overall methodological approach previously outlined, being more useful to compare the relative performances of competing models, than to evaluate a model's ability to reproduce reality. Nonetheless, increasing attention is paid in the current literature to more formal evaluation procedures; see, for instance, Canova (1995), Diebold *et al.* (1994), Smith (1995), and Watson (1993). For a recent survey, see Canova and Ortega (1996).

## 8.6 Calibration

Going back to our model, the complete list of parameters we have to pin down is the following: the intertemporal elasticity of substitution; $\widetilde{\beta}$, the intertemporal discount factor; $\theta$, the relative weight of real money balances in the felicity function; $\alpha$, the technology coefficient; $\delta$, the depreciation rate; $\gamma$, the long-run growth rate; $\eta$, the unconditional mean of money growth; $\rho$, the persistence parameter for TFP; and $\varsigma$, the persistence parameter for money growth; lastly $\sigma_a^2$ and $\sigma_\eta^2$ are the variances of shocks to TFP and money growth respectively.[6]

Some of these parameters can be estimated from the available data, while others can be recovered from available microeconometric evidence. In particular, the long-run quarterly growth rate $\gamma$ is estimated by fitting a linear trend to the logarithm of quarterly GDP; Cooley and Prescott (1995) obtain $\gamma = 1.004$. The literature provides a whole set of empirical estimates of the elasticity of intertemporal substitution, as discussed in Kocherlakota (1996); most authors agree on a figure that lies between 1 and 5, so we chose the standard value of 2 for our experiments.

A large subset of parameters, containing $\widetilde{\beta}$, $\theta$, $\alpha$, and $\delta$, are left for our calibration exercise. As already anticipated, we choose values for these parameters that make the model reproduce some long-run features of actual US data. First of all, then, we have to find out what the long-run features of the model are.

The Cobb–Douglas technology implies a labour share in income that is constant and equal to $\alpha$. Cooley and Prescott (1995) carefully reconstruct a consistent measure of total income and capital income, obtaining a long-run capital share equal to 0.4. We borrow their result and choose $\alpha = 0.6$.

We then impose a certainty equivalence assumption, assuring in this way that the unconditional mean of the invariant distribution, to which the solution tends in the long run, is equal to the steady-state of the deterministic version of our system. The steady-state of this deterministic system can easily be computed dropping all expectations and time indices from (8.21)–(8.26):

$$c^{-\mu} = \lambda, \tag{8.32}$$

$$(1-\alpha)\frac{y}{k} + 1 - \delta = \frac{\gamma}{\widetilde{\beta}}, \tag{8.33}$$

$$\theta p^{\mu} = \left(\frac{\eta}{\widetilde{\beta}} - 1\right)\lambda, \tag{8.34}$$

$$1 + r = \frac{\gamma}{\widetilde{\beta}}, \tag{8.35}$$

[6] The adopted solution method, and in particular the certainty equivalence assumption, implies that the stochastic properties of the model will not depend on the absolute values of the standard deviations, but may only depend on their relative size.

$$\gamma = 1 - \delta + \frac{i}{k}, \tag{8.36}$$

$$\gamma b = \frac{1-\eta}{p} + \frac{\gamma}{\widetilde{\beta}} b - \nu. \tag{8.37}$$

Equations (8.32)–(8.37) implicitly define the steady-state values for the control, endogenous state and costate variables. Furthermore, we may easily obtain a closed form solution for the steady-state capital-output ratio, the income velocity of money, the consumption share in total income, and the government bond-output ratio. From (8.37) we get:

$$\frac{k}{y} = \frac{\widetilde{\beta}(1-\alpha)}{\gamma - \widetilde{\beta}(1+\delta)}. \tag{8.38}$$

Combining (8.32) and (8.34), we obtain:

$$\frac{c}{y}\frac{y}{m} = \left(\frac{\eta - \widetilde{\beta}}{\widetilde{\beta}\theta}\right)^{\frac{1}{\mu}}. \tag{8.39}$$

Solving (8.36) for the investment-capital ratio delivers:

$$\frac{i}{k} = \gamma - 1 + \delta, \tag{8.40}$$

finally, from (8.37):

$$\frac{b}{y} = \left[\frac{\nu}{y} - (1-\eta)\frac{m}{y}\right]\frac{\gamma\widetilde{\beta}}{1-\widetilde{\beta}}. \tag{8.41}$$

Combining (8.38) and (8.40) we derive an expression for the investment share $i/y = (i/k)(k/y)$ and indirectly for the consumption share in income, $c/y = 1 - (i/y)$.

Empirical estimates of the long-run capital-output ratio, the income velocity, and the consumption share are readily available. In particular, Cooley and Prescott (1995) obtain a long-run quarterly capital-output ratio equal to 13.28 and a consumption share equal to 0.75; Gavin and Kydland (1999) report a long-run M1 income velocity equal to 5.3.

Manipulating (8.38)–(8.41), we can express the parameters $\widetilde{\beta}$, $\theta$, $\delta$, as a function of these observable long-run properties:

$$\delta = 1 - \gamma + \left(1 - \frac{c}{y}\right)\frac{y}{k}, \tag{8.42}$$

$$\widetilde{\beta} = \frac{\gamma}{(1-\alpha)\frac{y}{k} + 1 - \delta}, \tag{8.43}$$

$$\theta = \frac{\eta - \widetilde{\beta}}{\widetilde{\beta}}\left(\frac{y}{c}\frac{m}{y}\right)^{\mu}. \tag{8.44}$$

The implied values are $\delta = 0.015$, $\widetilde{\beta} = 0.989$, $\theta = 1.22$.

Finally, the stochastic process driving TFP can be estimated by fitting an AR model on the standard Solow residual. Symmetrically, the stochastic process for the money growth rate can be estimated simply by fitting an AR model on the logarithm of the actual M1 growth rate. Again, Cooley and Prescott (1995) obtain $\rho = 0.95$ and $\sigma^2 = 0.007$, while Cooley and Hansen (1995) obtain $\eta = 1.013$, $\zeta = 0.49$ and $\sigma_\eta^2 = 0.009$. Equipped with these parametric values we can solve the model and evaluate its performance against the data.

## 8.7 Model solution

To obtain the decision rules, we apply the solution procedure originally proposed by King, Plosser and Rebelo (1988). As anticipated in the previous section, we start by imposing a certainty equivalence. This step provides us with a point in $R_+^8$, the deterministic steady state, that corresponds to the system's unconditional mean. Assuming that the system's dynamics take place in a small ball around the steady state, we may approximate the non-linear system with a first-order Taylor expansion centred on the steady state itself. Actually, we log-linearize the system, obtaining a linear system of expectational difference equations that explains the variables' percentage deviations from the deterministic steady state. We then solve this linear system with the standard Blanchard–Kahn (1981) algorithm. Once an approximated solution is available, we perform a number of numerical exercises, as impulse response analysis and Monte Carlo simulations, and evaluate the results. As a consequence, the unconditional mean of the invariant distribution to which the solution tends in the long run corresponds to the deterministic steady state. Then, we linearize the system around the steady state and solve it with the Blanchard–Kahn algorithm.

### 8.7.1 *Log-linearization*

Consider a deterministic version of the first-order conditions:

$$c_t^{-\mu} = \lambda_t, \tag{8.45}$$

$$\lambda_{t+1}\left[(1-\alpha)\, a_{t+1} k_{t+1}^{-\alpha} + 1 - \delta\right] = \frac{\gamma}{\tilde{\beta}} \lambda_t, \tag{8.46}$$

$$\theta p_{t+1}^{\mu} + \lambda_{t+1} = \frac{\eta_t}{\tilde{\beta}} \frac{p_{t+1}}{p_t} \lambda_t, \tag{8.47}$$

$$\lambda_{t+1}\left(1 + r_{t+1}\right) = \frac{\gamma}{\tilde{\beta}} \lambda_t, \tag{8.48}$$

$$\gamma k_{t+1} = (1-\delta)\, k_t + \alpha k_t^{1-\alpha} - c_t, \tag{8.49}$$

$$\gamma b_{t+1} = \frac{1-\eta_t}{p_t} + (1 + r_t)\, b_t - \nu. \tag{8.50}$$

We linearly approximate conditions (8.45)–(8.50) with a first-order Taylor approximation around the deterministic steady state, expressing the approximated conditions in percentage deviations from the steady state itself.

Consider equation (8.45), and rewrite it as:[7]

$$e^{-\mu\widetilde{c}_t} = e^{\widetilde{\lambda}_t}, \tag{8.51}$$

where for a generic variable $x_t$, $\widetilde{x}_t = \ln(x_t)$. The first-order Taylor approximation of (8.51) around the logarithms of steady-state values $\widetilde{c}$, $\widetilde{\lambda}$, is equal to:[8]

$$-\mu e^{-\mu\widetilde{c}}\left(\widetilde{c}_t - \widetilde{c}\right) = e^{\widetilde{\lambda}}\left(\widetilde{\lambda}_t - \widetilde{\lambda}\right). \tag{8.52}$$

Since in the steady state, $\exp(-\mu\widetilde{c}) = \exp\left(\widetilde{\lambda}\right)$, and since $\widetilde{x}_t - \widetilde{x} = \ln(x_t/x)$, condition (8.52) can be simplified as:

$$-\mu\widehat{c}_t = \widehat{\lambda}_t, \tag{8.53}$$

where $\widehat{x}_t = \ln(x_t/x)$. Equation (8.53) is a log-linearized version of condition (8.45), expressed in percentage deviation from the steady state, since $\widehat{x}_t$ is approximately equal to $(x_t - x)/x$.

Now consider condition (8.46), and rewrite it as:

$$e^{\widetilde{\lambda}_{t+1}}\left[(1-\alpha)e^{\widetilde{a}_{t+1}}e^{-\alpha\widetilde{k}_{t+1}} + 1 - \delta\right] = \frac{\gamma}{\overline{\beta}}e^{\widetilde{\lambda}_t}.$$

The first-order Taylor approximation of (8.52) around the steady state is:

$$\begin{aligned}\frac{\gamma}{\overline{\beta}}e^{\widetilde{\lambda}}\left(\widetilde{\lambda}_t - \widetilde{\lambda}\right) &= e^{\widetilde{\lambda}}\left(\widetilde{\lambda}_{t+1} - \widetilde{\lambda}\right)\left[(1-\alpha)e^{\widetilde{a}}e^{-\alpha\widetilde{k}} + 1 - \delta\right] \\ &\quad + (1-\alpha)e^{\widetilde{\lambda}}e^{-\alpha\widetilde{k}}e^{\widetilde{a}}\left(\widetilde{a}_{t+1} - \widetilde{a}\right) - e^{\widetilde{\lambda}}e^{-\alpha\widetilde{k}}e^{\widetilde{a}}(1-\alpha)\alpha\left(\widetilde{k}_{t+1} - \widetilde{k}\right),\end{aligned}$$

which is equivalent to:

$$\begin{aligned}\frac{\gamma}{\overline{\beta}}\widehat{\lambda}_t &= \widehat{\lambda}_{t+1}\left[(1-\alpha)\frac{y}{k} + 1 - \delta\right] + (1-\alpha)\frac{y}{k}\widehat{a}_{t+1} \\ &\quad -\alpha(1-\alpha)\frac{y}{k}\widehat{k}_{t+1}.\end{aligned} \tag{8.54}$$

We know that in the steady state:

$$\left[(1-\alpha)\frac{y}{k} + 1 - \delta\right] = \frac{\gamma}{\overline{\beta}},$$

we can divide both the left-hand side and the right-hand side of (8.54) by $(1-\alpha)(y/k)$, to obtain:

[7] Along an optimal path both $c_t$ and $\lambda_t$ are strictly positive.

[8] The first-order Taylor expansion of a non-linear function $f(x)$ around a point $x_0$ is given by $f(x) = \Delta f(x_0)(x - x_0) + \epsilon(x)$. This implies that $f(x) \approx \Delta f(x_0)(x - x_0)$.

$$-\alpha\widehat{k}_{t+1}+\overline{\omega}\widehat{\lambda}_{t+1}-\overline{\omega}\widehat{\lambda}_t=-\widehat{a}_{t+1}, \tag{8.55}$$

where,

$$\overline{\omega}=\frac{k}{y}\frac{\gamma}{\widetilde{\beta}(1-\alpha)}.$$

Note that in equation (8.55), all endogenous state and costate variables are grouped on the left-hand side, while the exogenous state variable is isolated on the right-hand side.

Conditions (8.47) and (8.48) are log-linearly approximated by:

$$\left[\mu\left(1-\frac{\widetilde{\beta}}{\eta}\right)-1\right]\widehat{p}_{t+1}+\widehat{p}_t+\frac{\widetilde{\beta}}{\eta}\widehat{\lambda}_{t+1}-\widehat{\lambda}_t=\widehat{\eta}_t, \tag{8.56}$$

$$\frac{r}{1+r}\widehat{r}_{t+1}+\widehat{\lambda}_{t+1}-\widehat{\lambda}_t=0. \tag{8.57}$$

Finally, conditions (8.49) and (8.50) are log-linearly approximated by:

$$\gamma\frac{k}{y}\widehat{k}_{t+1}-\left[(1-\delta)\frac{k}{y}+1-\alpha\right]\widehat{k}_t=-\frac{c}{y}\widehat{c}_t+\widehat{a}_t \tag{8.58}$$

$$\gamma\widehat{b}_{t+1}-(1+r)\widehat{b}_t+(1-\eta)\varphi\widehat{p}_t-r\widehat{r}_t=-\eta\varphi\widehat{\eta}_t \tag{8.59}$$

where $\varphi=(m/y)(y/b)$.

The exogenous processes for technology and money can be re-written as

$$\widehat{a}_{t+1}=\rho\widehat{a}_t+\epsilon_t \tag{8.60}$$

$$\widehat{\eta}_{t+1}=\zeta\widehat{\eta}_t+\epsilon_t. \tag{8.61}$$

### 8.7.2 *The linearized system*

The linearized first-order conditions and the two exogenous processes for money and technology form a system of eight dynamic equations for which we have to find a solution:

$$\begin{aligned}
\mu\widehat{c}_t+\widehat{\lambda}_t&=0, \qquad (8.62)\\
-\alpha\widehat{k}_{t+1}+\overline{\omega}\widehat{\lambda}_{t+1}-\overline{\omega}\widehat{\lambda}_t&=-\widehat{a}_{t+1},\\
\left[\mu\left(1-\frac{\widetilde{\beta}}{\eta}\right)-1\right]\widehat{p}_{t+1}+\widehat{p}_t+\frac{\widetilde{\beta}}{\eta}\widehat{\lambda}_{t+1}-\widehat{\lambda}_t&=\widehat{\eta}_t,\\
\frac{r}{1+r}\widehat{r}_{t+1}+\widehat{\lambda}_{t+1}-\widehat{\lambda}_t&=0,\\
\gamma\frac{k}{y}\widehat{k}_{t+1}-\left[(1-\delta)\frac{k}{y}+1-\alpha\right]\widehat{k}_t+\frac{c}{y}\widehat{c}_t&=\widehat{a}_t,\\
\gamma\widehat{b}_{t+1}-(1+r)\widehat{b}_t+(1-\eta)\varphi\widehat{p}_t-r\widehat{r}_t&=-\eta\varphi\widehat{\eta}_t,\\
\widehat{a}_{t+1}&=\rho\widehat{a}_t+\epsilon^a_t,\\
\widehat{\eta}_{t+1}&=\zeta\widehat{\eta}_t+\epsilon^m_t.
\end{aligned}$$

Substituting for $\widehat{\lambda}_t$ in terms of $\widehat{c}_t$ from the first equation, we re-write (8.62) as:

$$\begin{aligned}
-\alpha\widehat{k}_{t+1} - \overline{\omega}\mu\widehat{c}_{t+1} + \overline{\omega}\mu\widehat{c}_t &= -\widehat{a}_{t+1}, \qquad (8.63)\\
\left[\mu\left(1-\frac{\widetilde{\beta}}{\eta}\right)-1\right]\widehat{p}_{t+1} + \widehat{p}_t - \frac{\widetilde{\beta}}{\eta}\mu\widehat{c}_{t+1} + \mu\widehat{c}_t &= \widehat{\eta}_t,\\
\frac{r}{1+r}\widehat{r}_{t+1} - \mu\widehat{c}_{t+1} + \mu\widehat{c}_t &= 0,\\
\gamma\frac{k}{y}\widehat{k}_{t+1} - \left[(1-\delta)\frac{k}{y} + 1 - \alpha\right]\widehat{k}_t + \frac{c}{y}\widehat{c}_t &= \widehat{a}_t,\\
\gamma\widehat{b}_{t+1} - (1+r)\widehat{b}_t + (1-\eta)\varphi\widehat{p}_t - r\widehat{r}_t &= -\eta\varphi\widehat{\eta}_t,\\
\widehat{a}_{t+1} &= \rho\widehat{a}_t + \epsilon_t^a,\\
\widehat{\eta}_{t+1} &= \zeta\widehat{\eta}_t + \epsilon_t^m.
\end{aligned}$$

Now, by defining $\widehat{\mathbf{s}}_t = \left[\widehat{k}_t \mid \widehat{b}_t \mid \widehat{p}_t \mid \widehat{r}_t \mid \widehat{c}_t\right]'$, and $\widehat{\mathbf{e}}_t = [\widehat{a}_t \mid \widehat{\eta}_t]$, we can rewrite (8.63) as:

$$\begin{aligned}
\mathbf{M}_s^0\widehat{\mathbf{s}}_{t+1} &= \mathbf{M}_s^1\widehat{\mathbf{s}}_t + \mathbf{M}_e^0\widehat{\mathbf{e}}_{t+1} + \mathbf{M}_e^1\widehat{\mathbf{e}}_t, \qquad (8.64)\\
\widehat{\mathbf{e}}_{t+1} &= \mathbf{P}\widehat{\mathbf{e}}_t,
\end{aligned}$$

where:

$$\mathbf{M}_s^0 = \begin{bmatrix} -\alpha & 0 & 0 & 0 & -\overline{\omega}\mu \\ 0 & 0 & \mu\left(1-\frac{\widetilde{\beta}}{\eta}\right)-1 & 0 & -\frac{\widetilde{\beta}}{\eta}\mu \\ 0 & 0 & 0 & \frac{r}{1+r} & -\mu \\ \gamma\frac{k}{y} & 0 & 0 & 0 & 0 \\ 0 & \gamma & 0 & 0 & 0 \end{bmatrix}$$

$$\mathbf{M}_s^1 = \begin{bmatrix} 0 & 0 & 0 & 0 & -\overline{\omega}\mu \\ 0 & 0 & -1 & 0 & -\mu \\ 0 & 0 & 0 & 0 & -\mu \\ (1-\delta)\frac{k}{y}+1-\alpha & 0 & 0 & 0 & -\frac{c}{y} \\ 0 & (1+r) & -(1-\eta)\varphi & r & 0 \end{bmatrix}$$

$$\mathbf{M}_e^0 = \begin{bmatrix} -1 & 0 \\ 0 & 0 \\ 0 & 0 \\ 0 & 0 \\ 0 & 0 \end{bmatrix}, \ \mathbf{M}_e^1 = \begin{bmatrix} 0 & 0 \\ 0 & 1 \\ 0 & 0 \\ 1 & 0 \\ 0 & -\eta\varphi \end{bmatrix}, \ \mathbf{P} = \begin{bmatrix} \rho & 0 \\ 0 & \zeta \end{bmatrix}$$

Under our certainty equivalence assumption, randomness can be reintroduced simply by taking the conditional expectation of (8.64):

$$\begin{aligned}
\mathbf{M}_s^0 E_t\left(\widehat{\mathbf{s}}_{t+1}\right) &= \mathbf{M}_s^1\widehat{\mathbf{s}}_t + \mathbf{M}_e^0 E_t\left(\widehat{\mathbf{e}}_{t+1}\right) + \mathbf{M}_e^1\widehat{\mathbf{e}}_t, \qquad (8.65)\\
\widehat{\mathbf{e}}_{t+1} &= \mathbf{P}\widehat{\mathbf{e}}_t.
\end{aligned}$$

As $E_t\hat{\mathbf{e}}_{t+1} = \mathbf{P}\hat{\mathbf{e}}_t$, (8.65) becomes:[9]

$$E_t\left(\hat{\mathbf{s}}_{t+1}\right) = \mathbf{W}\hat{\mathbf{s}}_t + \mathbf{A}\hat{\mathbf{e}}_t, \tag{8.66}$$
$$\mathbf{W} = \left(\mathbf{M}_s^0\right)^{-1}\mathbf{M}_s^1,$$
$$\mathbf{A} = \left(\mathbf{M}_s^0\right)^{-1}\left(\mathbf{M}_e^0\mathbf{P} + \mathbf{M}_e^1\right),$$

(8.66) is a linear system of expectational difference equations. We solve it by applying the algorithm proposed by Blanchard and Kahn, which has become of common use in the analysis of forward-looking monetary models (see, for example, Fuhrer and Moore 1995).

### 8.7.3 *The Blanchard–Kahn algorithm*

If $\mathbf{P}$ is the modal matrix of $\mathbf{W}$ and $\boldsymbol{\mu}$ its canonical form (with the eigenvalues on the diagonal ordered in ascending absolute value), and if $\mathbf{P}$ is invertible, we may decompose $\mathbf{W}$ as $\mathbf{W} = \mathbf{P}\boldsymbol{\mu}\mathbf{P}^{-1}$. We partition the vector of endogenous state variables as $\hat{\mathbf{s}}_t' = \left[\hat{\mathbf{s}}_{1t} \mid \hat{\mathbf{s}}_{2t}\right]'$, where $\hat{\mathbf{s}}_{1t}' = \left[\hat{k}_t \mid \hat{b}_t\right]'$ contains the backward-looking variables, and $\hat{\mathbf{s}}_{2t}' = \left[\hat{p}_t \mid \hat{r}_t \mid \hat{c}_t\right]'$ the forward-looking ones. Let us furthermore partition the matrices $\mathbf{W}$, $\boldsymbol{\mu}$ , $\mathbf{P}^{-1}$ and $\mathbf{A}$ as:

$$\mathbf{W} = \begin{bmatrix} \mathbf{w}_{11} & \mathbf{w}_{12} \\ \mathbf{w}_{21} & \mathbf{w}_{22} \end{bmatrix}, \quad \mathbf{P}^{-1} = \begin{bmatrix} \mathbf{q}_{11} & \mathbf{q}_{12} \\ \mathbf{q}_{21} & \mathbf{q}_{22} \end{bmatrix}, \quad \boldsymbol{\mu} = \begin{bmatrix} \boldsymbol{\mu}_1 & 0 \\ 0 & \boldsymbol{\mu}_2 \end{bmatrix}, \quad \mathbf{A} = \begin{bmatrix} \mathbf{a}_1 \\ \mathbf{a}_2 \end{bmatrix}. \tag{8.67}$$

The dynamics of (8.66) is governed by the eigenvalues of $\mathbf{W}$. In order to have a unique initial vector of values for the forward-looking variables compatible with the transversality conditions we need the system to be saddle-point stable. Such a result is achieved when the first two eigenvalues of $\mathbf{W}$ are stable (strictly less than one in absolute value) and the last three are unstable.

Pre-multiplying (8.66) by $\mathbf{P}^{-1}$, we can transform the original system into a new one containing two decoupled vectors of difference equations:

$$E_t\left(\hat{\mathbf{z}}_{t+1}\right) = \boldsymbol{\mu}\hat{\mathbf{z}}_t + \mathbf{B}\hat{\mathbf{e}}_t, \tag{8.68}$$

where $\hat{\mathbf{z}}_t = \mathbf{P}^{-1}\hat{\mathbf{s}}_t$ and $\mathbf{B} = \mathbf{P}^{-1}\mathbf{A}$.

The backward-looking sub-system is equivalent to:

$$E_t\left(\hat{\mathbf{z}}_{1t+1}\right) = \boldsymbol{\mu}_1\hat{\mathbf{z}}_{1t} + \mathbf{b}_1\hat{\mathbf{e}}_t, \tag{8.69}$$

where $b_1$ is implicitly defined by $\mathbf{B} = \left[\mathbf{b}_1 \mid \mathbf{b}_2\right]'$. Since the eigenvalues in $\boldsymbol{\mu}_1$ are less than one in absolute value, (8.69) is stable in the forward direction; furthermore, since $\hat{\mathbf{s}}_{1t}$ is predetermined, the initial conditions completely determine its solution.

[9] Under the maintained hypothesis that $M_s^0$ is invertible.

Conversely, the forward-looking sub-system:

$$E_t(\widehat{\mathbf{z}}_{2t+1}) = \boldsymbol{\mu}_2 \widehat{\mathbf{z}}_{2t} + \mathbf{b}_2 \widehat{\mathbf{e}}_t, \tag{8.70}$$

is stable in the backward direction, since the elements of $\boldsymbol{\mu}_2$ exceed one in absolute value. Thus it is necessary to impose a terminal rather than an initial condition.

Rewrite (8.70) as:

$$\widehat{\mathbf{z}}_{2t} = \boldsymbol{\mu}_2^{-1} E_t(\widehat{\mathbf{z}}_{2t+1}) - \boldsymbol{\mu}_2^{-1} \mathbf{b}_2 \widehat{\mathbf{e}}_t = \mathbf{d}_1 E_t(\widehat{\mathbf{z}}_{2t+1}) + \mathbf{d}_2 \widehat{\mathbf{e}}_t. \tag{8.71}$$

Applying the recursive substitution method described in Sargent (1987) we solve (8.71) as:

$$\widehat{\mathbf{z}}_{2t} = -\sum_{k=0}^{\infty} \mathbf{d}_1^k \mathbf{d}_2 E_t(\widehat{\mathbf{e}}_{t+k}) = -\sum_{k=0}^{\infty} \mathbf{d}_1^k \mathbf{d}_2 \mathbf{P}^k \widehat{\mathbf{e}}_t = L_{ee} \widehat{\mathbf{e}}_t. \tag{8.72}$$

Applying the VEC operator to $L_{ee}$ we derive $\overrightarrow{L}_{ee}$, as the value of $L_{ee}$ when $k$ goes to infinite:

$$\overrightarrow{L}_{ee} = -(I - \mathbf{P}' \otimes \mathbf{d}_1)^{-1} \mathbf{d}_2. \tag{8.73}$$

By construction:

$$\begin{aligned} \widehat{\mathbf{z}}_{1t} &= \mathbf{q}_{11} \widehat{\mathbf{s}}_{1t} + \mathbf{q}_{12} \widehat{\mathbf{s}}_{2t}, \\ \widehat{\mathbf{z}}_{2t} &= \mathbf{q}_{21} \widehat{\mathbf{s}}_{1t} + \mathbf{q}_{22} \widehat{\mathbf{s}}_{2t}. \end{aligned} \tag{8.74}$$

We can solve the second expression in (8.74) for $\widehat{\mathbf{s}}_{2t}$:

$$\widehat{\mathbf{s}}_{2t} = \mathbf{q}_{22}^{-1} \widehat{\mathbf{z}}_{2t} - \mathbf{q}_{22}^{-1} \mathbf{q}_{21} \widehat{\mathbf{s}}_{1t}, \tag{8.75}$$

or,

$$\widehat{\mathbf{s}}_{2t} = \mathbf{L}_s \widehat{\mathbf{s}}_{1t} + \mathbf{L}_e \widetilde{\mathbf{e}}_t = \mathbf{L}_\nu \widetilde{\boldsymbol{\nu}}_t, \tag{8.76}$$

where $\mathbf{L}_e = \mathbf{q}_{22}^{-1} \mathbf{L}_{ee}$, $\mathbf{L}_s = -\mathbf{q}_{22}^{-1} \mathbf{q}_{21}$, $\mathbf{L}_\nu = [\mathbf{L}_s \mid \mathbf{L}_e]$, and $\widetilde{\boldsymbol{\nu}}_t = [\widehat{\mathbf{s}}_{1t} \mid \widehat{\mathbf{e}}_t]'$.

For the first two equations of the original system, (8.66), given by:

$$E_t(\widehat{\mathbf{s}}_{1t+1}) = \mathbf{w}_{11} \widehat{\mathbf{s}}_{1t} + \mathbf{w}_{12} \widehat{\mathbf{s}}_{2t} + \mathbf{a}_1 \widehat{\mathbf{e}}_t \tag{8.77}$$

we know that $\widehat{\mathbf{s}}_{1t}$ is predetermined in the Blanchard–Kahn sense (expectational error equal to zero), and we can rewrite (8.77) as:

$$\widehat{\mathbf{s}}_{1t+1} = \mathbf{w}_{11} \widehat{\mathbf{s}}_{1t} + \mathbf{w}_{12} \widehat{\mathbf{s}}_{2t} + \mathbf{a}_1 \widehat{\mathbf{e}}_t. \tag{8.78}$$

By substituting (8.76) into (8.78) we have:

$$\widehat{\mathbf{s}}_{1t+1} = (\mathbf{w}_{11} + \mathbf{w}_{12}\mathbf{L}_s)\,\widehat{\mathbf{s}}_{1t} + (\mathbf{w}_{12}\mathbf{L}_e + \mathbf{a}_1)\,\widehat{\mathbf{e}}_t. \tag{8.79}$$

Combining (8.79) with the stochastic processes for money and technology we have:

$$\widetilde{\boldsymbol{\nu}}_{t+1} = \mathbf{M}_\nu \widetilde{\boldsymbol{\nu}}_t + \mathbf{u}_t, \tag{8.80}$$

where:

$$\mathbf{M}_\nu = \begin{bmatrix} (\mathbf{w}_{11} + \mathbf{w}_{12}\mathbf{L}_s) & (\mathbf{w}_{12}\mathbf{L}_e + \mathbf{a}_1) \\ 0 & \mathbf{P} \end{bmatrix}, \mathbf{u}_t = \begin{bmatrix} \mathbf{0} \\ \boldsymbol{\epsilon}_t \end{bmatrix}, \tag{8.81}$$

$$\widetilde{\boldsymbol{\nu}}_t = \begin{bmatrix} \widehat{\mathbf{s}}_{1t} \\ \widehat{\mathbf{e}}_t \end{bmatrix}, \boldsymbol{\epsilon}_t = \begin{bmatrix} \epsilon_t^a \\ \epsilon_t^m \end{bmatrix}. \tag{8.82}$$

System (8.80) describes a first-order vector autoregression; iterating on it and taking (8.76) into account we recover the sequence of probability distributions that represents the (approximated) solution to our non-linear system of stochastic difference equations.

Having found a solution, there are two more variables of interest we would like to track, namely output and investment,[10] defined as:

$$\begin{aligned} y_t &= a_t k_t^{1-\alpha}, \\ i_t &= a_t k_t^{1-\alpha} - c_t. \end{aligned} \tag{8.83}$$

Log-linearization of (8.83) delivers:

$$\begin{aligned} \widehat{y}_t &= \widehat{a}_t + (1-\alpha)\,\widehat{k}_t, \\ \widehat{i}_t &= \frac{y}{i}\widehat{a}_t + (1-\alpha)\,\frac{y}{i}\widehat{k}_t - \frac{c}{i}\widehat{c}_t. \end{aligned} \tag{8.84}$$

And the path for output and investment is immediately available from the solution of our system.

## 8.8 Implementation

The procedure described in the previous section can be implemented using Matlab matrix programming language. We provide procedures for the solution of a more general problem with respect to the one we have described in the previous section. In fact we consider our model as a special case of a generic forward-looking system in which variables can be organized as controls, endogenous states costates and exogenous states, and the Blanchard–Kahn methodology is applicable. The implementation requires the files main.m, kpr.m, and bk.m. The file main.m contains all the building blocks needed to run the King–Plosser–Rebelo procedure.

[10]Note that the real wage is obtained by considering a multiple of output. The dynamic properties of output and real wages coincide, and we do not study real wages separately.

```
% PART 1
name=['k ';'b ';'a ';'e ';'c ';'y ';'i ';'p ';'r ';'l '];
kp=1; bp=2; ap=3; ep=4; cp=5; yp=6; ip=7; pp=8; rp=9; lp=10;
nc=1; ns=2; nl=3; nn=2; nxf=2; nvar=ns+nl+nc+nn+nxf; nt=nl+ns;
% PART 2
mu=2; % risk aversion
sn=0.6; % alpha
sc=0.75; % c/y share
g=1.004; % growth rate
rky=13.28; % capital-output ratio
rmy=5.3; % money income velocity
rby=0.6; % bonds-output ratio
eta=1.013; % money growth rate
rho=[0.95 0;0 0.49]; % persistence of shocks
covar=zeros(ns+nn);
covar(ns+1:ns+nn,ns+1:ns+nn)=[0.007,0;0,0.009];
% PART 3
sk=1-sn; % 1-alpha
si=1-sc; % i/y share
d=1-g+si/rky; % delta
be=g/(sk/rky+1-d); % beta tilde
r=(g-be)/be; % real int. rate
theta=((eta-be)/be)*(rmy/sc)^mu; % pref. param.
capd=g/be*rky/sk; % capital delta
vphi=(1-be)/((eta-1)*g*be); % var. phi
rby=(eta-1)*rmy*((g*be)/(1-be)); % b/y ratio
% PART 4
muu=-mu;
mus=[0,0,0,0,1];
mue=[0,0];
ms0=[-sn,0,0,0,vpi;0,0,mu*(1-be/eta)-1,0,be/eta;...
0,0,0,r/(1+r),1; g*rky,0,0,0,0; 0,g,0,0,0];
ms1=[0,0,0,0,-vpi; 0,0,1,0,-1; 0,0,0,0,-1;...
-(1-d)*rky-sk,0,0,0,0; 0,-g/be,(1-eta)*vphi,-r,0];
mu0=[0;0;0;0;0];
mu1=[0;0;0;-sc;0];
me0=[-1,0;0,0;0,0;0,0;0,0];
me1=[0,0;0,1;0,0;1,0;0,-eta*vphi];
fvu=[0;-sc/si];
fvv=[sk,0,1,0;sk/si,0,1/si,0];
fvl=[0,0,0;0,0,0];
```

PART 1 of the program defines a vector name that contains the definition of variables; it then specifies the position of each variable in the system. Variables are then divided into controls, endogenous states, costates, exogenous states and other variables of interest: **nc** is the number of controls, **ns** the number of endogenous states, **nl** the number of costates, **nn** the number of exogenous states, and **nxf** the number of variables of interest. Finally, it stores the total number of variables in the system, **nvar**, and the total number of endogenous state and costate variables, **nt**.

Recall our system:

$$
\begin{aligned}
\mu\widehat{c}_t + \widehat{\lambda}_t &= 0, \\
-\alpha\widehat{k}_{t+1} + \overline{\omega}\widehat{\lambda}_{t+1} - \overline{\omega}\widehat{\lambda}_t &= -\widehat{a}_{t+1}, \\
\left[\mu\left(1 - \frac{\widetilde{\beta}}{\eta}\right) - 1\right]\widehat{p}_{t+1} + \widehat{p}_t + \frac{\widetilde{\beta}}{\eta}\widehat{\lambda}_{t+1} - \widehat{\lambda}_t &= \widehat{\eta}_t, \\
\frac{r}{1+r}\widehat{r}_{t+1} + \widehat{\lambda}_{t+1} - \widehat{\lambda}_t &= 0, \\
\gamma\frac{k}{y}\widehat{k}_{t+1} - \left[(1-\delta)\frac{k}{y} + 1 - \alpha\right]\widehat{k}_t + \frac{c}{y}\widehat{c}_t &= \widehat{a}_t, \\
\gamma\widehat{b}_{t+1} - (1+r)\widehat{b}_t + (1-\eta)\varphi\widehat{p}_t - r\widehat{r}_t &= -\eta\varphi\widehat{\eta}_t, \\
\widehat{a}_{t+1} &= \rho\widehat{a}_t + \epsilon_t^a, \\
\widehat{\eta}_{t+1} &= \zeta\widehat{\eta}_t + \epsilon_t^m.
\end{aligned}
$$

$\widehat{u}_t = [\widehat{c}_t]$ is the vector containing the only control, $\widehat{\mathbf{s}}_t = \left[\widehat{k}_t\ \widehat{b}_t\ \widehat{p}_t\ \widehat{r}_t\ \widehat{\lambda}_t\right]'$ is the vector containing the subvector $\widehat{\mathbf{s}}_{1t} = \left[\widehat{k}_t\ \widehat{b}_t\right]'$ of the two endogenous states and the subvector $\widehat{\mathbf{s}}_{2t} = \left[\widehat{p}_t\ \widehat{r}_t\ \widehat{\lambda}_t\right]$ of the three costates, lastly $\widehat{\mathbf{e}}_t = \left[\widehat{a}_t\ \widehat{\eta}_t\right]$ is the vector containing the exogenous states. In addition we define a vector $\widehat{\mathbf{f}}_t = \left[\widehat{y}_t\ \widehat{i}_t\right]'$, with the two other variables of interest.

PART 2 of the program stores the complete parameterization used in our exercise, and creates the covariance matrix, denoted **covar**, of the vector of innovations $\mathbf{u}_t$ in (8.80). PART 3 solves the steady state and obtains the value of all calibrated parameters. Finally, PART 4 stores the matrices that describe the linearized system that will be solved by the King–Plosser–Rebelo procedure. Note that we can re-write the first equation of our system as:

$$
M_{uu}\widehat{u}_t = \mathbf{M}_{us}\widehat{\mathbf{s}}_t + \mathbf{M}_{ue}\widehat{e}_t, \tag{8.85}
$$

where $M_{uu} = [-\mu]$, $\mathbf{M}_{us} = [0 \mid 0 \mid 0 \mid 0 \mid 1]$, and $\mathbf{M}_{ue} = [0 \mid 0]$.

The equations for the variables contained in the vector $\widehat{\mathbf{s}}_t$ can then be written as:

$$
\left(\mathbf{M}_{ss}^0 + \mathbf{M}_{ss}^1 L\right)\widehat{\mathbf{s}}_{t+1} = \left(\mathbf{M}_{su}^0 + \mathbf{M}_{su}^1\right)\widehat{u}_{t+1} + \left(\mathbf{M}_{se}^0 + \mathbf{M}_{se}^1 L\right)\widehat{\mathbf{e}}_{t+1}, \tag{8.86}
$$

where L is the lag operator and:

$$\mathbf{M}^0_{ss} = \begin{bmatrix} -\alpha & 0 & 0 & 0 & \overline{\omega} \\ 0 & 0 & \mu\left(1-\frac{\widetilde{\beta}}{\eta}\right)-1 & 0 & \frac{\widetilde{\beta}}{\eta} \\ 0 & 0 & 0 & \frac{r}{1+r} & 1 \\ \gamma\frac{k}{y} & 0 & 0 & 0 & 0 \\ 0 & \gamma & 0 & 0 & 0 \end{bmatrix}$$

$$M^1_{ss} = \begin{bmatrix} 0 & 0 & 0 & 0 & -\overline{\omega} \\ 0 & 0 & 1 & 0 & -1 \\ 0 & 0 & 0 & 0 & -1 \\ -(1-\delta)\frac{k}{y}+1-\alpha & 0 & 0 & 0 & 0 \\ 0 & -(1+r) & (1-\eta)\varphi & -r & 0 \end{bmatrix}$$

$$\mathbf{M}^0_{su} = \begin{bmatrix} 0 \\ 0 \\ 0 \\ 0 \\ 0 \end{bmatrix}, \ \mathbf{M}^1_{su} = \begin{bmatrix} 0 \\ 0 \\ 0 \\ -\frac{c}{y} \\ 0 \end{bmatrix}, \ \mathbf{M}^0_{se} = \begin{bmatrix} -1 & 0 \\ 0 & 0 \\ 0 & 0 \\ 0 & 0 \\ 0 & 0 \end{bmatrix}, \ \mathbf{M}^1_{se} = \begin{bmatrix} 0 & 0 \\ 0 & 1 \\ 0 & 0 \\ 1 & 0 \\ 0 & -\eta\varphi \end{bmatrix}.$$

As far as the other variables of interest are concerned we have:

$$\widehat{\mathbf{f}}_t = \mathbf{FV}_u \widehat{u}_t + \mathbf{FV}_\nu \widehat{\nu}_t + \mathbf{FV}_l \widehat{\mathbf{s}}_{2t},$$

where $\widehat{\mathbf{f}}_t = \left[\widehat{y}_t \ \widehat{i}_t\right]'$, and

$$\mathbf{FV}_u = \begin{bmatrix} 0 \\ -\frac{c}{i} \end{bmatrix}, \ \mathbf{FV}_\nu = \begin{bmatrix} 1-\alpha & 0 & 1 & 0 \\ (1-\alpha)\frac{y}{i} & 0 & \frac{y}{i} & 0 \end{bmatrix}, \ \mathbf{FV}_l = \begin{bmatrix} 0 & 0 & 0 \\ 0 & 0 & 0 \end{bmatrix}.$$

At this stage the King–Plosser–Rebelo procedure can be implemented by calling two external functions. The first one is kpr.m.

```
function [h,mv]=kpr(muu,mus,mue,mu0,mu1,ms0,ms1,me0,me1,fvu,fvv,fv
nl=size(fvl,2); nt=size(mus,2); ns=nt-nl;
qus=muu\mus;
que=muu\mue;
qus1=qus(:,1:ns);
qus2=qus(:,ns+1:nt);
msss0=ms0-mu0*qus;
msss1=ms1-mu1*qus;
msse0=me0+mu0*que;
msse1=me1+mu1*que;
w=-msss0\msss1;
a=msss0\(msse0*rho+msse1);
[lv,mv]=bk(w,a,rho,ns);
uv=[[qus1,que]+qus2*lv];
```

```
fv=fvu*uv+fvv+fvl*lv;
h=[uv;fv;lv];
end;
```

The King–Plosser–Rebelo functions assume $M_{uu}$ invertible and solve (8.85) for $\widehat{u}_t$:

$$\widehat{u}_t = \mathbf{Q}_{us}\widehat{\mathbf{s}}_t + \mathbf{Q}_{ue}\widehat{\mathbf{e}}_t, \tag{8.87}$$

where $\mathbf{Q}_{us} = M_{uu}^{-1}\mathbf{M}_{us}$ and $\mathbf{Q}_{ue} = M_{uu}^{-1}\mathbf{M}_{ue}$. Using (8.87) at date $t+1$ into (8.86) we get:

$$\begin{aligned}\left(\mathbf{M}_{ss}^0 + \mathbf{M}_{ss}^1 L\right)\widehat{\mathbf{s}}_{t+1} &= \left(\mathbf{M}_{su}^0 + \mathbf{M}_{su}^1 L\right)\left(\mathbf{Q}_{us}\widehat{\mathbf{s}}_{t+1} + \mathbf{Q}_{ue}\widehat{\mathbf{e}}_{t+1}\right)\\ &\quad + \left(\mathbf{M}_{se}^0 + \mathbf{M}_{se}^1 L\right)\widehat{\mathbf{e}}_{t+1}.\end{aligned}$$

Rearranging terms, we have:

$$\left(\mathbf{M}_s^0 + \mathbf{M}_s^1 L\right)\widehat{\mathbf{s}}_{t+1} = \left(\mathbf{M}_e^0 + \mathbf{M}_e^1 L\right)\widehat{\mathbf{e}}_{t+1},$$

where

$$\begin{aligned}\mathbf{M}_s^0 &= \mathbf{M}_{ss}^0 - \mathbf{M}_{su}^0\mathbf{Q}_{us},\\ \mathbf{M}_s^1 &= \mathbf{M}_{ss}^1 - \mathbf{M}_{su}^1\mathbf{Q}_{us},\\ \mathbf{M}_e^0 &= \mathbf{M}_{se}^0 + \mathbf{M}_{su}^0\mathbf{Q}_{ue},\\ \mathbf{M}_e^1 &= \mathbf{M}_{se}^1 + \mathbf{M}_{su}^1\mathbf{Q}_{ue}.\end{aligned}$$

If $\mathbf{M}_s^0$ is invertible, we can solve for $\widehat{\mathbf{s}}_{t+1}$, obtaining:

$$\widehat{\mathbf{s}}_{t+1} = \mathbf{W}\widehat{\mathbf{s}}_t + \mathbf{R}\widehat{\mathbf{e}}_{t+1} + \mathbf{Q}\widehat{\mathbf{e}}_t, \tag{8.88}$$

where $\mathbf{W} = -\left(\mathbf{M}_{ss}^0\right)^{-1}\mathbf{M}_{ss}^1$, $\mathbf{R} = \left(\mathbf{M}_{ss}^0\right)^{-1}\mathbf{M}_{se}^0$, and $\mathbf{Q} = \left(\mathbf{M}_{ss}^0\right)^{-1}\mathbf{M}_{se}^1$.

Under our certainty equivalence assumption, randomness is reintroduced by simply taking the conditional expectation of (8.88):

$$E_t\left(\widehat{\mathbf{s}}_{t+1}\right) = \mathbf{W}\widehat{\mathbf{s}}_t + \mathbf{R}E_t\left(\widehat{\mathbf{e}}_{t+1}\right) + \mathbf{Q}\widehat{\mathbf{e}}_t. \tag{8.89}$$

As $E_t\left(\widehat{\mathbf{e}}_{t+1}\right) = \mathbf{P}\widehat{\mathbf{e}}_t$, (8.89) becomes

$$E_t\left(\widehat{\mathbf{s}}_{t+1}\right) = \mathbf{W}\widehat{\mathbf{s}}_t + \mathbf{A}\widehat{\mathbf{e}}_t,$$

where $\mathbf{A} = \mathbf{RP} + \mathbf{Q}$.

We are now ready to call the bk.m function to apply the Blanchard–Kahn solution algorithm:

```
function [lv,mv]=bk(w,a,rho,ns)
nt=size(w,1); nl=nt-ns; nn=size(rho,1);
w11=w(1:ns,1:ns);
```

```
w12=w(1:ns,ns+1:nt);
[evec,eval]=eig(w);
[mu1,ind]=sort(abs(diag(eval)));
mu=diag(eval);
mu=mu(ind);
p=evec(:,ind);
mu2=diag(mu(ns+1:nt));
ps=p\eye(size(p));
b=ps*a;
d1=mu2\eye(size(mu2));
d2=d1*b(ns+1:nt,:);
lee=-(eye(nl*nn)-kron(rho',d1))\d2(:);
lee=reshape(lee,nl,nn);
ls=-ps(ns+1:nt,ns+1:nt)\ps(ns+1:nt,1:ns);
le=ps(ns+1:nt,ns+1:nt)\lee;
lv=[ls,le];
mv=[w11+w12*ls,w12*le+a(1:ns,:);zeros(nn,ns),rho];
end;
```

We have retrieved all the matrices that characterize the approximated solution.

## 8.9 Model evaluation

In Chapter 6 we introduced VAR models of the monetary transmission mechanism as the statistical framework to produce stylized facts for the evaluation of theoretical models. We have stressed the importance of identifying models via theory-independent restrictions and we have illustrated how stylized facts on the monetary transmission mechanism can be described by impulse response functions. We have also emphasized that the derivation of the responses of variables included in VAR models to unexpected monetary shocks is not meant to be a policy experiment but rather a benchmark against which to assess the performance of theoretical models. Our solution of the theoretical model discussed in this chapter delivers us a VAR on which theory-based parameters restrictions are imposed. We can then use the comparison of impulse responses derived from the theory-independent VAR and from the solution of our theoretical model as a model evaluation device. Corroboration of the theoretical model is achieved when the responses of variables to shocks in the theoretical model match the stylized facts derived within the empirical VAR. If the theoretical model performs consistently with the data, then it can be used for policy analysis. Policy analysis can be validly performed by considering experiments in the modification of systematic and non-systematic components of variables. The micro-foundation of the model and the separation of deep parameters describing taste and technology from expectational parameters guarantees the robustness of policy experiment against the Lucas critique.

Therefore we proceed to model evaluation by considering that, in the light of the VAR-based evidence, a theoretical model of the monetary transmission mechanism should be consistent at least with three stylized facts: i) after a monetary policy shock, the aggregate price level initial reaction is extremely limited; ii) the interest rate initially increases; iii) aggregate output initially falls, but then recovers, so that the long-run effect of a monetary shock on this variable is zero.

The first experiment we would like to perform with our simplified monetary model economy is to compute the model's impulse response functions and compare them with the impulse response functions of an estimated VAR. The Matlab file performing this task is called impulse.m.

```
clear; main;
n=61; t=1:n-1; pr=0;
shockto=['A ';'Eta'];
sim=zeros(nvar,n);
[h,mv]=kpr(muu,mus,mue,mu0,mu1,ms0,ms1,me0,me1,fvu,fvv,fvl,rho);
for i=1:2;
sck=zeros(nn+ns,n+1);
sck(i+2,1)=1;
s=sck(:,1);
for j=1:n;
sim(:,j)=[s;h*s];
s=mv*s+sck(:,j+1);
end;
for j=1:n-1;
pi(j)=sim(ep,j)+sim(pp,j+1)-sim(pp,j);
end;
sim=sim(:,1:n-1);
subplot(2,2,1), hnd=plot(t,sim(yp,:)','k-',t,sim(cp,:)',
'k-.',t,sim(ip,:)','k:');
legend(hnd,'y','c','i',1);
title(['Shock to ' shockto(i,:)]);
ylabel('% Deviation');
subplot(2,2,2), hnd=plot(t,sim(kp,:)','k-',t,sim(bp,:)','k:');
legend(hnd,'k','b',1);
subplot(2,2,3), hnd=plot(t,sim(pp,:)','k-',t,pi,'k:');
legend(hnd,'p','pi',1);
subplot(2,2,4), hnd=plot(t,sim(rp,:)','k-');
legend(hnd,'r',1);
if pr==0; pause; else
eval(['print -dbitmap fig' num2str(i)]);
end;
end;
```

The procedure begins by clearing the workspace and recalling the main.m file. Then, we choose a 60-quarters simulation horizon and create a vector `t` that will act as a time index, and set to zero a particular flag, called `pr`, that controls the display procedure (if `pr` is set to one, the figures are plotted on the screen and saved on disk as bitmaps). Finally, we define the vector `shockto` containing the names of the state variables we are going to shock, and allocate some memory in advance for the matrix `sim`, which will contain the simulated series, in order to speed up computation.

Once the initial steps have been completed, we recall the file kpr.m to solve our log-linearized system. The solution is summarized by the matrices `mv` and `h`. We proceed to shock our two exogenous state variables: TFP, and the growth rate of nominal money balances. We start a loop, which is repeated twice, and build a matrix of innovations, `sck`; the matrix `sck` is a matrix of zeros, with only one strictly positive element, corresponding to the initial shock to either TFP or money growth. Then, we interactively simulate the linearized system, recover the inflation rate, and adjust the sample end-point. We are now ready to plot the results, and save the figures as bitmaps if the flag `pr` is set to one. These bitmaps are shown in Figures 8.3 and 8.4.

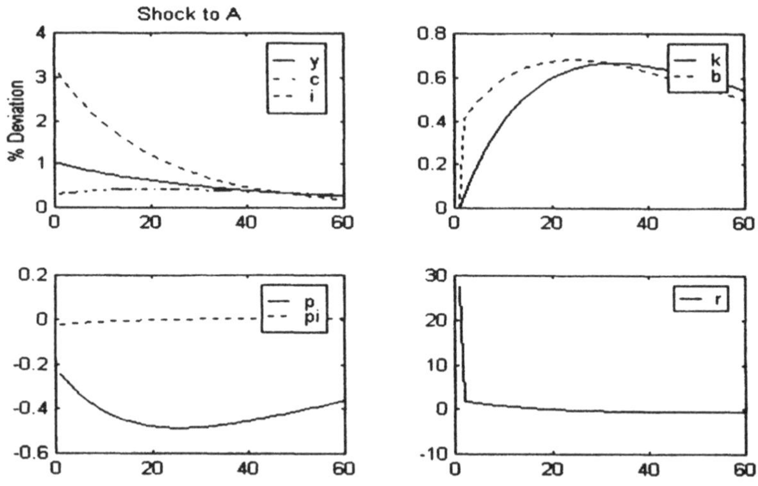


FIG. 8.3. The effect of a shock to total factor productivity in our model economy

Figure 8.3 shows the model's reaction to a positive shock to TFP.The unexpected increase in TFP induces a parallel increase in current output, since the current capital stock is fixed. As the productivity shock is highly persistent, TFP converges slowly to its steady-state level. Also consumption and investment increase on impact, but consumption's reaction is less pronounced, since the representative agent wants to smooth consumption over time; furthermore, the consumption path's slope increases on impact, since the rate of return on physical capital, which depends on its marginal productivity, is higher than in the steady state. The accumulation of physical capital and the decrease in TFP jointly drive down the rate of return, back to its steady-state level and further down. At this point, the rate of return being lower than in the steady state, the slope of the consumption path becomes negative. Since consumption and investment are jointly higher than output, the capital stock is eaten up. The marginal productivity of capital increases and converges back to its steady-state level. Consumption, output, investment, and capital converge slowly to their steady-state levels.

Consider now the nominal variables and the stock of government bonds. On impact, a positive income effect increases the demand for real money balances, while the nominal money supply still grows at the steady-state rate. The price level has to decrease on impact to balance demand and supply of real money balances. The further dynamics of the price level is driven by the dynamics of the shadow price of installed physical capital, i.e. by the costate variable. Also the value of the interest rate on government bonds is fully determined by the shadow price of capital from date 1 onwards. To balance the government budget constraint, the stock of government bonds has to follow a particular path from date 1 onwards, since both the price level and the interest rate depend only on the costate variable. At date 0, the interest rate on government bonds has to balance the government budget constraint for the price level and the required level of investment in government bonds. From date 1 onwards, then, the dynamics of the nominal variables and of the stock of government bonds is fully determined by the path of the shadow value of physical capital. Figure 8.4, instead, shows the model's reaction to a positive shock to the growth rate of the nominal money balances. As we can see, the real side does not absolutely react to monetary shocks. Since the demand for money balances remains unchanged, the sudden increase in the nominal money supply has to be counterbalanced by a sharp increase in the price level. From date 1 onwards, the interest rate on government bonds returns to its steady-state value, since the shadow price of capital remains constant; the stock of government bonds, then, has to balance the government budget constraint for the given price level, whose dynamics depend only on the dynamics of the growth rate of the nominal money stock. At date 0, the interest rate has to jump sharply in order to balance the government budget constraint for the required level of investment in government bonds and the price level.

Impulse response functions summarized in Figure 8.4 are in sharp contrast with the stylized facts proposed by the VAR approach. We may compare Figure 8.4 with, for instance, Figure 6.4. In the VAR model, the effect of a monetary shock on output is nearly zero on impact, but then clearly positive in the short run, and again zero in the long run. The effect on the price level is extremely small on impact, but increasing over time.

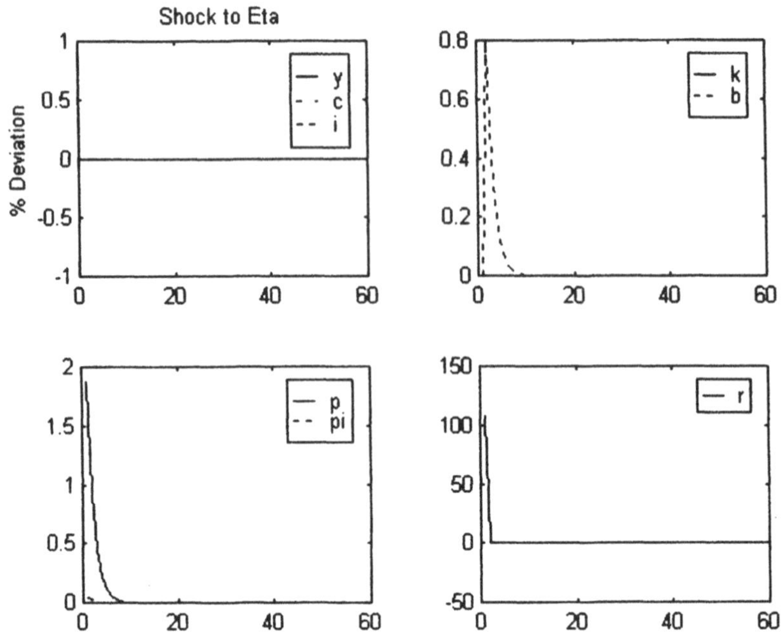


FIG. 8.4. The effect of a shock to money supply in our model economy

The same applies to the interest rate, whose reaction to a monetary shock is small on impact but then increases over time. In our model, the output level simply does not react to monetary shocks, while both the price level and the interest rate increase sharply on impact and then return to their steady-state levels.

Evidently enough, the model is completely unable to reproduce the stylized facts regarding the dynamic relationship between the output level, the price index, and the interest rate on government bonds. This result is, however, not surprising. In our framework, all kinds of friction or market imperfections are ruled out, and the role of money is limited, since it simply reduces the transaction costs associated with shopping. The model's equilibrium outcome, then, should be more appropriately considered as an approximation of the long-run behaviour of the US economy. If this is the case, however, the model at hand is not the right one to study the cyclical properties of the US nominal variables, and, in particular, the transmission mechanism of monetary policy.

To reinforce these conclusions, we briefly examine the small sample stochastic properties of our model, performing some Monte Carlo experiments. In other words, we draw from a random number generator a finite sequence of innovations, corresponding to a 100-quarters simulation horizon, and iterate to derive the simulation series for all exogenous and endogenous variables. To isolate the dynamics at business cycles frequencies, we filter the simulated series applying the so-called Hodrick–Prescott (H-P) filter, with a smoothing parameter equal to 1600. Then, we calculate the statistics of interest, as the relative standard deviation of each variable with regard to output, the autocorrelation coefficient, and the correlation coefficient with output. We repeat this procedure for at least 1000 times, storing the results of each round in a matrix. Finally, we summarize the empirical distribution of our statistics of interest calculating their mean, standard deviation, and so on, across the 1000 replications.

The Matlab program that performs these experiments is simulate.m.

```
%PART 1
clear; main;
nexp=1000; n=101;
v1=[cp;ip;pp;rp;kp;bp;ap;ep];
v2=[yp;v1];
m_std=zeros(size(v1,1),nexp); m_cor=zeros(size(v1,1),nexp);
m_auc=zeros(size(v2,1),nexp); inf_st=zeros(3,nexp);
p_st=zeros(3,nexp); sim=zeros(nvar,n); inf=zeros(n,1);
[h,mv]=kpr(muu,mus,mue,mu0,mu1,ms0,ms1,me0,me1,fvu,fvv,fvl,rho);
rn=1;
while rn<=nexp
sck=covar*randn(ns+nn,n+1); s=sck(:,1);
for j=1:n;
sim(:,j)=[s;h*s]; s=mv*s+sck(:,j+1);
end;
for j=1:n-1;
inf(j)=sim(ep,j)+sim(pp,j+1)-sim(pp,j);
end;
sim=sim(:,1:n-1); inf=inf(1:n-1);
sim_hp=hpf(sim',1600); inf_hp=hpf(inf,1600);
m_std(:,rn)=(std(sim_hp(:,v1))/std(sim_hp(:,yp)))';
m_auc(:,rn)=acor(sim_hp(:,v2),1)';
x=corrcoef(sim_hp);
m_cor(:,rn)=x(v1,yp);
inf_st(1,rn)=std(inf_hp)/std(sim_hp(:,yp));
inf_st(2,rn)=acor(inf_hp,1)';
x=corrcoef(inf_hp,sim_hp(:,yp));
inf_st(3,rn)=x(1,2);
rn=rn+1;
end;
%PART 2
stdm(:,1)=mean(m_std')'; stdm(:,2)=median(m_std')';
stdm(:,3)=std(m_std')'; stdm(:,4)=min(m_std')';
stdm(:,5)=max(m_std')';
```

```
au(:,1)=mean(m_auc')'; au(:,2)=median(m_auc')';
au(:,3)=std(m_auc')'; au(:,4)=min(m_auc')';
au(:,5)=max(m_auc')';
cor(:,1)=mean(m_cor')'; cor(:,2)=median(m_cor')';
cor(:,3)=std(m_cor')'; cor(:,4)=min(m_cor')';
cor(:,5)=max(m_cor')';
for j=1:3
st_inf(j,1)=mean(inf_st(j,:)); st_inf(j,2)=median(inf_st(j,:));
st_inf(j,3)=std(inf_st(j,:)); st_inf(j,4)=min(inf_st(j,:));
st_inf(j,5)=max(inf_st(j,:));
end;
%PART 3
delete output.txt;
diary output.txt;
t=' '; clc;
disp(['Performed simulations: ' num2str(nexp)]);
disp(' '); disp(' '); disp('Relative Standard deviations:');
disp(' ');
tit='Var. Avg Med Std Min Max';
f='%3.2f\t'; disp(tit); disp(' ');
disp([name(v1,:) t(ones(size(v1,1),1),:) num2str(stdm,f)]);
disp(['PI ' t num2str(st_inf(1,:),f)]);
disp(' '); disp('Autocorrelations:');
disp(' '); disp(tit); disp(' ');
disp([name(v2,:) t(ones(size(v2,1),1),:) num2str(au,f)]);
disp(['PI ' t num2str(st_inf(2,:),f)]); disp(' ');
disp('Correlations with Output:');
disp(' '); disp(tit); disp(' ');
disp([name(v1,:) t(ones(size(v1,1),1),:) num2str(cor,f)]);
disp(['PI ' t num2str(st_inf(3,:),f)]); disp(' ');
diary off;
```

In PART 1 we start by clearing the workspace and recalling the file main.m. Then, we define the number of rounds, `nexp`, and the simulation horizon, n (we need a further quarter to recover the inflation rate). We create a vector `v1` that identifies the variables for which we want to calculate the relative volatility and the correlation with output, and a vector `v2` that identifies the variables for which we want to calculate the autocorrelation coefficient. Finally, we allocate memory for the matrices containing the results of our experiments.

We are now ready to recall the King–Plosser–Rebelo solution procedure and start our sequence of experiments. We create a matrix of normally distributed innovations, denoted by `sck`, and simulate interactively the system. Then, we recover the inflation rate and adjust the sample endpoint. Finally, the simulated series are H-P filtered (by recalling the Hpf.m procedure), to isolate the business cycle frequencies. We can now calculate the statistics of interest, and store them in the matrices previously defined. The whole procedure is repeated **nexp** times.

In PART 2 of the program, we describe the empirical distribution of the statistics of interest, storing the average, the standard deviation, the maximum and the minimum.

In PART 3 we print on the screen and save the results of our Monte-Carlo experiments as an ASCII file.

The results are summarized in Tables 8.1–8.3. In Table 8.1, we report the stochastic properties of the model under our benchmark parameterization, when both exogenous state variables, TFP and the growth rate of nominal money balances, are hit by random shocks.

TABLE 8.1. Stochastic properties (benchmark parameterization)

| Var. | Vol. | Std | Auto | Std | Cor. | Std |
|---|---|---|---|---|---|---|
| $y$ | | | 0.67 | 0.06 | | |
| $c$ | 0.32 | 0.01 | 0.71 | 0.08 | 0.97 | 0.01 |
| $i$ | 3.08 | 0.01 | 0.67 | 0.08 | 1.00 | 0.00 |
| $k$ | 0.20 | 0.03 | 0.93 | 0.03 | -0.01 | 0.06 |
| $b$ | 0.95 | 0.12 | 0.43 | 0.09 | 0.27 | 0.13 |
| $a$ | 1.00 | 0.00 | 0.67 | 0.08 | 1.00 | 0.00 |
| $\eta$ | 1.06 | 0.17 | 0.35 | 0.09 | 0.00 | 0.14 |
| $\rho$ | 2.00 | 0.31 | 0.35 | 0.09 | -0.13 | 0.13 |
| $\pi$ | 1.87 | 0.29 | -0.06 | 0.09 | 0.02 | 0.10 |

The real side of the model performs as the standard stochastic Brock–Mirman model, being able to reproduce quite well the main features of the US real business cycle. Note that the price level is more volatile than output, it is slightly autocorrelated, and it is negatively correlated with output. Furthermore, note that the inflation rate is uncorrelated with both its own past values and with current output. Table 8.2, instead, shows the model's properties when only real shocks are present.

TABLE 8.2. Stochastic properties (only real shocks)

| Var. | Vol. | Std | Auto | Std | Cor. | Std |
|---|---|---|---|---|---|---|
| $y$ | | | 0.68 | 0.08 | | |
| $c$ | 0.32 | 0.01 | 0.71 | 0.08 | 0.97 | 0.01 |
| $i$ | 3.08 | 0.01 | 0.67 | 0.08 | 1.00 | 0.00 |
| $k$ | 0.20 | 0.03 | 0.93 | 0.03 | -0.01 | 0.07 |
| $b$ | 0.44 | 0.01 | 0.72 | 0.08 | 0.58 | 0.07 |
| $a$ | 1.00 | 0.00 | 0.67 | 0.08 | 1.00 | 0.00 |
| $\eta$ | 0.00 | 0.00 | 0.00 | 0.00 | 0.00 | 0.00 |
| $\rho$ | 0.27 | 0.01 | 0.74 | 0.07 | -0.92 | 0.02 |
| $\pi$ | 0.19 | 0.02 | -0.05 | 0.10 | 0.24 | 0.08 |

As we can see, the properties of the real variables, except the stock of government bonds, is left unchanged, while the behaviour of the nominal variables changes dramatically. The relative volatility of the price level drops sharply, its autocorrelation increases, and its correlation with output reaches almost $-1$. The inflation rate becomes slightly positively correlated with output. Table 8.3, finally, shows the model's properties when only monetary policy shocks are present.

TABLE 8.3. Stochastic properties (only monetary shocks)

| Var. | Vol. | Std | Auto | Std | Cor. | Std |
|---|---|---|---|---|---|---|
| $y$ | | | 0.00 | 0.00 | | |
| $c$ | 0.00 | 0.00 | 0.00 | 0.00 | 0.00 | 0.00 |
| $i$ | 0.00 | 0.00 | 0.00 | 0.00 | 0.00 | 0.00 |
| $k$ | 0.00 | 0.00 | 0.00 | 0.00 | 0.00 | 0.00 |
| $b$ | $\infty$ | 0.00 | 0.34 | 0.09 | 0.00 | 0.00 |
| $a$ | 0.00 | 0.00 | 0.00 | 0.00 | 0.00 | 0.00 |
| $\eta$ | $\infty$ | 0.00 | 0.34 | 0.09 | 0.00 | 0.00 |
| $\rho$ | $\infty$ | 0.01 | 0.34 | 0.09 | 0.00 | 0.00 |
| $\pi$ | $\infty$ | 0.02 | -0.06 | 0.10 | 0.00 | 0.00 |

Evidently, monetary policy shocks influence only the nominal variables, leaving the real side completely unaffected.

## 8.10 Policy analysis

The results discussed in the previous section make clear that the proposed model design cannot be used for monetary policy analysis. McCallum (1999) and McCallum and Nelson (1999*b*) perform policy analyses by using the following modified version of the model:

$$y_t = E_t y_{t+1} - \frac{1}{\mu}\left(i_t - E_t \pi_{t+1}\right), \tag{8.90}$$

$$\pi_t = \beta E_t \pi_{t+1} + \gamma_1 y_t - \gamma_2 a_t, \tag{8.91}$$

$$a_t = \rho a_{t-1} + \epsilon_t^a, \tag{8.92}$$

$$i_t = \mu_0 + \mu_3 i_{t-1} + (1 - \mu_3)\left((1 + \mu_1) E_t \pi_{t+1} + \mu_2 y_t\right) + \epsilon_t^m. \tag{8.93}$$

Equation (8.90) is the forward-looking IS equation consistent with the optimization problem in our model economy, (8.91) is an aggregate supply equation, which introduces some degree of price stickiness to make it consistent with the stylized facts on the monetary transmission mechanism, (8.92) describes technological shocks exactly as in the model economy while (8.93) is a central bank reaction function, consistent with inflation targeting which substitutes the forward-looking LM equation. As the central bank targets interest rates the effect of the monetary policy can be evaluated from the LM equation. In fact this relation only defines the quantity of money that the central bank has to supply in order to keep its target for the interest rate and it has no relevance for the analysis of monetary policy. The solution of this new system delivers a VAR featuring impulse responses consistent with the stylized facts from the data. Having corroborated the model by analysing responses to shocks, it is possible to proceed to policy simulation. McCallum stresses the importance of analysing systematic monetary policy and evaluates the impact on the system of different choices for the parameters $\mu_0$, $\mu_1$, $\mu_2$, $\mu_3$ in the central bank's reaction function. As we have already noted, this is perfectly compatible with the use of impulse responses to monetary policy shocks as a model evaluation device. The main limitation of this modified model is that it is not derived explicitly from an intertemporal optimization problem. In particular, we have seen how a reaction function such as (8.93) can be derived by solving an intertemporal optimization problem for a strict or a flexible inflation targeter. The functional specification of the (8.93) requires some preference for interest rate smoothing by the central bank. Moreover, the parameters $\mu_0$, $\mu_1$, $\mu_2$, $\mu_3$ describing the optimal response by the monetary policy-maker to macroeconomic conditions are convolutions of the central bank's preferences and the parameters determining the structure of the economy. As a consequence, McCallum's proposal for the simulation of systematic monetary policy could be further refined by explicitly identifying the central banker's preferences to consider the impact of their modifications.[11] Comparison of optimal with sub-optimal monetary policies could also be interesting for the evaluation of the cost of sub-optimal policies.

## 8.11 References


Bénassy, J. P. (1995). 'Money and Wage Contracts in an Optimizing Model of the Business Cycle'. *Journal of Monetary Economics*, 35: 303–315.

Blanchard, O. P., and Kahn, C. (1981). 'The Solution of Linear Difference Models under Rational Expectations'. *Econometrica*, 48: 1305–1311.

Campbell, J. Y. (1994). 'Inspecting the Mechanism: an Analytical Approach to the Stochastic Growth Model'. *Journal of Monetary Economics*, 33: 463–506.

Canova, F. (1994). 'Statistical Inference in Calibrated Models'. *Journal of Applied Econometrics*, 9: S123–S144.

Canova, F. (1995). 'Sensitivity Analysis and Model Evaluation in Simulated Dynamic General Equilibrium Economies'. *International Economic Review*, 36: 477–501.

Canova, F., and Ortega, E. (1999). 'Testing Calibrated General Equilibrium Models'. In R. Mariano, T. Schuermann, and M. Weeks (eds), *Simulation Based Inference in Econometrics: Methods and Applications*. Cambridge University Press.


[11] In the website associated with the book we make available an exercise aimed at showing how the optimal policy response is derived and what the impact of uncertainty is on the optimal policy response. Marco Aiolfi has kindly provided both the exercise, and the Matlab code for the solution, which are made available in the files ex1chap8.pdf and ex1chap8.m.

Christano, L. J., Eichenbaum, M., and Evans, C. (1998) 'Monetary Policy shocks: what have we learned and to what end?'. NBER working paper 6400.

Christano, L. J., Eichenbaum, M., and Evans, C. (1996). 'Modeling Money'. Mimeo.

Christano, L. J., and Eichenbaum, M. (1992). Current Business Cycle Theories and Aggregate Labor Market Fluctuations. *American Economic Review*, 82: 430–450.

Cooley, T. F. (1995). *Frontiers of Business Cycle Research*. Princeton: Princeton University Press.

Cooley, T. F. (1997). 'Calibrated Models'. *Oxford Review of Economic Policy*, 13: 55–69.

Cooley, T. F., and Hansen, G. (1995). 'Money and the Business Cycles'. In T. Cooley, (ed), *Frontiers of Business Cycle Research*. New Jersey: Princeton University Press.

Cooley, T. F., and Prescott, E. (1995). 'Economic Growth and Business Cycles'. In T. S. Cooley, (ed), *Frontiers of Business Cycle Research*. 1–38. New Jersey: Princeton University Press.

DeJong, D., Ingram, B., and Whiteman, C. (1996). 'A Bayesian Approach to Calibration'. *Journal of Business and Economic Statistics*, 14: 1-9.

Diebold, F., Ohanian, L., and Berkowitz, J. (1995). 'Dynamic Equilibrium Economies: A Framework for Comparing Models and Data'. *Review of Economic Studies*, 65: 433-451.

Eichenbaum, M. (1991). 'Real Business Cycle Theory: Wisdom or Whimsey?' *Journal of Economic Dynamics and Control*, 5: 607-626.

Eichenbaum, M. (1995). 'Some Comments on the Role of Econometrics in Economic Theory'. *Economic Journal*, 105: 1609-1621.

Fuhrer, J. C., and Moore, G. R. (1995). 'Monetary Policy Trade-offs and the Correlation Between Nominal Interest Rates and Real Output'. *American Economic Review*, 85: 219-239.

Gallant, A. R. (1995). 'Comments on Calibration'. Unpublished.

Gavin, W., and Kydland, F. (1999). 'Endogenous Money Supply and the Business Cycle'. *Review of Economic Dynamics*, 2: 347-369.

Haavelmo, T. (1944). 'The Probability Approach in Econometrics'. Supplement to *Econometrica*, 12: 1-118.

Hansen, L. (1982). 'Large Sample properties of Generalized Methods of Moments Estimators'. *Econometrica*, 50: 1029-1054.

Hansen, L. P., and Heckman, J. (1996). 'The Empirical Foundations of Calibration'. *The Journal of Economic Perspectives*, 10: 87-104.

Kim, K., and Pagan, A. R. (1995). 'The Econometric Analysis of Calibrated Macroeconomic Models'. In M.H. Pesaran and M. Wickens (eds.). 356-390

*Handbook of Applied Econometrics. Macroeconomics.* Blackwell Handbooks in Economics, Oxford: Basil Blackwell.

King, G., Plosser I., and Rebelo, S. (1988). 'Production, Growth and Business Cycles I: the Basic Neoclassical Model'. *Journal of Monetary Economics*, 21: 195-232.

Kocherlakota, N. (1996). 'The Equity Premium: it's Still a Puzzle'. *Journal of Economic Literature*, 34: 42-71.

Kydland, F., and Prescott, P. (1982). 'Time to Build and Aggregate Fluctuations'. *Econometrica*, 50: 1345-1370.

Kydland, F., and Prescott, P. (1996). 'The Computational Experiment: an Econometric Tool'. *Journal of Economic Perspectives*, 10: 69-85.

McCallum, B. T. (1999). 'Analysis of the Monetary Transmission Mechanism: Methodological Issues'. Paper presented at the Deutsche Bundesbank conference 'The Monetary Transmission Process: Recent Developments and Lessons for Europe', Frankfurt, March 26-27.

McCallum, B. T., and Nelson, E. (1999a). 'An optimizing IS-LM specification for monetary policy and business cycle analysis'. *Journal of Money Credit and Banking*, 31.

McCallum, B. T., and Nelson, E. (1999b). 'Performance of operational monetary policy rules in an estimated semi–classical structural model'. In Taylor, J. B. (ed.), *Monetary Policy Rules*. Chicago: Univeristy of Chicago Press.

Sargent, T. (1987). *Dynamic Macroeconomic Theory*. Cambridge, Massachussets: Harvard University Press.

Sims, C. (1996). 'Macroeconomics and Methodology'. *Journal of Economic Perspectives*, 10: 105–120.

Smith, G. W. (1995). 'Discussion of the Econometrics of the General Equilibrium Approach to Business Cycles'. In K. D. Hoover,(ed.), *Macroeconometrics: Developments, Tensions, and Prospects*. Boston: Kluwer.

Taylor, J. B., and Uhlig, H. (1990). 'Solving Non-Linear Stochastic Growth Models: A Comparison of Alternative Solution Methods'. *Journal of Business Economics and Statistics*, 8: 1–17.

Watson, M. W. (1993). 'Measures of Fit for Calibrated Models'. *Journal of Political Economy*, 101: 1011–41.

Wickens, M. (1995). 'Real Business Cycle Analysis: A Needed Revolution in Macroeconometrics'. *The Economic Journal*, 105: 1637–1648.

# INDEX


aggregation, 227
Amisano G., 98, 203
Andrews D., 140, 224
ARCH models, 106
artificial economies, 241
autocovariances, 222
autoregressive model
  Solow residual, 255

Bénassy J.-P., 247
Baba Y., 158
Bagliano F.-C., 169, 185, 192
Barghava A., 47
Barro R., 26
Bartlett weights, 228
baseline model, 140
Bernanke B., 166
Beveridge S., 50
Blanchard O., 169, 255, 259
Bollerslev T., 106
borrowed reserves targeting, 168
Brunner K., 191
budget constraint
  government, 244
Bundesbank, 196
  Council meetings, 200
business cycle, 214, 248
business cycle frequencies, 272

calibrated parameters, 263
calibration, 241, 249
  approach, 250
Campbell J., 227, 234
Canova F., 252
capital share, 253
central bank behaviour, 230
certainty equivalence, 217, 253, 255
Chow, 139
Christiano L., 162, 164, 245, 251
Christiano L. J., 96, 97
Clarida R., 100, 229, 232
closed form solution, 216
Cobb-Douglas production function, 251
Cochrane-Orcutt estimator, 147
cointegration, 158
common factor restrictions, 147
congruency, 153, 248
constant relative risk aversion, 215
constraint
  budget, 243
  cash in advance, 241
consumption function, 216, 217
Cooley T., 249–254
Cowles Commission, 103, 132
Cuddington J. T., 52
Cumby R., 225
Cushman D., 184

Datastream, 196
Davidson R., 224
De Jong B., 252
Deaton A., 226
deep parameters, 250
DGP, 134, 218, 248
diagnostic tests, 137, 248
  ARCH, 138
  heteroscedasticity, 137
  normality, 138
  parameters constancy, 139
  residual correlation, 137
Dickey-Fuller tests, 47
Diebold C., 251
discount factor, 229
disposable income, 227
Doornik J., 72, 138
dynamic econometric models, 158
dynamic equilibrium, 245
dynamic multipliers, 119, 154, 163

E-Views, 154, 224, 229
econometric policy evaluation, 132, 146, 162
Eichenbaum M., 96, 97, 162, 164, 180, 245, 249, 251, 252
eigenvalues, 259
encompassing, 150
Engle, 138
Engle R., 150, 158
Engle R. F., 106
equilibrium real interest rate, 234
Ericsson N., 150
error correction mechanism, 218
estimation
  and calibration, 251
  approach, 248
  covariance matrix in GMM, 222
  Euler equations, 219, 228
  GIVE, 221
  GMM, 165, 214

heteroscedasticity consistent estimators, 224
OLS, 5, 234
TSLS, 229
two-step two-stages least squares, 225
Euler equations, 214, 216
parameters instability, 227
Evans C., 96, 97, 162, 180, 245
exchange rate puzzle, 181
exchange rate targeting, 185
exogeneity, 144
ECM representations, 146
sequential cut, 145
strong exogeneity, 145
super exogeneity, 145
testing exogeneity, 149
weak exogeneity, 145
expectational model, 173
expected inflation, 234

Farmer R., 164
Farmer R. E. A., 97
Faust J., 1, 159
Fed behaviour
and long-term interest rates, 234
Federal funds future, 191
Federal funds target, 234
Federal funds targeting, 168
FIML, 154
first-order conditions, 244, 246
fluctuations
in income and consumption, 248
FOMC, 196
forecasting, 248
forward discount puzzle, 181

Galì J., 100, 229, 232
Garber P., 227
Gavin W., 252
general equilibrium models
parameterization and estimation, 214
Gertler M., 100, 229, 232
Ghysels E., 227
Giannini C., 66, 98, 203
Giavazzi F., 172
GMM, 235
empirical applications, 227
monetary policy rules, 229
testing the validity of instruments, 220
GMM approach
applications, 215
Godfrey, 137
Goldberger A. S., 103
Goodfriend M., 97, 164, 234
government bonds, 242
Granger causality, 145
growth, 250
long-run balanced, 250

Haavelmo T., 135, 249
Hall R., 227
Hamilton J., 66
Hansen G., 252
Hansen H., 72, 138
Hansen L., 220, 228, 251
Harvey A. C., 55
Hatanaka M., 45
Hausman J., 149
Hendry D.F., 72, 91, 92, 116, 132, 139, 150, 152, 158, 183
Heston, 3
historical decomposition, 174
Hodrick R. J., 54
Hodrick-Prescott filter, 54, 271
Horvath M. T. K., 79
households, 243
Huizinga H., 225

identification, 86, 162, 219
Choleski decompositition, 165
cointegrated VARs, 171
contemporaneous restrictions, 166
structural VARs with long-run restrictions, 169
VAR models, 164
impulse response analysis, 174, 275
impulse response functions, 266
inflation rate, 245
inflation scares, 234
inflation targeting, 222
strict and flexible, 236
initial conditions, 260
instantaneous forward rates, 192
instruments
choice, 233
validity, 229
interest rate rules, 235
interest rate smoothing, 229, 237
interest rate targeting, 153, 232
intertemporal discount factor, 253
intertemporal elasticity of substitution, 253
intertemporal optimization, 214, 247, 275
central banks, 235
representative consumer, 215
with liquidity constraints, 225
investment, 247
investment-capital ratio, 254
Irons J., 150
IS-LM
forward-looking, 241, 248

Jaeger A., 55
Jappelli T., 227
Johansen S., 61–63, 65, 67, 74, 75, 170
Johnston, 103
Juselius K., 66, 72

Kahn C., 255, 259
Kaldor N., 250
Keynesian macroeconomics, 214
Kim I., 45
Kim S., 182
King R., 97, 164, 227, 255
Kiviet, 137
Kocherlakota N., 253
Kydland F., 249, 252

lag truncation parameter, 224
Lagrange multipliers, 216
Leeper E., 176, 191, 231
Leeper E. M., 72, 121
likelihood function, 134
linear approximation, 255
Lippi M., 174
liquidity effect, 164
liquidity puzzle, 177
LSE, 249
LSE methodology, 132
Lucas critique, 133, 152, 162, 173, 214, 266
  testing, 156
Lucas R., 162, 164, 236
Lucas R. E., 29, 92, 93, 96, 97, 99, 130
Lucas R.E., 26

M1, 252
MacKinnon J., 224
macroeconomic policy
  simulation of ad-hoc models, 218
macroeconomic time-series
  real and simulated, 227
Maddala G. S., 45
Malcolm, 170
Mankiw G., 3, 4, 9, 24, 25, 27, 28, 225, 227
Mankiw R., 214
market imperfections, 225
Matlab, 261, 267
McCallum B., 173, 241, 242, 247, 248, 274, 275
measurement and theory, 250
Mellander E., 171
method of moments estimation
  and calibration, 251
microeconomic foundations, 249
Microfit, 228
Mihov I., 166
model evaluation, 155, 266, 267, 275
model identification, 266
Monetary Condition Indexes, 184
monetary model economy, 267
monetary policy, 245
  closed economies, 176
  expectations, 196
  German, 188
  measures, 191
  narrative approach, 191
  non-VAR measures, 201
  open economies, 179
  shocks, 275
  systematic, 275
  US, 188
monetary policy rules, 214, 222
  and VARs, 172
monetary transmission mechanism, 136, 153, 164
  open economy, 185, 206
  stylized facts, 179
  theoretical models, 267
  VAR models, 237
money
  in the utility function, 241
money demand, 159
money growth, 253
Monte Carlo, 270
Monte Carlo simulations, 255
Mosconi R., 72, 170
moving average structures, 222
multivariate stochastic process, 248

Nelson C.R., 50, 193
Nelson E., 241, 242, 247, 248, 274
neo-classical economics, 217
neo-classical macroeconomics, 214
Newey W., 224
Nielsen B. G., 74
no-Ponzi game, 244
non-borrowed reserves targeting, 168
numerical exercises, 252
numerical solution, 226

Obstfeld M., 225
oil investment, 227
Oliner S., 227
Orphanides A., 232
Ortega E., 252
Osterwald-Lenum M., 74
output gap, 222
  capacity utilization rate, 232
  Hodrick-Prescott filter, 232
  measurement, 232

Pagan, 137

Pagano M., 227
panel data, 227
parameters
  deep, 225
  deep and expectational, 214
  taste and technology, 227
Pc-FIML, 140
permanent income, 217
persistence
  in policy rates, 229
Pesaran M.H., 1, 91, 226, 227
Phillips P. C. B., 79
Pindyck R.S., 103
Plosser C., 255
policy analysis, 241, 266
policy experiments, 266
policy regimes, 142
policy simulation, 162
preferences
  monetary policy-makers, 275
Prescott E., 54, 249, 252, 254
price puzzle, 177
price stickiness, 274

Quah D., 169

random number generator, 270
rational expectations, 214, 246
RATS, 170
reaction function, 222, 275
  Fed, 183
real business cycle, 252
real interest rate, 246
real money balances, 246, 253
Rebelo S., 255
reduced form, 248
reduction process, 134
regime shifts, 174
Reichlin L., 174
Reimers H. E., 79
rejection
  of an economic model, 249
restrictions, 248
reverse regression, 148
risk aversion
  coefficient of, 229
Romer C., 191
Romer D., 3, 4, 9, 24, 25, 27, 28, 191
Rotemberg J., 214
Roubini N., 182
Rovelli R., 237
Rubinfeld D.L., 103
Rudebusch G., 47, 191, 227

saddle-point stability, 259
Saikkonen P., 79
Sala-i-Martin X., 26
Sargan D., 19, 91, 109, 110, 221
Sargan J. D., 47
Sargent T., 247, 260
seigniorage, 246
shocks, 164
  demand and supply, 169
  exchange rate, 185
  growth rate of money, 269
  identification of monetary policy, 196
  monetary policy, 168, 267
  permanent and transitory, 171
  supply side, 241
  total factor productivity, 268
Sichel D., 227
Siegel A.F., 193
Sims C., 29, 72, 79, 92, 93, 121, 129, 162, 165, 176, 178, 231
simulation, 248
  effects of monetary policy, 154
Singleton P., 228
Skinner T., 192
Smets F., 184
Smith R., 1, 91, 226
Soderlind P., 192
Solow R., 1, 27
Solow residuals, 251
Spanos A., 91, 132, 133
Spaventa L., 172
specification, 162
spectrum, 251
Starr R., 158
stationarity, 135
steady state
  deterministic, 255
steady-state, 253
stochastic difference equations, 246
stochastic optimal control, 243
stochastic process, 261
Stock J. H., 60, 79
Strongin S., 168
structural breaks, 48
structural disturbances, 164
structural model, 248
structural parameters, 218
stylized facts, 241, 266
Summers, 3
Summers L., 214
super neutrality, 249
Svensson L.E.O., 99, 100, 157, 192, 235–237

target inflation rate, 231
Taylor expansion, 255

Taylor J., 230
technical progress, 243
term premium, 234
terminal conditions, 260
test
  validity of instruments, 221
theoretical framework, 250
total factor productivity, 242, 253
transversality conditions, 244, 246

US data, 253

validation, 132
  of reduced forms, 134
VAR, 267
  cointegration, 208
  statistical adequacy, 208
  uncertainty, 208
VAR approach, 162
VAR models
  monetary transmission mechanism, 166
VAR residuals, 164
variance decomposition, 174
velocity
  income, 254
Vredin A., 171

Walsh C., 142
Warne A., 171
Watson M., 79, 252
Weil D., 3, 4, 9, 24, 25, 27, 28
West K., 224
White, 138
White A., 106
White H., 224
Whiteman C., 1, 159
Winters L. A., 52
Wold decomposition theorem, 37
Wu, 149

Zeldes R., 227
Zettelmeyer J., 192
Zha T., 72, 121, 176, 184, 231

Lightning Source UK Ltd.
Milton Keynes UK
UKOW06f1044110816

280437UK00001B/52/P

9 780198 296850